SQL

9th Edition

by Allen G. Taylor
Author of SQL All-in-One For Dummies

for **dummies®**
A Wiley Brand

SQL For Dummies® 9th Edition

Published by: **John Wiley & Sons, Inc.**, 111 River Street, Hoboken, NJ 07030-5774, www.wiley.com

Copyright © 2019 by John Wiley & Sons, Inc., Hoboken, New Jersey

Published simultaneously in Canada

For general information on our other products and services, please contact our Customer Care Department within the U.S. at 877-762-2974, outside the U.S. at 317-572-3993, or fax 317-572-4002. For technical support, please visit https://hub.wiley.com/community/support/dummies.

Wiley publishes in a variety of print and electronic formats and by print-on-demand. Some material included with standard print versions of this book may not be included in e-books or in print-on-demand. If this book refers to media such as a CD or DVD that is not included in the version you purchased, you may download this material at http://booksupport.wiley.com. For more information about Wiley products, visit www.wiley.com.

Library of Congress Control Number: 2018960776

ISBN: 978-1-119-52707-7 (pbk); ISBN: 978-1-119-52708-4 (ePDF); ISBN: 978-1-119-52709-1 (ePub)

Manufactured in the United States of America

C10005914_110718

Contents at a Glance

Table of Contents

Introduction

Welcome to database development using SQL, the industry-standard database query language. Many database management system (DBMS) tools run on a variety of hardware platforms. The differences among the tools can be great, but all serious products have one thing in common: They support SQL data access and manipulation. If you know SQL, you can build relational databases and get useful information out of them.

About This Book

Relational database management systems are vital to many organizations. People often think that creating and maintaining these systems must be extremely complex activities — the domain of database gurus who possess enlightenment beyond that of mere mortals. This book sweeps away the database mystique. In this book, you

>> Get to the roots of databases.

>> Find out how a DBMS is structured.

>> Discover the major functional components of SQL.

>> Build a database.

>> Protect a database from harm.

>> Operate on database data.

>> Determine how to get the information you want out of a database.

The purpose of this book is to help you build relational databases and get valuable information out of them by using SQL. SQL is the international standard language used to create and maintain relational databases. This edition covers the latest version of the standard, SQL:2016.

This book doesn't tell you how to design a database (I do that in *Database Development For Dummies*, also published by Wiley). Here I assume that you or somebody else has already created a valid design. I then illustrate how you implement that design by using SQL. If you suspect that you don't have a good database design, then by all means fix your design before you try to build the database. The earlier you detect and correct problems in a development project, the cheaper the corrections will be.

Foolish Assumptions

If you need to store or retrieve data from a DBMS, you can do a much better job with a working knowledge of SQL. You don't need to be a programmer to use SQL, and you don't need to know programming languages, such as Java, C, or BASIC. SQL's syntax is like that of English. If you *are* a programmer, you can incorporate SQL into your programs. SQL adds powerful data manipulation and retrieval capabilities to conventional languages. This book tells you what you need to know to use SQL's rich assortment of tools and features inside your programs.

Icons Used in This Book

When something in this book is particularly valuable, we go out of our way to make sure that it stands out. We use these cool icons to mark text that (for one reason or another) *really* needs your attention. Here's a quick preview of the ones waiting for you in this book and what they mean.

TIP

Tips save you a lot of time and keep you out of trouble.

REMEMBER

Pay attention to the information marked by this icon — you may need it later.

WARNING

Heeding the advice that this icon points to can save you from major grief. Ignore it at your peril.

TECHNICAL STUFF

This icon alerts you to the presence of technical details that are interesting but not absolutely essential to understanding the topic being discussed.

Beyond the Book

In addition to the content in this book, you'll find some extra content available at the www.dummies.com website:

>> **For the Cheat Sheet for this book**, visit www.dummies.com/ and search for SQL For Dummies 9E cheat sheet.

>> **For updates to this book, if any, visit the** www.dummies.com store and search for SQL For Dummies 9E.

Where to Go from Here

Now for the fun part! Databases are the best tools ever invented for keeping track of the things you care about. After you understand databases and can use SQL to make them do your bidding, you wield tremendous power. Co-workers come to you when they need critical information. Managers seek your advice. Youngsters ask for your autograph. But most importantly, you know, at a very deep level, how your organization really works.

1
Getting Started with SQL

Chapter **1**

Relational Database Fundamentals

QL (pronounced *ess-que-ell*, not *see'qwl*, though database geeks still argue about that) is a language specifically designed with databases in mind. SQL enables people to create databases, add new data to them, maintain the data in them, and retrieve selected parts of the data. Developed in the 1970s at IBM, SQL has grown and advanced over the years to become the industry standard. It is governed by a formal standard maintained by the International Standards Organization (ISO).

Various kinds of databases exist, each adhering to a different model of how the data in the database is organized.

SQL was originally developed to operate on data in databases that follow the *relational model*. Recently, the international SQL standard has incorporated part of the *object model*, resulting in hybrid structures called object-relational databases. In this chapter, I discuss data storage, devote a section to how the relational model compares with other major models, and provide a look at the important features of relational databases.

Before I talk about SQL, however, I want to nail down what I mean by the term *database*. Its meaning has changed, just as computers have changed the way people record and maintain information.

Keeping Track of Things

Today people use computers to perform many tasks formerly done with other tools. Computers have replaced typewriters for creating and modifying documents. They've surpassed calculators as the best way to do math. They've also replaced millions of pieces of paper, file folders, and file cabinets as the principal storage medium for important information. Compared with those old tools, of course, computers do much more, much faster — and with greater accuracy. These increased benefits do come at a cost, however: Computer users no longer have direct physical access to their data.

When computers occasionally fail, office workers may wonder whether computerization really improved anything at all. In the old days, a manila file folder "crashed" only if you dropped it — then you merely knelt down, picked up the papers, and put them back in the folder. Barring earthquakes or other major disasters, file cabinets never "went down," and they never gave you an error message. A hard-drive crash is another matter entirely: You can't "pick up" lost bits and bytes. Mechanical, electrical, and human failures can make your data go away into the Great Beyond, never to return. Backing up your data frequently is one thing you can do to enhance your peace of mind. Another thing you can do is store your data in the cloud and let your cloud provider do the backing up.

Taking the necessary precautions to protect yourself from accidental data loss allows you to start cashing in on the greater speed and accuracy that computers provide.

If you're storing important data, you have four main concerns:

>> Storing data must be quick and easy because you're likely to do it often.

>> The storage medium must be reliable. You don't want to come back later and find some (or all) of your data missing.

>> Data retrieval must be quick and easy, regardless of how many items you store.

>> You need an easy way to separate the exact information you want *now* from the tons of data that you *don't* want right now.

State-of-the-art computer databases satisfy these four criteria. If you store more than a dozen or so data items, you probably want to store those items in a database.

What Is a Database?

The term *database* has fallen into loose use lately, losing much of its original meaning. To some people, a database is any collection of data items (phone books, laundry lists, parchment scrolls . . . whatever). Other people define the term more strictly.

In this book, I define a *database* as a self-describing collection of integrated records. And yes, that does imply computer technology, complete with programming languages such as SQL.

REMEMBER

A *record* is a representation of some physical or conceptual object. Say, for example, that you want to keep track of a business's customers. You assign a record for each customer. Each record has multiple *attributes*, such as name, address, and telephone number. Individual names, addresses, and so on are the *data*.

A database consists of both data and *metadata*. Metadata is the data that describes the data's structure within a database. If you know how your data is arranged, then you can retrieve it. Because the database contains a description of its own structure, it's *self-describing*. The database is *integrated* because it includes not only data items but also the relationships among data items.

The database stores metadata in an area called the *data dictionary*, which describes the tables, columns, indexes, constraints, and other items that make up the database.

Because a flat-file system (described later in this chapter) has no metadata, applications written to work with flat files must contain the equivalent of the metadata as part of the application program.

Database Size and Complexity

Databases come in all sizes, from simple collections of a few records to mammoth systems holding millions of records. Most databases fall into one of three categories, which are based on the size of the database itself, the size of the equipment it runs on, and the size of the organization that is maintaining it:

>> A **personal database** is designed for use by a single person on a single computer. Such a database usually has a rather simple structure and a relatively small size.

>> A **departmental or workgroup database** is used by the members of a single department or workgroup within an organization. This type of database is generally larger than a personal database and is necessarily more complex; such a database must handle multiple users trying to access the same data at the same time.

>> An **enterprise database** can be huge. Enterprise databases may model the critical information flow of entire large organizations.

What Is a Database Management System?

Glad you asked. A *database management system* (DBMS) is a set of programs used to define, administer, and process databases and their associated applications. The database being managed is, in essence, a structure that you build to hold valuable data. A DBMS is the tool you use to build that structure and operate on the data contained within the database.

You can find many DBMS programs on the market today. Some run on large and powerful machines, and some on personal computers, notebooks, and tablets. Some even run on smartphones. A strong trend, however, is for such products to work on multiple platforms or on networks that contain different classes of machines. An even stronger trend is to store data in data centers or even to store it out in the *cloud,* which could be a public cloud run by a large company such as Amazon, Google, or Microsoft, via the Internet, or it could be a private cloud operated by the same organization that is storing the data on its own intranet.

These days, *cloud* is a buzzword that is bandied about incessantly in techie circles. Like the puffy white things up in the sky, it has indistinct edges and seems to float somewhere out there. In reality, it is a collection of computing resources that is accessible via a browser, either over the Internet or on a private intranet. The thing that distinguishes the computing resources in the cloud from similar computing resources in a physical data center is the fact that the resources are accessible via a browser rather than an application program that directly accesses those resources.

REMEMBER

A DBMS that runs on platforms of multiple classes, large and small, is called *scalable*.

Whatever the size of the computer that hosts the database — and regardless of whether the machine is connected to a network — the flow of information between database and user is always the same. Figure 1-1 shows that the user communicates with the database through the DBMS. The DBMS masks the physical details of the database storage so that the application need only concern itself with the logical characteristics of the data, not with how the data is stored.

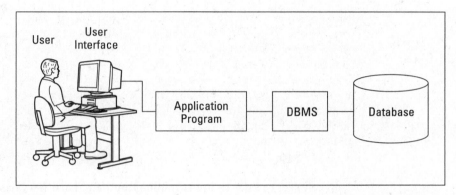

FIGURE 1-1:
A block diagram of a DBMS-based information system.

THE VALUE IS NOT IN THE DATA, BUT IN THE STRUCTURE

Years ago, some clever person calculated that if you reduce human beings to their components of carbon, hydrogen, oxygen, and nitrogen atoms (plus traces of others), they would be worth only 97 cents. However droll this assessment, it's misleading. People aren't composed of mere isolated collections of atoms. Our atoms combine into enzymes, proteins, hormones, and many other substances that would cost millions of dollars per ounce on the pharmaceutical market. The precise structure of these combinations of atoms is what gives them greater value. By analogy, database structure makes possible the interpretation of seemingly meaningless data. The structure brings to the surface patterns, trends, and tendencies in the data. Unstructured data — like uncombined atoms — has little or no value.

Flat Files

Where structured data is concerned, the flat file is as simple as it gets. No, a flat file isn't a folder that's been squashed under a stack of books. *Flat files* are so called because they have minimal structure. If they were buildings, they'd barely stick up from the ground. A flat file is simply a collection of data records, one after another, in a specified format — the data, the whole data, and nothing but the data — in effect, a list. In computer terms, a flat file is simple. Because the file doesn't store structural information (metadata), its overhead (stuff in the file that is not data but takes up storage space) is minimal.

Say that you want to keep track of the names and addresses of your company's customers in a flat file system. The system may have a structure something like this:

```
Harold Percival   26262 S. Howards Mill Rd   Westminster   CA92683
Jerry Appel       32323 S. River Lane Rd      Santa Ana     CA92705
Adrian Hansen     232 Glenwood Court          Anaheim       CA92640
John Baker        2222 Lafayette St           Garden Grove  CA92643
Michael Pens      77730 S. New Era Rd         Irvine        CA92715
Bob Michimoto     25252 S. Kelmsley Dr        Stanton       CA92610
Linda Smith       444 S.E. Seventh St         Costa Mesa    CA92635
Robert Funnell    2424 Sheri Court            Anaheim       CA92640
Bill Checkal      9595 Curry Dr               Stanton       CA92610
Jed Style         3535 Randall St             Santa Ana     CA92705
```

As you can see, the file contains nothing but data. Each field has a fixed length (the Name field, for example, is always exactly 15 characters long), and no structure separates one field from another. The person who created the database assigned field positions and lengths. Any program using this file must "know" how each field was assigned, because that information is not contained in the database itself.

Such low overhead means that operating on flat files can be very fast. On the minus side, however, application programs must include logic that manipulates the file's data at a very detailed level. The application must know exactly where and how the file stores its data. Thus, for small systems, flat files work fine. The larger a system is, however, the more cumbersome a flat-file system becomes.

TIP

Using a database instead of a flat-file system eliminates duplication of effort. Although database files themselves may have more overhead, the applications can be more portable across various hardware platforms and operating systems. A database also makes writing application programs easier because the programmer doesn't need to know the physical details of where and how the data is stored.

The reason databases eliminate duplication of effort is because the DBMS handles the data-manipulation details. Applications written to operate on flat files must include those details in the application code. If multiple applications all access the same flat-file data, these applications must all (redundantly) include that data-manipulation code. If you're using a DBMS, however, you don't need to include such code in the applications at all.

Clearly, if a flat-file-based application includes data-manipulation code that runs only on a particular operating system (OS), migrating the application to a different OS is a headache waiting to happen. You must change all the OS-specific code — and that's just for openers. Migrating a similar DBMS-based application to another OS is much simpler — fewer complicated steps, fewer aspirin consumed.

Database Models

The first databases, back at the dawn of time (1950s), were structured according to a hierarchical model. They suffered from redundancy problems, and their structural inflexibility made database modification difficult. They were soon followed by databases that adhered to the network model, which strove to eliminate the main disadvantages of the hierarchical model. Network databases have minimal redundancy but pay for that advantage with structural complexity.

Some years later, Dr. E. F. Codd at IBM developed the *relational* model, which featured minimal redundancy and an easily understood structure. The SQL language was developed to operate on relational databases. Relational databases eventually consigned the hierarchical and network databases to the dustbin of history.

TECHNICAL STUFF

A relatively new phenomenon is the emergence of the so-called NoSQL databases, which lack the structure of the relational databases and do not use the SQL language. I don't cover NoSQL databases in this book. If this topic interests you, check out *NoSQL For Dummies*, by Adam Fowler (Wiley Publishing, Inc.).

Relational model

Dr. Codd first formulated the relational database model in 1970, and this model started appearing in products about a decade later. Ironically, IBM did not deliver the first relational DBMS. That distinction went to a small start-up company, which named its product Oracle.

Relational databases have almost completely replaced earlier database types. That's largely because you can change the structure of a relational database without having to change or modify applications that were based on the old structures. Suppose, for example, that you add one or more new columns to a database table. You don't need to change any previously written applications that process that table — unless, of course, you alter one or more of the columns that those applications use.

WARNING

Of course, if you remove a column that an existing application uses, you experience problems no matter what database model you follow. One of the quickest ways to make a database application crash is to ask it to retrieve a piece of data that your database doesn't contain.

Components of a relational database

Relational databases gain their flexibility because their data resides in tables that are largely independent of each other. You can add, delete, or change data in a table without affecting the data in the other tables, provided that the affected table is not a *parent* of any of the other tables. (Parent-child table relationships are explained in Chapter 5, and no, they don't involve discussing allowances over dinner.) In this section, I show what these tables consist of and how they relate to the other parts of a relational database.

Dealing with your relations

At holiday time, many of my relatives come to my house and sit down at my table. Databases have relations, too, but each of their relations has its *own* table. A relational database is made up of one or more relations.

REMEMBER

A *relation* is a two-dimensional array of rows and columns, containing single-valued entries and no duplicate rows. Each cell in the array can have only one value, and no two rows may be identical. If that's a little hard to picture, here's an example that will put you in the right ballpark. . . .

Most people are familiar with *two-dimensional* arrays of rows and columns, in the form of electronic spreadsheets such as Microsoft Excel. A major-league baseball player's offensive statistics, as listed on the back of a baseball card, are an example of such an array. On the baseball card are columns for year, team, games played, at-bats, hits, runs scored, runs batted in, doubles, triples, home runs, bases on balls, steals, and batting average. A row covers each year that the player has played in the Major Leagues. You can also store this data in a relation (a table), which has the same basic structure. Figure 1-2 shows a relational database table holding the offensive statistics for a single major-league player. In practice, such a table would hold the statistics for an entire team — or perhaps the whole league.

FIGURE 1-2:
A table
showing
a baseball
player's
offensive
statistics.

Player	Year	Team	Game	At Bat	Hits	Runs	RBI	2B	3B	HR	Walk	Steals	Bat. Avg.
Roberts	1988	Padres	5	9	3	1	0	0	0	0	1	0	.333
Roberts	1989	Padres	117	329	99	81	25	15	8	3	49	21	.301
Roberts	1990	Padres	149	556	172	104	44	36	3	9	55	46	.309

Columns in the array are *self-consistent:* A column has the same meaning in every row. If a column contains a player's last name in one row, the column must contain a player's last name in all rows. The order in which the rows and columns appear in the array has no significance. As far as the DBMS is concerned, it doesn't matter which column is first, which is next, and which is last. The same is true of rows. The DBMS processes the table the same way regardless of the organization.

Every column in a database table embodies a single attribute of the table, just like that baseball card. The column's meaning is the same for every row of the table. A table may, for example, contain the names, addresses, and telephone numbers of all an organization's customers. Each row in the table (also called a *record*, or a *tuple*) holds the data for a single customer. Each column holds a single *attribute* — such as customer number, customer name, customer street, customer city, customer state, customer postal code, or customer telephone number. Figure 1-3 shows some of the rows and columns of such a table.

REMEMBER

The *relations* in this database model correspond to *tables* in any database based on the model. Try to say that ten times fast.

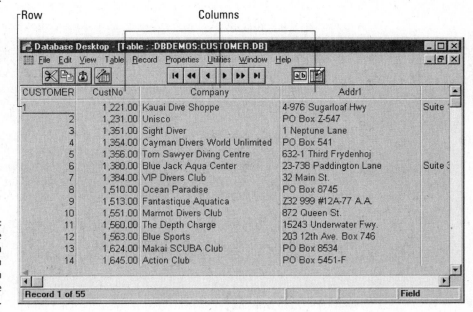

FIGURE 1-3:
Each database
row contains a
record; each
database column
holds a single
attribute.

Enjoy the view

One of my favorite views is of the Yosemite Valley from the mouth of the Wawona Tunnel, late on a spring afternoon. Golden light bathes the sheer face of El Capitan, Half Dome glistens in the distance, and Bridal Veil Falls forms a silver cascade of sparkling water, while wispy clouds weave a tapestry across the sky. Databases have views as well — even if they're not quite that picturesque. The beauty of database views is their sheer usefulness when you're working with your data.

Tables can contain many columns and rows. Sometimes all that data interests you, and sometimes it doesn't. Only some columns of a table may interest you, or perhaps you want to see only rows that satisfy a certain condition. Some columns of one table and some other columns of a related table may interest you. To eliminate data that isn't relevant to your current needs, you can create a *view* — a subset of a database that an application can process. It may contain parts of one or more tables.

REMEMBER

Views are sometimes called *virtual tables.* To the application or the user, views behave the same as tables. Views, however, have no independent existence. Views allow you to look at data, but views are not part of the data.

Say, for example, that you're working with a database that has a CUSTOMER table and an INVOICE table. The CUSTOMER table has the columns CustomerID, FirstName, LastName, Street, City, State, Zipcode, and Phone. The INVOICE table has the columns InvoiceNumber, CustomerID, Date, TotalSale, Total Remitted, and FormOfPayment.

A national sales manager wants to look at a screen that contains only the customer's first name, last name, and telephone number. Creating from the CUSTOMER table a view that contains only the FirstName, LastName, and Phone columns enables the manager to view what he or she needs without having to see all the unwanted data in the other columns. Figure 1-4 shows the derivation of the national sales manager's view.

A branch manager may want to look at the names and phone numbers of all customers whose zip codes fall between 90000 and 93999 (southern and central California). A view that places a restriction on the rows it retrieves, as well as the columns it displays, does the job. Figure 1-5 shows the sources for the columns in the branch manager's view.

The accounts-payable manager may want to look at customer names from the CUSTOMER table and Date, TotalSale, TotalRemitted, and FormOfPayment from the INVOICE table, where TotalRemitted is less than TotalSale. The latter would be the case if full payment hasn't yet been made. This need requires a view that draws from both tables. Figure 1-6 shows data flowing into the accounts-payable manager's view from both the CUSTOMER and INVOICE tables.

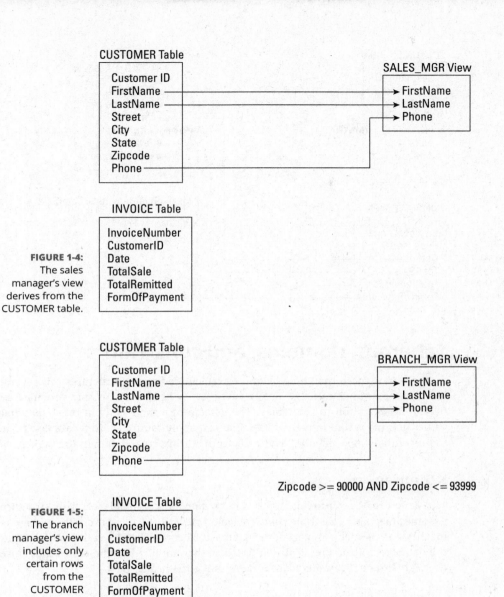

CUSTOMER Table

Customer ID
FirstName
LastName
Street
City
State
Zipcode
Phone

SALES_MGR View

FirstName
LastName
Phone

INVOICE Table

InvoiceNumber
CustomerID
Date
TotalSale
TotalRemitted
FormOfPayment

FIGURE 1-4:
The sales manager's view derives from the CUSTOMER table.

CUSTOMER Table

Customer ID
FirstName
LastName
Street
City
State
Zipcode
Phone

BRANCH_MGR View

FirstName
LastName
Phone

Zipcode >= 90000 AND Zipcode <= 93999

INVOICE Table

InvoiceNumber
CustomerID
Date
TotalSale
TotalRemitted
FormOfPayment

FIGURE 1-5:
The branch manager's view includes only certain rows from the CUSTOMER table.

Views are useful because they enable you to extract and format database data without physically altering the stored data. They also protect the data that you *don't* want to show, because they don't contain it. Chapter 6 illustrates how to create a view by using SQL.

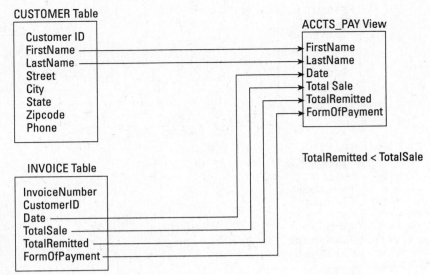

FIGURE 1-6:
The accounts-
payable
manager's
view draws
from two tables.

Schemas, domains, and constraints

A database is more than a collection of tables. Additional structures, on several levels, help to maintain the data's integrity. A database's *schema* provides an overall organization to the tables. The *domain* of a table column tells you what values you may store in the column. You can apply *constraints* to a database table to prevent anyone (including yourself) from storing invalid data in the table.

Schemas

The structure of an entire database is its *schema*, or *conceptual view*. This structure is sometimes also called the *complete logical view* of the database. The schema is metadata — as such, it's part of the database. The metadata itself, which describes the database's structure, is stored in tables that are just like the tables that store the regular data. Even metadata is data; that's the beauty of it.

Domains

An attribute of a relation (that is, a column of a table) can assume some finite number of values. The set of all such values is the *domain* of the attribute.

Say, for example, that you're an automobile dealer who handles the newly intro-duced Curarri GT 4000 sports coupe. You keep track of the cars you have in stock in a database table that you name INVENTORY. You name one of the table columns `Color`, which holds the exterior color of each car. The GT 4000 comes in only four colors: blazing crimson, midnight black, snowflake white, and metallic gray. Those four colors are the domain of the `Color` attribute.

Constraints

Constraints are an important, although often overlooked, component of a database. Constraints are rules that determine what values the table attributes can assume.

By applying tight constraints to a column, you can prevent people from entering invalid data into that column. Of course, every value that is legitimately in the domain of the column must satisfy all the column's constraints. As I mention in the preceding section, a column's domain is the set of all values that the column can contain. A constraint is a restriction on what a column may contain. The characteristics of a table column, plus the constraints that apply to that column, determine the column's domain.

In the auto dealership example, you can constrain the database to accept only those four values (mentioned in the preceding section) in the Color column. If a data entry operator then tries to enter in the Color column a value of, for example, forest green, the system refuses to accept the entry. Data entry can't proceed until the operator enters a valid value into the Color field.

You may wonder what happens when Curarri AutoWerks decides to offer a forest-green version of the GT 4000 as a mid-year option. The answer is (drum roll, please) job security for database-maintenance programmers. This kind of thing happens all the time and requires updates to the database structure. Only people who know how to modify the database structure (such as you) will be able to prevent a major snafu.

The object model challenged the relational model

The relational model has been fantastically successful in a wide variety of application areas. However, it does not do everything that anyone would ever want. The limitations have been made more visible by the rise in popularity of object-oriented programming languages such as C++, Java, and C#. Such languages are capable of handling more complex problems than traditional languages due to their advanced features, such as user-extensible type systems, encapsulation, inheritance, dynamic binding of methods, complex and composite objects, and object identity.

I am not going to explain all that jargon in this book (although I do touch on some of these terms later). Suffice it to say that the classic relational model doesn't mesh well with many of these features. As a result, database management systems based on the object model have been developed. However, the idea never really took off. Although object-oriented programming languages have become very popular, object-oriented databases have not.

Final score: Relational databases 1, object-oriented databases 0.

The object-relational model

Database designers, like everyone else, are constantly searching for the best of all possible worlds. They mused, "Wouldn't it be great if we could have the advantages of an object-oriented database system and still retain compatibility with the relational system that we know and love?" This kind of thinking led to the hybrid object-relational model. Object-relational DBMSs extend the relational model to include support for object-oriented data modeling. Object-oriented features have been added to the international SQL standard, allowing relational DBMS vendors to transform their products into object-relational DBMSs, while retaining compatibility with the standard. Thus, whereas the SQL-92 standard describes a purely relational database model, SQL:1999 describes an object-relational database model. SQL:2003 has more object-oriented features, and subsequent versions of the SQL standard have gone even further in that direction.

In this book, I describe ISO/IEC international standard SQL. (If you're curious, IEC stands for International Electrotechnical Commission, but nobody really cares about that. How many people know what the letters in the acronym LASER stand for?) The system described by the ISO/IEC SQL standard is primarily a relational database model. I also include the object-oriented extensions to the standard that were introduced in SQL:1999 and the additional extensions included in later versions. The object-oriented features of the new standard allow developers to apply SQL databases to problems that are too complex to address with the older, purely relational, paradigm. Vendors of DBMS systems are incorporating the object-oriented features in the ISO standard into their products. Some of these features have been present for years, but others are yet to be included.

Database Design Considerations

A database is a representation of a physical or conceptual structure, such as an organization, an automobile assembly, or the performance statistics of all the major-league baseball clubs. The accuracy of the representation depends on the level of detail of the database design. The amount of effort that you put into database design should depend on the type of information you want to get out of the database. Too much detail is a waste of effort, time, and hard-drive space. Too little detail may render the database worthless.

TIP

Decide how much detail you need now and how much you may need in the future — and then provide exactly that level of detail in your design (no more and no less). But don't be surprised if you have to adjust the design eventually to meet changing real-world needs.

REMEMBER

Today's database management systems, complete with attractive graphical user interfaces and intuitive design tools, can give the would-be database designer a false sense of security. These systems make designing a database seem comparable to building a spreadsheet or engaging in some other relatively straightforward task. No such luck. Database design is difficult. If you do it incorrectly, not only is your database likely to suffer from poor performance, but it also may well become gradually more corrupt as time goes on. Often the problem doesn't turn up until after you devote a great deal of effort to data entry. By the time you know that you have a problem, it's already serious. In many cases, the only solution is to completely redesign the database and reenter all the data. The up side is that by the time you finish your second version of the same database, you realize how much better you understand database design.

Chapter **2**

SQL Fundamentals

S QL is a flexible language that you can use in a variety of ways. It's the most widely used tool for communicating with a relational database. In this chapter, I explain what SQL is and isn't — specifically, what distinguishes SQL from other types of computer languages. Then I introduce the commands and data types that standard SQL supports and I explain two key concepts: *null values* and *constraints.* Finally, I give an overview of how SQL fits into the client/server environment, as well as the Internet and organizational intranets.

What SQL Is and Isn't

The first thing to understand about SQL is that SQL isn't a *procedural language,* as are Python, C, C++, C#, and Java. To solve a problem in a procedural language, you write a *procedure* — a sequence of commands that performs one specific operation after another until the task is complete. The procedure may be a straightforward linear sequence or may loop back on itself, but in either case, the programmer specifies the order of execution.

SQL, on the other hand, is *nonprocedural.* To solve a problem using SQL, simply tell SQL *what* you want (as if you were talking to Aladdin's genie) instead of telling the system *how to get* you what you want. The database management system (DBMS) decides the best way to get you what you request.

All right. I just told you that SQL is not a procedural language — and that's essentially true. However, millions of programmers out there (and you're probably one of them) are accustomed to solving problems in a procedural manner. So, in recent years, there has been a lot of pressure to add some procedural functionality to SQL — and SQL now incorporates features of a procedural language: BEGIN blocks, IF statements, functions, and (yes) procedures. With these facilities added, you can store programs at the server, where multiple clients can use your programs repeatedly.

To illustrate what I mean by "tell the system what you want," suppose you have an EMPLOYEE table from which you want to retrieve the rows that correspond to all your senior people. You want to define a senior person as anyone older than age 40 or anyone earning more than $100,000 per year. You can make the desired retrieval by using the following query:

```
SELECT * FROM EMPLOYEE WHERE Age > 40 OR Salary > 100000 ;
```

This statement retrieves all rows from the EMPLOYEE table where either the value in the Age column is greater than 40 or the value in the Salary column is greater than 100,000. In SQL, you don't have to specify how the information is retrieved. The database engine examines the database and decides for itself how to fulfill your request. You need only specify what data you want to retrieve.

REMEMBER

A *query* is a question you ask the database. If any of the data in the database satisfies the conditions of your query, SQL retrieves that data.

Current SQL implementations lack many of the basic programming constructs that are fundamental to most other languages. Real-world applications usually require at least some of these programming constructs, which is why SQL is actually a data *sublanguage.* Even with the extensions that were added in 1999, 2003, 2005, 2008, and 2011, you still have to use SQL in combination with a procedural language (such as C++) to create a complete application.

You can extract information from a database in one of two ways:

>> **Make an *ad hoc query* from your keyboard by just typing an SQL statement and reading the results from the screen.** Queries from the keyboard are appropriate when you want a quick answer to a specific question. To meet an immediate need, you may require information that you never needed before from a database. You're likely never to need that information again, either, but you need it now. Enter the appropriate SQL query statement from the keyboard, and in due time, the result appears on your screen.

>> **Execute a program that collects information from the database and then reports on the information either onscreen or in a printed report.** Incorporating an SQL query directly into a program is a good way to run a complex query that you're likely to run again in the future. That way, you can formulate a query just once for use as often as you want. Chapter 16 explains how to incorporate SQL code into programs written in another programming language.

A (Very) Little History

SQL originated in one of IBM's research laboratories, as did relational database theory. In the early 1970s, as IBM researchers developed early relational DBMS (or RDBMS) systems, they created a data sublanguage to operate on these systems. They named the pre-release version of this sublanguage *SEQUEL* (*S*tructured *E*nglish *QUE*ry *L*anguage). However, when it came time to formally release their query language as a product, they found that another company had already trademarked the product name "Sequel." Therefore, the marketing geniuses at IBM decided to give the released product a name that was different from SEQUEL but still recognizable as a member of the same family. So they named it SQL, pronounced *ess-que-ell*. Although the official pronunciation is ess-que-ell, people had become accustomed to pronouncing it "Sequel" in the early pre-release days and continued to do so. That practice has persisted to the present day; some people will say "Sequel" and others will say "S-Q-L," but they are both talking about the same thing.

TECHNICAL STUFF

The syntax of SQL is a form of structured English, which is where its original name came from. However, SQL is not a structured *language* in the sense that computer scientists understand that term. Thus, despite the assumptions of many people, SQL is not an acronym standing for "structured query language." It is a sequence of three letters that don't stand for anything, just like the name of the C language does not stand for anything.

IBM's work with relational databases and SQL was well known in the industry even before IBM introduced its SQL/DS relational database (RDBMS) product in 1981. By that time, Relational Software, Inc. (now Oracle Corporation) had already released its first RDBMS. These early products immediately set the standard for a new class of database management systems. They incorporated SQL, which became the de facto standard for data sublanguages. Vendors of other relational database management systems came out with their own versions of SQL. Typically, these other implementations contained all the core functionality of the IBM products, extended in ways that took advantage of the particular strengths of their own RDBMS product. As a result, although nearly all vendors used some form of SQL, compatibility between platforms was poor.

REMEMBER

An *implementation* is a specific RDBMS running on a specific hardware platform.

Soon a movement began, to create a universally recognized SQL standard to which everyone could adhere. In 1986, ANSI (the American National Standards Institute) released a formal standard it named *SQL-86*. ANSI updated that standard in 1989 to *SQL-89* and again in 1992 to *SQL-92*. As DBMS vendors proceed through new releases of their products, they try to bring their implementations ever closer to this standard. This effort has brought the goal of true SQL portability much closer to reality.

REMEMBER

The most recent full version of the SQL standard is SQL:2016 (ISO/IEC 9075-X:2016). In this book, I describe SQL as SQL:2016 defines the language. Every specific SQL implementation differs from the standard to a certain extent. Because the complete SQL standard is comprehensive, currently available implementations are unlikely to support it fully. However, DBMS vendors are working to support a core subset of the standard SQL language. The full ISO/IEC standard is available for purchase at `www.iso.org/search.html?q=iso%209075`, but you probably don't want to buy it unless you intend to create your own ISO/IEC SQL standard database management system. The standard is *highly* technical and virtually incomprehensible to anyone other than a computer language scholar.

SQL Statements

The SQL command language consists of a limited number of statements that perform three functions of data handling: Some of them define data, some manipulate data, and others control data. I cover the data-definition statements and data-manipulation statements in Chapters 4 through 12; I detail the data-control statements in Chapter 14.

To comply with SQL:2016, an implementation must include a basic set of core features. It may also include extensions to the core set (which the SQL:2016 specification also describes). Table 2-1 lists the core plus the extended SQL:2016 statements. It's quite a list. If you're among those programmers who love to try out new capabilities, rejoice.

TABLE 2-1 ## SQL:2016 Statements

ADD	DEALLOCATE PREPARE	FREE LOCATOR
ALLOCATE CURSOR	DECLARE	GET DESCRIPTOR
ALLOCATE DESCRIPTOR	DECLARE LOCAL TEMPORARY TABLE	GET DIAGNOSTICS
ALTER DOMAIN	DELETE	GRANT PRIVILEGE
ALTER ROUTINE	DESCRIBE INPUT	GRANT ROLE
ALTER SEQUENCE GENERATOR	DESCRIBE OUTPUT	HOLD LOCATOR
ALTER TABLE	DISCONNECT	INSERT
ALTER TRANSFORM	DROP	MERGE
ALTER TYPE	DROP ASSERTION	OPEN
CALL	DROP ATTRIBUTE	PREPARE
CLOSE	DROP CAST	RELEASE SAVEPOINT
COMMIT	DROP CHARACTER SET	RETURN
CONNECT	DROP COLLATION	REVOKE
CREATE	DROP COLUMN	ROLLBACK
CREATE ASSERTION	DROP CONSTRAINT	SAVEPOINT
CREATE CAST	DROP DEFAULT	SELECT
CREATE CHARACTER SET	DROP DOMAIN	SET CATALOG
CREATE COLLATION	DROP METHOD	SET CONNECTION
CREATE DOMAIN	DROP ORDERING	SET CONSTRAINTS
CREATE FUNCTION	DROP ROLE	SET DESCRIPTOR
CREATE METHOD	DROP ROUTINE	SET NAMES

(continued)

TABLE 2-1 *(continued)*

CREATE ORDERING	DROP SCHEMA	SET PATH
CREATE PROCEDURE	DROP SCOPE	SET ROLE
CREATE ROLE	DROP SEQUENCE	SET SCHEMA
CREATE SCHEMA	DROP TABLE	SET SESSION AUTHORIZATION
CREATE SEQUENCE	DROP TRANSFORM	SET SESSION CHARACTERISTICS
CREATE TABLE	DROP TRANSLATION	SET SESSION COLLATION
CREATE TRANSFORM	DROP TRIGGER	SET TIME ZONE
CREATE TRANSLATION	DROP TYPE	SET TRANSACTION
CREATE TRIGGER	DROP VIEW	SET TRANSFORM GROUP
CREATE TYPE	EXECUTE IMMEDIATE	START TRANSACTION
CREATE VIEW	FETCH	UPDATE
DEALLOCATE DESCRIPTOR		

Reserved Words

In addition to the statements, a number of other words have a special significance within SQL. These words, along with the statements, are reserved for specific uses, so you can't use them as variable names or in any other way that differs from their intended use. You can easily see why tables, columns, and variables should not be given names that appear on the reserved word list. Imagine the confusion that a statement such as the following would cause:

```
SELECT SELECT FROM SELECT WHERE SELECT = WHERE ;
```

'Nuff said. A complete list of SQL reserved words appears in Appendix A.

Data Types

Depending on their histories, different SQL implementations support a variety of data types. The SQL specification recognizes seven predefined general types:

- » Numerics
- » Binary
- » Strings
- » Booleans
- » Datetimes
- » Intervals
- » XML

Within each of these general types may be several subtypes (exact numerics, approximate numerics, character strings, bit strings, large object strings). In addition to the built-in, predefined types, SQL supports collection types, constructed types, and user-defined types, all of which I discuss later in this chapter.

TIP

If you use an SQL implementation that supports data types that aren't described in the SQL specification, you can keep your database more portable by avoiding these undescribed data types. Before you decide to create and use a user-defined data type, make sure that any DBMS you may want to port to in the future also supports user-defined types.

Exact numerics

As you can probably guess from the name, the *exact numeric* data types enable you to express the value of a number exactly. Five data types fall into this category:

- » INTEGER
- » SMALLINT
- » BIGINT
- » NUMERIC
- » DECIMAL
- » DECFLOAT

INTEGER data type

Data of the INTEGER type has no fractional part, and its precision depends on the specific SQL implementation. As the database developer, you can't specify the precision.

The *precision* of a number is the maximum number of significant digits the number can have.

SMALLINT data type

The SMALLINT data type is also for integers, but the precision of a SMALLINT in a specific implementation can't be any larger than the precision of an INTEGER on the same implementation. In many implementations, SMALLINT and INTEGER are the same.

If you're defining a database table column to hold integer data and you know that the range of values in the column won't exceed the precision of SMALLINT data on your implementation, assign the column the SMALLINT type rather than the INTEGER type. This assignment may enable your DBMS to conserve storage space.

BIGINT data type

The BIGINT data type is defined as a type whose precision is at least as great as that of the INTEGER type (it may be greater). The exact precision of a BIGINT data type depends on the SQL implementation used.

NUMERIC data type

NUMERIC data can have a fractional component in addition to its integer component. You can specify both the precision and the scale of NUMERIC data. (Precision, remember, is the maximum number of significant digits possible.)

The *scale* of a number is the number of digits in its fractional part. The scale of a number can't be negative or larger than that number's precision.

If you specify the NUMERIC data type, your SQL implementation gives you exactly the precision and scale that you request. You may specify NUMERIC and get a default precision and scale, or NUMERIC (p) and get your specified precision and the default scale, or NUMERIC (p,s) and get both your specified precision and your specified scale. The parameters p and s are placeholders that would be replaced by actual values in a data declaration.

Say, for example, that the NUMERIC data type's default precision for your SQL implementation is 12 and the default scale is 6. If you specify a database column as having a NUMERIC data type, the column can hold numbers up to 999,999.999999. If, on the other hand, you specify a data type of NUMERIC (10) for a column, that column can hold only numbers with a maximum value of 9,999.999999. The parameter (10) specifies the maximum number of digits possible in the number. If you specify a data type of NUMERIC (10,2) for a column, that column can hold numbers with a maximum value of 99,999,999.99. In this case, you may still have ten total digits, but only two of those digits can fall to the right of the decimal point.

TIP

NUMERIC data is used for values such as 595.72. That value has a precision of 5 (the total number of digits) and a scale of 2 (the number of digits to the right of the decimal point). A data type of NUMERIC (5,2) is appropriate for such numbers.

DECIMAL data type

The DECIMAL data type is similar to NUMERIC. This data type can have a fractional component, and you can specify its precision and scale. The difference is that your implementation may specify a precision greater than what you specify — if so, the implementation uses the greater precision. If you do not specify precision or scale, the implementation uses default values, as it does with the NUMERIC type.

An item that you specify as NUMERIC (5,2) can never contain a number with an absolute value greater than 999.99. An item that you specify as DECIMAL (5,2) can always hold values *up to* 999.99, but if your SQL implementation permits larger values, then the DBMS won't reject values larger than 999.99.

TIP

Use the NUMERIC or DECIMAL type if your data has fractional positions, and use the INTEGER, SMALLINT, or BIGINT type if your data always consists of whole numbers. Use the NUMERIC type rather than the DECIMAL type if you want to maximize portability, because a value that you define as NUMERIC (5,2), for example, holds the same range of values on all systems.

DECFLOAT data type

The DECFLOAT data type is new in SQL: 2016. Unlike the REAL and DOUBLE PRECISION data types, which are approximate numeric types and only provide binary approximations of decimal data, DECFLOAT combines the accuracy of the exact numeric DECIMAL data type with the performance advantages of the FLOAT data type. This is important for business applications, where approximations are not acceptable.

Approximate numerics

Some quantities have such a large range of possible values (many orders of magnitude) that a computer with a given register size can't represent all the values exactly. (Examples of *register sizes* are 32 bits, 64 bits, and 128 bits.) Usually in such cases, exactness isn't necessary, and a close approximation is acceptable. SQL defines three approximate NUMERIC data types to handle this kind of data: REAL, DOUBLE PRECISION, and FLOAT (as detailed in the next three subsections).

REAL data type

The REAL data type gives you a single-precision, floating-point number — the precision of which depends on the SQL implementation. In general, the hardware you use determines precision. A 64-bit machine, for example, gives you more precision than does a 32-bit machine.

REMEMBER

A *floating-point number* is a number that contains a decimal point. The decimal point can "float" to different locations in the number, depending on the number's value. Examples include 3.1, 3.14, and 3.14159 — and yes, all three can be used as values for Π — each with a different precision.

DOUBLE PRECISION data type

The DOUBLE PRECISION data type gives you a double-precision floating-point number, the precision of which again depends on the implementation. Surprisingly, the meaning of the word DOUBLE also depends on the implementation. Double-precision arithmetic is primarily employed by scientific users. Different scientific disciplines require different levels of precision. Some SQL implementations cater to one category of users, and other implementations cater to other categories of users.

In some systems, the DOUBLE PRECISION type has exactly twice the capacity of the REAL data type for both mantissa and exponent. (In case you've forgotten what you learned in high school, you can represent any number as a *mantissa* multiplied by ten raised to the power given by an exponent. You can write 6,626, for example, as 6.626E3. The number 6.626 is the mantissa, which you multiply by ten raised to the third power; in that case, 3 is the exponent.)

You gain no benefit by representing numbers that are fairly close to 1 (such as 6,626 or even 6,626,000) with an approximate NUMERIC data type. Exact numeric types work just as well — and after all, they're exact. For numbers that are either very near 0 or much larger than 1, however, such as 6.626E-34 (a very small number), you must use an approximate NUMERIC type. Exact NUMERIC data types can't hold such numbers. On other systems, the DOUBLE PRECISION type gives you somewhat more than twice the mantissa capacity — and somewhat less than twice the exponent capacity as the REAL type. On yet another type of system, the DOUBLE PRECISION type gives double the mantissa capacity but the same exponent capacity as the REAL type. In this case, accuracy doubles, but range does not.

REMEMBER

The SQL specification doesn't try to dictate, arbitrate, or establish by fiat what DOUBLE PRECISION means. The specification requires only that the precision *of a* DOUBLE PRECISION number be greater than the precision *of a* REAL number. Although this constraint is rather weak, it's probably the best possible, given the great differences you encounter in hardware.

FLOAT data type

The FLOAT data type is most useful if you think that you may someday migrate your database to a hardware platform with register sizes different from those available on your current platform. By using the FLOAT data type, you can specify a precision — for example, FLOAT (5). If your hardware supports the specified precision with its single-precision circuitry, then your present system uses single-precision arithmetic. If, after you migrate your database, the specified precision requires double-precision arithmetic, then the system uses double-precision arithmetic.

Using FLOAT rather than REAL or DOUBLE PRECISION makes moving your databases to other hardware easier. That's because the FLOAT data type enables you to specify precision and lets the hardware fuss over whether to use single- or double-precision arithmetic. (Remember, the precision of REAL and DOUBLE PRECISION numbers is hardware-dependent.)

If you aren't sure whether to use the exact NUMERIC data types (that is, NUMERIC and DECIMAL) or the approximate NUMERIC data types (that is, FLOAT and REAL), use the exact NUMERIC types. Exact data types demand fewer system resources — and, of course, give exact (rather than approximate) results. If the range of possible values of your data is large enough to require you to use approximate data types, you can probably determine this fact in advance.

Character strings

Databases store many types of data, including graphic images, sounds, and animations. I expect odors to come next. Can you imagine a three-dimensional 1920-x-1080, 24-bit color image of a large slice of pepperoni pizza on your screen, while an odor sample taken at DiFilippi's Pizza Grotto replays through your super-multimedia card? Such a setup may get frustrating — at least until you can afford to add taste-type data to your system as well. Alas, you can expect to wait a long time before odor and taste become standard SQL data types. These days, the data types that you use most commonly — after the NUMERIC types, of course — are the character-string types.

You have three main types of CHARACTER data:

>> Fixed character data (CHARACTER or CHAR)

>> Varying character data (CHARACTER VARYING or VARCHAR)

>> Character large-object data (CHARACTER LARGE OBJECT or CLOB)

You also have three variants of these types of character data:

>> NATIONAL CHARACTER

>> NATIONAL CHARACTER VARYING

>> NATIONAL CHARACTER LARGE OBJECT

Details coming right up.

CHARACTER data type

If you define the data type of a column as CHARACTER or CHAR, you can specify the number of characters the column holds by using the syntax CHAR (x), where x is the number of characters. If you specify a column's data type as CHAR (16), for example, the maximum length of any data you can enter in the column is 16 characters. If you don't specify an argument (that is, you don't provide a value in place of the x, SQL assumes a field length of one character. If you enter data into a CHARACTER field of a specified length and you enter fewer characters than the specified number, SQL fills the remaining character spaces with blanks.

CHARACTER VARYING data type

The CHARACTER VARYING data type is useful if entries in a column can vary in length but you don't want SQL to pad the field with blanks. This data type enables you to store exactly the number of characters that the user enters. No default value exists for this data type. To specify this data type, use the form CHARACTER VARYING (x) or VARCHAR (x), where x is the maximum number of characters permitted.

CHARACTER LARGE OBJECT data type

The CHARACTER LARGE OBJECT (CLOB) data type was introduced with SQL:1999. As its name implies, it's used with huge character strings that are too large for the CHARACTER type. CLOBs behave much like ordinary character strings, but there are restrictions on what you can do with them.

For one thing, a CLOB may not be used in a PRIMARY KEY, FOREIGN KEY, or UNIQUE predicate. Furthermore, it may not be used in a comparison other than one for either equality or inequality. Because of their large size, applications generally do not transfer CLOBs to or from a database. Instead, a special client-side data type called a *CLOB locator* is used to manipulate the CLOB data. It's a parameter whose value identifies a large character-string object.

A *predicate* is a statement that may either be logically True or logically False.

NATIONAL CHARACTER, NATIONAL CHARACTER VARYING, and NATIONAL CHARACTER LARGE OBJECT data types

Various languages have some characters that differ from any characters in another language. For example, German has some special characters not present in the English-language character set. Some languages, such as Russian, have a very different character set from that of English. For example, if you specify the English character set as the default for your system, you can use alternative character sets because the NATIONAL CHARACTER, NATIONAL CHARACTER VARYING, and NATIONAL CHARACTER LARGE OBJECT data types function the same as the CHARACTER, CHARACTER VARYING, and CHARACTER LARGE OBJECT data types — the only difference is that the character set you're specifying is different from the default character set.

You can specify the character set as you define a table column. If you want, each column can use a different character set. The following example of a table-creation statement uses multiple character sets:

```
CREATE TABLE XLATE (
    LANGUAGE_1 CHARACTER (40),
    LANGUAGE_2 CHARACTER VARYING (40) CHARACTER SET GREEK,
    LANGUAGE_3 NATIONAL CHARACTER (40),
    LANGUAGE_4 CHARACTER (40)   CHARACTER SET KANJI
    ) ;
```

Here the LANGUAGE_1 column contains characters in the implementation's default character set. The LANGUAGE_3 column contains characters in the implementation's national character set. The LANGUAGE_2 column contains Greek characters. And the LANGUAGE_4 column contains Kanji characters. After a long absence, Asian character sets, such as Kanji, are now available in many DBMS products.

Binary strings

The BINARY string data types were introduced in SQL:2008. Considering that binary data has been fundamental to digital computers since the Atanasoff-Berry Computer of the 1930s, this recognition of the importance of binary data seems a little late in coming to SQL. (Better late than never, I suppose.) There are three different binary types, BINARY, BINARY VARYING, and BINARY LARGE OBJECT.

BINARY data type

If you define the data type of a column as BINARY, you can specify the number of bytes (octets) the column holds by using the syntax BINARY (x), where x is the number of bytes. If you specify a column's data type as BINARY (16), for example, the binary string must be 16 bytes in length. BINARY data must be entered as bytes, starting with byte one.

BINARY VARYING data type

Use the BINARY VARYING or VARBINARY type when the length of a binary string is a variable. To specify this data type, use the form BINARY VARYING (x) or VARBINARY (x), where x is the maximum number of bytes permitted. The minimum size of the string is zero and the maximum size is x.

BINARY LARGE OBJECT data type

The BINARY LARGE OBJECT (BLOB) data type is used with huge binary strings that are too large for the BINARY type. Graphical images and music files are examples of huge binary strings. BLOBs behave much like ordinary binary strings, but SQL puts some restrictions on what you can do with them.

For one thing, you can't use a BLOB in a PRIMARY KEY, FOREIGN KEY, or UNIQUE predicate. Furthermore, no BLOBs are allowed in comparisons other than those for equality or inequality. BLOBs are large, so applications generally don't transfer actual BLOBs to or from a database. Instead, they use a special client-side data type called a *BLOB locator* to manipulate the BLOB data. The locator is a parameter whose value identifies a binary large object.

Booleans

The BOOLEAN data type consists of the distinct truth values *True* and *False*, as well as *Unknown*. If either a Boolean True or False value is compared to a NULL or Unknown truth value, the result will have the Unknown value.

Datetimes

The SQL standard defines five data types that deal with dates and times; they're called *datetime data types,* or simply *datetimes.* Considerable overlap exists among these data types, so some implementations you encounter may not support all five.

WARNING

Implementations that do not fully support all five data types for dates and times may have problems with databases that you try to migrate from another implementation. If you have trouble with a migration, check the source and the destination implementations to see how they represent dates and times.

DATE data type

The DATE type stores year, month, and day values of a date, in that order. The year value is four digits long, and the month and day values are both two digits long. A DATE value can represent any date from the year 0001 to the year 9999. The length of a DATE is ten positions, as in 1957-08-14.

TIME WITHOUT TIME ZONE data type

The TIME WITHOUT TIME ZONE data type stores hour, minute, and second values of time. The hours and minutes occupy two digits. The seconds value may be only two digits but may also expand to include an optional fractional part. Therefore, this data type can represent a time such as (for example) 32 minutes and 58.436 seconds past 9:00 a.m. as 09:32:58.436.

The precision of the fractional part is implementation-dependent but is at least six digits long. A TIME WITHOUT TIME ZONE value takes up eight positions (including colons) when the value has no fractional part, or nine positions (including the decimal point) plus the number of fractional digits when the value does include a fractional part. You specify TIME WITHOUT TIME ZONE type data either as TIME, which gives you the default of no fractional digits, or as TIME WITHOUT TIME ZONE (p), where p is the number of digit positions to the right of the decimal. The example in the preceding paragraph represents a data type of TIME WITHOUT TIME ZONE (3).

TIMESTAMP WITHOUT TIME ZONE data type

TIMESTAMP WITHOUT TIME ZONE data includes both date and time information. The lengths and the restrictions on the values of the components of TIMESTAMP WITHOUT TIME ZONE data are the same as they are for DATE and TIME WITHOUT TIME ZONE data, except for one difference: The default length of the fractional part of the time component of a TIMESTAMP WITHOUT TIME ZONE is six digits rather than zero.

If the value has no fractional digits, the length of a TIMESTAMP WITHOUT TIME ZONE is 19 positions — ten date positions, one space as a separator, and eight time positions, in that order. If fractional digits are present (six digits is the default), the length is 20 positions plus the number of fractional digits. The 20th position is for the decimal point. You specify a field as TIMESTAMP WITHOUT TIME ZONE type by using either TIMESTAMP WITHOUT TIME ZONE or TIMESTAMP WITHOUT TIME ZONE (p), where p is the number of fractional digit positions. The value of p can't be negative, and the implementation determines its maximum value.

TIME WITH TIME ZONE data type

The `TIME WITH TIME ZONE` data type is the same as the `TIME WITHOUT TIME ZONE` data type except this type adds information about the offset from *Universal Time* (UTC, the successor of Greenwich Mean Time or GMT). The value of the offset may range anywhere from −12:59 to +13:00. This additional information takes up six additional digit positions following the time — a hyphen as a separator, a plus or minus sign, and then the offset in hours (two digits) and minutes (two digits) with a colon in between the hours and minutes. A `TIME WITH TIME ZONE` value with no fractional part (the default) is 14 positions long. If you specify a fractional part, the field length is 15 positions plus the number of fractional digits.

TIMESTAMP WITH TIME ZONE data type

The `TIMESTAMP WITH TIME ZONE` data type functions the same as the `TIMESTAMP WITHOUT TIME ZONE` data type except that this data type also adds information about the offset from Universal Time. The additional information takes up six additional digit positions following the timestamp. (See the preceding section for the form of the time-zone information.) Including time-zone data sets up 25 positions for a field with no fractional part and 26 positions (plus the number of fractional digits) for fields that do include a fractional part. (Six is the default number of fractional digits.)

Intervals

The *interval* data types relate closely to the datetime data types. An interval is the difference between two datetime values. In many applications that deal with dates, times, or both, you sometimes need to determine the interval between two dates or two times.

SQL recognizes two distinct types of intervals: the *year-month* interval and the *day-time* interval. A year-month interval is the number of years and months between two dates. A day-time interval is the number of days, hours, minutes, and seconds between two instants within a month. You can't mix calculations involving a year-month interval with calculations involving a day-time interval, because months come in varying lengths (28, 29, 30, or 31 days long).

XML type

XML is an acronym for eXtensible Markup Language, which defines a set of rules for adding markup to data. The markup structures the data in a way that conveys what the data means. XML enables the sharing of data between very different platforms.

The XML data type has a tree structure, so a root node may have child nodes, which may, in turn, have children of their own. First introduced in SQL:2003, the XML type was fleshed out in SQL/XML:2005, and further augmented in SQL:2008. The 2005 edition defined five parameterized subtypes, while retaining the original plain-vanilla XML type. XML values can exist as instances of two or even more types, because some of the subtypes are subtypes of other subtypes. (Maybe I should call them sub-subtypes, or even sub-sub-subtypes. Fortunately, SQL:2008 defined a standard way of referring to subtypes.)

The primary modifiers of the XML type are SEQUENCE, CONTENT, and DOCUMENT. The secondary modifiers are UNTYPED, ANY, and XMLSCHEMA. Figure 2-1 shows the tree-like structure illustrating the hierarchical relationships among the subtypes.

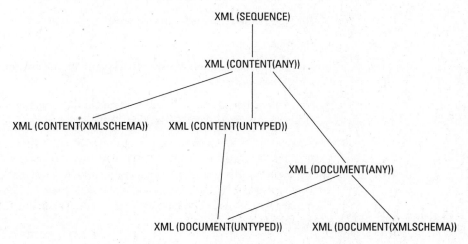

FIGURE 2-1:
The relationships of the XML subtypes.

The following list is a rundown of the XML types you should be familiar with. Don't freak out if it looks like Greek (or worse yet, Linear A) to you. I give a more detailed explanation of these types in Chapter 18. I've organized the list to begin with the most basic types and end with the most complicated:

REMEMBER

>> XML(SEQUENCE): Every value in XML is either an SQL NULL value or an XQuery sequence. That way, every XML value is an instance of the XML(SEQUENCE) type. *XQuery* is a query language specifically designed to extract information from XML data. This is the most basic XML type.

XML(SEQUENCE) is the least restrictive of the XML types. It can accept values that are not well-formed XML values. The other XML types, on the other hand, aren't quite so forgiving.

» `XML(CONTENT(ANY))`: This is a slightly more restrictive type than `XML(SEQUENCE)`. Every XML value that is either a `NULL` value or an XQuery document node (or a child of that document node) is an instance of this type. Every instance of `XML(CONTENT(ANY))` is also an instance of `XML(SEQUENCE)`. XML values of the `XML(CONTENT(ANY))` type are not necessarily well formed, either. Such values may be intermediate results in a query that are later reduced to well-formed values.

» `XML(CONTENT(UNTYPED))`: This is more restrictive than `XML(ANY CONTENT)`, and thus any value of the `XML(CONTENT(UNTYPED))` type is also an instance of the `XML(CONTENT(ANY))` type and the `XML(SEQUENCE)` type. Every XML value that is either the null value or a non-null value of type `XML(CONTENT(ANY))` is an XQuery document node **D**, such that the following is true for every XQuery element node contained in the XQuery tree **T** rooted in **D**:

- The type-name property is `xdt:untyped`.

- The **nilled** property is `False`.

- For every XQuery attribute node contained in **T**, the type property is `xdt:untypedAtomic`.

- For every XQuery attribute node contained in **T**, the type property is a value of type-name `XML(CONTENT(UNTYPED))`.

» `XML(CONTENT(XMLSCHEMA))`: This is a second subtype of `XML(CONTENT (ANY))` besides `XML(CONTENT(UNTYPED))`. As such it is also a subtype of `XML(SEQUENCE)`. Every XML value that is either the null value or a non-null value of type `XML(CONTENT(ANY))` and is also an XQuery document node **D** such that every XQuery element node that is contained in the XQuery tree **T** rooted in **D**:

- Is valid according to the XML Schema **S**, or

- Is valid according to an XML namespace **N** in an XML Schema **S**, or

- Is valid according to a global element declaration schema component **E** in an XML schema **S**, or

- Is a value of type `XML(CONTENT(XMLSCHEMA))`, whose type descriptor includes the registered XML Schema descriptor of **S**, and, if **N** is specified, the XML namespace URI of **N**, or if **E** is specified, the XML namespace URI of **E** and the XML NCName of **E**.

» `XML(DOCUMENT(ANY))`: This is another subtype of the `XML(CONTENT(ANY))` type with the added restriction that instances of `XML(DOCUMENT(ANY))` are document nodes that have exactly one XQuery element node, zero or more XQuery comment nodes, and zero or more XQuery processing instruction nodes.

>> XML(DOCUMENT(UNTYPED)): Every value that is either the NULL value or a non-null value of type XML(CONTENT(UNTYPED)) that is an XQuery document node whose children property has exactly one XQuery element node, zero or more XQuery comment nodes, and zero or more XQuery processing instruction nodes is a value of type XML(DOCUMENT(UNTYPED)). All instances of XML(DOCUMENT(UNTYPED)) are also instances of XML(CONTENT(UNTYPED)). Furthermore, all instances of XML(DOCUMENT(UNTYPED)) are also instances of XML(DOCUMENT(ANY)). XML(DOCUMENT(UNTYPED)) is the most restrictive of the subtypes, sharing the restrictions of all the other subtypes. Any document that qualifies as an XML(DOCUMENT(UNTYPED)) is also an instance of all the other XML subtypes.

ROW types

The ROW data type was introduced with SQL:1999. It's not that easy to understand, and as a beginning to intermediate SQL programmer, you may never use it. After all, people got by without it just fine between 1986 and 1999.

One notable thing about the ROW data type is that it violates the rules of normalization that E. F. Codd declared in the early days of relational database theory. (I talk more about those rules in Chapter 5.) One of the defining characteristics of first normal form is that a field in a table row may not be multivalued. A field may contain one and only one value. However, the ROW data type allows you to declare an entire row of data to be contained within a single field in a single row of a table — in other words, a row nested within a row.

REMEMBER

The *normal forms,* first articulated by Dr. Codd, are defining characteristics of relational databases. Inclusion of the ROW type in the SQL standard was the first attempt to broaden SQL beyond the pure relational model.

Consider the following SQL statement, which defines a ROW type for a person's address information:

```
CREATE ROW TYPE addr_typ (
    Street      CHARACTER VARYING (25),
    City        CHARACTER VARYING(20),
    State       CHARACTER (2),
    PostalCode  CHARACTER VARYING (9)
    ) ;
```

After it's defined, the new ROW type can be used in a table definition:

```
CREATE TABLE CUSTOMER (
    CustID          INTEGER        PRIMARY KEY,
    LastName        CHARACTER VARYING (25),
    FirstName       CHARACTER VARYING (20),
    Address         addr_typ,
    Phone           CHARACTER VARYING (15)
    ) ;
```

The advantage here is that if you're maintaining address information for multiple entities — such as customers, vendors, employees, and stockholders — you need define the details of the address specification only once: in the ROW type definition.

Collection types

After SQL broke out of the relational straightjacket with SQL:1999, data types that violate first normal form became possible. It became possible for a field to contain a whole collection of objects rather than just one. The ARRAY type was introduced in SQL:1999, and the MULTISET type was introduced in SQL:2003.

Two collections may be compared to each other only if they are both the same type, either ARRAY or MULTISET, and if their element types are comparable. Because arrays have a defined element order, corresponding elements from the arrays can be compared. Multisets have no defined element order, but you can compare them if (a) an enumeration exists for each multiset being compared and (b) the enumerations can be paired.

ARRAY type

The ARRAY data type violates first normal form (1NF), but in a different way than the way the ROW type violates 1NF. The ARRAY type, a collection type, is not a distinct type in the same sense that CHARACTER and NUMERIC are distinct data types. An ARRAY type merely allows one of the other types to have multiple values within a single field of a table. For example, say your organization needs to be able to contact customers whether they're at work, at home, or on the road. You want to maintain multiple telephone numbers for them. You can do this by declaring the Phone attribute as an array, as shown in the following code:

```
CREATE TABLE CUSTOMER (
    CustID          INTEGER        PRIMARY KEY,
    LastName        CHARACTER VARYING (25),
    FirstName       CHARACTER VARYING (20),
```

```
Address          addr_typ,
Phone            CHARACTER VARYING (15) ARRAY [3]
) ;
```

The ARRAY [3] notation allows you to store up to three telephone numbers in the CUSTOMER table. The three telephone numbers represent an example of a repeating group. *Repeating groups* are a no-no according to classical relational database theory, but this is one of several examples of cases where SQL:1999 broke the rules. When Dr. Codd first specified the rules of normalization, he traded off functional flexibility for data integrity. SQL:1999 took back some of that functional flexibility, at the cost of some added structural complexity.

REMEMBER

The increased structural complexity could translate into compromised data integrity if you are not fully aware of all the effects of the actions you perform on your database. Arrays are ordered, in that each element in an array is associated with *exactly one* ordinal position in the array.

An array is an ordered collection of values, and the *cardinality* of an array is the number of elements in the array. An SQL array can have any cardinality from zero up to and including some declared maximum number of elements. This means that the cardinality of a column of the array type can vary from one row to the next. An array can be atomically null, in which case its cardinality would also be null. A null array is not the same as an empty array, whose cardinality would be zero. An array that has only null elements would have a cardinality greater than zero. For example, an array with five null elements would have a cardinality of five.

If an array has a cardinality that is less than the declared maximum, the unused cells in the array are considered to be nonexistent. They are not considered to contain null values; they just aren't there at all.

You can access individual elements in an array by enclosing their subscripts in square brackets. If you have an array named Phone, then Phone [3] would refer to the third element of the Phone array.

Since SQL:1999, it has been possible to find out the cardinality of an array by invoking the CARDINALITY function. SQL:2011 added the ability to discover the maximum cardinality of an array by using the ARRAY_MAX_CARDINALITY function. This is very useful because it enables you to write general-purpose routines that apply to arrays with different maximum cardinalities. Routines with hard-coded maximum cardinalities apply only to arrays that have a given maximum cardinality and would have to be rewritten for arrays of any other maximum cardinality.

Whereas SQL:1999 introduced the ARRAY data type and the ability to address individual elements within an array, it did not make any provision for removing elements from an array. That oversight was corrected in SQL:2011 with the introduction of the TRIM_ARRAY function, which enables you to remove elements from the end of an array.

MULTISET type

A *multiset* is an unordered collection. Specific elements of the multiset may not be referenced; usually that's because those elements are not assigned specific ordinal positions in the multiset.

REF types

REF types are not part of core SQL. This means that a DBMS may claim compliance with the SQL standard without implementing REF types at all. The REF type is not a distinct data type in the sense that CHARACTER and NUMERIC are. Instead, it's a *pointer* to a data item, a row type, or an abstract data type that resides in a row of a table (a site). Dereferencing the pointer can retrieve the value stored at the target site.

If you're confused, don't worry, because you're not alone. Using the REF types requires a working knowledge of object-oriented programming (OOP) principles. This book refrains from wading too deeply into the murky waters of OOP. In fact, because the REF types are not a part of core SQL, you may be better off if you don't use them. If you want maximum portability across DBMS platforms, stick to core SQL.

User-defined types

User-defined types (UDTs) represent another example of features that arrived in SQL:1999 that come from the object-oriented programming world. As an SQL programmer, you are no longer restricted to the data types defined in the SQL specification. You can define your own data types, using the principles of abstract data types (ADTs) found in such object-oriented programming languages as C++.

One of the most important benefits of UDTs is the fact that you can use them to eliminate the *impedance mismatch* between SQL and the host language that is "wrapped around" the SQL. A long-standing problem with SQL has been the fact the SQL's predefined data types do not match the data types of the host languages within which SQL statements are embedded. Now, with UDTs, a database programmer can create data types within SQL that match the data types of the host language.

A UDT has attributes and methods, which are encapsulated within the UDT. The outside world can see the attribute definitions and the results of the methods — but the specific implementations of the methods are hidden from view. Access to the attributes and methods of a UDT can be further restricted by specifying that they are public, private, or protected:

>> **Public** attributes or methods are available to all users of a UDT.

>> **Private** attributes or methods are available only to the UDT itself.

>> **Protected** attributes or methods are available only to the UDT itself or its subtypes.

You see from this that a UDT in SQL behaves much like a class in an object-oriented programming language. Two forms of user-defined types exist: distinct types and structured types.

Distinct types

Distinct types are the simpler of the two forms of user-defined types. A distinct type's defining feature is that it's expressed as a single data type. It is constructed from one of the predefined data types, called the *source type.* Multiple distinct types that are all based on a single source type are distinct from each other; thus, they are not directly comparable. For example, you can use distinct types to distinguish between different currencies. Consider the following type definition:

```
CREATE DISTINCT TYPE USdollar AS DECIMAL (9,2) ;
```

This definition creates a new data type for U.S. dollars (USdollar), based on the predefined DECIMAL data type. You can create another distinct type in a similar manner:

```
CREATE DISTINCT TYPE Euro AS DECIMAL (9,2) ;
```

You can now create tables that use these new types:

```
CREATE TABLE USInvoice (
    InvID       INTEGER       PRIMARY KEY,
    CustID      INTEGER,
    EmpID       INTEGER,
    TotalSale   USdollar,
    Tax         USdollar,
    Shipping    USdollar,
    GrandTotal  USdollar
    ) ;
```

```
CREATE TABLE EuroInvoice (
    InvID       INTEGER       PRIMARY KEY,
    CustID      INTEGER,
    EmpID       INTEGER,
    TotalSale   Euro,
```

```
Tax          Euro,
Shipping     Euro,
GrandTotal   Euro
) ;
```

The USdollar type and the Euro type are both based on the DECIMAL type, but instances of one cannot be directly compared with instances of the other or with instances of the DECIMAL type. In SQL, as in the real world, it is possible to convert U.S. dollars into euros, but doing so requires a special operation (CAST). After conversion is complete, comparisons are possible.

Structured types

The second form of user-defined type — the structured type — is expressed as a list of attribute definitions and methods instead of being based on a single predefined source type.

CONSTRUCTORS

When you create a structured UDT, the DBMS automatically creates a constructor function for it, giving it the same name as the UDT. The constructor's job is to initialize the attributes of the UDT to their default values.

MUTATORS AND OBSERVERS

When you create a structured UDT, the DBMS automatically creates a mutator function and an observer function. A *mutator,* when invoked, changes the value of an attribute of a structured type. An *observer* function is the opposite of a mutator function; its job is to retrieve the value of an attribute of a structured type. You can include observer functions in SELECT statements to retrieve values from a database.

SUBTYPES AND SUPERTYPES

A hierarchical relationship can exist between two structured types. For example, a type named MusicCDudt has a subtype named RockCDudt and another subtype named ClassicalCDudt. MusicCDudt is the supertype of those two subtypes. RockCDudt is a *proper subtype* of MusicCDudt if there is no subtype of MusicCDudt that is a supertype of RockCDudt. If RockCDudt has a subtype named Heavy MetalCDudt, HeavyMetalCDudt is also a subtype of MusicCDudt, but it is not a proper subtype of MusicCDudt.

A structured type that has no supertype is called a *maximal supertype,* and a structured type that has no subtypes is called a *leaf subtype.*

EXAMPLE OF A STRUCTURED TYPE

You can create structured UDTs in the following way:

```
/* Create a UDT named MusicCDudt */
CREATE TYPE MusicCDudt AS
/* Specify attributes */
Title              CHAR(40),
Cost               DECIMAL(9,2),
SuggestedPrice     DECIMAL(9,2)
/* Allow for subtypes */
NOT FINAL ;

CREATE TYPE RockCDudt UNDER MusicCDudt NOT FINAL ;
```

The subtype RockCDudt inherits the attributes of its supertype MusicCDudt.

```
CREATE TYPE HeavyMetalCDudt UNDER RockCDudt FINAL ;
```

Now that you have the types, you can create tables that use them. Here's an example:

```
CREATE TABLE METALSKU (
        Album       HeavyMetalCDudt,
        SKU         INTEGER) ;
```

Now you can add rows to the new table:

```
BEGIN
        /* Declare a temporary variable a */
        DECLARE a = HeavyMetalCDudt ;
        /* Execute the constructor function */
        SET a = HeavyMetalCDudt() ;
            /* Execute first mutator function */
            SET a = a.title('Edward the Great') ;
            /* Execute second mutator function */
            SET a = a.cost(7.50) ;
            /* Execute third mutator function */
            SET a = a.suggestedprice(15.99) ;
              INSERT INTO METALSKU VALUES (a, 31415926) ;
        END
```

User-defined types sourced from collection types

In the earlier section "Distinct types," I illustrate how you can create a user-defined type from a predefined type, using the example of creating a USDollar type from the DECIMAL type. This capability was introduced in SQL:1999. SQL:2011 expanded on this capability by enabling you to create a new user-defined type from a collection type. This enables the developer to define methods on the array as a whole, not just on the individual elements of the array, as allowed by SQL:1999.

Data type summary

Table 2-2 lists various data types and displays literals that conform to each type.

TABLE 2-2   ## Data Types

Data Type	Example Value
CHARACTER (20)	'Amateur Radio '
VARCHAR (20)	'Amateur Radio'
CLOB (1000000)	'This character string is a million characters long ...'
SMALLINT, BIGINT, or INTEGER	7500
NUMERIC, DECIMAL, or DECFLOAT	3425.432
REAL, FLOAT, or DOUBLE PRECISION	6.626E-34
BINARY (1)	'01100011'
VARBINARY (4)	'01100011110001101110011O'
BLOB (1000000)	'10010011101010110101010101010101...'
BOOLEAN	'TRUE'
DATE	DATE '1957-08-14'
TIME (2) WITHOUT TIME ZONE	TIME '12:46:02.43' WITHOUT TIME ZONE
TIME (3) WITH TIME ZONE	TIME '12:46:02.432-08:00' WITH TIME ZONE
TIMESTAMP WITHOUT TIME ZONE (0)	TIMESTAMP '1957-08-14 12:46:02' WITHOUT TIME ZONE

Data Type	Example Value
TIMESTAMP WITH TIME ZONE (0)	TIMESTAMP '1957-08-14 12:46:02-08:00' WITH TIME ZONE
INTERVAL DAY	INTERVAL '4' DAY
XML(SEQUENCE)	<Client>Vince Tenetria</Client>
ROW	ROW (Street VARCHAR (25), City VARCHAR (20), State CHAR (2), PostalCode VARCHAR (9))
ARRAY	INTEGER ARRAY [15]
MULTISET	No literal applies to the MULTISET type
REF	Not a type, but a pointer
USER DEFINED TYPE	Currency type based on DECIMAL

[1] Argument specifies number of fractional digits.

REMEMBER

Your SQL implementation may not support all the data types that I describe in this section. Furthermore, your implementation may support nonstandard data types that I don't describe here. (Your mileage may vary, and so on. You know the drill.)

Null Values

REMEMBER

If a database field contains a data item, that field has a specific value. A field that does not contain a data item is said to have a *null value.* Keep in mind that

>> In a numeric field, a null value is not the same as a value of zero.

>> In a character field, a null value is not the same as a blank.

Both a numeric zero and a blank character are definite values. A null value indicates that a field's value is undefined — its value is not known.

Many situations exist in which a field may have a null value. The following list describes a few of these situations and gives an example of each:

>> **The value exists, but you don't know what the value is yet.** You set NUMBER to null in the Lifeforms row of the Exoplanets table before astronomers have discovered unequivocal evidence of life beyond our solar system in the Milky Way galaxy.

>> **The value doesn't exist yet.** You set TOTAL_SOLD to null in the SQL For Dummies, 9th Edition row of the BOOKS table because the first set of quarterly sales figures is not yet reported.

>> **The field isn't applicable for this specific row.** You set SEX to null in the C3PO row of the EMPLOYEE table because C3PO is a droid that has no gender. (You knew that.)

>> **The value is out of range.** You set SALARY to null in the Oprah Winfrey row of the EMPLOYEE table because you designed the SALARY column as type NUMERIC (8,2) and Oprah's contract calls for pay in excess of $999,999.99. (You knew that too.)

TIP

A field can have a null value for many different reasons. Don't jump to any hasty conclusions about what any particular null value means.

Constraints

Constraints are restrictions that you apply to the data that someone can enter into a database table. You may know, for example, that entries in a given numeric column must fall within a certain range. If anyone makes an entry that falls outside that range, then that entry must be an error. Applying a range constraint to the column prevents this type of error from happening.

Traditionally, the application program that uses the database applies any constraints to a database. The most recent DBMS products, however, enable you to apply constraints directly to the database. This approach has several advantages. If multiple applications use the same database, you apply the constraints only once (rather than multiple times). Also, adding constraints at the database level is usually simpler than adding them to an application. Often all you do is tack the appropriate clause onto your CREATE statement.

I discuss constraints and *assertions* (which are constraints that apply to more than one table) in detail in Chapter 5.

Using SQL in a Client/Server System

SQL is a data sublanguage that works on a standalone system or on a multiuser system. SQL works particularly well on a client/server system. On such a system, users on multiple client machines that connect to a server machine can access — via a local-area network (LAN) or other communications channel — a database that resides on the server to which they're connected. The application program on a client machine contains SQL data-manipulation commands. The portion of the DBMS residing on the client sends these commands to the server across the communications channel that connects the server to the client. At the server, the server portion of the DBMS interprets and executes the SQL command and then sends the results back to the client across the communication channel. You can encode very complex operations into SQL at the client, and then decode and perform those operations at the server. This type of setup results in the most effective use of the bandwidth of that communication channel.

The server

Unless it receives a request from a client, the server does nothing; it just stands around and waits. If multiple clients require service at the same time, however, servers must respond quickly. Servers generally differ from client machines in terms of how much data they handle. They have large amounts of very fast disk storage, optimized for fast data access and retrieval. And because they must handle traffic coming in simultaneously from multiple client machines, servers need fast multi-core processors.

What the server is

The *server* (short for *database server*) is the part of a client/server system that holds the database. The server also holds the server software — the part of a database management system that interprets commands coming in from the clients and translates these commands into operations in the database. The server software also formats the results of retrieval requests and sends the results back to the requesting client.

What the server does

The server's job is relatively simple and straightforward. All a server needs to do is read, interpret, and execute commands that come to it across the network from clients. Those commands are in one of several data sublanguages.

A sublanguage doesn't qualify as a complete language — it implements only part of a language. A data sublanguage may, for example, deal only with data handling. The sublanguage has operations for inserting, updating, deleting, and selecting data, but may not have flow control structures such as DO loops, local variables, functions, procedures, or input/output to printers. SQL is the most common data sublanguage in use today and has become an industry standard. In fact, SQL has supplanted proprietary data sublanguages on machines in all performance classes. With SQL:1999, SQL acquired many of the features missing from traditional sublanguages. However, SQL is still not a complete general-purpose programming language; it must be combined with a host language to create a database application.

The client

The *client* part of a client/server system consists of a hardware component and a software component. The hardware component is the client computer and its interface to the local-area network. This client hardware may be very similar (or even identical) to the server hardware. The software is the distinguishing component of the client.

What the client is

The client's primary job is to provide a user interface. As far as the user is concerned, the client machine *is* the computer, and the user interface *is* the application. The user may not even realize that the process involves a server. The server is usually out of sight — often in another room. Aside from the user interface, the client also contains the application program and the client part of the DBMS. The application program performs the specific task you require (say, in accounts receivable or order entry). The client part of the DBMS executes the application program's commands and exchanges data and SQL data-manipulation commands with the server part of the DBMS.

What the client does

The client part of a DBMS displays information onscreen and responds to user input transmitted via the keyboard, mouse, or other input device. The client may also process data coming in from a telecommunications link or from other stations on the network. The client part of the DBMS does all the application-specific "thinking." To a developer, the client part of a DBMS is the interesting part. The server part just handles the requests of the client part in a repetitive, mechanical fashion.

Using SQL on the Internet or an Intranet

Database operation on the Internet (now often called "the cloud") and on intranets differs fundamentally from database operation in a traditional client/server system. The difference is primarily on the client end. In a traditional client/server system, much of the functionality of the DBMS resides on the client machine. On an Internet-based database system, most or all of the DBMS resides on the server. The client may host nothing more than a web browser. At most, the client holds a browser and a browser extension, such as a Firefox add-on or an ActiveX control. Thus, the conceptual "center of mass" of the system shifts toward the server. This shift has several advantages:

>> The client portion of the system (browser) is low-cost or even free.

>> You have a standardized user interface.

>> The client is easy to maintain.

>> You have a standardized client/server relationship.

>> You have a common means of displaying multimedia data.

The main disadvantages of performing database manipulations over the Internet involve security and data integrity:

>> To protect information from unwanted access or tampering, both the web server and the client browser must support strong encryption.

>> Browsers don't perform adequate data-entry validation checks.

>> Database tables residing on different servers may become desynchronized.

Client and server extensions designed to address these concerns make the Internet a feasible location for production database applications. The architecture of an intranet is similar to that of the Internet, but security is less of a concern. Because the organization maintaining the intranet has physical control over all the client machines — as well as the servers and the network that connects these components together — an intranet suffers much less exposure to the efforts of malicious hackers. Data-entry errors and database desynchronization, however, do remain concerns.

Chapter **3**

The Components of SQL

SQL is a special-purpose language designed for the creation and maintenance of data in relational databases. Although the vendors of relational database management systems have their own SQL implementations, an ISO/IEC standard (revised in 2016) defines and controls what SQL is. All implementations differ from the standard to varying degrees. Close adherence to the standard is the key to running a database (and its associated applications) on more than one platform.

Although SQL isn't a general-purpose programming language, it contains some impressive tools. Three languages within the language offer everything you need to create, modify, maintain, and provide security for a relational database:

» **The Data Definition Language (DDL):** The part of SQL that you use to create (completely define) a database, modify its structure, and destroy it when you no longer need it.

» **The Data Manipulation Language (DML):** The part of SQL that performs database maintenance. Using this powerful tool, you can specify what you want to do with the data in your database — enter it, change it, remove it, or retrieve it.

» **The Data Control Language (DCL):** The part of SQL that protects your database from becoming corrupted. Used correctly, the DCL provides security for your database; the amount of protection depends on the implementation. If your implementation doesn't provide sufficient protection, you must add that protection to your application program.

This chapter introduces the DDL, DML, and DCL.

Data Definition Language

The Data Definition Language (DDL) is the part of SQL you use to create, change, or destroy the basic elements of a relational database. Basic elements include tables, views, schemas, catalogs, clusters, and possibly other things as well. In the following sections, I discuss the containment hierarchy that relates these elements to each other and look at the commands that operate on these elements.

In Chapter 1, I mention tables and schemas, noting that a *schema* is an overall structure that includes tables within it. Tables and schemas are two elements of a relational database's *containment hierarchy.* You can break down the containment hierarchy as follows:

» Tables contain columns and rows.

» Schemas contain tables and views.

» Catalogs contain schemas.

The database itself contains catalogs. Sometimes the database is referred to as a *cluster.* I mention clusters again later in this chapter, in the section on ordering by catalog.

When "Just do it!" is not good advice

Suppose you set out to create a database for your organization. Excited by the prospect of building a useful, valuable, and totally righteous structure of great importance to your company's future, you sit down at your computer and start entering SQL CREATE statements. Right?

Well, no. Not quite. In fact, that's a prescription for disaster. Many database-development projects go awry from the start as excitement and enthusiasm overtake careful planning. Even if you have a clear idea of how to structure your database, *write everything down on paper* before touching your keyboard.

Here's where database development bears some resemblance to a game of chess. In the middle of a complicated and competitive chess game, you may see what looks like a good move. The urge to make that move can be overwhelming. However, the odds are good that you've missed something. Grandmasters advise newer players — only partly in jest — to sit on their hands. If sitting on your hands prevents you from making an ill-advised move, then so be it: Sit on your hands. If you study the position a little longer, you might find an even better move — or you might even see a brilliant counter move that your opponent can make. Plunging into creating a database without sufficient forethought can lead to a database structure that, at best, is suboptimal. At worst, it could be disastrous, an open invitation to data corruption. Sitting on your hands probably won't help, but it *will* help to pick up a pencil in one of those hands and start mapping your database plan on paper. For help in deciding what to include in your plan, check out my book *Database Development For Dummies,* which covers planning in depth.

Keep in mind the following procedures when planning your database:

>> Identify all tables.

>> Define the columns that each table must contain.

>> Give each table a *primary key* that you can guarantee is unique. (I discuss primary keys in Chapters 4 and 5.)

>> Make sure that every table in the database has at least one column in common with (at least) one other table in the database. These shared columns serve as logical links that enable you to relate information in one table to the corresponding information in another table.

>> Put each table in *third normal form* (3NF) or better, to ensure the prevention of insertion, deletion, and update anomalies. (I discuss database normalization in Chapter 5.)

After you complete the design on paper and verify that it's sound, you're ready to transfer the design to the computer. You can do this bit of magic by typing SQL CREATE statements. More likely, you will use your DBMS's graphical user interface (GUI) to create the elements of your design. If you do use a GUI, your input will be converted "under the covers" into SQL by your DBMS.

Creating tables

A database table looks a lot like a spreadsheet table: a two-dimensional array made up of rows and columns. You can create a table by using the SQL CREATE TABLE command. Within the command, you specify the name and data type of each column.

After you create a table, you can start loading it with data. (Loading data is a DML, not a DDL, function.) If requirements change, you can change a table's structure by using the ALTER TABLE command. If a table outlives its usefulness or becomes obsolete, you can eliminate it with the DROP command. The various forms of the CREATE and ALTER commands, together with the DROP command, make up SQL's DDL.

Suppose you're a database designer and you don't want your database tables to turn to guacamole as you make updates over time. You decide to structure your database tables according to the best normalized form so that you can maintain data integrity.

REMEMBER

Normalization, an extensive field of study in its own right, is a way of structuring database tables so that updates don't introduce anomalies. Each table you create contains columns that correspond to attributes that are tightly linked to each other.

You may, for example, create a CUSTOMER table with the attributes CUSTOMER. CustomerID, CUSTOMER.FirstName, CUSTOMER.LastName, CUSTOMER.Street, CUSTOMER.City, CUSTOMER.State, CUSTOMER.Zipcode, and CUSTOMER.Phone. All these attributes are more closely related to the customer entity than to any other entity in a database that may contain many tables. These attributes contain all the relatively permanent customer information that your organization keeps on file.

Most database management systems provide a graphical tool for creating database tables. You can also create such tables by using an SQL command. The following example demonstrates a command that creates your CUSTOMER table:

```
CREATE TABLE CUSTOMER (
    CustomerID      INTEGER         NOT NULL,
    FirstName       CHAR (15),
    LastName        CHAR (20)       NOT NULL,
    Street          CHAR (25),
    City            CHAR (20),
    State           CHAR (2),
    Zipcode         CHAR (10),
    Phone           CHAR (13) ) ;
```

For each column, you specify its name (for example, CustomerID), its data type (for example, INTEGER), and possibly one or more constraints (for example, NOT NULL).

Figure 3-1 shows a portion of the CUSTOMER table with some sample data.

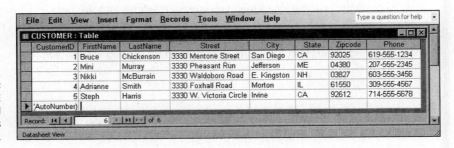

FIGURE 3-1:
Use the CREATE TABLE command to create this CUSTOMER table.

REMEMBER

If the SQL implementation you use doesn't fully implement the latest version of ISO/IEC standard SQL, the syntax you need to use may differ from the syntax that I give in this book. Read the user documentation that came with your DBMS for specific information.

A room with a view

At times, you want to retrieve specific information from the CUSTOMER table. You don't want to look at everything — only specific columns and rows. What you need is a view.

A *view* is a virtual table. In most implementations, a view has no independent physical existence. The view's definition exists only in the database's metadata, but the data comes from the table or tables from which you derive the view. The view's data is not physically duplicated somewhere else in online disk storage. Some views consist of specific columns and rows of a single table. Others, known as *multi-table views,* draw from two or more tables.

Single-table view

Sometimes when you have a question, the data that gives you the answer resides in a single table in your database. If the information you want exists in a single table, you can create a single-table view of the data. For example, suppose you want to look at the names and telephone numbers of all customers who live in the state of New Hampshire. You can create a view from the CUSTOMER table that contains only the data you want. The following SQL statement creates this view:

```
CREATE VIEW NH_CUST AS
    SELECT CUSTOMER.FirstName,
           CUSTOMER.LastName,
           CUSTOMER.Phone
        FROM CUSTOMER
        WHERE CUSTOMER.State = 'NH' ;
```

Figure 3-2 shows how you derive the view from the CUSTOMER table.

TIP

This code is correct, but a little on the wordy side. You can accomplish the same task with less typing if your SQL implementation assumes that all table references are the same as the ones in the FROM clause. If your system makes that reasonable default assumption, you can reduce the statement to the following lines:

```
CREATE VIEW NH_CUST AS
    SELECT FirstName, LastName, Phone
        FROM CUSTOMER
        WHERE STATE = 'NH';
```

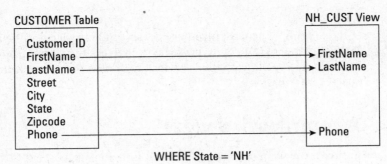

FIGURE 3-2:
You derive
the NH_CUST
view from the
CUSTOMER table.

CUSTOMER Table

Customer ID
FirstName
LastName
Street
City
State
Zipcode
Phone

NH_CUST View

FirstName
LastName

Phone

WHERE State = 'NH'

Although the second version is easier to write and read, it's more vulnerable to disruption from ALTER TABLE commands. Such disruption isn't a problem for this simple case, which has no JOIN, but views with JOINs are more robust when they use fully qualified names. I cover JOINs in Chapter 11.

Creating a multi-table view

Quite often, you need to pull data from two or more tables to answer your question. Suppose, for example, that you work for a sporting goods store, and you want to send a promotional mailing to all the customers who have bought ski equipment since the store opened last year. You need information from the CUSTOMER table, the PRODUCT table, the INVOICE table, and the INVOICE_LINE table. You can create a multi-table view that shows the data you need. After you create the view, you can use that same view again and again. Each time you use the view, it reflects any changes that occurred in the underlying tables since you last used the view.

The database for this sporting goods store contains four tables: CUSTOMER, PRODUCT, INVOICE, and INVOICE_LINE. The tables are structured as shown in Table 3-1.

Notice that some of the columns in Table 3-1 contain the constraint NOT NULL. These columns are either the primary keys of their respective tables or columns that you decide *must* contain a value. A table's primary key must uniquely identify each row. To do that, the primary key must contain a non-null value in every row. (I discuss keys in detail in Chapter 5.)

TIP

The tables relate to each other through the columns that they have in common. The following list describes these relationships (as shown in Figure 3-3):

>> The CUSTOMER table bears a *one-to-many relationship* to the INVOICE table. One customer can make multiple purchases, generating multiple invoices. Each invoice, however, deals with one, and only one, customer.

TABLE 3-1   **Sporting Goods Store Database Tables**

Table	Column	Data Type	Constraint
CUSTOMER	CustomerID	INTEGER	NOT NULL
	FirstName	CHAR (15)	
	LastName	CHAR (20)	NOT NULL
	Street	CHAR (25)	
	City	CHAR (20)	
	State	CHAR (2)	
	Zipcode	CHAR (10)	
	Phone	CHAR (13)	
PRODUCT	ProductID	INTEGER	NOT NULL
	Name	CHAR (25)	
	Description	CHAR (30)	
	Category	CHAR (15)	
	VendorID	INTEGER	
	VendorName	CHAR (30)	
INVOICE	InvoiceNumber	INTEGER	NOT NULL
	CustomerID	INTEGER	
	InvoiceDate	DATE	
	TotalSale	NUMERIC (9,2)	
	TotalRemitted	NUMERIC (9,2)	
	FormOfPayment	CHAR (10)	
INVOICE_LINE	LineNumber	INTEGER	NOT NULL
	InvoiceNumber	INTEGER	NOT NULL
	ProductID	INTEGER	NOT NULL
	Quantity	INTEGER	
	SalePrice	NUMERIC (9,2)	

» The INVOICE table bears a one-to-many relationship to the INVOICE_LINE table. An invoice may have multiple lines, but each line appears on one, and only one, invoice.

» The PRODUCT table also bears a one-to-many relationship to the INVOICE_ LINE table. A product may appear on more than one line on one or more invoices. Each line, however, deals with one, and only one, product.

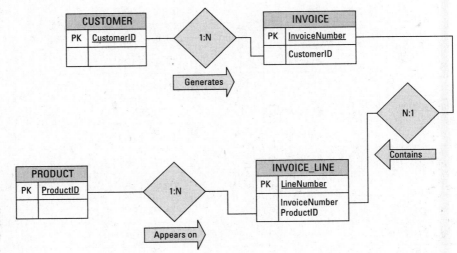

FIGURE 3-3: A sporting goods store's database structure.

The CUSTOMER table links to the INVOICE table by the common `CustomerID` column. The INVOICE table links to the INVOICE_LINE table by the common `InvoiceNumber` column. The PRODUCT table links to the INVOICE_LINE table by the common `ProductID` column. These links are what make this database a *relational* database.

To access the information about customers who bought ski equipment, you need `FirstName`, `LastName`, `Street`, `City`, `State`, and `Zipcode` from the CUSTOMER table; `Category` from the PRODUCT table; `InvoiceNumber` from the INVOICE table; and `LineNumber` from the INVOICE_LINE table. You can create the view you want in stages by using the following statements:

```
CREATE VIEW SKI_CUST1 AS
    SELECT FirstName,
        LastName,
        Street,
        City,
        State,
```

```
          Zipcode,
          InvoiceNumber
      FROM CUSTOMER JOIN INVOICE
      USING (CustomerID) ;
CREATE VIEW SKI_CUST2 AS
      SELECT FirstName,
          LastName,
          Street,
          City,
          State,
          Zipcode,
          ProductID
      FROM SKI_CUST1 JOIN INVOICE_LINE
      USING (InvoiceNumber) ;
CREATE VIEW SKI_CUST3 AS
      SELECT FirstName,
          LastName,
          Street,
          City,
          State,
          Zipcode,
          Category
      FROM SKI_CUST2 JOIN PRODUCT
      USING (ProductID) ;
CREATE VIEW SKI_CUST AS
      SELECT DISTINCT FirstName,
          LastName,
          Street,
          City,
          State,
          Zipcode
      FROM SKI_CUST3
      WHERE CATEGORY = 'Ski' ;
```

These CREATE VIEW statements combine data from multiple tables by using the
JOIN operator. Figure 3-4 diagrams the process.

Here's a rundown of the four CREATE VIEW statements:

>> The first statement combines columns from the CUSTOMER table with a
   column of the INVOICE table to create the SKI_CUST1 view.

>> The second statement combines SKI_CUST1 with a column from the INVOICE_
   LINE table to create the SKI_CUST2 view.

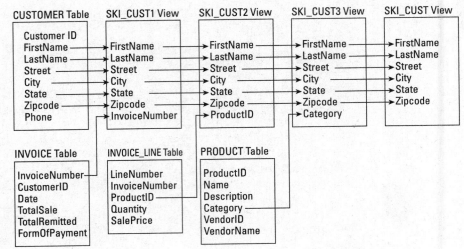

CUSTOMER Table | SKI_CUST1 View | SKI_CUST2 View | SKI_CUST3 View | SKI_CUST View

CUSTOMER Table
- Customer ID
- FirstName
- LastName
- Street
- City
- State
- Zipcode
- Phone

SKI_CUST1 View
- FirstName
- LastName
- Street
- City
- State
- Zipcode
- InvoiceNumber

SKI_CUST2 View
- FirstName
- LastName
- Street
- City
- State
- Zipcode
- ProductID

SKI_CUST3 View
- FirstName
- LastName
- Street
- City
- State
- Zipcode
- Category

SKI_CUST View
- FirstName
- LastName
- Street
- City
- State
- Zipcode

INVOICE Table
- InvoiceNumber
- CustomerID
- Date
- TotalSale
- TotalRemitted
- FormOfPayment

INVOICE_LINE Table
- LineNumber
- InvoiceNumber
- ProductID
- Quantity
- SalePrice

PRODUCT Table
- ProductID
- Name
- Description
- Category
- VendorID
- VendorName

FIGURE 3-4: Creating a multi-table view by using JOINs.

>> The third statement combines SKI_CUST2 with a column from the PRODUCT table to create the SKI_CUST3 view.

>> The fourth statement filters out all rows that don't have a category of Ski. The result is a view (SKI_CUST) that contains the names and addresses of all customers who bought at least one product in the Ski category.

The DISTINCT keyword in the fourth CREATE VIEW's SELECT clause ensures that you have only one entry for each customer, even if some customers made multiple purchases of ski items. (I cover JOINs in detail in Chapter 11.)

It's possible to create a multi-table view with a single SQL statement. However, if you think that one or all of the preceding statements are complex, imagine how complex a single statement would be that performed all these functions. I tend to prefer simplicity over complexity, so whenever possible, I choose the simplest way to perform a function, even if it is not the most "efficient."

Collecting tables into schemas

A table consists of rows and columns and usually deals with a specific type of entity, such as customers, products, or invoices. Useful work generally requires information about several (or many) related entities. Organizationally, you collect the tables that you associate with these entities according to a logical schema. A *logical schema* is the organizational structure of a collection of related tables.

REMEMBER

A database also has a *physical schema* — which represents the physical arrangement of the data and its associated items (such as indexes) on the system's storage devices. When I mention "the schema" of a database, I'm referring to the logical schema, not the physical schema.

On a system where several unrelated projects may co-reside, you can assign all related tables to one schema. You can collect other groups of tables into schemas of their own.

TIP

Be sure to name your schemas to ensure that no one accidentally mixes tables from one project with tables from another. Each project has its own associated schema; you can distinguish it from other schemas by name. Seeing certain table names (such as CUSTOMER, PRODUCT, and so on) appear in multiple projects, however, is common. If any chance exists of a naming ambiguity, qualify your table name by using its schema name as well (as in SCHEMA_NAME.TABLE_NAME). If you don't qualify a table name, SQL assigns that table to the default schema.

Ordering by catalog

For really large database systems, multiple schemas may not be sufficient. In a large distributed database environment with many users, you may even find duplicated schema names. To prevent this situation, SQL adds another level to the containment hierarchy: the catalog. A *catalog* is a named collection of schemas.

You can *qualify* a table name by using a catalog name and a schema name. This safeguard is the best way to ensure that no one confuses the table in one schema with a table that has the same name in some other schema that has the same schema name. (Say what? Well, some folks just have a really hard time thinking up different names.) The catalog-qualified name appears in the following format:

```
CATALOG_NAME.SCHEMA_NAME.TABLE_NAME
```

TIP

At the top of the database containment hierarchy are *clusters.* Systems rarely require use of the full scope of the containment hierarchy; going to the catalog level is enough in most cases. A catalog contains schemas; a schema contains tables and views; tables and views contain columns and rows.

The catalog also contains the *information schema.* The information schema contains the system tables. The system tables hold the metadata associated with the other schemas. In Chapter 1, I define a database as a self-describing collection of integrated records. The metadata contained in the system tables is what makes the database self-describing.

Because catalogs are identified by name, you can have multiple catalogs in a database. Each catalog can have multiple schemas, and each schema can have multiple tables. Of course, each table can have multiple columns and rows. The hierarchical relationships are shown in Figure 3-5.

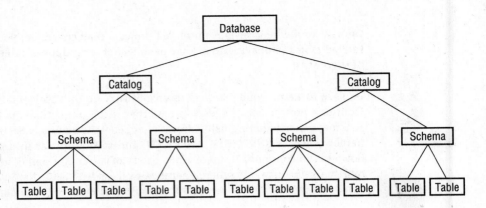

FIGURE 3-5:
The hierarchical
structure of a
typical SQL
database.

Getting familiar with DDL statements

SQL's Data Definition Language (DDL) deals with the structure of a database. It's distinct from the Data Manipulation Language (described later in this chapter), which deals with the data contained within that structure. The DDL consists of these three statements:

>> CREATE: You use the various forms of this statement to build the essential structures of the database.

>> ALTER: You use this statement to change structures that you have created.

>> DROP: You apply this statement to structures created with the CREATE statement, to destroy them.

In the following sections, I give you brief descriptions of the DDL statements. In Chapters 4 and 5, I use these statements in examples.

CREATE

You can apply the SQL CREATE statement to a large number of SQL objects, including schemas, domains, tables, and views. By using the CREATE SCHEMA statement, you can not only create a schema, but also identify its owner and specify a default character set. Here's an example of such a statement:

```
CREATE SCHEMA SALES
    AUTHORIZATION SALES_MGR
    DEFAULT CHARACTER SET ASCII_FULL ;
```

Use the CREATE DOMAIN statement to apply constraints to column values. The constraints you apply to a domain determine what objects the domain can and cannot contain. You can create domains after you establish a schema. The following example shows how to use this statement:

```
CREATE DOMAIN Age AS INTEGER
    CHECK (AGE > 20) ;
```

You create tables by using the CREATE TABLE statement, and you create views by using the CREATE VIEW statement. Earlier in this chapter, I show you examples of these two statements. When you use the CREATE TABLE statement, you can specify constraints on the new table's columns at the same time.

TIP

Sometimes you may want to specify constraints that don't specifically attach to a table but apply to an entire schema. You can use the CREATE ASSERTION statement to specify such constraints.

You also have CREATE CHARACTER SET, CREATE COLLATION, and CREATE TRANSLATION statements, which give you the flexibility of creating new character sets, collation sequences, or translation tables. (*Collation sequences* define the order in which you carry out comparisons or sorts. *Translation tables* control the conversion of character strings from one character set to another.) You can create a number of other things (which I won't go into here), as you can deduce if you flip to Chapter 2 for a glance at Table 2-1.

ALTER

After you create a table, you're not necessarily stuck with that exact table forever. As you use the table, you may discover that it's not everything you need it to be. You can use the ALTER TABLE statement to change the table by adding, changing, or deleting a column in the table. Besides tables, you can also ALTER columns and domains.

DROP

Removing a table from a database schema is easy. Just use a DROP TABLE <tablename> statement. You erase all data from the table, as well as the metadata that defines the table in the data dictionary. It's almost as if the table never existed. You can also use the DROP statement to get rid of anything that was created by a CREATE statement.

REMEMBER

DROP won't work if it breaks referential integrity. I discuss referential integrity later in this chapter.

Data Manipulation Language

Although the DDL is the part of SQL that creates, modifies, or destroys database structures, it doesn't deal with data itself. Handling data is the job of the Data Manipulation Language (DML). Some DML statements read like ordinary English-language sentences and are easy to understand. Unfortunately, because SQL gives you very fine-grained control of your data, other DML statements can be fiendishly complex.

If a DML statement includes multiple expressions, clauses, predicates (more about them later in this chapter), or subqueries, understanding what that statement is trying to do can be a challenge. After you deal with some of these statements, you may even consider switching to an easier line of work, such as brain surgery or quantum electrodynamics. Fortunately, such drastic action isn't necessary. You can understand complex SQL statements by breaking them down into their basic components and analyzing them one chunk at a time.

The DML statements you can use are `INSERT`, `UPDATE`, `DELETE`, `MERGE`, and `SELECT`. These statements can consist of a variety of parts, including multiple clauses. Each clause may incorporate value expressions, logical connectives, predicates, aggregate functions, and subqueries. You can make fine discriminations among database records and extract more information from your data by including these clauses in your statements. In Chapter 6, I discuss the operation of the DML commands, and in Chapters 7 through 13, I delve into the details of these commands.

Value expressions

You can use *value expressions* to combine two or more values. Several kinds of value expressions exist, corresponding to the different data types:

>> Numeric

>> String

>> Datetime

>> Interval

>> Boolean

>> User-defined

>> Row

>> Collection

The Boolean, user-defined, row, and collection types were introduced with SQL:1999. Some implementations may not support them all yet. If you want to use these data types, make sure your implementation includes the ones you want to use.

Numeric value expressions

To combine numeric values, use the addition (+), subtraction (–), multiplication (∗), and division (/) operators. The following lines are examples of numeric value expressions:

```
12 - 7
15/3 - 4
6 * (8 + 2)
```

The values in these examples are *numeric literals*. These values may also be column names, parameters, host variables, or subqueries — provided that those column names, parameters, host variables, or subqueries evaluate to a numeric value. The following are some examples:

```
SUBTOTAL + TAX + SHIPPING
6 * MILES/HOURS
:months/12
```

The colon in the last example signals that the following term (months) is either a parameter or a host variable.

String value expressions

String value expressions may include the *concatenation operator* (||). Use concatenation to join two text strings, as shown in Table 3-2.

TABLE 3-2

Examples of String Concatenation

Expression	Result
'military ' || 'intelligence'	'military intelligence'
CITY|| ' ' ||STATE|| ' '||ZIP	A single string with city, state, and zip code, each separated by a single space.

REMEMBER

Some SQL implementations use + as the concatenation operator rather than ||. Check your documentation to see which operator your implementation uses.

Some implementations may include string operators other than concatenation, but ISO-standard SQL doesn't support such operators. Concatenation applies to binary strings as well as to text strings.

Datetime and interval value expressions

Datetime value expressions deal with (surprise!) dates and times. Data of DATE, TIME, TIMESTAMP, and INTERVAL types may appear in datetime value expressions. The result of a datetime value expression is always another datetime. You can add or subtract an interval from a datetime and specify time zone information.

Here's an example of a datetime value expression:

```
DueDate + INTERVAL '7' DAY
```

A library may use such an expression to determine when to send a late notice. The following example specifies a time rather than a date:

```
TIME '18:55:48' AT LOCAL
```

TIP

The AT LOCAL keywords indicate that the time refers to the local time zone.

Interval value expressions deal with the difference (how much time passes) between one datetime and another. You have two kinds of intervals: *year-month* and *day-time.* You can't mix the two in an expression.

As an example of an interval, suppose someone returns a library book after the due date. By using an interval value expression such as that of the following example, you can calculate how many days late the book is and assess a fine accordingly:

```
(DateReturned - DateDue) DAY
```

Because an interval may be of either the year-month or the day-time variety, you need to specify which kind to use. (In the preceding example, I specify DAY.)

Boolean value expressions

A *Boolean value expression* tests the truth value of a predicate. The following is an example of a Boolean value expression:

```
(Class = SENIOR) IS TRUE
```

If this were a condition on the retrieval of rows from a student table, only rows containing the records of seniors would be retrieved. To retrieve the records of all non-seniors, you could use the following:

```
NOT (Class = SENIOR) IS TRUE
```

Alternatively, you could use:

```
(Class = SENIOR) IS FALSE
```

To retrieve every row that has a null value in the CLASS column, use:

```
(Class = SENIOR) IS UNKNOWN
```

User-defined type value expressions

I describe user-defined data types in Chapter 2. If necessary, you can define your own data types instead of having to settle for those provided by "stock" SQL. Expressions that incorporate data elements of such a user-defined type must evaluate to an element of the same type.

Row value expressions

A *row value expression*, not surprisingly, specifies a row value. The row value may consist of one value expression, or two or more comma-delimited value expressions. For example:

```
('Joseph Tykociner', 'Professor Emeritus', 1918)
```

This is a row in a faculty table, showing a faculty member's name, rank, and year of hire.

Collection value expressions

A *collection value expression* evaluates to an array.

Reference value expressions

A *reference value expression* evaluates to a value that references some other database component, such as a table column.

Predicates

Predicates are SQL equivalents of logical propositions. The following statement is an example of a proposition:

"The student is a senior."

In a table containing information about students, the domain of the CLASS column may be SENIOR, JUNIOR, SOPHOMORE, FRESHMAN, or NULL. You can use the predicate CLASS = SENIOR to filter out rows for which the predicate is False, retaining only those for which the predicate is True. Sometimes the value of a predicate in a row is Unknown (NULL). In those cases, you may choose either to discard the row or to retain it. (After all, the student *could* be a senior.) The correct course of action depends on the situation.

Class = SENIOR is an example of a *comparison predicate.* SQL has six comparison operators. A simple comparison predicate uses one of these operators. Table 3-3 shows the comparison predicates and some legitimate as well as bogus examples of their use.

WARNING

In the preceding example, only the first two entries in Table 3-3 (Class = SENIOR and Class <> SENIOR) make sense. SOPHOMORE is considered greater than SENIOR because SO comes after SE in the default collation sequence, which sorts in ascending alphabetical order. This interpretation, however, is probably not the one you want.

TABLE 3-3

Comparison Operators and Comparison Predicates

Operator	Comparison	Expression
=	Equal to	Class = SENIOR
<>	Not equal to	Class <> SENIOR
<	Less than	Class < SENIOR
>	Greater than	Class > SENIOR
<=	Less than or equal to	Class <= SENIOR
>=	Greater than or equal to	Class >= SENIOR

Logical connectives

Logical connectives enable you to build complex predicates out of simple ones. Say, for example, that you want to identify child prodigies in a database of high-school students. Two propositions that could identify these students may read as follows:

"The student is a senior."

"The student's age is less than 14 years."

You can use the logical connective AND to create a compound predicate that isolates the student records that you want, as in the following example:

```
Class = SENIOR AND Age < 14
```

If you use the AND connective, both component predicates must be true for the compound predicate to be true. Use the OR connective when you want the compound predicate to evaluate to true if either component predicate is true. NOT is the third logical connective. Strictly speaking, NOT doesn't connect two predicates, but instead reverses the truth value of the single predicate to which you apply it. Take, for example, the following expression:

```
NOT (Class = SENIOR)
```

This expression is true only if Class is not equal to SENIOR.

Set functions

Sometimes the information you want to extract from a table doesn't relate to individual rows but rather to sets of rows. SQL provides *set* (or *aggregate*) *functions* to deal with such situations. These functions are COUNT, MAX, MIN, SUM, and AVG. Each function performs an action that draws data from a set of rows rather than from a single row.

COUNT

The COUNT function returns the number of rows in the specified table. To count the number of precocious seniors in my example high-school database, use the following statement:

```
SELECT COUNT (*)
     FROM STUDENT
     WHERE Grade = 12 AND Age <14 ;
```

MAX

Use the MAX function to return the maximum value that occurs in the specified column. Suppose you want to find the oldest student enrolled in your school. The following statement returns the appropriate row:

```
SELECT FirstName, LastName, Age
    FROM STUDENT
    WHERE Age = (SELECT MAX(Age) FROM STUDENT);
```

This statement returns all students whose ages are equal to the maximum age. That is, if the age of the oldest student is 23, this statement returns the first and last names and the age of all students who are 23 years old.

This query uses a subquery. The subquery SELECT MAX(Age) FROM STUDENT is embedded within the main query. I talk about subqueries (also called *nested queries*) in Chapter 12.

MIN

The MIN function works just like MAX except that MIN looks for the minimum value in the specified column rather than the maximum. To find the youngest student enrolled, you can use the following query:

```
SELECT FirstName, LastName, Age
    FROM STUDENT
    WHERE Age = (SELECT MIN(Age) FROM STUDENT);
```

This query returns all students whose age is equal to the age of the youngest student.

SUM

The SUM function adds up the values in a specified column. The column must be one of the numeric data types, and the value of the sum must be within the range of that type. Thus, if the column is of type SMALLINT, the sum must be no larger than the upper limit of the SMALLINT data type. In the retail database from earlier in this chapter, the INVOICE table contains a record of all sales. To find the total dollar value of all sales recorded in the database, use the SUM function as follows:

```
SELECT SUM(TotalSale) FROM INVOICE;
```

AVG

The AVG function returns the average of all the values in the specified column. As does the SUM function, AVG applies only to columns with a numeric data type.

To find the value of the average sale, considering all transactions in the database, use the AVG function like this:

```
SELECT AVG(TotalSale) FROM INVOICE
```

Nulls have no value, so if any of the rows in the TotalSale column contain null values, those rows are ignored in the computation of the value of the average sale.

LISTAGG

The LISTAGG function, new in SQL 2016, transforms values from a group of rows in a table into a list of values, delimited by a separator that you specify. LISTAGG is often used to transform the values in table rows into a string of comma separated values (CSV), or some similar format that is more easily read by humans.

WARNING

LISTAGG does not escape the separators, making it impossible to tell if a character encountered is indeed an escape character, or merely an instance of that character that happens to be part of a value. Only use LISTAGG when you can be sure that your chosen separator character does not appear in any of the data you are aggregating.

LISTAGG is an ordered set function. The ordering is accomplished by use of a WITHIN GROUP clause. Basic syntax is:

```
LISTAGG (<expression>, <separator>) WITHIN GROUP (ORDER BY ...)
```

The <expression> cannot contain window functions, aggregate functions, or subqueries. The <separator> must be a character literal.

LISTAGG removes NULL values before aggregating the rest of the values. If no non-null values remain after that removal, the result of the LISTAGG operation is a NULL value.

If the DISTINCT keyword is used, duplicate values as well as NULL values will be removed. The syntax is:

```
LISTAGG (DISTINCT <expression>, <separator>) ...
```

LISTAGG, introduced in SQL:2016, is an optional feature of standard SQL, and is, as yet, not present in all implementations. In those implementations where it is present, check system documentation for additional clauses that may give additional functionality.

Subqueries

Subqueries, as you can see in the "Set functions" section earlier in this chapter, are queries within a query. Anywhere you can use an expression in an SQL statement, you can also use a subquery (except in a LISTAGG function, as mentioned previously). Subqueries are powerful tools for relating information in one table to information in another table; you can embed (or *nest*) a query into one table, within a query into another table. By nesting one subquery within another, you enable the access of information from two or more tables to generate a final result. When you use subqueries correctly, you can retrieve just about any information you want from a database. Don't worry about how many levels of subqueries your database supports. When you start building nested subqueries, you will run out of comprehension of what you are doing long before your database runs out of levels of subqueries that it supports.

Data Control Language

The Data Control Language (DCL) has four commands: COMMIT, ROLLBACK, GRANT, and REVOKE. These commands protect the database from harm, both accidental and intentional.

Transactions

Your database is most vulnerable to damage while you or someone else is changing it. Even in a single-user system, making a change can be dangerous to a database. If a software or hardware failure occurs while the change is in progress, a database may be left in an indeterminate state that's somewhere between where it was before the change operation started and where it would be if the change operation completed successfully.

SQL protects your database by restricting operations that can change it so they can occur only within transactions. During a transaction, SQL records every operation performed on the data in a log file. If anything interrupts the transaction before the COMMIT statement ends the transaction, you can restore the system to its original state by issuing a ROLLBACK statement. The ROLLBACK processes the transaction log in reverse, undoing all the actions that took place in the transaction. After you roll back the database to its state before the transaction began, you can clear up whatever caused the problem and attempt the transaction again.

TIP

If it's possible for a hardware or software problem to occur, your database is susceptible to damage. To minimize the chance of damage, today's DBMSs close the window of vulnerability as much as possible by performing all operations that affect the database within a transaction and then committing all these operations at once, at the end of the transaction. Modern database management systems use logging in conjunction with transactions to guarantee that hardware, software, or operational problems won't damage data. After a transaction has been committed, it's safe from all but the most catastrophic of system failures. Prior to commitment, incomplete transactions can be rolled back to their starting points and applied again, after the problem is corrected.

In a multiuser system, database corruption or incorrect results are possible even if no hardware or software failures occur. Interactions between two or more users who access the same table at the same time can cause serious problems. By restricting changes so that they occur only *within* transactions, SQL addresses these problems, as well.

By putting all operations that affect the database into transactions, you can isolate the actions of one user from those of another user. Such isolation is critical if you want to make sure that the results you obtain from the database are accurate.

TECHNICAL STUFF

You may wonder how the interaction of two users can produce inaccurate results. Here's a funny/scary example: Suppose Donna reads a record in a database table. An instant later (more or less), David changes the value of a numeric field in that record. Now Donna writes a value back into that field, based on the value that she read initially. Because Donna is unaware of David's change, the value after Donna's write operation is incorrect.

Another problem can result if Donna writes to a record and then David reads that record. If Donna rolls back her transaction, David is unaware of the rollback and bases his actions on the value that he read, which doesn't reflect the value that's in the database after the rollback. This sounds like the plot for an episode of *I Love Lucy* — it makes for good comedy but lousy data management.

Users and privileges

Another major threat to data integrity is the users themselves. Some people should have no access to the data. Others should have only restricted access to some of the data but no access to the rest. Some (hint: *not* very many) should have unlimited access to everything in the database. You need a system for classifying users and for assigning access privileges to the users in different categories.

The creator of a schema specifies who is considered its owner. As the owner of a schema, you can grant access privileges to the users you specify. Any privileges that you don't explicitly grant are withheld. You can also revoke privileges that you've already granted. A user must pass an authentication procedure to prove his identity before he can access the files you authorize him to use. The specifics of that procedure depend on the implementation.

SQL gives you the capability to protect the following database objects:

>> Tables

>> Columns

>> Views

>> Domains

>> Character sets

>> Collations

>> Translations

I discuss character sets, collations, and translations in Chapter 5.

SQL supports several different kinds of protection: *seeing, adding, modifying, deleting, referencing,* and *using* databases. It also supports protections associated with the execution of external routines.

TIP

You permit access by using the GRANT statement and remove access by using the REVOKE statement. By controlling the use of the SELECT statement, the DCL controls who can see a database object such as a table, column, or view. Controlling the INSERT statement determines who can add new rows in a table. Restricting the use of the UPDATE statement to authorized users gives you control of who can modify table rows; restricting the DELETE statement controls who can delete table rows.

If one table in a database contains as a foreign key a column that is a primary key in another table in the database, you can add a constraint to the first table so that it references the second table. (Chapter 5 describes foreign keys.) When one table references another, a user of the first table may be able to deduce information about the contents of the second. As the owner of the second table, you may want to prevent such snooping. The GRANT REFERENCES statement gives you that power. The following section discusses the problem of a renegade reference — and how the GRANT REFERENCES statement prevents it. By using the GRANT USAGE statement, you can control who can use — or even see — the contents of a domain, character set, collation, or translation. (I cover provisions for security in Chapter 14.)

Table 3-4 summarizes the SQL statements that you use to grant and revoke privileges.

TABLE 3-4　　　　**Types of Protection**

Protection Operation	Statement
Enable user to see a table	GRANT SELECT
Prevent user from seeing a table	REVOKE SELECT
Enable user to add rows to a table	GRANT INSERT
Prevent user from adding rows to a table	REVOKE INSERT
Enable user to change data in table rows	GRANT UPDATE
Prevent user from changing data in table rows	REVOKE UPDATE
Enable user to delete table rows	GRANT DELETE
Prevent user from deleting table rows	REVOKE DELETE
Enable user to reference a table	GRANT REFERENCES
Prevent user from referencing a table	REVOKE REFERENCES
Enable user to use a domain, character set, translation, or collation	GRANT USAGE ON DOMAIN, GRANT USAGE ON CHARACTER SET, GRANT USAGE ON COLLATION, GRANT USAGE ON TRANSLATION
Prevent user from using a domain, character set, collation, or translation	REVOKE USAGE ON DOMAIN, REVOKE USAGE ON CHARACTER SET, REVOKE USAGE ON COLLATION, REVOKE USAGE ON TRANSLATION

You can give different levels of access to different people, depending on their needs. The following commands offer a few examples of this capability:

```
GRANT SELECT
     ON CUSTOMER
     TO SALES_MANAGER;
```

The preceding example enables one person — the sales manager — to see the CUSTOMER table.

The following example enables anyone with access to the system to see the retail price list:

```
GRANT SELECT
     ON RETAIL_PRICE_LIST
     TO PUBLIC;
```

The following example enables the sales manager to modify the retail price list. She can change the contents of existing rows, but she can't add or delete rows:

```
GRANT UPDATE
    ON RETAIL_PRICE_LIST
    TO SALES_MANAGER;
```

The following example enables the sales manager to add new rows to the retail price list:

```
GRANT INSERT
    ON RETAIL_PRICE_LIST
    TO SALES_MANAGER;
```

Now, thanks to this last example, the sales manager can delete unwanted rows from the table, too:

```
GRANT DELETE
    ON RETAIL_PRICE_LIST
    TO SALES MANAGER;
```

Referential integrity constraints can jeopardize your data

You may think that if you can control who sees, creates, modifies, and deletes data in a table, you're well protected. Against *most* threats, you are. A knowledgeable hacker, however, can still ransack the house by using an indirect method.

A correctly designed relational database has *referential integrity,* which means that the data in one table in the database is consistent with the data in all the other tables. To ensure referential integrity, database designers apply constraints to tables that restrict the data that users can enter into the tables. But here's the downside of that protection: If you have a database with referential integrity constraints, a user can possibly create a new table that uses a column in a confidential table as a foreign key. That column then serves as a link through which someone can possibly steal confidential information. Oops.

Say, for example, that you're a famous Wall Street stock analyst. Many people believe in the accuracy of your stock picks, so whenever you recommend a stock to your subscribers, many people buy that stock, and its value increases. You keep your analysis in a database, which contains a table named FOUR_STAR. Your top recommendations for your next newsletter are in that table. Naturally, you restrict access to FOUR_STAR so that word doesn't leak out to the investing public before your paying subscribers receive the newsletter.

You're still vulnerable, however, if anyone else can create a new table that uses the stock name field of FOUR_STAR as a foreign key, as shown in the following command example:

```
CREATE TABLE HOT_STOCKS (
    Stock CHARACTER (30) REFERENCES FOUR_STAR
    );
```

The hacker can now try to insert the name of every stock on the New York Stock Exchange, American Stock Exchange, and NASDAQ into the table. Those inserts that succeed tell the hacker which stocks match the stocks that you name in your confidential table. It doesn't take long for the hacker to extract your entire list of stocks.

You can protect yourself from hacks such as the one in the preceding example by being very careful about entering statements like the following:

```
GRANT REFERENCES (Stock)
    ON FOUR_STAR
    TO SECRET_HACKER;
```

WARNING

Clearly I'm exaggerating here. You would never grant any kind of access to a critical table to an untrustworthy person, would you? Not if you realized what you were doing. However, hackers today are not just clever technically. They are also masters of *social engineering*, the art of misleading people into doing what they ordinarily would not do. Ramp up to full alert whenever a smooth talker mentions *anything* related to your confidential information.

TIP

Avoid granting privileges to people who may abuse them. True, people don't come with guarantees printed on their foreheads. But if you wouldn't lend your new car to a person for a long trip, you probably shouldn't grant him the REFERENCES privilege on an important table, either.

The preceding example offers one good reason for maintaining careful control of the REFERENCES privilege. Here are two other reasons why you should maintain careful control of REFERENCES:

>> If the other person specifies a constraint in HOT STOCKS by using a RESTRICT option and you try to delete a row from your table, the DBMS tells you that you can't, because doing so would violate a referential integrity constraint.

>> If you want to use the DROP command to destroy your table, you find you must get the other person to DROP his constraint (or his table) first.

REMEMBER

The bottom line: Enabling another person to specify integrity constraints on your table not only introduces a potential security breach, but also means that the other user sometimes gets in your way.

Delegating responsibility for security

To keep your system secure, you must severely restrict the access privileges you grant, as well as the people to whom you grant these privileges. But people who can't do their work because they lack access are likely to hassle you constantly. To preserve your sanity, you'll probably need to delegate some of the responsibility for maintaining database security. SQL provides for such delegation through the WITH GRANT OPTION clause. Consider the following example:

```
GRANT UPDATE
    ON RETAIL_PRICE_LIST
    TO SALES_MANAGER WITH GRANT OPTION;
```

This statement is similar to the previous GRANT UPDATE example in that the statement enables the sales manager to update the retail price list. The WITH GRANT OPTION clause also gives her the right to grant the update privilege to anyone she wants. If you use this form of the GRANT statement, you must not only trust the grantee to use the privilege wisely, but also trust her to choose wisely in granting the privilege to others.

WARNING

The ultimate in trust — therefore the ultimate in vulnerability — is to execute a statement such as the following:

```
GRANT ALL PRIVILEGES
    ON FOUR_STAR
    TO Benedict_Arnold WITH GRANT OPTION;
```

Be *extremely* careful about using statements such as this one. Granting all privileges, along with the grant option, leaves you maximally exposed. Benedict Arnold was one of George Washington's trusted generals during the American Revolutionary War. He defected to the British, thus becoming the most reviled traitor in American history. You don't want something like that to happen to you.

Using SQL to Build Databases

2

Chapter **4**

Building and Maintaining a Simple Database Structure

Computer history changes so fast that sometimes the rapid turnover of technological generations can be confusing. High-level (so-called *third-generation*) languages such as FORTRAN, COBOL, BASIC, Pascal, and C were the first languages used to build and change large databases. Later languages included some specifically designed for use with databases — such as dBASE, Paradox, and R:BASE. (So were these third-and-a-half-generation languages? Never mind.) The next step in this progression was the emergence of development environments such as Access, PowerBuilder, and C++ Builder, the so-called fourth-generation languages (4GLs). Now things have moved beyond the numbered generations to rapid application development (RAD) tools and integrated development environments (IDEs) such as Eclipse and Visual Studio .NET, which can be used with any of a number of languages (such as C, C++, C#, Python, Java, Visual Basic, or PHP). You use them to assemble application components into production applications.

REMEMBER

Because SQL is not a complete language, it doesn't fit tidily into one of the generational categories I just mentioned. Nor is it an IDE. It makes use of commands in the manner of a third-generation language, but it is essentially nonprocedural, like a fourth-generation language. No matter how you classify SQL, you can use it in conjunction with an IDE or with older third- and fourth-generation development tools. You can write the SQL code yourself, or you can move objects around onscreen and have the development environment generate equivalent code for you. The commands that go out to the remote database are pure SQL in either case.

In this chapter, I take you through the process of using a RAD tool to build, alter, and drop a simple table, and then I discuss how to build, alter, and drop the same table using SQL.

Using a RAD Tool to Build a Simple Database

People use databases because they want to keep track of important information. Sometimes the information that they want to track is simple, and sometimes it's not. A good database management system provides what you need in either case. Some DBMSs give you SQL. Others, such as RAD tools, give you an object-oriented graphical environment. Some DBMSs support both approaches. In the following sections, I show you how to build a simple single-table database by using a graphical database design tool. I use Microsoft Access in my examples, but the procedure is similar for other Windows-based development environments.

Deciding what to track

The first step when you create a database is to decide what you want to track. For example, imagine you've just won $248 million in the Powerball lottery. (It's okay to *imagine* something like this. In real life, it's about as likely as finding your car squashed by a giant meteorite.) Friends and acquaintances that you haven't heard from in years are suddenly coming out of the woodwork. Some have surefire, can't-miss business opportunities in which they want you to invest. Others represent worthy causes that could benefit from your support. As a good steward of your new wealth, you realize that some business opportunities aren't as good as others, and some causes aren't as worthy as others. You decide to put all the options into a database, so you can keep track of them and make fair and equitable judgments.

You decide to track the following information about your friends and relations:

>> First name
>> Last name

» Address

» City

» State or province

» Postal code

» Phone

» How known (your relationship to the person)

» Proposal

» Business or charity

You decide to put all the listed items into a single database table; you don't need something elaborate.

Creating a database table

When you fire up your Access 2016 or 2019 development environment, you're greeted by the screen shown in Figure 4-1. From there, you can build a database table in several different ways. I start with Datasheet view because that approach shows you how to create a database from the ground up. Read on.

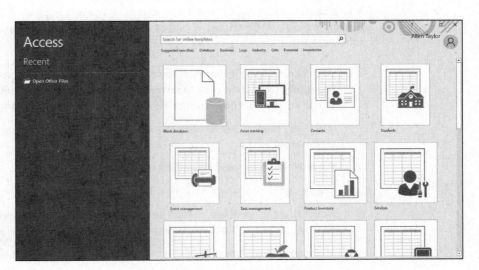

FIGURE 4-1:
The Microsoft Access opening screen.

Building a database table in Datasheet view

By default, Access 2016 opens in Datasheet view. To build an Access database in Datasheet view, double-click the Blank Desktop Database template.

Your Access datasheet stands ready for you to start entering data into Table 1, the first table in your database, as shown in Figure 4-2. You can change the table name to something more meaningful later. Access gives your new database the default name Database1 (or Database31 if you've already created 30 databases and not bothered to give them meaningful names). It's better to give the database a meaningful name at the outset just to avoid confusion.

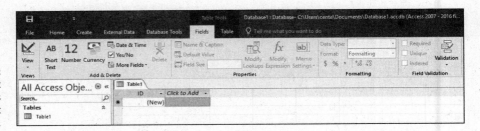

FIGURE 4-2:
The Datasheet view in the Access development environment.

TIP

That's the start-from-scratch method, but you have several different ways to create an Access database table. This next one uses Design view.

Building a database table in Design view

In Datasheet view (refer to Figure 4-2), building a database table is pretty easy: You just start entering data. That approach, however, is prone to errors, because details are easy to overlook. A better way to create a table is in Design view by following these steps:

1. **With Access open in Datasheet view (the default), click the Hometab on the Ribbon and then click View below the icon in the upper left corner of the window. Choose Design View from the drop-down menu.**

   When you choose Design View, a dialog box pops up and asks you to enter a table name.

2. **Enter POWER (for your Powerball winnings) and click OK.**

   The Design view (shown in Figure 4-3) appears.

   Notice that the window is divided into functional areas. Two of them are especially useful in building database tables:

   - *Design view options:* A menu across the top of the window offers Home, Create, External Data, Database Tools, and Design options. When the Ribbon is displayed, the tools available in Design view are represented by the icons just below the menu. In Figure 4-3, the highlighting shows that the Design tab and the Primary Key icon are selected.

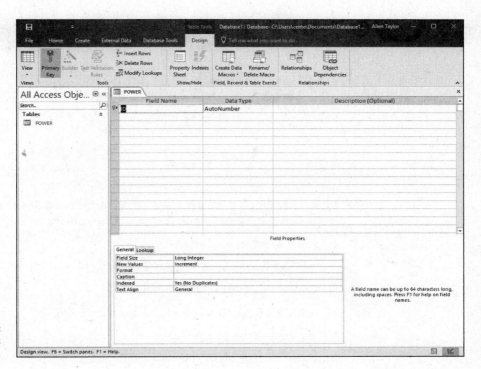

FIGURE 4-3:
The Design view's starting screen.

- *Field Properties pane:* In this area for defining database fields, the cursor is blinking in the Field Name column of the first row. Access is suggesting that you specify a primary key here, name it **ID**, and give it the AutoNumber data type.

TIP

AutoNumber, an Access data type, isn't a standard SQL type; it increments an integer in the field by one automatically every time you add a new record to a table. This data type guarantees that the field you use as a primary key won't be duplicated and will thus stay unique. Most other RAD tools that you might encounter will have a similar autoincrementing data type.

3. **In the Field Properties area, change the primary key's Field Name from** ID **to** ProposalNumber.

TIP

The suggested Field Name for the primary key, ID, just isn't very informative. If you get into the habit of changing it to something more meaningful (and/or providing additional information in the Description column), it's easier to keep track of what the fields in your database are for. Here the field name is sufficiently descriptive.

Figure 4-4 shows the database table's design at this point.

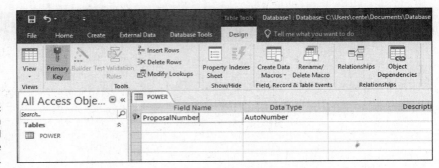

FIGURE 4-4:
Using a descriptive field name to define the primary key.

4. **In the Field Properties pane, check the assumptions that Access has made automatically about the** `ProposalNumber` **field.**

   Figure 4-4 shows the following assumptions:

   - The Field Size has been set to Long Integer.

   - New Values are obtained by incrementing.

   - Indexing is called for and duplicates are not allowed.

   - Text alignment is general.

   As is often the case, the assumptions Access makes are fine for what you want to do. If any of the assumptions are incorrect, you can override them by entering new values.

5. **Specify the rest of the fields you want this table to have.**

   Figure 4-5 shows Design view after you've entered the `FirstName` field.

TIP

   The data type for `FirstName` is `Short Text`, rather than `AutoNumber`, so the field properties that apply to it are different. Here Access has given `FirstName` the default Field Size for short text data, which is 255 characters. I don't know too many people whose first names are that long. Access is smart enough to allocate only as much memory space as is needed for an entry. It does not blindly allocate 255 bytes regardless of what you enter. However, other development environments might not have this capability. I like to assign reasonable values to field lengths. This keeps me out of trouble when I move from one development environment to another.

FIGURE 4-5:
The table-creation window after FirstName has been defined.

Field Name	Data Type	Description (Optional)
ProposalNumber	AutoNumber	
FirstName	Short Text	

THINKING AHEAD AS YOU DESIGN YOUR TABLE

In some development environments (other than Microsoft Access), reducing the size of the FirstName field to 15 saves 240 bytes for *every record in the database* if you're using ASCII (UTF-8) characters, 480 bytes if you're using UTF-16 characters, or 960 bytes if you're using UTF-32 characters. It adds up. While you're at it, take a look at other default assumptions for some other field properties, and try to anticipate how you might use them as the database grows. Some of these fields require attention right away to make them more efficient (FirstName is a handy example); others apply only to relatively obscure cases.

You may notice one other field property that comes up a lot: the Indexed property. If you don't anticipate having to retrieve a record by a given field, then don't waste processing power indexing it. Note, however, that in a large table with many rows, you can speed up retrievals immensely by indexing the field you use to identify the record you want to retrieve. The devil — or, in this case, a potential performance boost — is in the details when you're designing your database tables.

Here the default Access assumption is that FirstName is not a required field. You could enter a record in the POWER table and leave the FirstName field blank, which takes into account folks who go by only one name, such as Bjork, Prince, or Madonna.

6. **Change the Field Size for FirstName to 15.**

For a rundown on why this is a good idea, see the accompanying sidebar, "Thinking ahead as you design your table."

7. **To ensure that you can retrieve a record quickly from the POWER table by LastName (which *is* likely), change the Indexed property for LastName to Yes (Duplicates OK), as shown in Figure 4-6.**

The figure shows some changes I've made in the Field Properties pane:

- I've reduced the maximum field size from 255 to 20.

- I've changed Required to Yes, Allow Zero Length to No, and Indexed to Yes (Duplicates OK). I want every proposal to include the last name of the person responsible for it. A name of zero length is not allowed, and the LastName field will be indexed.

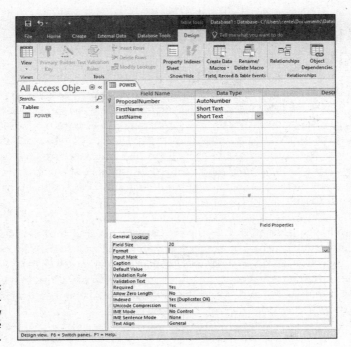

FIGURE 4-6:
The table-
creation window
after LastName
has been defined.

REMEMBER

- I allow duplicates; two or more proposers might have the same last name. This is practically certain in the case of the POWER table; I expect proposals from all three of my brothers, as well as my sons and unmarried daughter, not to mention my cousins.

- The Yes (No Duplicates) option, which I did *not* choose, would be appropriate for a field that is the primary key of a table, but LastName is not the primary key of this table. A table's primary key should never contain duplicates.

8. **Enter the rest of the fields, changing the default Field Size to something appropriate in all cases.**

   Figure 4-7 shows the result.

TIP

As you can see in Figure 4-7, the field for business or charity (BusinessOrCharity) is not indexed. There's no point in indexing a field that has only two possible entries; indexing doesn't narrow down the selection enough to be worth the performance hit you get from adding indexing.

TECHNICAL STUFF

Access uses the term *field* rather than *attribute* or *column*. The program's original file-processing systems weren't relational and used the file, field, and record terminology that are common for flat-file systems.

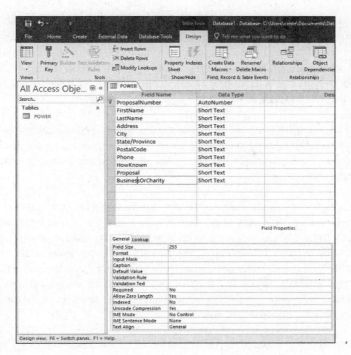

FIGURE 4-7:
The table-creation window after all fields are defined.

9. **Save your table by clicking on the diskette icon in the upper left corner of the window.**

TIP

Keeping one eye on the future is wise as you develop your database. It's a good idea (for example) to save frequently as you develop; just click that diskette icon now and then. Doing so could save you a lot of tedious rework in the event of a power outage or other untoward event. Also, though it won't destroy the planet if you give the same name to a database and to one of the tables that the database contains, it might be mildly confusing for later administrators and users. As a rule, it's handier (and kinder) to just come up with two different names.

After you save your table, you may find that you need to tweak your original design, as I describe in the next section, "Altering the table structure."

Altering the table structure

Often newly created database tables need some tweaking. If you're working for someone else, your client may come to you after you create the database and tell you that she wants to keep track of another data item — perhaps several more. That means you must go back to the drawing board.

If you're building a database for your own use, deficiencies in its structure inevitably become apparent *after* you create the structure (it's probably a clause in

Murphy's Law). For example, say you start getting proposals from other countries and need to add a Country column. Or you have an older database that didn't include email addresses — time to bring it up to date. In this section, I show you how to use Access to modify a table. Other RAD tools have comparable capabilities and work in a similar fashion.

TIP

If a time comes when you need to update your database tables, take a moment to assess all the fields you could be using. For example, you may as well add a second Address field for people with complex addresses and a Country field for proposals from other countries.

TIP

Although it is fairly easy to update database tables, you should avoid doing so whenever possible. Any applications that depend on the old database structure are likely to break and will have to be fixed. If you have a lot of applications, this task could be a major undertaking. Try to anticipate expansions that might be needed in the future and make provisions for them. Carrying along a little extra overhead in the database is usually preferable to updating a slew of applications written several years ago. The knowledge of how they work is probably long gone, and they may be essentially unfixable.

To insert new rows and accommodate changes, open the table and follow these steps:

1. **In the table-creation window, right-click in the small colored square to the left of the City field to select that row and choose Insert Rows from the menu that pops up.**

A blank row appears above the cursor position and pushes down all the existing rows, as shown in Figure 4-8.

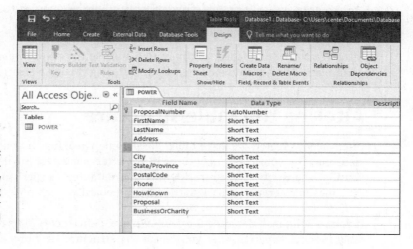

FIGURE 4-8:
The table-creation window after opening up space for a second address line.

2. **Enter the fields you want to add to your table.**

I added an Address2 field above the City field and a Country field above the Phone field.

3. **After you finish your modifications, save the table before closing it.**

The result should look similar to Figure 4-9.

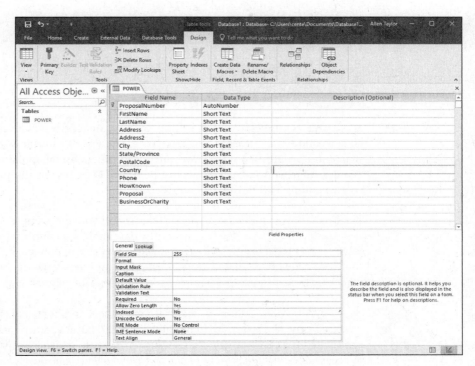

FIGURE 4-9:
Your revised
table definition
should look
similar to this.

Creating an index

In any database, you need a quick way to access records of interest. (This is never truer than when you win the lottery — the number of investment and charitable proposals you receive could easily grow into the thousands.) Say, for example, that you want to look at all the proposals from people claiming to be your brother, son, father, mother, or other appropriately named persons. Assuming none of your relatives have changed their last names for theatrical or professional reasons, you can isolate these proposals by basing your retrieval on the contents of the LastName field, as shown in the following SQL ad hoc query:

```
SELECT * FROM POWER
    WHERE LastName = 'Marx' ;
```

That strategy may not work for the proposals made by half-brothers, half-sisters, sisters-in-law, and brothers-in-law, so you need to look at a different field, as shown in the following example:

```
SELECT * FROM POWER
    WHERE LastName = 'Marx'
        OR
        HowKnown = 'brother-in-law'
        OR
        HowKnown = 'sister-in-law'
        OR
        HowKnown = 'half-sister'
        OR
        HowKnown = 'half-brother' ;
```

SQL scans the table a row at a time, looking for entries that satisfy the WHERE clause condition. If the POWER table is large (tens of thousands of records), you may end up waiting a while. You can speed things up by applying *indexes* to the POWER table. (An *index* is a table of pointers. Each row in the index points to a corresponding row in the data table.)

You can define an index for all the different ways you may want to access your data. If you add, change, or delete rows in the data table, you don't have to re-sort the table — you need only update the indexes. You can update an index much faster than you can sort a table. After you establish an index with the desired ordering, you can use that index to access rows in the data table almost instantaneously.

TIP

Because the ProposalNumber field is unique as well as short, using that field is the quickest way to access an individual record. Those qualities make it an ideal candidate for a primary key. And because primary keys are usually the fastest way to access data, *the primary key of any and every table should always be indexed;* Access indexes primary keys automatically. To use this field, however, you must know the ProposalNumber of the record you want. You may want to create additional indexes based on other fields, such as LastName, PostalCode, or HowKnown. For a table that you index on LastName, after a search finds the first row containing a LastName of Marx, the search has found them all. The index keys for all the Marx rows are stored one right after another. You can retrieve Chico, Groucho, Harpo, Zeppo, and Karl almost as fast as you could get the data on Chico alone.

Indexes add overhead to your system, which slows down operations. You must balance this slowdown against the speed you gain by accessing records through an index.

Here are some tips for picking good indexing fields:

>> Indexing the fields you frequently use to access records is always a good idea. You can speedily access records without too much latency.

>> Don't bother creating indexes for fields that you *never* use as retrieval keys. Creating needless indexes is a waste of time and memory space, and you gain nothing.

>> Don't create indexes for fields that don't differentiate one record from a lot of others. For example, the BusinessOrCharity field merely divides the table records into two categories; it doesn't make a good index.

The effectiveness of an index varies from one implementation to another. If you migrate a database from one platform to another, the indexes that gave the best performance on the first system may not perform the best on the new platform. In fact, the performance may be worse than if you hadn't indexed the database at all. Try various indexing schemes to see which one gives you the best overall performance, and then optimize your indexes so that neither retrieval speed nor update speed suffer from the migration.

To create indexes for the POWER table, just select Yes for Indexed in the Field Properties pane of the table creation window.

Access does two handy tricks automatically: It creates an index for PostalCode (because that field is often used for retrievals) *and* it indexes the primary key. (Ah, progress. Gotta love it.)

PostalCode isn't a primary key and isn't necessarily unique; the opposite is true for ProposalNumber. You already created an index for LastName. Do the same for HowKnown because both are likely to be used for retrievals. Be sure to specify (Duplicates OK) when you create an index for the HowKnown field. You want to be able to include all your brothers and sisters.

After you create all your indexes, don't forget to save the new table structure before closing it.

If you use a RAD tool other than Microsoft Access, the info in this section doesn't apply to you. However, the overall process is fairly similar.

Deleting a table

In the course of creating a table (such as the POWER table I describe in this chapter) with the exact structure you want, you may have to create a few intermediate versions along the way. Having these variant tables on your system may confuse people later, so delete them now while they're still fresh in your mind. To do so, right-click the table you want to delete from the All Tables list on the left side of the window. A menu pops up, and one of the options it offers is Delete. When you click Delete, as shown in Figure 4-10, the table is removed from the database.

WARNING

Be *really* sure of what you're doing. When you click Delete, that table, and all the work you put into it, will be gone.

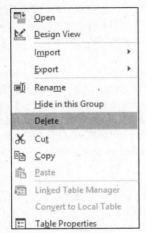

FIGURE 4-10:
Select Delete to delete a table.

REMEMBER

If Access deletes a table, it deletes all subsidiary tables as well, including any indexes the table may have.

Building POWER with SQL's DDL

All the database-definition functions you can perform with a RAD tool (such as Access) are also possible if you're using SQL to build your table. Of course, using SQL isn't as glamorous — instead of clicking menu choices with the mouse, you enter commands from the keyboard. People who prefer to manipulate visual objects find the RAD tools easy to understand and use. People who are happier stringing words together into logical statements find SQL commands easier to use.

TIP

Becoming proficient at using both methods is worthwhile because some things are more easily represented by using the object-oriented (mouse) technique and others are more easily handled by typing in SQL commands.

In the following sections, I use SQL to create the same table as before, and then I do the same alteration and deletion operations I did with the RAD tool in the first part of this chapter.

Using SQL with Microsoft Access

Access is designed as a rapid application development (RAD) tool that does not require programming. You can write and execute SQL statements in Access, but you must use a back-door method to do it. To open a basic editor where you can enter SQL code, follow these steps:

1. **Open your database and click the CREATE tab to display the Ribbon across the top of the window.**

2. **Click Query Design in the Queries section.**

The Show Table dialog box appears.

3. **Select the POWER table. Click the Add button and then click the Close button to close the dialog box.**

Doing so produces the display shown in Figure 4-11.

A picture of the POWER table and its attributes appears in the upper part of the work area and a Query By Example (QBE) grid appears below it. Access expects you to enter a query now by using the QBE grid. (You *could* do that, sure, but it wouldn't tell you anything about how to use SQL in the Access environment.)

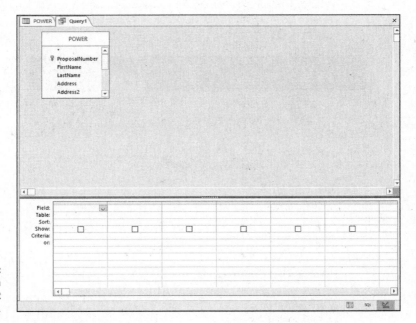

4. **Click the Home tab and then pull down the View menu in the left corner of the Ribbon.**

A menu drops down, displaying the different views available to you in query mode, as shown in Figure 4-12.

One of those views is SQL View.

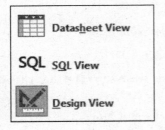

FIGURE 4-12:
The database views available in Query mode.

5. **Click SQL View to display the SQL View Object tab.**

As Figure 4-13 shows, the SQL View Object tab has made the (very rational) assumption that you want to retrieve some information from the POWER table, so it has written the first part for you. It doesn't know exactly what you want to retrieve, so it displays only the part it feels confident about.

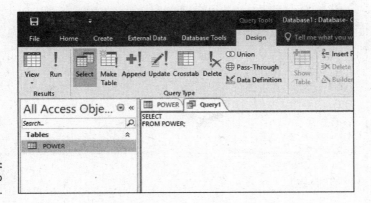

FIGURE 4-13:
The Object tab in SQL view.

Here's what it's written so far:

```
SELECT
FROM POWER ;
```

6. **Fill in an asterisk (*) in the blank area in the first line and add a WHERE clause after the FROM line.**

If you had already entered some data into the POWER table, you could make a retrieval with something like:

```
SELECT *
FROM POWER
   WHERE LastName = 'Marx' ;
```

Be sure the semicolon (;) is the last thing in the SQL statement. You need to move it down from just after POWER to the end of the next line down.

7. **When you're finished, make sure the Query1 tab is selected and then click the floppy-diskette Save icon.**

Access asks you for a name for the query you have just created.

8. **Enter a name to replace the default Query1 and then click OK.**

Your statement is saved and can be executed as a query later.

Creating a table

Whether you're working with Access or a full-featured enterprise-level DBMS — such as Microsoft SQL Server, Oracle, or IBM DB2 — to create a database table with SQL, you must enter the same information that you'd enter if you created the table with a RAD tool. The difference is that the RAD tool helps you by providing a visual interface — in the form of a table-creation dialog box (or some similar data-entry skeleton) — and by preventing you from entering invalid field names, types, or sizes.

REMEMBER

SQL doesn't give you as much help. You must know what you're doing at the outset; figuring things out along the way can lead to less-than-desirable database results. You must enter the entire CREATE TABLE statement before SQL even looks at it, let alone gives you any indication of whether you made errors in the statement.

In ISO/IEC standard SQL, the statement that creates a proposal-tracking table (identical to the one created earlier in the chapter) uses the following syntax:

```
CREATE TABLE POWERSQL (
   ProposalNumber      INTEGER     PRIMARY KEY,
   FirstName           CHAR (15),
   LastName            CHAR (20),
   Address             CHAR (30),
```

```
    City                CHAR (25),
    StateProvince       CHAR (2),
    PostalCode          CHAR (10),
    Country             CHAR (30),
    Phone               CHAR (14),
    HowKnown            CHAR (30),
    Proposal            CHAR (50),
    BusinessOrCharity   CHAR (1) );
```

The information in the SQL statement is essentially the same information you enter using Access's graphical user interface. The nice thing about SQL is that the language is universal. The same standard syntax works regardless of what standard-compliant DBMS product you use.

In Access 2016, creating database objects such as tables is a little more complicated. You can't just type a CREATE statement (such as the one just given) into the SQL View Object tab. That's because the SQL View Object tab is available only as a query tool; you must take a few extra actions to inform Access that you're about to enter a data-definition query rather than a normal query that requests information from the database. A further complication: Because table creation is an action that could possibly compromise database security, it's disallowed by default. You must tell Access that this is a trusted database before it will accept a data-definition query.

1. **Click the Create tab on the Ribbon to display the icons for creation functionality.**

2. **Click Query Design in the Queries section.**

   This displays the Show Table dialog box, which at this point contains POWER.

3. **Select POWER and click the Add button.**

   As you've seen in the previous example, a picture of the POWER table and its attributes appears in the upper half of the work area.

4. **Click the Close button on the Show Table dialog box.**

5. **Click the Home tab and then pull down the View menu at the left end of the Ribbon and choose SQL View from the menu.**

   As in the previous example, Access has "helped" you by putting SELECT FROM POWER in the SQL editor. This time you don't want the help.

6. Delete `SELECT FROM POWER` and (in its place) enter the data-definition query given earlier, as follows:

```
CREATE TABLE POWERSQL (
        ProposalNumber        INTEGER        PRIMARY KEY,
        FirstName             CHAR (15),
        LastName              CHAR (20),
        Address               CHAR (30),
        City                  CHAR (25),
        StateProvince         CHAR (2),
        PostalCode            CHAR (10),
        Country               CHAR (30),
        Phone                 CHAR (14),
        HowKnown              CHAR (30),
        Proposal              CHAR (50),
        BusinessOrCharity     CHAR (1) );
```

At this point, your screen should look something like Figure 4-14.

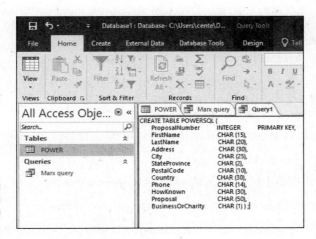

FIGURE 4-14: Data-definition query to create a table.

7. After clicking the Design tab of the Ribbon, click the red exclamation point Run icon.

Doing so runs the query, which creates the POWERSQL table (as shown in Figure 4-15).

You should see POWERSQL listed under All Access Objects in the column at the left edge of the window. In which case, you're golden. Or you may not see the table in the All Access Objects list. In that case, read (and slog) on.

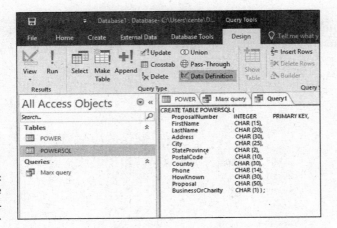

FIGURE 4-15:
Behold the
POWERSQL
table.

WARNING

Access 2016 goes to great lengths to protect you from malicious hackers and from your own inadvertent mistakes. Because running a data-definition query is potentially dangerous to the database, Access has a default that prevents the query from running. If this has happened to you, POWERSQL *won't* appear in the column at the left of the window, because the query won't have been executed. Instead, the Message Bar may appear below the Ribbon, with this terse message:

```
Security Warning: Certain content in the database has
          been disabled.
```

If you see this message, move on to the next steps.

8. **Click the File tab and, from the menu of the left edge, choose Options.**

   The Access Options dialog box appears.

9. **Select Trust Center from the Access Options dialog box.**

10. **Click the Trust Center Settings button when it appears.**

11. **Select Message Bar from the menu on the left and then specify Show the Message Bar by clicking its option button if it isn't already selected.**

12. **Click your way back to the place where you can execute the data-definition query that creates the POWERSQL table.**

13. **Execute the query.**

REMEMBER

Becoming proficient in SQL has long-term payoffs because it will be around for a long time. The effort you put into becoming an expert in a specific development tool is likely to yield a lower return on investment. No matter how wonderful the latest RAD tool may be, it will be superseded by newer technology within three to five years. If you can recover your investment in the tool in that time, great! Use it. If not, you may be wise to stick with the tried and true. Train your people in SQL, and your training investment will pay dividends over a much longer period.

Creating an index

Indexes are an important part of any relational database. They serve as pointers into the tables that contain the data of interest. By using an index, you can go directly to a specific record without having to scan the table sequentially, one record at a time, to find that record. For really large tables, indexes are a necessity; without indexes, you may need to wait *years* rather than seconds for a result. (Well, okay, maybe you wouldn't actually wait *years*. Some retrievals, however, may actually take that long if you let them keep running. Unless you have nothing better to do with your computer's time, you'd probably do best to abort the retrieval and do without the result. Life goes on.)

Amazingly, the SQL standard doesn't provide a means to create an index. The DBMS vendors provide their own implementations of the function. Because these implementations aren't standardized, they may differ from one another. Most vendors provide the index-creation function by adding a CREATE INDEX command to SQL.

WARNING

Even though two vendors may use the same words for the command (CREATE INDEX), the way the command operates may not be the same. You're likely to find quite a few implementation-dependent clauses. Carefully study your DBMS documentation to determine how to create indexes.

Altering the table structure

To change the structure of an existing table, you can use SQL's ALTER TABLE command. Interactive SQL at your client station is not as convenient as a RAD tool. The RAD tool displays your table's structure, which you can then modify. Using SQL, you must know in advance the table's structure and how you want to modify it. At the screen prompt, you must enter the appropriate command to perform the alteration. If, however, you want to embed the table-alteration instructions in an application program, then using SQL is usually the easiest way to do so.

To add a second address field to the POWERSQL table, use the following DDL command:

```
ALTER TABLE POWERSQL
    ADD COLUMN Address2 CHAR (30);
```

You don't need to be an SQL guru to decipher this code. Even professed computer illiterates can probably figure this one out. The command alters a table named POWERSQL by adding a column to the table. The column is named Address2, is of the CHAR data type, and is at most 30 characters long. This example demonstrates how easily you can change the structure of database tables by using SQL DDL commands.

Standard SQL provides the preceding statement for adding a column to a table and allows you to drop an existing column in a similar manner, as in the following code:

```
ALTER TABLE POWERSQL
   DROP COLUMN Address2;
```

Deleting a table

Deleting database tables that you no longer need is easy. Just use the DROP TABLE command, as follows:

```
DROP TABLE POWERSQL;
```

What could be simpler? If you DROP a table, you erase all its data and its metadata. No vestige of the table remains. This works great most of the time. The only time it doesn't is if another table in the database references the one you are trying to delete. This is called a *referential integrity constraint*. In such a case, SQL will spit out an error message rather than delete the table.

Deleting an index

WARNING

If you delete a table by issuing a DROP TABLE command, you also delete any indexes associated with that table. Sometimes, however, you may want to keep a table but remove an index from it. The SQL standard doesn't define a DROP INDEX command, but most implementations include that command anyway. Such a command comes in handy if your system slows to a crawl and you discover that your tables aren't optimally indexed. Correcting an index problem can dramatically improve performance — which will delight users who've become accustomed to response times reminiscent of pouring molasses on a cold day in Vermont.

Portability Considerations

Any SQL implementation you're likely to use may have extensions that give it capabilities that the SQL standard doesn't cover. Some of these features may appear in the next release of the SQL standard. Others are unique to a particular implementation and are probably destined to stay that way.

Often extensions make it easier to create an application that meets your needs, and you'll find yourself tempted to use them. Using the extensions may be your best course, but be aware of the tradeoffs: If you ever want to migrate your application to another SQL implementation, you may have to rewrite those sections in which you used extensions that your new environment doesn't support.

TIP

The more you know about existing implementations and development trends, the better the decisions you'll make. Think about the probability of such a migration in the future — and also about whether the extension you're considering is unique to your implementation or fairly widespread. Foregoing use of an extension may be better in the long run, even if its use might save you some time now. On the other hand, you may find no reason not to use the extension. Your call.

Chapter **5**

Building a Multi-table Relational Database

In this chapter, I take you through an example of how to design a multi-table database. The first step to designing any database is to identify what to include and what not to include. The next steps involve deciding how the included items relate to each other and then setting up tables accordingly. I also discuss how to use *keys*, which enable you to access individual records and indexes quickly.

A database must do more than merely hold your data. It must also protect the data from becoming corrupted. In the latter part of this chapter, I discuss how to protect the integrity of your data. *Normalization* is one of the key methods you can use to protect the integrity of a database. I discuss the various normal forms and point out the kinds of problems that normalization solves.

Designing a Database

To design a database, follow these basic steps (I go into detail about each step in the sections that follow this list):

1. **Decide what objects you want to include in your database.**

2. **Determine which of these objects should be tables and which should be columns within those tables.**

3. **Define tables based on how you need to organize the objects.**

   Optionally, you may want to designate a table column or a combination of columns as a key. *Keys* provide a fast way to locate a row of interest in a table.

The following sections discuss these steps in detail, as well as some other technical issues that arise during database design.

Step 1: Defining objects

The first step in designing a database is deciding which aspects of the system are important enough to include in the model. Treat each aspect as an object and create a list of all the objects you can think of. At this stage, don't try to decide how these objects relate to each other. Just try to list them all.

TIP

You may find it helpful to gather a diverse team of people who, in one way or another, are familiar with the system you're modeling. These people can brainstorm and respond to each other's ideas. Working together, you'll probably develop a more complete and accurate set of important objects than you would on your own.

When you have a reasonably complete set of objects, move on to the next step: deciding how these objects relate to each other. Some of the objects are major entities (more about those in a minute) that are crucial to giving you the results you want. Other objects are subsidiary to those major entities. Ultimately you may decide that some objects don't belong in the model at all.

Step 2: Identifying tables and columns

Major entities translate into database tables. Each major entity has a set of *attributes* — the table columns. Many business databases, for example, have a CUSTOMER table that keeps track of customers' names, addresses, and other permanent information. Each attribute of a customer — such as name, street, city, state, zip code, phone number, and email address — becomes a column (and a column heading) in the CUSTOMER table.

If you're hoping to find a set of rules to help you identify which objects should be tables and which of the attributes in the system belong to which tables, think again: You may have some reasons for assigning a given attribute to one table and other reasons for assigning *the same attribute* to another table. You must base your judgment on two goals:

>> The information you want to get from the database

>> How you want to use that information

WARNING

When deciding how to structure database tables, involve the future users of the database as well as the people who will make decisions based on database information. If you come up with what you think is a reasonable structure, but it isn't consistent with the way that people will use the information, your system will be frustrating to use at best — and could even produce wrong information, which is even worse. Don't let this happen! Put careful effort into deciding how to structure your tables.

Take a look at an example to demonstrate the thought process that goes into creating a multi-table database. Suppose you just established VetLab, a clinical microbiology laboratory that tests biological specimens sent in by veterinarians. You want to track several things, including the following:

>> Clients

>> Tests that you perform

>> Employees

>> Orders

>> Results

Each of these entities has associated attributes. Each client has a name, an address, and other contact information. Each test has a name and a standard charge. Each employee has contact information as well as a job classification and pay rate. For each order, you need to know who ordered it, when it was ordered, and what test was ordered. For each test result, you need to know the outcome of the test, whether the results were preliminary or final, and the test order number.

Step 3: Defining tables

Now you want to define a table for each entity and a column for each attribute. Table 5-1 shows how you may define the VetLab tables I introduce in the previous section.

TABLE 5-1

VetLab Tables

Table	Columns
CLIENT	Client Name
	Address 1
	Address 2
	City
	State
	Postal Code
	Phone
	Fax
	Contact Person
TESTS	Test Name
	Standard Charge
EMPLOYEE	Employee Name
	Address 1
	Address 2
	City
	State
	Postal Code
	Home Phone
	Office Extension
	Hire Date
	Job Classification
	Hourly/Salary/Commission
ORDERS	Order Number
	Client Name
	Test Ordered
	Responsible Salesperson
	Order Date

Table	Columns
RESULTS	Result Number
	Order Number
	Result
	Date Reported
	Preliminary/Final

You can create the tables defined in Table 5-1 by using either a rapid application development (RAD) tool or by using SQL's Data Definition Language (DDL), as shown in the following code:

```
CREATE TABLE CLIENT (
     ClientName       CHAR (30)       NOT NULL,
     Address1         CHAR (30),
     Address2         CHAR (30),
     City             CHAR (25),
     State            CHAR (2),
     PostalCode       CHAR (10),
     Phone            CHAR (13),
     Fax              CHAR (13),
     ContactPerson    CHAR (30) ) ;

CREATE TABLE TESTS (
     TestName         CHAR (30)       NOT NULL,
     StandardCharge   CHAR (30) ) ;

CREATE TABLE EMPLOYEE (
     EmployeeName     CHAR (30)       NOT NULL,
     Address1         CHAR (30),
     Address2         CHAR (30),
     City             CHAR (25),
     State            CHAR (2),
     PostalCode       CHAR (10),
     HomePhone        CHAR (13),
     OfficeExtension  CHAR (4),
     HireDate         DATE,
     JobClassification CHAR (10),
     HourSalComm      CHAR (1) ) ;
```

```
CREATE TABLE ORDERS (
       OrderNumber         INTEGER              NOT NULL,
       ClientName          CHAR (30),
       TestOrdered         CHAR (30),
       Salesperson         CHAR (30),
       OrderDate           DATE ) ;

CREATE TABLE RESULTS (
       ResultNumber        INTEGER              NOT NULL,
       OrderNumber         INTEGER,
       Result              CHAR(50),
       DateReported        DATE,
       PrelimFinal         CHAR (1) ) ;
```

These tables relate to each other by the attributes (columns) that they share, as the following list describes:

>> The CLIENT table links to the ORDERS table by the ClientName column.

>> The TESTS table links to the ORDERS table by the TestName (TestOrdered) column.

>> The EMPLOYEE table links to the ORDERS table by the EmployeeName (Salesperson) column.

>> The RESULTS table links to the ORDERS table by the OrderNumber column.

If you want a table to serve as an integral part of a relational database, link that table to at least one other table in the database, using a common column. Figure 5-1 illustrates the relationships between the tables.

The links in Figure 5-1 illustrate four different *one-to-many* relationships. The diamond in the middle of each relationship shows the maximum cardinality of each end of the relationship. The number 1 denotes the "one" side of the relationship, and N denotes the "many" side.

>> One client can place many orders, but each order is made by one, and only one, client.

>> Each test can appear on many orders, but each order calls for one, and only one, test.

>> Each order is booked by one, and only one, employee (or salesperson), but each salesperson can (and, you hope, does) book multiple orders.

>> Each order can produce several preliminary test results and a final result, but each result is associated with one, and only one, order.

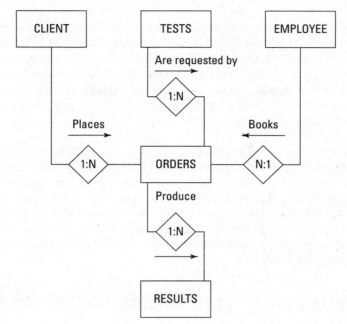

FIGURE 5-1:
VetLab database
tables and links.

As you can see in the code, the attribute that links one table to another can have a different name in each table. Both attributes must, however, have matching data types. At this point, I have not included any referential integrity constraints, wanting to avoid hitting you with too many ideas at once. I cover referential integrity later in this chapter, after I have laid the foundation for understanding it.

Domains, character sets, collations, and translations

Although tables are the main components of a database, additional elements play a part, too. In Chapter 1, I define the *domain* of a column in a table as the set of all values that the column may assume. Establishing clear-cut domains for the columns in a table, by defining constraints, is an important part of designing a database.

People who communicate in standard American English aren't the only ones who use relational databases. Other languages — even some that use other character sets — work equally well. Even if your data is in English, some applications may still require a specialized character set. SQL enables you to specify the character set you want to use. In fact, you can use a different character set for each column in a table if you need to. This flexibility is generally unavailable in languages other than SQL.

A *collation,* or *collating sequence,* is a set of rules that determines how strings in a character set compare with one another. Every character set has a default collation. In the default collation of the ASCII character set, *A* comes before *B,* and *B* comes before *C.* A comparison, therefore, considers *A* as less than *B* and considers *C* as greater than *B.* SQL enables you to apply different collations to a character set. This degree of flexibility isn't generally available in other languages, so you now have another reason to love SQL.

Sometimes you encode data in a database in one character set but want to deal with the data in another character set. Perhaps you have data in the German character set (for example) but your printer doesn't support German characters that aren't included in the ASCII character set. SQL allows *translation* of character strings from one character set to another. A translation may change one character into two, as when a German *ü* becomes an ASCII *ue,* or change lowercase characters to uppercase. You can even translate one alphabet into another (for example, Hebrew into ASCII).

Getting into your database fast with keys

A good rule for database design is to make sure that every row in a database table is distinguishable from every other row; each row should be unique. Sometimes you may want to extract data from your database for a specific purpose (such as a statistical analysis), and in doing so, end up creating tables in which the rows aren't necessarily unique. For such a limited purpose, this sort of duplication doesn't matter. Tables that you may use in more than one way, however, should not contain duplicate rows.

A *key* is an attribute (or combination of attributes) that uniquely identifies a row in a table. To access a row in a database, you must have some way of distinguishing that row from all the other rows. Because keys must be unique, they provide such an access mechanism.

REMEMBER

Furthermore, a key must never contain a null value. If you use null keys, you may not be able to distinguish between two rows that contain a null key field.

In the veterinary-lab example, you can designate appropriate columns as keys. In the CLIENT table, `ClientName` is a good key. This key can distinguish each individual client from all other clients. Therefore, entering a value in this column becomes mandatory for every row in the table. `TestName` and `EmployeeName` make good keys for the TESTS and EMPLOYEE tables. `OrderNumber` and `ResultNumber` make good keys for the ORDERS and RESULTS tables. Make sure that you enter a unique value for every row.

You can have two kinds of keys: *primary keys* and *foreign keys.* The keys I discuss in the preceding paragraph are examples of primary keys; they guarantee uniqueness. I zero in on primary and foreign keys in the next two sections.

Primary keys

A *primary key* is a column or combination of columns in a table with values that uniquely identify the rows in the table. To incorporate the idea of keys into the VetLab database, you can specify the primary key of a table as you create the table. In the following example, a single column is sufficient (assuming that all of VetLab's clients have unique names):

```
CREATE TABLE CLIENT (
    ClientName          CHAR (30)     PRIMARY KEY,
    Address1            CHAR (30),
    Address2            CHAR (30),
    City                CHAR (25),
    State               CHAR (2),
    PostalCode          CHAR (10),
    Phone               CHAR (13),
    Fax                 CHAR (13),
    ContactPerson       CHAR (30)
    ) ;
```

The constraint PRIMARY KEY replaces the constraint NOT NULL, given in the earlier definition of the CLIENT table. The PRIMARY KEY constraint implies the NOT NULL constraint, because a primary key can't have a null value.

Although most DBMSs allow you to create a table without a primary key, all tables in a database should have one. With that in mind, replace the NOT NULL constraint in all your tables. In my example, the TESTS, EMPLOYEE, ORDERS, and RESULTS tables should have the PRIMARY KEY constraint, as in the following example:

```
CREATE TABLE TESTS (
    TestName            CHAR (30)     PRIMARY KEY,
    StandardCharge      CHAR (30) ) ;
```

Sometimes no single column in a table can guarantee uniqueness. In such cases, you can use a *composite key* — a combination of columns that guarantee uniqueness when used together. Imagine that some of VetLab's clients are chains that have offices in several cities. ClientName isn't sufficient to distinguish between two branch offices of the same client. To handle this situation, you can define a composite key as follows:

```
CREATE TABLE CLIENT (
    ClientName          CHAR (30)       NOT NULL,
    Address1            CHAR (30),
    Address2            CHAR (30),
    City                CHAR (25)       NOT NULL,
    State               CHAR (2),
    PostalCode          CHAR (10),
    Phone               CHAR (13),
    Fax                 CHAR (13),
    ContactPerson       CHAR (30),
    CONSTRAINT BranchPK    PRIMARY KEY
      (ClientName, City)
    ) ;
```

As an alternative to using a composite key to uniquely identify a record, you can let your DBMS assign one automatically, as Access does in suggesting that the first field in a new table be named ID and be of the AutoNumber type. Such a key has no meaning in and of itself. Its only purpose is to be a unique identifier.

Foreign keys

A *foreign key* is a column or group of columns in a table that corresponds to or references a primary key in another table in the database. A foreign key doesn't have to be unique, but it must uniquely identify the column(s) in the table that the key references.

If the `ClientName` column is the primary key in the CLIENT table (for example), every row in the CLIENT table must have a unique value in the `ClientName` column. `ClientName` is a foreign key in the ORDERS table. This foreign key corresponds to the primary key of the CLIENT table, but the key doesn't have to be unique in the ORDERS table. In fact, you hope the foreign key *isn't* unique; if each of your clients gave you only one order and then never ordered again, you'd go out of business rather quickly. You hope that many rows in the ORDERS table correspond with each row in the CLIENT table, indicating that nearly all your clients are repeat customers.

The following definition of the ORDERS table shows how you can add the concept of foreign keys to a `CREATE` statement:

```
CREATE TABLE ORDERS (
    OrderNumber     INTEGER         PRIMARY KEY,
    ClientName      CHAR (30),
```

```
TestOrdered        CHAR (30),
Salesperson        CHAR (30),
OrderDate          DATE,
CONSTRAINT NameFK FOREIGN KEY (ClientName)
  REFERENCES CLIENT (ClientName),
CONSTRAINT TestFK FOREIGN KEY (TestOrdered)
  REFERENCES TESTS (TestName),
CONSTRAINT SalesFK FOREIGN KEY (Salesperson)
  REFERENCES EMPLOYEE (EmployeeName)
) ;
```

In this example, foreign keys in the ORDERS table link that table to the primary keys of the CLIENT, TESTS, and EMPLOYEE tables.

Working with Indexes

The SQL specification doesn't address the topic of indexes, but that omission doesn't mean that indexes are rare or even optional parts of a database system. Every SQL implementation supports indexes, but you'll find no universal agreement on how to support them. In Chapter 4, I show you how to create an index by using Microsoft Access, a rapid application development (RAD) tool. Refer to the documentation for other database management systems (DBMSs) to see how those systems implements indexes.

What's an index, anyway?

Data generally appears in a table in the order in which you originally entered the information. That order may have nothing to do with the order in which you later want to process the data. Say, for example, that you want to process your CLIENT table in ClientName order. The computer must first sort the table in ClientName order. Sorting the data this way takes time. The larger the table, the longer the sort takes. What if you have a table with 100,000 rows? Or a table with a million rows? In some applications, such table sizes are not rare. The best sort algorithms would have to make some 20 million comparisons and millions of swaps to put the table in the desired order. Even if you're using a very fast computer, you may not want to wait that long.

Indexes can be a great timesaver. An *index* is a subsidiary or *support table* that goes along with a data table. For every row in the data table, you have a corresponding row in the index table. The order of the rows in the index table is different.

Table 5-2 is a small example of a data table for the veterinary lab.

TABLE 5-2   ## CLIENT Table

ClientName	Address1	Address2	City	State
Butternut Animal Clinic	5 Butternut Lane		Hudson	NH
Amber Veterinary, Inc.	470 Kolvir Circle		Amber	MI
Vets R Us	2300 Geoffrey Road	Suite 230	Anaheim	CA
Doggie Doctor	32 Terry Terrace		Nutley	NJ
The Equestrian Center	Veterinary	7890 Paddock Parkway	Gallup	NM
Dolphin Institute	1002 Marine Drive		Key West	FL
J. C. Campbell, Credit Vet	2500 Main Street		Los Angeles	CA
Wenger's Worm Farm	15 Bait Boulevard		Sedona	AZ

Here the rows are not in alphabetical order by ClientName. In fact, they aren't in any useful order at all. The rows are simply in the order in which somebody entered the data.

An index for this CLIENT table may look like Table 5-3.

TABLE 5-3   ## Client Name Index for the CLIENT Table

ClientName	Pointer to Data Table
Amber Veterinary, Inc.	2
Butternut Animal Clinic	1
Doggie Doctor	4
Dolphin Institute	6
J. C. Campbell, Credit Vet	7
The Equestrian Center	5
Vets R Us	3
Wenger's Worm Farm	8

The index contains the field that forms the basis of the index (in this case, ClientName) and a pointer into the data table. The pointer in each index row gives the row number of the corresponding row in the data table.

Why you should want an index

If you want to process a table in ClientName order, and you have an index arranged in ClientName order, you can perform your operation almost as fast as you could if the data table itself were already in ClientName order. You can work through the index, moving immediately to each index row's corresponding data record by using the pointer in the index.

If you use an index, the table processing time is proportional to N, where N is the number of records in the table. Without an index, the processing time for the same operation is proportional to $N \lg N$, where $\lg N$ is the logarithm of N to the base 2. For small tables, the difference is insignificant, but for large tables, the difference is great. On large tables, some operations aren't practical to perform without the help of indexes.

Suppose you have a table containing 1,000,000 records (N = 1,000,000), and processing each record takes one millisecond (one-thousandth of a second). If you have an index, processing the entire table takes only 1,000 seconds — less than 17 minutes. Without an index, you need to go through the table approximately 1,000,000 × 20 times to achieve the same result. This process would take 20,000 seconds — more than five and a half hours. I think you can agree that the difference between 17 minutes and five and a half hours is substantial. That's just one example of the difference indexing makes on processing records.

Maintaining an index

After you create an index, you must maintain it. Fortunately, you don't have to think too much about maintenance — your DBMS maintains your indexes for you automatically, by updating them every time you update the corresponding data tables. This process takes some extra time, but it's worth it. When you create an index and your DBMS maintains it, the index is always available to speed up your data processing, no matter how many times you need to call on it.

TIP

The best time to create an index is at the same time you create its corresponding data table. If you create the index early and the DBMS starts maintaining it at the same time, you don't need to undergo the pain of building the index later; the entire operation takes place in a single, long session. Try to anticipate all the ways that you may want to access your data, and then create an index *for each possibility*.

Some DBMS products give you the capability to turn off index maintenance. You may want to do so in some real-time applications where updating indexes takes a great deal of time and you have precious little to spare. You may even elect to update the indexes as a separate operation during off-peak hours. As usual, "do what works for you" is the rule.

WARNING

Don't fall into the trap of creating an index for retrieval orders that you're unlikely ever to use. Index maintenance is an extra operation that the computer must perform every time it modifies the index field or adds or deletes a data table row — and this operation affects performance. For optimal performance, create only those indexes that you expect to use as retrieval keys — and only for tables containing a large number of rows. Otherwise indexes can degrade performance.

TIP

You may need to compile something such as a monthly or quarterly report that requires the data in an odd order that you don't ordinarily need. Create an index just before running that periodic report, run the report, and then drop the index so the DBMS isn't burdened with maintaining the index during the long period between reports.

Maintaining Data Integrity

A database is valuable only if you're reasonably sure that the data it contains is correct. In medical, aircraft, and spacecraft databases, for example, incorrect data can lead to loss of life. Incorrect data in other applications may have less severe consequences but can still prove damaging. Database designers must do their best to make sure that incorrect data never enters the databases they produce. This isn't always possible, but it *is* possible to at least make sure the data that is entered is valid. Maintaining *data integrity* means making sure any data that is entered into a database system satisfies the constraints that have been established for it. For example, if a database field is of the Date type, the DBMS should reject any entry into that field that is not a valid date.

Some problems can't be stopped at the database level. The application programmer must intercept these problems before they can damage the database. Everyone responsible for dealing with the database in any way must remain conscious of the threats to data integrity and take appropriate action to nullify those threats.

Databases can experience several distinctly different kinds of integrity — and a number of problems that can affect integrity. In the following sections, I discuss three types of integrity: *entity, domain,* and *referential.* I also look at some of the problems that can threaten database integrity.

Entity integrity

Every table in a database corresponds to an entity in the real world. That entity may be physical or conceptual, but in some sense, the entity's existence is independent of the database. A table has *entity integrity* if the table is entirely consistent with the entity that it models. To have entity integrity, a table must have a primary key that uniquely identifies each row in the table. Without a primary key, you can't be sure that the row retrieved is the one you want.

To maintain entity integrity, be sure to specify that the column (or group of columns) making up the primary key is NOT NULL. In addition, you must constrain the primary key to be UNIQUE. Some SQL implementations enable you to add such constraints to the table definition. With other implementations, however, you must apply the constraint later, after you specify how to add, change, or delete data from the table.

TIP

The best way to ensure that your primary key is both NOT NULL and UNIQUE is to give the key the PRIMARY KEY constraint when you create the table, as shown in the following example:

```
CREATE TABLE CLIENT (
    ClientName       CHAR (30)      PRIMARY KEY,
    Address1         CHAR (30),
    Address2         CHAR (30),
    City             CHAR (25),
    State            CHAR (2),
    PostalCode       CHAR (10),
    Phone            CHAR (13),
    Fax              CHAR (13),
    ContactPerson    CHAR (30)
    ) ;
```

An alternative is to use NOT NULL in combination with UNIQUE, as shown in the following example:

```
CREATE TABLE CLIENT (
    ClientName       CHAR (30)      NOT NULL,
    Address1         CHAR (30),
    Address2         CHAR (30),
    City             CHAR (25),
    State            CHAR (2),
    PostalCode       CHAR (10),
    Phone            CHAR (13),
    Fax              CHAR (13),
    ContactPerson    CHAR (30),
    UNIQUE (ClientName) ) ;
```

Domain integrity

You usually can't guarantee that any given data item in a database is correct, but you *can* determine whether a data item is valid. Many data items have a limited number of possible values. If you make an entry that is not one of the possible values, that entry must be an error. The United States, for example, has 50 states plus the District of Columbia, Puerto Rico, and a few possessions. Each of these areas has a two-character code that the U.S. Postal Service recognizes. If your database has a State column, you can enforce *domain integrity* by requiring that any entry into that column be one of the recognized two-character codes. If an operator enters a code that's not on the list of valid codes, that entry breaches domain integrity. If you test for domain integrity, you can refuse to accept any operation that causes such a breach.

Domain integrity concerns arise if you add new data to a table by using either the INSERT statement or the UPDATE statement. You can specify a domain for a column by using a CREATE DOMAIN statement before you use that column in a CREATE TABLE statement, as shown in the following example, which creates a table for major league baseball teams:

```
CREATE DOMAIN LeagueDom CHAR (8)
    CHECK (VALUE IN ('American', 'National'));
CREATE TABLE TEAM (
    TeamName          CHAR (20)          NOT NULL,
    League            LeagueDom          NOT NULL
    ) ;
```

The domain of the League column includes only two valid values: American and National. Your DBMS doesn't enable you to commit an entry or update to the TEAM table unless the League column of the row you're adding has a value of either 'American' or 'National'.

Referential integrity

Even if every table in your system has entity integrity and domain integrity, you may still have a problem because of inconsistencies in the way one table relates to another. In most well-designed multi-table databases, every table contains at least one column that refers to a column in another table in the database. These references are important for maintaining the overall integrity of the database. The same references, however, make update anomalies possible. *Update anomalies* are problems that can occur after you update the data in a row of a database table. The next several sections look at a typical example and suggest how to deal with it.

Trouble between parent and child tables

The relationships among tables are generally not bidirectional. One table is usually dependent on the other. Say, for example, that you have a database with a CLIENT table and an ORDERS table. You may conceivably enter a client into the CLIENT table before she makes any orders. You can't, however, enter an order into the ORDERS table unless you already have an entry in the CLIENT table for the client who's making that order. The ORDERS table is dependent on the CLIENT table. This kind of arrangement is often called a *parent-child relationship*, where CLIENT is the parent table and ORDERS is the child table. The child is dependent on the parent.

TIP

Generally, the primary key of the parent table is a column (or group of columns) that appears in the child table. Within the child table, that same column (or group) is a foreign key. Keep in mind, however, that a foreign key need not be unique.

Update anomalies arise in several ways between parent and child tables. A client moves away, for example, and you want to delete her information from your database. If she has already made some orders (which you recorded in the ORDERS table), deleting her from the CLIENT table could present a problem. You'd have records in the ORDERS (child) table for which you have no corresponding records in the CLIENT (parent) table. Similar problems can arise if you add a record to a child table without making a corresponding addition to the parent table.

REMEMBER

The corresponding foreign keys in all child tables must reflect any changes to the primary key of a row in a parent table; otherwise an update anomaly results.

Cascading deletions — use with care

You can eliminate most referential integrity problems by carefully controlling the update process. In some cases, you must *cascade* deletions from a parent table to its children. To cascade a deletion when you delete a row from a parent table, you also delete all the rows in its child tables whose foreign keys match the primary key of the deleted row in the parent table. Take a look at the following example:

```
CREATE TABLE CLIENT (
    ClientName        CHAR (30)     PRIMARY KEY,
    Address1          CHAR (30),
    Address2          CHAR (30),
    City              CHAR (25)     NOT NULL,
    State             CHAR (2),
    PostalCode        CHAR (10),
    Phone             CHAR (13),
    Fax               CHAR (13),
    ContactPerson     CHAR (30)
    ) ;
```

```
CREATE TABLE TESTS (
    TestName              CHAR (30)      PRIMARY KEY,
    StandardCharge        CHAR (30)
    ) ;


CREATE TABLE EMPLOYEE (
    EmployeeName          CHAR (30)      PRIMARY KEY,
    ADDRESS1              CHAR (30),
    Address2              CHAR (30),
    City                  CHAR (25),
    State                 CHAR (2),
    PostalCode            CHAR (10),
    HomePhone             CHAR (13),
    OfficeExtension       CHAR (4),
    HireDate              DATE,
    JobClassification     CHAR (10),
    HourSalComm           CHAR (1)
    ) ;


CREATE TABLE ORDERS (
    OrderNumber           INTEGER               PRIMARY KEY,
    ClientName            CHAR (30),
    TestOrdered           CHAR (30),
    Salesperson           CHAR (30),
    OrderDate             DATE,
    CONSTRAINT NameFK FOREIGN KEY (ClientName)
      REFERENCES CLIENT (ClientName)
        ON DELETE CASCADE,
    CONSTRAINT TestFK FOREIGN KEY (TestOrdered)
      REFERENCES TESTS (TestName)
        ON DELETE CASCADE,
    CONSTRAINT SalesFK FOREIGN KEY (Salesperson)
      REFERENCES EMPLOYEE (EmployeeName)
        ON DELETE CASCADE
    ) ;
```

The constraint NameFK names ClientName as a foreign key that references the
ClientName column in the CLIENT table. If you delete a row in the CLIENT table,
you also automatically delete all rows in the ORDERS table that have the same
value in the ClientName column as those in the ClientName column of the CLIENT
table. The deletion cascades down from the CLIENT table to the ORDERS table. The
same is true for the foreign keys in the ORDERS table that refer to the primary
keys of the TESTS and EMPLOYEE tables.

Alternative ways to control update anomalies

You may not want to cascade a deletion. Instead, you may want to change the child table's foreign key to a NULL value. Consider the following variant of the previous example:

```
CREATE TABLE ORDERS (
    OrderNumber       INTEGER            PRIMARY KEY,
    ClientName        CHAR (30),
    TestOrdered       CHAR (30),
    SalesPerson       CHAR (30),
    OrderDate         DATE,
    CONSTRAINT NameFK FOREIGN KEY (ClientName)
      REFERENCES CLIENT (ClientName),
    CONSTRAINT TestFK FOREIGN KEY (TestOrdered)
      REFERENCES TESTS (TestName),
    CONSTRAINT SalesFK FOREIGN KEY (Salesperson)
      REFERENCES EMPLOYEE (EmployeeName)
        ON DELETE SET NULL
    ) ;
```

The constraint SalesFK names the Salesperson column as a foreign key that references the EmployeeName column of the EMPLOYEE table. If a salesperson leaves the company, you delete her row in the EMPLOYEE table. New salespeople are eventually assigned to her accounts, but for now, deleting her name from the EMPLOYEE table causes all of her orders in the ORDER table to receive a null value in the Salesperson column.

TIP

You can also keep inconsistent data out of a database by using one of these methods:

>> **Refuse to permit an addition to a child table until a corresponding row exists in its parent table.** If you refuse to permit rows in a child table without a corresponding row in a parent table, you prevent the occurrence of "orphan" rows in the child table. This refusal helps maintain consistency across tables.

>> **Refuse to permit changes to a table's primary key.** If you refuse to permit changes to a table's primary key, you don't need to worry about updating foreign keys in other tables that depend on that primary key.

Just when you thought it was safe . . .

The one thing you can count on in databases (as in life) is change. Wouldn't you know? You create a database, complete with tables, constraints, and rows and rows of data. Then word comes down from management that the structure needs to be changed. How do you add a new column to a table that already exists? How do you delete one that you don't need any more? SQL to the rescue!

Adding a column to an existing table

Suppose your company institutes a policy of having a party for every employee on his or her birthday. To give the party coordinator the advance warning she needs when she plans these parties, you have to add a Birthday column to the EMPLOYEE table. As they say in the Bahamas, "No problem!" Just use the ALTER TABLE statement. Here's how:

```
ALTER TABLE EMPLOYEE
   ADD COLUMN Birthday DATE ;
```

Now all you need do is add the birthday information to each row in the table, and you can party on. (By the way, *where* did you say you work?)

Deleting a column from an existing table

Now suppose that an economic downturn hits your company and it can no longer afford to fund lavish birthday parties. Even in a bad economy, DJ fees have gone through the roof. No more parties means no more need to retain birthday data. With the ALTER TABLE statement, you can handle this situation too.

```
ALTER TABLE EMPLOYEE
   DROP COLUMN Birthday ;
```

Ah, well, it was fun while it lasted.

Potential problem areas

Data integrity is subject to assault from a variety of quarters. Some of these problems arise only in multi-table databases; others can happen even in databases that contain only a single table. You want to recognize and minimize all these potential threats.

Bad input data

The source documents or data files that you use to populate your database may contain bad data. This data may be a corrupted version of the correct data, or it may not be the data you want. A *range check* tells you whether the data has domain integrity. This type of check catches some — but not all — problems. (For example, incorrect field values that are within the acceptable range — but still incorrect — aren't identified as problems.)

Operator error

Your source data may be correct, but the data entry operator may incorrectly transcribe the data. This type of error can lead to the same kinds of problems as bad input data. Some of the solutions are the same, too. Range checks help, but they're not foolproof. Another solution is to have a second operator independently validate all the data. This approach is costly because independent validation takes twice the number of people and twice the time. But in some cases where data integrity is critical, the extra effort and expense may prove worthwhile.

Mechanical failure

If you experience a mechanical failure, such as a disk crash, the data in the table may be destroyed. Good backups are your main defense against this problem.

Malice

Consider the possibility that someone may *want* to corrupt your data. Your first line of defense against intentional corruption is to deny database access to anyone who may have a malicious intent and to restrict authorized users so that they can access only the data they need. Your second defense is to maintain data backups in a safe place. Periodically re-evaluate the security features of your installation. Being just a little paranoid doesn't hurt.

Data redundancy

Data redundancy — the same data items cropping up in multiple places — is a big problem with the hierarchical database model, but the problem can plague relational databases, too. Not only does such redundancy waste storage space and slow down processing, but it can also lead to serious data corruption. If you store the same data item in two different tables in a database, the item in one of those tables may change while the corresponding item in the other table remains the same. This situation generates a discrepancy, and you may have no way of determining which version is correct. That's a good reason to keep data redundancy to a minimum.

REMEMBER

Although a certain amount of redundancy is necessary for the primary key of one table to serve as a foreign key in another, you should try to avoid the repetition of any data items beyond that.

WARNING

After you eliminate most redundancy from a database design, you may find that performance is now unacceptable. Operators often purposefully use a little redundancy to speed up processing. In the VetLab database, for example, the ORDERS table contains only the client's name to identify the source of each order. If you prepare an order, you must join the ORDERS table with the CLIENT table to get the client's address. If this joining of tables makes the program that prints orders run too slowly, you may decide to store the client's address redundantly in the ORDERS table as well as in the CLIENT table. Then, at least, you can print the orders faster — but at the expense of slowing down and complicating any updating of the client's address.

TIP

A common practice is to initially design a database with little redundancy and with high degrees of normalization, and then, after finding that important applications run slowly, to selectively add redundancy and denormalize. The key word here is *selectively*. The redundancy that you add back in must have a specific purpose, and because you're acutely aware of both the redundancy and the hazard it represents, you take appropriate measures to ensure that the redundancy doesn't cause more problems than it solves. (For more information, jump ahead a bit to the "Normalizing the Database" section.)

Exceeding the capacity of your DBMS

A database system might work properly for years and then start experiencing intermittent errors that become progressively more serious. This may be a sign that you're approaching one of the system's capacity limits. There are, after all, limits to the number of rows that a table may have. There are also limits on columns, constraints, and various other database features. Check the current size and content of your database against the specifications listed in the documentation of your DBMS. If you're near the limit in any area, consider upgrading to a system with a higher capacity. Or you may want to archive older data that is no longer active and then delete it from your database.

Constraints

Earlier in this chapter, I talk about constraints as mechanisms for ensuring that the data you enter into a table column falls within the domain of that column. A *constraint* is an application rule that the DBMS enforces. After you define a database, you can include constraints (such as NOT NULL) in a table definition. The DBMS makes sure that you can never commit any transaction that violates a constraint.

REMEMBER

You have three kinds of constraints:

>> A **column constraint** imposes a condition on a column in a table.

>> A **table constraint** puts a specified constraint on an entire table.

>> An **assertion** is a constraint that can affect more than one table.

Column constraints

An example of a column constraint is shown in the following Data Definition Language (DDL) statement:

```
CREATE TABLE CLIENT (
    ClientName        CHAR (30)      NOT NULL,
    Address1          CHAR (30),
    Address2          CHAR (30),
    City              CHAR (25),
    State             CHAR (2),
    PostalCode        CHAR (10),
    Phone             CHAR (13),
    Fax               CHAR (13),
    ContactPerson     CHAR (30)
    ) ;
```

The statement applies the constraint NOT NULL to the ClientName column, specifying that ClientName may not assume a null value. UNIQUE is another constraint that you can apply to a column. This constraint specifies that every value in the column must be unique. The CHECK constraint is particularly useful because it can take any valid expression as an argument. Consider the following example:

```
CREATE TABLE TESTS (
    TestName          CHAR (30)      NOT NULL,
    StandardCharge    NUMERIC (6,2)
        CHECK (StandardCharge >= 0.0
          AND StandardCharge <= 200.0)
    ) ;
```

VetLab's standard charge for a test must always be greater than or equal to zero. And none of the standard tests costs more than $200. The CHECK clause refuses to accept any entries that fall outside the range 0 <= StandardCharge <= 200. Another way of stating the same constraint is as follows:

```
CHECK (StandardCharge BETWEEN 0.0 AND 200.0)
```

Table constraints

The PRIMARY KEY constraint specifies that the column to which it applies is a primary key. This constraint applies to the entire table and is equivalent to a combination of the NOT NULL and UNIQUE column constraints. You can specify this constraint in a CREATE statement, as shown in the following example:

```
CREATE TABLE CLIENT (
    ClientName      CHAR (30)    PRIMARY KEY,
    Address1        CHAR (30),
    Address2        CHAR (30),
    City            CHAR (25),
    State           CHAR (2),
    PostalCode      CHAR (10),
    Phone           CHAR (13),
    Fax             CHAR (13),
    ContactPerson   CHAR (30)
    ) ;
```

Named constraints, such as the NameFK constraint in the example in the earlier "Cascading deletions — use with care" section, can have some additional functionality. Suppose, for example, that you want to do a bulk load of several thousand prospective clients into your PROSPECT table. You have a file that contains mostly prospects in the United States, but with a few Canadian prospects sprinkled throughout the file. Normally, you want to restrict your PROSPECT table to include only U.S. prospects, but you don't want this bulk load to be interrupted every time it hits one of the Canadian records. (Canadian postal codes include letters as well as numbers, but U.S. zip codes contain only numbers.) You can choose to not enforce a constraint on PostalCode until the bulk load is complete, and then you can restore constraint enforcement later.

Initially, your PROSPECT table was created with the following CREATE TABLE statement:

```
CREATE TABLE PROSPECT (
    ClientName      CHAR (30)    PRIMARY KEY,
    Address1        CHAR (30),
    Address2        CHAR (30),
    City            CHAR (25),
    State           CHAR (2),
    PostalCode      CHAR (10),
    Phone           CHAR (13),
    Fax             CHAR (13),
    ContactPerson   CHAR (30),
    CONSTRAINT Zip CHECK (PostalCode BETWEEN 0 AND 99999)
    ) ;
```

Before the bulk load, you can turn off the enforcement of the `Zip` constraint:

```
ALTER TABLE PROSPECT
    CONSTRAINT Zip NOT ENFORCED;
```

After the bulk load is complete, you can restore enforcement of the constraint:

```
ALTER TABLE PROSPECT
    CONSTRAINT Zip ENFORCED;
```

At this point you can eliminate any rows that do not satisfy the constraint with:

```
DELETE FROM PROSPECT
    WHERE PostalCode NOT BETWEEN 0 AND 99999 ;
```

Assertions

An *assertion* specifies a restriction for more than one table. The following example uses a search condition drawn from two tables to create an assertion:

```
CREATE TABLE ORDERS (
    OrderNumber        INTEGER          NOT NULL,
    ClientName         CHAR (30),
    TestOrdered        CHAR (30),
    Salesperson        CHAR (30),
    OrderDate          DATE
    ) ;

CREATE TABLE RESULTS (
    ResultNumber       INTEGER          NOT NULL,
    OrderNumber        INTEGER,
    Result             CHAR (50),
    DateOrdered        DATE,
    PrelimFinal        CHAR (1)
    ) ;

CREATE ASSERTION
    CHECK (NOT EXISTS (SELECT * FROM ORDERS, RESULTS
        WHERE ORDERS.OrderNumber = RESULTS.OrderNumber
        AND ORDERS.OrderDate > RESULTS.DateReported)) ;
```

This assertion ensures that test results aren't reported before the test is ordered.

Normalizing the Database

Some ways of organizing data are better than others. Some are more logical. Some are simpler. Some are better at preventing inconsistencies when you start using the database. Yep, modifying a database opens another whole nest of troubles and (fortunately) their solutions, known respectively as . . .

Modification anomalies and normal forms

A host of problems — called *modification anomalies* — can plague a database if you don't structure the database correctly. To prevent these problems, you can *normalize* the database structure. Normalization generally entails splitting one database table into two simpler tables.

Modification anomalies are so named because they are generated by the addition of, change to, or deletion of data from a database table.

To illustrate how modification anomalies can occur, consider the table shown in Figure 5-2.

	SALES	
Customer_ID	Product	Price
1001	Laundry detergent	12
1007	Toothpaste	3
1010	Chlorine bleach	4
1024	Toothpaste	3

FIGURE 5-2: This SALES table leads to modification anomalies.

Suppose, for example, that your company sells household cleaning and personal-care products, and you charge all customers the same price for each product. The SALES table keeps track of everything for you. Now assume that customer 1001 moves out of the area and no longer is a customer. You don't care what he's bought in the past, because he's not going to buy anything from your company again. You want to delete his row from the table. If you do so, however, you don't just lose the fact that customer 1001 has bought laundry detergent; you also lose the fact that laundry detergent costs $12. This situation is called a *deletion anomaly*. In deleting one fact (that customer 1001 bought laundry detergent), you inadvertently delete another fact (that laundry detergent costs $12).

You can use the same table to illustrate an insertion anomaly. For example, suppose you want to add stick deodorant to your product line at a price of $2. You can't add this data to the SALES table until a customer buys stick deodorant.

The problem with the SALES table in the figure is that this table deals with more than one thing: It covers not just which products customers buy, but also what the products cost. To eliminate the anomalies, you can split the SALES table into two tables, each dealing with only one theme or idea, as shown in Figure 5-3.

CUST_PURCH		PROD_PRICE	
Customer_ID	Product	Product	Price
1001	Laundry detergent	Laundry detergent	12
1007	Toothpaste	Toothpaste	3
1010	Chlorine bleach	Chlorine bleach	4
1024	Toothpaste		

FIGURE 5-3: Splitting the SALES table into two tables.

Figure 5-3 shows the SALES table divided into two tables:

>> CUST_PURCH, which deals with the single idea of customer purchases.

>> PROD_PRICE, which deals with the single idea of product pricing.

You can now delete the row for customer 1001 from CUST_PURCH without losing the fact that laundry detergent costs $12. (The cost of laundry detergent is now stored in PROD_PRICE.) You can also add stick deodorant to PROD_PRICE even if nobody has bought the product. Purchase information is stored elsewhere, in the CUST_PURCH table.

The process of breaking up a table into multiple tables, each of which has a single theme, is called *normalization.* A normalization operation that solves one problem may not affect other problems. You may have to perform several successive normalization operations to reduce each resulting table to a single theme. Each database table should deal with one — and only one — main theme. Sometimes (as you probably guessed) determining that a table *really* deals with two or more themes can be difficult.

TECHNICAL STUFF

You can classify tables according to the types of modification anomalies to which they're subject. In a 1970 paper, E. F. Codd, the first to describe the relational model, identified three sources of modification anomalies and defined first, second, and third *normal forms* (1NF, 2NF, 3NF) as remedies to those types of anomalies. In the ensuing years, Codd and others discovered additional types of anomalies and specified new normal forms to deal with them. The Boyce–Codd normal form (BCNF), the fourth normal form (4NF), and the fifth normal form (5NF) each afforded a higher degree of protection against modification anomalies. Not until 1981, however, did a paper, written by Ronald Fagin, describe domain-key normal form or DK/NF (which gets a whole section to itself later in this chapter). Using this last normal form enables you to *guarantee* that a table is free of modification anomalies.

The normal forms are *nested* in the sense that a table that's in 2NF is automatically *also* in 1NF. Similarly, a table in 3NF is automatically in 2NF, and so on. For most practical applications, putting a database in 3NF is sufficient to ensure a high degree of integrity. To be absolutely sure of its integrity, you must put the database into DK/NF; for more about why, flip ahead to the "Domain-key normal form (DK/NF)" section.

TIP

After you normalize a database as much as possible, you may want to make selected denormalizations to improve performance. If you do, be aware of the types of anomalies that may now become possible.

First normal form

To be in first normal form (1NF), a table must have the following qualities:

>> The table is two-dimensional with rows and columns.

>> Each row contains data that pertains to some thing or portion of a thing.

>> Each column contains data for a single attribute of the thing it's describing.

>> Each cell (intersection of a row and a column) of the table must have only a single value.

>> Entries in any column must all be of the same kind. If, for example, the entry in one row of a column contains an employee name, all the other rows must contain employee names in that column, too.

>> Each column must have a unique name.

>> No two rows may be identical (that is, each row must be unique).

>> The order of the columns and the order of the rows are not significant.

A table (relation) in first normal form is immune to some kinds of modification anomalies but is still subject to others. The SALES table shown in Figure 5-2 is in first normal form, and as discussed previously, the table is subject to deletion and insertion anomalies. First normal form may prove useful in some applications but unreliable in others.

Second normal form

To appreciate second normal form, you must understand the idea of functional dependency. A *functional dependency* is a relationship between or among attributes. One attribute is functionally dependent on another if the value of the second attribute determines the value of the first attribute. If you know the value of the second attribute, you can determine the value of the first attribute.

Suppose, for example, that a table has attributes (columns) `StandardCharge`, `NumberOfTests`, and `TotalCharge` that relate through the following equation:

```
TotalCharge = StandardCharge * NumberOfTests
```

`TotalCharge` is functionally dependent on both `StandardCharge` and `NumberOf Tests`. If you know the values of `StandardCharge` and `NumberOfTests`, you can determine the value of `TotalCharge`.

Every table in first normal form must have a unique primary key. That key may consist of one or more than one column. A key consisting of more than one column is called a *composite key*. To be in second normal form (2NF), all non-key attributes (columns) must depend on the entire key. Thus, every relation that is in 1NF with a single attribute key is automatically in second normal form. If a relation has a composite key, all non-key attributes must depend on all components of the key. If you have a table where some non-key attributes don't depend on all components of the key, break the table up into two or more tables so that — in each of the new tables — all non-key attributes depend on all components of the primary key.

Sound confusing? Look at an example to clarify matters. Consider a table like the SALES table back in Figure 5-2. Instead of recording only a single purchase for each customer, you add a row every time a customer buys an item for the first time. An additional difference is that charter customers (those with `Customer_ID` values of 1001 to 1007) get a discount off the normal price. Figure 5-4 shows some of this table's rows.

SALES_TRACK		
Customer_ID	Product	Price
1001	Laundry detergent	11.00
1007	Toothpaste	2.70
1010	Chlorine bleach	4.00
1024	Toothpaste	3.00
1010	Laundry detergent	12.00
1001	Toothpaste	2.70

FIGURE 5-4:
In the SALES_
TRACK table, the
Customer_ID and
Product columns
constitute a
composite key.

In Figure 5-4, `Customer_ID` does not uniquely identify a row. In two rows, `Customer_ID` is 1001. In two other rows, `Customer_ID` is 1010. The combination of the `Customer_ID` column and the `Product` column uniquely identifies a row. These two columns together are a composite key.

If not for the fact that some customers qualify for a discount and others don't, the table wouldn't be in second normal form, because `Price` (a non-key attribute) would depend only on part of the key (`Product`). Because some customers do qualify for a discount, `Price` depends on both `CustomerID` and `Product`, and the table is in second normal form.

Third normal form

Tables in second normal form are especially vulnerable to some types of modification anomalies — namely, those that come from transitive dependencies.

REMEMBER

A *transitive dependency* occurs when one attribute depends on a second attribute, which depends on a third attribute. Deletions in a table with such a dependency chain can cause unwanted information loss. A relation in third normal form is a relation in second normal form with no transitive dependencies.

Look again at the SALES table in Figure 5-2, which you know is in first normal form. As long as you constrain entries to permit only one row for each `Customer_ID`, you have a single-attribute primary key, and the table is in second normal form. However, the table is still subject to anomalies. What if customer 1010 is unhappy with the chlorine bleach, for example, and returns the item for a refund? You want to remove the third row from the table, which records the fact that customer 1010 bought chlorine bleach. You have a problem: If you remove that row, you also lose the fact that chlorine bleach has a price of $4. This situation is an example of a transitive dependency. Price depends on Product, which, in turn, depends on the primary key Customer_ID.

Breaking the SALES table into two tables solves the transitive dependency problem. The two tables shown in Figure 5-3, CUST_PURCH and PROD_PRICE, make up a database that's in third normal form.

Domain-key normal form (DK/NF)

After a database is in third normal form, you've eliminated most, but not all, chances of modification anomalies. Normal forms beyond the third are defined to squash those few remaining bugs. Boyce–Codd normal form (BCNF), fourth normal form (4NF), and fifth normal form (5NF) are examples of such forms. Each form eliminates a possible modification anomaly but doesn't guarantee prevention of all possible modification anomalies. Domain-key normal form, however, provides such a guarantee.

REMEMBER

A relation is in *domain-key normal form (DK/NF)* if every constraint on the relation is a logical consequence of the definition of keys and domains. A *constraint* in this definition is any rule that's precise enough that you can evaluate whether it's true. A *key* is a unique identifier of a row in a table. A *domain* is the set of permitted values of an attribute.

Look again at the database in Figure 5-2, which is in 1NF, to see what you must do to put that database in DK/NF.

Table:	SALES (Customer_ID, Product, Price)
Key:	Customer_ID
Constraints:	1. Customer_ID determines Product
	2. Product determines Price
	3. Customer_ID must be an integer > 1000

To enforce Constraint 3 (that Customer_ID must be an integer greater than 1000), you can simply define the domain for Customer_ID to incorporate this constraint. That makes the constraint a logical consequence of the domain of the Customer ID column. Product depends on Customer_ID, and Customer_ID is a key, so you have no problem with Constraint 1, which is a logical consequence of the definition of the key. Constraint 2 *is* a problem. Price depends on (is a logical consequence of) Product, and Product isn't a key. The solution is to divide the SALES table into two tables. One table uses Customer_ID as a key, and the other uses Product as a key. This setup is what you have in Figure 5-3. The database in Figure 5-3, besides being in 3NF, is also in DK/NF.

REMEMBER

Design your databases so they're in DK/NF if possible. If you can do that, then enforcing key and domain restrictions causes all constraints to be met, and modification anomalies aren't possible. If a database's structure is designed in a way that prevents you from putting it into DK/NF, then you must build the constraints into the application program that uses the database. The database itself doesn't guarantee that the constraints will be met.

Abnormal form

As in life, so in databases: Sometimes being abnormal pays off. You can get carried away with normalization and go too far. You can break up a database into so many tables that the entire thing becomes unwieldy and inefficient. Performance can plummet. Often the optimal structure for your database is somewhat denormalized. In fact, practical databases (the really big ones, anyway) are almost never normalized all the way to DK/NF. You want to normalize the databases you design as much as possible, however, to eliminate the possibility of data corruption that results from modification anomalies.

After you normalize the database as far as you can, make some retrievals as a dry run. If performance isn't satisfactory, examine your design to see whether selective denormalization would improve performance without sacrificing integrity. By carefully adding redundancy in strategic locations and denormalizing *just enough*, you can arrive at a database that's both efficient and safe from anomalies.

3
Storing and Retrieving Data

» Retrieving the data you want from a table

» Displaying only selected information from one or more tables

» Updating the information in tables and views

» Adding a new row to a table

» Changing some or all the data in a table row

» Deleting a table row

Chapter **6**

Manipulating Database Data

hapters 3 and 4 reveal that creating a sound database structure is critical to maintaining data integrity. The stuff you're really interested in, however, is the data itself — not its structure. At any given time, you probably want to do one of four things with data: add it to tables, retrieve and display it, change it, or delete it from tables.

In principle, database manipulation is quite simple. Understanding how to add data to a table isn't difficult — you can add your data either one row at a time or in a batch. Changing, deleting, or retrieving one or more table rows is also easy in practice. The main challenge to database manipulation is *selecting* the rows that you want to change, delete, or retrieve. The data you want may reside in a database that contains a large volume of data you *don't* want right now. Fortunately, if you can specify what you want by using an SQL SELECT statement, the computer does all the searching for you. I guess that means manipulating a database with

SQL is a piece of cake. Adding, changing, deleting, and retrieving are all easy! (Hmmm. Perhaps "easy" might be a slight exaggeration.) At least you get to start off easy with simple data retrieval.

Retrieving Data

The data-manipulation task that users perform most frequently is retrieving selected information from a database. You may want to retrieve the contents of one row out of thousands in a table. You may want to retrieve all rows that satisfy a condition or a combination of conditions. You may even want to retrieve all rows in the table. One SQL statement, the SELECT statement, performs all these tasks for you.

The simplest use of the SELECT statement is to retrieve all the data in all the rows of a specified table. To do so, use the following syntax:

```
SELECT * FROM CUSTOMER ;
```

REMEMBER

The asterisk (*) is a wildcard character that means *everything*. In this context, the asterisk is a shorthand substitute for a listing of all the column names of the CUSTOMER table. After this statement is executed, all the data in all the rows and columns of the CUSTOMER table appear onscreen.

SELECT statements can be much more complicated than the statement in this example. In fact, some SELECT statements can be so complicated that they're virtually indecipherable. This potential complexity is a result of the fact that you can tack multiple modifying clauses onto the basic statement. Chapter 10 covers modifying clauses in detail; in this chapter, I briefly discuss the WHERE clause, which is the most commonly used method of restricting the rows that a SELECT statement returns.

A SELECT statement with a WHERE clause has the following general form:

```
SELECT column_list FROM table_name
    WHERE condition ;
```

The column list specifies which columns you want to display. The statement displays only the columns that you list. The FROM clause specifies from which table you want to display columns. The WHERE clause excludes rows that don't satisfy a specified condition. The condition may be simple (for example, WHERE CUSTOMER_ STATE = 'NH'), or it may be compound (for example, WHERE CUSTOMER_STATE='NH' AND STATUS='Active').

The following example shows a compound condition inside a SELECT statement:

```
SELECT FirstName, LastName, Phone FROM CUSTOMER
    WHERE State = 'NH'
    AND Status = 'Active' ;
```

This statement returns the names and phone numbers of all active customers living in New Hampshire. The AND keyword means that for a row to qualify for retrieval, that row must meet both conditions: State = 'NH' and Status = 'Active'.

Creating Views

The structure of a database that's designed according to sound principles — including appropriate normalization (see Chapter 5) — maximizes the integrity of the data. This structure, however, is often not the best way to look at the data. Several applications may use the same data, but each application may have a different emphasis. One of the most powerful features of SQL is its capability to display views of the data that are structured differently from how the database tables store the data. The tables you use as sources for columns and rows in a view are the *base tables*. Chapter 3 discusses views as part of the Data Definition Language (DDL); this section looks at views in the context of retrieving and manipulating data.

A SELECT statement always returns a result in the form of a virtual table. A *view* is a special kind of virtual table. You can distinguish a view from other virtual tables because the database's metadata holds the definition of a view. This distinction gives a view a degree of persistence that other virtual tables don't possess.

TIP

You can manipulate a view just as you can manipulate a real table. The difference is that a view's data doesn't have an independent existence. The view derives its data from the table or tables from which you draw the view's columns. Each application can have its own unique views of the same data.

Consider the VetLab database that I describe in Chapter 5. That database contains five tables: CLIENT, TESTS, EMPLOYEE, ORDERS, and RESULTS. Suppose the national marketing manager wants to see from which states the company's orders are coming. Some of this information lies in the CLIENT table; some lies in the ORDERS table. Suppose the quality-control officer wants to compare the order date of a test to the date on which the final test result came in. This comparison requires some data from the ORDERS table and some from the RESULTS table. To satisfy needs such as these, you can create views that give you exactly the data you want in each case.

From tables

For the marketing manager, you can create the view shown in Figure 6-1.

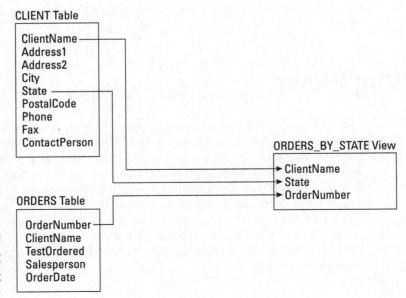

FIGURE 6-1: The ORDERS_BY_STATE view for the marketing manager.

The following statement creates the marketing manager's view:

```
CREATE VIEW ORDERS_BY_STATE
    (ClientName, State, OrderNumber)
  AS SELECT CLIENT.ClientName, State, OrderNumber
  FROM CLIENT, ORDERS
  WHERE CLIENT.ClientName = ORDERS.ClientName ;
```

The new view has three columns: ClientName, State, and OrderNumber. ClientName appears in both the CLIENT and ORDERS tables and serves as the link between the two tables. The new view draws State information from the CLIENT table and takes the OrderNumber from the ORDERS table. In the preceding example, you declare the names of the columns explicitly in the new view.

Note that I prefixed ClientName with the table that contains it, but I didn't do that for State and OrderNumber. That is because State appears only in the CLIENT table and OrderNumber appears only in the ORDERS table, so there is no ambiguity. However, ClientName appears in both CLIENT and ORDERS, so the additional identifier is needed.

REMEMBER

You don't need this declaration if the names are the same as the names of the corresponding columns in the source tables. The example in the following section shows a similar CREATE VIEW statement, except that the view column names are implied rather than explicitly stated.

With a selection condition

The quality-control officer requires a different view from the one that the marketing manager uses, as shown by the example in Figure 6-2.

Here's the code that creates the view in Figure 6-2:

```
CREATE VIEW REPORTING_LAG
  AS SELECT ORDERS.OrderNumber, OrderDate, DateReported
  FROM ORDERS, RESULTS
  WHERE ORDERS.OrderNumber = RESULTS.OrderNumber
  AND RESULTS.PreliminaryFinal = 'F' ;
```

This view contains order-date information from the ORDERS table and final-report-date information from the RESULTS table. Only rows that have an 'F' in the PreliminaryFinal column of the RESULTS table appear in the REPORTING LAG view. Note also that the column list in the ORDERS_BY_STATE view is optional. The REPORTING_LAG view works fine without such a list.

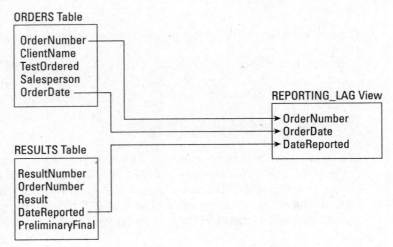

ORDERS Table

OrderNumber
ClientName
TestOrdered
Salesperson
OrderDate

REPORTING_LAG View

OrderNumber
OrderDate
DateReported

RESULTS Table

ResultNumber
OrderNumber
Result
DateReported
PreliminaryFinal

FIGURE 6-2:
The REPORTING_
LAG view for the
quality-control
officer.

With a modified attribute

The SELECT clauses in the examples in the two preceding sections contain only column names. You can include expressions in the SELECT clause as well. Suppose VetLab's owner is having a birthday and wants to give all his customers a 10-percent discount to celebrate. He can create a view based on the ORDERS table *and* the TESTS table. He may construct this table as shown in the following code example:

```
CREATE VIEW BIRTHDAY
    (ClientName, Test, OrderDate, BirthdayCharge)
    AS SELECT ClientName, TestOrdered, OrderDate,
        StandardCharge * .9
    FROM ORDERS, TESTS
    WHERE TestOrdered = TestName ;
```

Notice that the second column in the BIRTHDAY view — Test — corresponds to the TestOrdered column in the ORDERS table, which also corresponds to the TestName column in the TESTS table. Figure 6-3 shows how to create this view.

You can build a view based on multiple tables, as shown in the preceding examples, or you can build a view based on a single table. If you don't need some of the columns or rows in a table, create a view to remove these elements from sight and then deal with the view rather than the original table. This approach ensures that users see only the parts of the table that are relevant to the task at hand.

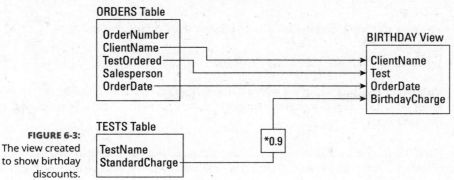

ORDERS Table

OrderNumber
ClientName
TestOrdered
Salesperson
OrderDate

BIRTHDAY View

ClientName
Test
OrderDate
BirthdayCharge

TESTS Table

TestName
StandardCharge

*0.9

FIGURE 6-3:
The view created
to show birthday
discounts.

TIP

Another reason for creating a view is to provide security for its underlying tables. You may want to make some columns in your tables available for inspection while hiding others. You can create a view that includes only those columns that you want to make available and then grant broad access to that view while restricting access to the tables from which you draw the view. (Chapter 14 explores database security and describes how to grant and revoke data-access privileges.)

Updating Views

After you create a table, that table is automatically capable of accommodating insertions, updates, and deletions. Views don't necessarily exhibit the same capability. If you update a view, you're actually updating its underlying table. Here are a few potential problems you may encounter when you update views:

>> **Some views may draw components from two or more tables.** If you update such a view, the underlying tables may not be updated properly.

>> **A view may include an expression in a SELECT list.** Because expressions don't map directly to rows in tables, your DBMS won't know how to update an expression.

Suppose you create a view by using the following statement:

```
CREATE VIEW COMP (EmpName, Pay)
    AS SELECT EmpName, Salary+Comm AS Pay
    FROM EMPLOYEE ;
```

You may think you can update Pay by using the following statement:

```
UPDATE COMP SET Pay = Pay + 100 ;
```

Unfortunately, this approach doesn't make any sense. That's because the underlying table has no Pay column. You can't update something that doesn't exist in the base table.

REMEMBER

Keep the following rule in mind whenever you consider updating views: You can't update a column in a view unless it corresponds to a column in an underlying base table.

Adding New Data

Every database table starts out empty. After you create a table, either by using SQL's DDL or a RAD tool, that table is nothing but a structured shell containing no data. To make the table useful, you must put some data into it. You may or may not have that data already stored in digital form. Your data may appear in one of the following forms:

>> **Not yet compiled in any digital format:** If your data is not already in digital form, someone will probably have to enter the data manually, one record at a time. You can also enter data by using optical scanners and voice-recognition systems, but the use of such devices for data entry is still not commonplace.

>> **Compiled in some sort of digital format:** If your data is already in digital form — but perhaps not in the format of the database tables you use — you have to translate the data into the appropriate format and then insert the data into the database.

>> **Compiled in the correct digital format:** If your data is already in digital form and in the correct format, you're ready to transfer it to a new database.

The following sections address adding data to a table when it exists in each of these three forms. Depending on the current form of the data, you may be able to transfer it to your database in one operation, or you may need to enter the data one record at a time. Each data record you enter corresponds to a single row in a database table.

Adding data one row at a time

Most DBMSs support form-based data entry. This feature enables you to create a screen form that has a field for every column in a database table. Field labels on the form enable you to determine easily what data goes into each field. The data-entry operator enters all the data for a single row into the form. After the DBMS accepts the new row, the system clears the form to accept another row. In this way, you can easily add data to a table one row at a time.

Form-based data entry is easy and less susceptible to data-entry errors than using a list of *comma-delimited values.* The main problem with form-based data entry is that it is nonstandard; each DBMS has its own method of creating forms. This diversity, however, is not a problem for the data-entry operator. You can make the form look generally the same from one DBMS to another. (The data-entry operator may not suffer too much, but the application developer must return to the bottom of the learning curve every time he or she changes development tools.) Another possible problem with form-based data entry is that some implementations may not permit a full range of validity checks on the data that you enter.

The best way to maintain a high level of data integrity in a database is to keep bad data out of the database. You can prevent the entry of some bad data by applying constraints to the fields on a data-entry form. This approach enables you to make sure that the database accepts only data values of the correct type and within a predefined range. Such constraints can't prevent all possible errors, but they can catch some of them.

TIP

If the form-design tool in your DBMS doesn't let you apply all the validity checks that you need to ensure data integrity, you may want to build your own screen, accept data entries into variables, and check the entries by using application program code. After you're sure that all the values entered for a table row are valid, you can then add that row by using the SQL INSERT command.

If you enter the data for a single row into a database table, the INSERT command uses the following syntax:

```
INSERT INTO table_1 [(column_1, column_2, ..., column_n)]
    VALUES (value_1, value_2, ..., value_n) ;
```

As indicated by the square brackets ([ ]), the listing of column names is optional. The default column list order is the order of the columns in the table. If you put the VALUES in the same order as the columns in the table, these elements go into the correct columns — whether you specify those columns explicitly or not. If you want to specify the VALUES in some order other than the order of the columns in the table, you must list the column names in the same order as the list of values in the VALUES clause.

To enter a record into the CUSTOMER table, for example, use the following syntax:

```
INSERT INTO CUSTOMER (CustomerID, FirstName, LastName,
    Street, City, State, Zipcode, Phone)
    VALUES (:vcustid, 'David', 'Taylor', '235 Loco Ave.',
    'El Pollo', 'CA', '92683', '(617) 555-1963') ;
```

The first VALUE in the third line, vcustid, is a variable that you increment with your program code after you enter each new row of the table. This approach guarantees that you have no duplication of the CustomerID (which is the primary key for this table and must be unique). The rest of the values are data items rather than variables that *contain* data items. Of course, you can hold the data for these columns in variables, too, if you want. The INSERT statement works equally well whether you use variables or an explicit copy of the data itself to form the arguments of the VALUES keyword.

Adding data only to selected columns

Sometimes you want to note the existence of an object even if you don't have all the facts on it yet. If you have a database table for such objects, you can insert a row for the new object without filling in the data in all the columns. If you want the table in first normal form, you must insert enough data to distinguish the new row from all the other rows in the table. (For the intricacies of the normal forms, including first, see Chapter 5.) Inserting the new row's primary key is sufficient for this purpose. In addition to the primary key, insert any other data that you have about the object. Columns in which you enter no data contain nulls.

The following example shows such a partial row entry:

```
INSERT INTO CUSTOMER (CustomerID, FirstName, LastName)
    VALUES (:vcustid, 'Tyson', 'Taylor') ;
```

You insert only the customer's unique identification number and name into the database table. The other columns in this row contain null values.

Adding a block of rows to a table

Loading a database table one row at a time by using INSERT statements can be tedious, particularly if that's all you do. Even entering the data into a carefully human-engineered ergonomic screen form gets tiring after a while. Clearly, if you have a reliable way to enter the data automatically, you'll find occasions in which automatic entry is better than having a person sit at a keyboard and type.

Automatic data entry is feasible, for example, if the data exists in electronic form because somebody has already entered the data manually. If so, there's no reason to repeat history. Transferring data from one data file to another is a task that a computer can perform with minimal human involvement. If you know the characteristics of the source data and the desired form of the destination table, a computer can (in principle) perform the data transfer automatically.

Copying from a foreign data file

Suppose you're building a database for a new application. Some data that you need already exists in a computer file. The file may be a flat file or a table in a database created by a DBMS different from the one you use. The data may be in ASCII or EBCDIC code or in some arcane proprietary format. What do you do?

The first things you do are hope and pray that the data you want is in a widely used format. If the data is in a popular format, you have a good chance of finding a format-conversion utility that can translate the data into one or more *other* popular formats. Your development environment can probably import at least one of these formats; if you're *really* lucky, your development environment can handle the current data format directly. On personal computers, the Access, SQL Server, and MySQL formats are the most widely used. If the data you want is in one of these formats, conversion should be easy. If the format of the data is less common, you may have to put it through a two-step conversion.

TIP

If the data is in an old, proprietary, or defunct format, as a last resort, you can turn to a professional data-translation service. These businesses specialize in translating computer data from one format to another. They deal with hundreds of formats — most of which nobody has ever heard of. Give one of these services a tape or disk containing the data in its original format, and you get back the same data translated into whatever format you specify.

Transferring all rows between tables

A less severe problem than dealing with foreign data is taking data that already exists in one table in your database and combining that data with compatible data in another table. This process works great if the structure of the second table is identical to the structure of the first table — that is, every column in the first table has a corresponding column in the second table, and the data types of the corresponding columns match. In that case, you can combine the contents of the two tables by using the UNION relational operator. The result is a *virtual table* (that is, one that has no independent existence) that contains data from both source tables. I discuss the relational operators, including UNION, in Chapter 11.

Transferring selected columns and rows between tables

Generally, the structure of the data in the source table isn't identical to the structure of the table into which you want to insert the data. Perhaps only some of the columns match, and these are the columns that you want to transfer. By combining SELECT statements with a UNION, you can specify which columns from the source tables to include in the virtual result table. By including WHERE clauses in the SELECT statements, you can restrict the rows that you place into the result table to those that satisfy specific conditions. (I cover WHERE clauses extensively in Chapter 10.)

Suppose that you have two tables, PROSPECT and CUSTOMER, and you want to list everyone living in the state of Maine who appears in either table. You can create a virtual result table that contains the desired information; just use the following command:

```
SELECT FirstName, LastName
    FROM PROSPECT
    WHERE State = 'ME'
UNION
SELECT FirstName, LastName
    FROM CUSTOMER
    WHERE State = 'ME' ;
```

Here's a closer look:

>> The SELECT statements specify that the columns included in the result table are FirstName and LastName.

>> The WHERE clauses restrict the rows included to those with the value 'ME' in the State column.

>> The State column isn't included in the results table but is present in both the PROSPECT and CUSTOMER tables.

>> The UNION operator combines the results of the SELECT statement on PROSPECT with the results of the SELECT on CUSTOMER, deletes any duplicate rows, and then displays the result.

TIP

Another way to copy data from one table in a database to another is to nest a SELECT statement within an INSERT statement. This method (known as a *subselect* and detailed in Chapter 12) doesn't create a virtual table; instead, it duplicates the selected data. You can take all the rows from the CUSTOMER table, for example, and insert those rows into the PROSPECT table. Of course, this works only if the structures of the CUSTOMER and PROSPECT tables are identical. If you want to place only those customers who live in Maine into the PROSPECT table, a simple SELECT with one condition in the WHERE clause does the trick, as shown in the following example:

```
INSERT INTO PROSPECT
    SELECT * FROM CUSTOMER
    WHERE State = 'ME' ;
```

Even though this operation creates redundant data (you're now storing customer data in both the PROSPECT table and the CUSTOMER table), you may want to do it anyway to improve the performance of retrievals. Beware of the redundancy, however! To maintain data consistency, make sure that you don't insert, update, or delete rows in one table without inserting, updating, or deleting the corresponding rows in the other table. Another potential problem is the possibility that the INSERT statement might generate duplicate primary keys. If even one preexisting prospect has a primary key of ProspectID that matches the corresponding primary key (CustomerID) of a customer you're trying to insert into the PROSPECT table, the insert operation will fail. If both tables have autoincrementing primary keys, you don't want them to start with the same number. Make sure the two blocks of numbers are far apart from each other.

Updating Existing Data

You can count on one thing in this world — change. If you don't like the current state of affairs, just wait a while. Before long, things will be different. Because the world is constantly changing, the databases used to model aspects of the world also need to change. A customer may change her address. The quantity of a product in stock may change (because, you hope, someone buys an item now and then). A basketball player's season performance statistics change each time he plays in another game. If your database contains such items, you need to update it periodically.

SQL provides the UPDATE statement for changing data in a table. By using a single UPDATE statement, you can change one, some, or all rows in a table. The UPDATE statement uses the following syntax:

```
UPDATE table_name
    SET column_1 = expression_1, column_2 = expression_2,
    ..., column_n = expression_n
    [WHERE predicates] ;
```

TIP

The WHERE clause is optional. This clause specifies the rows that you're updating. If you don't use a WHERE clause, all the rows in the table are updated. The SET clause specifies the new values for the columns that you're changing.

Consider the CUSTOMER table shown as Table 6-1.

TABLE 6-1

CUSTOMER Table

Name	City	Area Code	Telephone
Abe Abelson	Springfield	(714)	555-1111
Bill Bailey	Decatur	(714)	555-2222
Chuck Wood	Philo	(714)	555-3333
Don Stetson	Philo	(714)	555-4444
Dolph Stetson	Philo	(714)	555-5555

Customer lists change occasionally — as people move, change their phone numbers, and so on. Suppose that Abe Abelson moves from Springfield to Kankakee. You can update his record in the table by using the following UPDATE statement:

```
UPDATE CUSTOMER
    SET City = 'Kankakee', Telephone = '666-6666'
    WHERE Name = 'Abe Abelson' ;
```

This statement causes the changes shown in Table 6-2.

TABLE 6-2

CUSTOMER Table after UPDATE to One Row

Name	City	Area Code	Telephone
Abe Abelson	Kankakee	(714)	666-6666
Bill Bailey	Decatur	(714)	555-2222
Chuck Wood	Philo	(714)	555-3333
Don Stetson	Philo	(714)	555-4444
Dolph Stetson	Philo	(714)	555-5555

You can use a similar statement to update multiple rows. Assume that Philo is experiencing explosive population growth and now requires its own area code.

You can change all rows for customers who live in Philo by using a single UPDATE statement, as follows:

```
UPDATE CUSTOMER
   SET AreaCode = '(619)'
   WHERE City = 'Philo' ;
```

The table now looks like the one shown in Table 6-3.

TABLE 6-3

CUSTOMER Table after UPDATE to Several Rows

Name	City	Area Code	Telephone
Abe Abelson	Kankakee	(714)	666-6666
Bill Bailey	Decatur	(714)	555-2222
Chuck Wood	Philo	(619)	555-3333
Don Stetson	Philo	(619)	555-4444
Dolph Stetson	Philo	(619)	555-5555

Updating all the rows of a table is even easier than updating only some of the rows. You don't need to use a WHERE clause to restrict the statement. Imagine that the city of Rantoul has acquired major political clout and has now annexed not only Kankakee, Decatur, and Philo, but also all the cities and towns in the database. You can update all the rows by using a single statement, as follows:

```
UPDATE CUSTOMER
   SET City = 'Rantoul' ;
```

Table 6-4 shows the result.

TABLE 6-4

CUSTOMER Table after UPDATE to All Rows

Name	City	Area Code	Telephone
Abe Abelson	Rantoul	(714)	666-6666
Bill Bailey	Rantoul	(714)	555-2222
Chuck Wood	Rantoul	(619)	555-3333
Don Stetson	Rantoul	(619)	555-4444
Dolph Stetson	Rantoul	(619)	555-5555

When you use the WHERE clause with the UPDATE statement to restrict which rows are updated, the contents of the WHERE clause can be a *subselect* — a SELECT statement, the result of which is used as input by another SELECT statement.

For example, suppose that you're a wholesaler and your database includes a VENDOR table containing the names of all the manufacturers from whom you buy products. You also have a PRODUCT table containing the names of all the products that you sell and the prices that you charge for them. The VENDOR table has columns VendorID, VendorName, Street, City, State, and Zip. The PRODUCT table has ProductID, ProductName, VendorID, and SalePrice.

Your vendor, Cumulonimbus Corporation, decides to raise the prices of all its products by 10 percent. To maintain your profit margin, you must raise your prices on the products that you obtain from Cumulonimbus by 10 percent. You can do so by using the following UPDATE statement:

```
UPDATE PRODUCT
    SET SalePrice = (SalePrice * 1.1)
    WHERE VendorID IN
        (SELECT VendorID FROM VENDOR
        WHERE VendorName = 'Cumulonimbus Corporation') ;
```

The subselect finds the VendorID that corresponds to Cumulonimbus. You can then use the VendorID field in the PRODUCT table to find the rows that you want to update. The prices on all Cumulonimbus products increase by 10 percent; the prices on all other products stay the same. (I discuss subselects more extensively in Chapter 12.)

Transferring Data

In addition to using the INSERT and UPDATE statements, you can add data to a table or view by using the MERGE statement. You can MERGE data from a source table or view into a destination table or view. The MERGE can either insert new rows into the destination table or update existing rows. MERGE is a convenient way to take data that already exists somewhere in a database and copy it to a new location.

For example, consider the VetLab database that I describe in Chapter 5. Suppose some people in the EMPLOYEE table are salespeople who have taken orders, whereas others are non-sales employees or salespeople who have not yet taken an order. The year just concluded has been profitable, and you want to share some of that success with the employees. You decide to give a bonus of $100 to everyone who has taken at least one order and a bonus of $50 to everyone else. First, you create a BONUS table and insert into it a record for each employee who appears at least once in the ORDERS table, assigning each record a default bonus value of $100.

Next, you want to use the MERGE statement to insert new records for those employees who have not taken orders, giving them $50 bonuses. Here's some code that builds and fills the BONUS table:

```
CREATE TABLE BONUS (
    EmployeeName CHARACTER (30)       PRIMARY KEY,
    Bonus         NUMERIC             DEFAULT 100 ) ;

INSERT INTO BONUS (EmployeeName)
    (SELECT EmployeeName FROM EMPLOYEE, ORDERS
    WHERE EMPLOYEE.EmployeeName = ORDERS.Salesperson
    GROUP BY EMPLOYEE.EmployeeName) ;
```

You can now query the BONUS table to see what it holds:

```
SELECT * FROM BONUS ;

EmployeeName            Bonus
------------            ------------
Brynna Jones            100
Chris Bancroft          100
Greg Bosser             100
Kyle Weeks              100
```

Now, by executing a MERGE statement, you can give $50 bonuses to the rest of the employees:

```
MERGE INTO BONUS
    USING EMPLOYEE
    ON (BONUS.EmployeeName = EMPLOYEE.EmployeeName)
    WHEN NOT MATCHED THEN INSERT
        (BONUS.EmployeeName, BONUS.bonus)
        VALUES (EMPLOYEE.EmployeeName, 50) ;
```

Records for people in the EMPLOYEE table that don't match records for people already in the BONUS table are now inserted into the BONUS table. Now a query of the BONUS table gives the following result:

```
SELECT * FROM BONUS ;

EmployeeName            Bonus
---------------         ----------

Brynna Jones               100
Chris Bancroft             100
Greg Bosser                100
Kyle Weeks                 100
Neth Doze                   50
Matt Bak                    50
Sam Saylor                  50
Nic Foster                  50
```

The first four records, which were created with the INSERT statement, are in alphabetical order by employee name. The rest of the records, added by the MERGE statement, appear in whatever order they were listed in the EMPLOYEE table.

The MERGE statement is a relatively new addition to SQL and may not yet be supported by some DBMS products. Even newer is an additional capability of MERGE added in SQL:2011, paradoxically enabling you to delete records with a MERGE statement.

Suppose, after doing the INSERT, you decide that you do not want to give bonuses to people who have taken at least one order after all, but you do want to give a $50 bonus to everybody else. You can remove the sales bonuses and add the non-sales bonuses with the following MERGE statement:

```
MERGE INTO BONUS
    USING EMPLOYEE
    ON (BONUS.EmployeeName = EMPLOYEE.EmployeeName)
    WHEN MATCHED THEN DELETE
    WHEN NOT MATCHED THEN INSERT
        (BONUS.EmployeeName, BONUS.bonus)
        VALUES (EMPLOYEE.EmployeeName, 50);
```

The result is

```
SELECT * FROM BONUS;

EmployeeName            Bonus
---------------      -----------
Neth Doze                 50
Matt Bak                  50
Sam Saylor                50
Nic Foster                50
```

Deleting Obsolete Data

As time passes, data can get old and lose its usefulness. You may want to remove this outdated data from its table. Unneeded data in a table slows performance, consumes memory, and can confuse users. You may want to transfer older data to an archive table and then take the archive offline. That way, in the unlikely event that you ever need to look at that data again, you can recover it. In the meantime, it doesn't slow down your everyday processing. Whether or not you decide that obsolete data is worth archiving, you eventually come to the point where you want to delete that data. SQL provides for the removal of rows from database tables by use of the DELETE statement.

You can delete all the rows in a table by using an unqualified DELETE statement, or you can restrict the deletion to only selected rows by adding a WHERE clause. The syntax is similar to the syntax of a SELECT statement, except that you don't need to specify columns. After all, if you want to delete a table row, you probably want to remove all the data in that row's columns.

For example, suppose that your customer, David Taylor, just moved to Switzerland and isn't going to buy anything from you anymore. You can remove him from your CUSTOMER table by using the following statement:

```
DELETE FROM CUSTOMER
    WHERE FirstName = 'David' AND LastName = 'Taylor';
```

If you have only one customer named David Taylor, this statement makes the intended deletion. If you have two or more customers who share the name David Taylor (which, after all, is a fairly common name in English-speaking countries), you can add more conditions to the WHERE clause (such as STREET or PHONE or CUSTOMER_ID) to make sure that you delete only the customer you want to remove. If you don't add a WHERE clause, all customers named David Taylor will be deleted.

Chapter **7**

Handling Temporal Data

B efore SQL:2011, ISO/IEC standard SQL had no mechanism for dealing with data that was valid at one point in time but not valid at another. Any application that requires that an audit trail be kept needs that capability. This means that the burden of keeping track of what was true at a given time falls on the application programmer rather than the database. This sounds like a recipe for complicated, over-budget, late, and bug-infested applications.

Syntax was added to SQL:2011 that enables handling of temporal data without messing up the way code for non-temporal data is handled. This is a big advantage for anyone who wants to add temporal capability to an existing SQL database. Even though SQL:2011 standardized how to handle temporal data, it did not specify how temporal data templates should be formatted or parsed. That deficiency was finally remedied with SQL:2016.

What do I mean by the term *temporal data*? The ISO/IEC SQL:2011 standard does not use that term at all, but it is commonly used in the database community. In SQL:2011, temporal data is any data with one or more associated time periods during which that data is deemed to be effective or valid along some time dimension. In plain English, that means that with temporal data capability, you can determine when a predicate is true.

In this chapter, I introduce the concept of a period of time, defining it in a very specific way. We will look at various kinds of time and the effect that temporal data has on the definition of primary keys and referential integrity constraints. I then discuss the way that very complex data can be stored and operated on in bitemporal tables. Finally, I give the standard template placeholder arguments for date and time data.

Understanding Times and Periods

Although versions of the SQL standard prior to SQL:2011 provided for DATE, TIME, TIMESTAMP, and INTERVAL data types, they did not address the idea of a *time period* with a definite start time and a definite end time. One way of addressing this need is to define a new PERIOD data type. SQL:2011 however, did not do this. To introduce a new data type into SQL at this late stage in its development would wreak havoc with the ecosystem that has built up around SQL. Major surgery to virtually all existing database products would be required to add a new data type.

Instead of adding a PERIOD data type, SQL:2011 solved the problem by adding *period definitions* as metadata to tables. A period definition is a named table component, identifying a pair of columns that capture the period start and the period end time. The CREATE TABLE and ALTER TABLE statements used to create and modify tables were updated with new syntax to create or destroy the periods created by the period definitions.

A PERIOD is determined by two columns: a start column and an end column. These columns are conventional, just like the columns of the existing date data types, each with its own unique name. As mentioned previously, a period definition is a named table component. It occupies the same name space as column names, so it must not duplicate any existing column name.

SQL follows a closed-open model for periods, meaning that a period includes the start time but not the end time. For any table row, a period end time must be greater than its start time. This is a constraint that is enforced by the DBMS.

REMEMBER

There are two dimensions of time that are important when dealing with temporal data:

>> **Valid time** is the time period during which a row in a table correctly reflects reality.

>> **Transaction time** is the time period during which a row is committed to or recorded in a database.

The valid time and the transaction time for a row in a table need not be the same. For example, in a business database that records the period during which a contract is in effect, the information about the contract may be (and probably is) inserted before the contract start time.

As specified in SQL:2011, separate tables may be created and maintained to accommodate the two different kinds of time, or a single, bitemporal table (discussed later in this chapter) may serve the purpose. Transaction time information is kept in system-versioned tables, which contain the system-time period, denoted by the keyword SYSTEM_TIME. Valid time information, on the other hand, is maintained in tables that contain an application-time period. You can give an application-time period any name you want, provided the name is not already used for something else. You're allowed to define at most one system-time period and one application-time period.

Although temporal data support in SQL was introduced for the first time in SQL:2011, people have had to deal with temporal data long before the temporal constructs of SQL:2011 were included in any database products. This was typically done by defining two table columns, one for the start datetime and the other for the end datetime. The fact that SQL:2011 does not define a new PERIOD data type, but rather uses period definitions as metadata, means that existing tables with such start and end columns can easily be upgraded to incorporate the new capability. The logic for providing period information can be removed from existing application programs, simplifying them, speeding them up, and making them more reliable.

Working with Application-Time Period Tables

Consider an example using application-period time tables. Suppose a business wants to keep track of what department its employees belong to at any time throughout their period of employment. The business can do this by creating application-time period tables for employees and departments, like this:

```
CREATE TABLE employee_atpt(
    EmpID        INTEGER,
    EmpStart     DATE,
    EmpEnd       DATE,
    EmpDept      VARCHAR(30),
    PERIOD FOR EmpPeriod (EmpStart, EmpEnd)
    );
```

The starting datetime (`EmpStart` in the example) is included in the period, but the ending datetime (`EmpEnd` in the example) is not. This is what closed-open semantics means.

TECHNICAL STUFF

I haven't specified a primary key yet, because that is a little more involved when you're dealing with temporal data. I deal with that later in this chapter.

For now, put some data into this table and see what it looks like:

```
INSERT INTO employee_atpt
VALUES (12345, DATE '2018-01-01', DATE '9999-12-31', 'Sales');
```

The resulting table has one row, as shown in Table 7-1.

TABLE 7-1

The Application-Period Time Table Contains One Row

EmpID	EmpStart	EmpEnd	EmpDept
12345	2018-01-01	9999-12-31	Sales

The end date of 9999-12-31 indicates that this employee's tenure with the company has not ended yet. For simplicity, I have left off the hours, minutes, seconds, and fractional seconds in this and subsequent examples.

Now suppose that on March 15, 2018, employee 12345 is temporarily assigned to the Engineering department until July 15, 2018, returning to the Sales department thereafter. You can accomplish this with the following UPDATE statement:

```
UPDATE employee_atpt
    FOR PORTION OF EmpPeriod
        FROM DATE '2018-03-15'
        TO DATE '2018-07-15'
    SET EmpDept = 'Engineering'
    WHERE EmpID = 12345;
```

After the update, the table now has three rows, as shown in Table 7-2.

Assuming employee 12345 is still employed in the Sales department, the table accurately records her department membership from New Year's Day of 2018 up to the present time.

TABLE 7-2

Application-Time Period Table after an Update

EmpID	EmpStart	EmpEnd	EmpDept
12345	2018-01-01	2018-03-15	Sales
12345	2018-03-15	2018-07-15	Engineering
12345	2018-07-15	9999-12-31	Sales

If you can insert new data into a table and update existing data in the table, you'd better be able to delete data from the table, too. However, deleting data from an application-time period table can be a little more complicated than merely deleting rows from an ordinary, non-temporal table. As an example, suppose that employee 12345, instead of being transferred to the Engineering department on March 15 of 2018, leaves the company on that date and is rehired on July 15 of the same year. Initially, the application-time period table will have one row, as shown in Table 7-3.

TABLE 7-3

Application-Time Period Table before Update or Deletion

EmpID	EmpStart	EmpEnd	EmpDept
12345	2018-01-01	9999-12-31	Sales

A `DELETE` statement will update the table to show the period during which employee 12345 was gone:

```
DELETE employee_atpt
    FOR PORTION OF EmpPeriod
        FROM DATE '2018-03-15'
        TO DATE '2018-07-15'
    WHERE EmpID = 12345;
```

The resulting table will be like Table 7-4.

TABLE 7-4

Application-Time Period Table after Deletion

EmpID	EmpStart	EmpEnd	EmpDept
12345	2018-01-01	2018-03-15	Sales
12345	2018-07-15	9999-12-31	Sales

The table now reflects the time periods during which employee 12345 was employed by the company and shows the gap during which she was not employed by the company.

You may have noticed something puzzling about the tables shown in this section. In an ordinary, non-temporal table listing an organization's employees, the employee ID number is sufficient to serve as the table's primary key because it uniquely identifies each employee. However, an application-time period table of employees may contain multiple rows for a single employee. The employee ID number, by itself, is no longer usable as the table's primary key. The temporal data must be added to the mix.

Designating primary keys in application-time period tables

In Tables 7-2 and 7-4, it is clear that the employee ID (EmpID) does not guarantee uniqueness. There are multiple rows with the same EmpID. To guarantee that there is no duplication of rows, the start date (EmpStart) and end date (EmpEnd) must be included in the primary key. However, just including them is not sufficient. Consider Table 7-5, showing the case where employee 12345 was merely transferred to Engineering for a few months, and then returned to her home department.

TABLE 7-5

A Situation You May Not Want to Occur

EmpID	EmpStart	EmpEnd	EmpDept
12345	2018-01-01	9999-12-31	Sales
12345	2018-03-15	2018-07-15	Engineering

The two rows of the table are guaranteed to be unique by inclusion of EmpStart and EmpEnd in the primary key, but notice that the two time periods overlap. It looks like employee 12345 is a member of both the Sales department and the Engineering department from March 15, 2018 until July 15, 2018. In some organizations, this may be possible, but it adds complication and could lead to data corruption. Enforcing a constraint that says that an employee can be a member of only one department at a time is perhaps what most organizations would want to do. You can add such a constraint to a table with an ALTER TABLE statement such as the following:

```
ALTER TABLE employee_atpt
ADD PRIMARY KEY (EmpID, EmpPeriod WITHOUT OVERLAPS);
```

There's a better way to do things than creating a table first and adding its primary key constraint later — instead, you can include the primary key constraint in the original CREATE statement. It might look like the following:

```
CREATE TABLE employee_atpt (
    EmpID              INTEGER              NOT NULL,
    EmpStart           DATE                 NOT NULL,
    EmpEnd             DATE                 NOT NULL,
    EmpDept            VARCHAR(30),
      PERIOD FOR EmpPeriod (EmpStart, EmpEnd)
      PRIMARY KEY (EmpID, EmpPeriod WITHOUT OVERLAPS)
);
```

Now overlapping rows are prohibited. While I was at it, I added NOT NULL constraints to all the elements of the primary key. A null value in any of those fields would be a source of errors in the future. Normally, the DBMS will take care of this, but why take chances?

Applying referential integrity constraints to application-time period tables

Any database that is meant to maintain more than a simple list of items will probably require multiple tables. If a database has multiple tables, the relationships between the tables must be defined, and referential integrity constraints must be put into place.

In the example in this chapter, you have an employee application-time period table and a department application-time period table. There is a one-to-many relationship between the department table and the employee table, because a department may have multiple employees, but each employee belongs to one and only one department. This means that you need to put a foreign key into the employee table that references the primary key of the department table. With this in mind, create the employee table again, this time using a more complete CREATE statement, and create a department table in a similar manner:

```
CREATE TABLE employee_atpt (
    EmpID        INTEGER             NOT NULL,
    EmpStart     DATE                NOT NULL,
    EmpEnd       DATE                NOT NULL,
    EmpName      VARACHAR (30),
    EmpDept      VARCHAR (30),
    PERIOD FOR EmpPeriod (EmpStart, EmpEnd)
    PRIMARY KEY (EmpID, EmpPeriod WITHOUT OVERLAPS)
```

```
    FOREIGN KEY (EmpDept, PERIOD EmpPeriod)
        REFERENCES dept_atpt (DeptID, PERIOD DeptPeriod)
);

CREATE TABLE dept_atpt (
    DeptID          VARCHAR (30)            NOT NULL,
    Manager         VARCHAR (40)            NOT NULL,
    DeptStart       DATE                    NOT NULL,
    DeptEnd         DATE                    NOT NULL,
    PERIOD FOR DeptTime (DeptStart, DeptEnd),
    PRIMARY KEY (DeptID, DeptTime WITHOUT OVERLAPS)
);
```

Querying application-time period tables

Now, detailed information can be retrieved from the database by using SELECT statements that make use of the temporal data.

One thing you might want to do is to list all the people who are currently employed by the organization. Even before SQL:2011, you could do it with a statement similar to the following:

```
SELECT *
    FROM employee_atpt
    WHERE EmpStart <= CURRENT_DATE()
        AND EmpEnd > CURRENT_DATE();
```

With the new PERIOD syntax, you can get the same result a little more easily, like this:

```
SELECT *
    FROM employee_atpt
    WHERE EmpPERIOD CONTAINS CURRENT_DATE();
```

You can also retrieve employees who were employed during a specific period of time, like so:

```
SELECT *
    FROM employee_atpt
    WHERE EmpPeriod OVERLAPS
    PERIOD (DATE ('2018-01-01'), DATE ('2018-09-16'));
```

Other predicates besides `CONTAINS` and `OVERLAPS` that you can use in this context include `EQUALS`, `PRECEDES`, `SUCCEEDS`, `IMMEDIATELY PRECEDES`, and `IMMEDIATELY SUCCEEDS`.

These predicates operate as follows:

>> If one period EQUALS another, they are exactly the same.

>> If one period PRECEDES another, it comes somewhere before it.

>> If one period SUCCEEDS another, it comes somewhere after it.

>> If one period IMMEDIATELY PRECEDES another, it comes just before and is contiguous with it.

>> If one period IMMEDIATELY SUCCEEDS another, it comes just after and is contiguous with it.

Working with System-Versioned Tables

System-versioned tables have a different purpose than application-time period tables, and consequently work differently. Application-time period tables enable you to define periods of time and operate on the data that falls within those periods. In contrast, system-versioned tables are designed to create an auditable record of exactly when a data item was added to, changed within, or deleted from a database. For example, it is important for a bank to know exactly when a deposit or withdrawal was made, and this information must be kept for a period of time designated by law. Similarly, stock brokers need to track exactly when a purchase transaction was made. There are a number of similar cases, where knowing when a particular event occurred, down to a fraction of a second, is important.

Applications such as the bank application or the stock broker application have strict requirements:

>> Any update or delete operation must preserve the original state of the row before performing the update or delete operation.

>> The system, rather than the user, maintains the start and end times of the periods of the rows.

Original rows that have been subjected to an update or delete operation remain in the table and are henceforward referred to as *historical rows*. Users are prevented from modifying the contents of historical rows or the periods associated with any of the rows. Only the system, not the user, may update the periods of rows in a system-versioned table. This is done by updating the non-period columns of the table or as a result of row deletions.

These constraints guarantee that the history of data changes is immune to tampering, thus meeting audit standards and complying with government regulations.

System-versioned tables are distinguished from application-time period tables by a couple of differences in the CREATE statements that create them:

>> Whereas in an application-time period table the user can give any name to the period, in a system-versioned table, the period name must be SYSTEM_TIME.

>> The CREATE statement must include the keywords WITH SYSTEM VERSIONING. Although SQL:2011 allowed the data type for the period start and period end to be either DATE type or one of the timestamp types, you will almost always want to use one of the timestamp types, which give you a level of precision much finer than a day. Of course, whatever type you choose for the start column must also be used for the end column.

To illustrate the use of system-versioned tables, I continue to use employee and department examples. You can create a system-versioned table with the following code:

```
CREATE TABLE employee_sys (
    EmpID       INTEGER,
    Sys_Start TIMESTAMP(12) GENERATED ALWAYS AS ROW START,
    Sys_End TIMESTAMP(12) GENERATED ALWAYS AS ROW END,
    EmpName     VARCHAR(30),
    PERIOD FOR SYSTEM_TIME (SysStart, SysEnd)
) WITH SYSTEM VERSIONING;
```

A row in a system-versioned table is considered to be a current system row if the current time is contained in the system-time period. Otherwise it is considered to be a historical system row.

System-versioned tables are similar to application-time period tables in many respects, but there are also differences. Here are a few:

>> Users may not assign or change the values in the Sys_Start and Sys_End columns. These values are assigned and changed automatically by the DBMS. This situation is mandated by the keywords GENERATED ALWAYS.

>> When you use the INSERT operation to add something into a system-versioned table, the value in the Sys_Start column is automatically set to the transaction

timestamp, which is associated with every transaction. The value assigned to the Sys_End column is the highest value of that column's data type.

>> In system-versioned tables, the UPDATE and DELETE operations operate only on current system rows. Users may not update or delete historical system rows.

>> Users may not modify the system-time period start or end time of either current or historical system rows.

>> Whenever you either use the UPDATE or DELETE operation on a current-system row, a historical system row is automatically inserted.

An UPDATE statement on a system-versioned table first inserts a copy of the old row, with its system end time set to the transaction timestamp. This indicates that the row ceased to be current at that timestamp. Next, the DBMS performs the update, simultaneously changing the system-period start time to the transaction timestamp. Now the updated row is the current system row as of the transaction timestamp. UPDATE triggers for the rows in question will fire, but INSERT triggers will not fire even though historical rows are being inserted as a part of this operation. If you are wondering what triggers are, they are covered extensively in Chapter 23.

A DELETE operation on a system-versioned table doesn't actually delete the specified rows. Instead it changes the system-time period end time of those rows to the system timestamp. This indicates that those rows ceased to be current as of the transaction timestamp. Now those rows are part of the historical system rather than the current system. When you perform a DELETE operation, any DELETE triggers for the affected rows will fire.

Designating primary keys in system-versioned tables

Designating primary keys in system-versioned tables is a lot simpler than it is in application-time period tables. This is because you don't have to deal with time period issues. In system-versioned tables, the historical rows cannot be changed. Back when they were current rows, they were checked for uniqueness. Because they cannot be changed now, they don't need to be checked for uniqueness now either.

If you add a primary key constraint to an existing system-versioned table with an ALTER statement, because it applies only to the current rows, you need not include period information in the statement. For example:

```
ALTER TABLE employee_sys
   ADD PRIMARY KEY (EmpID);
```

That does the trick. Short and sweet.

Applying referential integrity constraints to system-versioned tables

Applying referential integrity constraints to system-versioned tables is also straightforward for the same reason. Here's an example of that:

```
ALTER TABLE employee_sys
    ADD FOREIGN KEY (EmpDept)
        REFERENCES dept_sys (DeptID);
```

Because only current rows are affected, you don't need to include the start and end of the period columns.

Querying system-versioned tables

Most queries of system-versioned tables are concerned with what was true at some point in time in the past or during some period of time in the past. To deal with these situations, SQL:2011 added some new syntax. To query a table for information about what was true at a specific point in time, the SYSTEM_TIME AS OF syntax is used. Suppose you want to know who was employed by the organization on July 15, 2017. You could find out with the following query:

```
SELECT EmpID, EmpName, Sys_Start, Sys_End
    FROM employee_sys FOR SYSTEM_TIME AS OF
        TIMESTAMP '2017-07-15 00:00:00';
```

This statement returns all rows whose start time is equal to or before the timestamp value and whose end time is later than the timestamp value.

To find what was true during a period of time, you can use a similar statement, with appropriate new syntax. Here's an example:

```
SELECT EmpID, EmpName, Sys_Start, Sys_End
    FROM employee_sys FOR SYSTEM_TIME FROM
        TIMESTAMP '2017-07-01 00:00:00' TO
        TIMESTAMP '2017-08-01 00:00:00';
```

This retrieval will include all the rows starting at the first timestamp, up to but *not* including the second timestamp.

If a query on a system-versioned table does not include a timestamp specification, the default case is to return only the current system rows. This case would be coded similar to the following:

```
SELECT EmpID, EmpName, Sys_Start, Sys_End
    FROM employee_sys;
```

If you want to retrieve all rows in a system-versioned table, both historical and current, you can do it with the following syntax:

```
SELECT EmpID, EmpName, Sys_Start, Sys_End
    FROM employee_sys FOR SYSTEM_TIME FROM
        TIMESTAMP '2017-07-01 00:00:00' TO
        TIMESTAMP '9999-12-31 24:59:59';
```

Tracking Even More Time Data with Bitemporal Tables

Sometimes you want to know both when an event occurred in the real world and when that event was recorded in the database. For cases such as this, you may use a table that is both a system-versioned table and an application-time period table. Such tables are known as bitemporal tables.

There are a number of cases where a bitemporal table might be called for. Suppose, for example, that one of your employees moves her residence across the state line from Oregon to Washington. You must take account of the fact that her state income tax withholding must change as of the official date of the move. However, it is unlikely that the change to the database will be made on exactly that same day. Both times need to be recorded, and a bitemporal table can do that recording very well. The system-versioned time period records when the change became known to the database, and the application-time period records when the move legally went into effect. Here's some example code to create such a table:

```
CREATE TABLE employee_bt (
    EmpID          INTEGER,
    EmpStart       DATE,
    EmpEnd         DATE,
    EmpDept        INTEGER,
    PERIOD FOR EmpPeriod (EmpStart, EmpEnd),
    Sys_Start TIMESTAMP (12) GENERATED ALWAYS
        AS ROW START,
```

```
      Sys_End TIMESTAMP (12) GENERATED ALWAYS
          AS ROW END,
      EmpName          VARCHAR (30),
      EmpStreet        VARCHAR (40),
      EmpCity          VARCHAR (30),
      EmpStateProv     VARCHAR (2),
      EmpPostalCode    VARCHAR (10),
      PERIOD FOR SYSTEM_TIME (Sys_Start, Sys_End),
      PRIMARY KEY (EmpID, EPeriod WITHOUT OVERLAPS),
      FOREIGN KEY (EDept, PERIOD EPeriod)
      REFERENCES Dept (DeptID, PERIOD DPeriod)
) WITH SYSTEM VERSIONING;
```

Bitemporal tables serve the purposes of both system-versioned tables and application-time tables. The user supplies values for the application-time period start and end columns. An INSERT operation in such a table automatically sets the value of the system-time period to the transaction timestamp. The value of the system-time period end column is automatically set to the highest value permitted for that column's data type.

UPDATE and DELETE operations work as they do for standard application-time period tables. As is true with system-versioned tables, UPDATE and DELETE operations affect only current rows, and with each such operation a historical row is automatically inserted.

A query made upon a bitemporal table can specify an application-time period, a system-versioned period, or both. Here's an example of the "both" case:

```
SELECT EmpID
    FROM employee_bt FOR SYSTEM TIME AS OF
        TIMESTAMP '2017-07-15 00:00:00'
    WHERE EmpID = 314159 AND
        EmpPeriod CONTAINS DATE '2017-06-20 00:00:00';
```

Formatting and Parsing Dates and Times

A language standard, such as the international SQL standard, should describe legal syntax for the language, and in addition, how to format language elements, such as dates and times. Amazingly, the SQL standard did not do this until SQL:2016. It's possible to express dates and times in a variety of ways, and the standard format in the USA, for example, is different from the standard format in Europe.

SQL:2016 specifies how to represent units of time in a template, to show how actual dates and/or times should be represented. For example, a data of September 16, 2018 could be represented as '09-16-2018' in an SQL statement. A template that shows the expected format for a date could be of the form 'MM-DD-YYYY'. This template tells the SQL programmer to express the data first as month, followed by day, and then by year. Alternatively, a template of 'DD-MM-YYYY' would tell the programmer to put the day first, followed by the month, and then the year. The MM, DD, and YYYY entries are placeholders that are to be replaced in an SQL statement by a specific month, day, and year.

In addition to MM, DD, and YYYY, there are several other placeholders that have specific meanings. Table 7-6 lists them, along with what they stand for.

TABLE 7-6

Template Placeholders and What They Stand For

Placeholder	Meaning
YYYY | YYY | YY | Y	Year
RRRR | RR	Rounded year
MM	Month
DD	Day of month
DDD	Day of year
HH | HH12	Hour, out of 12
HH24	Hour, out of 24
MI	Minute
SS	Second, out of minute
SSSS	Second, out of day
FF1 | FF2 | . . .. | FF9	Fraction of a second
A.M | P.M.	AM or PM
TZH	Time zone hour
TZM	Time zone minute

You can use format templates with these placeholders in the JSON path method datetime, as described in Chapter 19, and in a CAST expression, as described in Chapter 9.

Chapter **8**

Specifying Values

This book emphasizes the importance of database structure for maintaining database integrity. Although the significance of database structure is often overlooked, you must never forget that the most important thing is the data itself. After all, the values held in the cells that form the intersections of the database table's rows and columns are the raw materials from which you can derive meaningful relationships and trends.

You can represent values in several ways. You can represent them directly, or you can derive them with functions or expressions. This chapter describes the various kinds of values, as well as functions and expressions.

REMEMBER

Functions examine data and calculate a value based on the data. *Expressions* are combinations of data items that SQL evaluates to produce a single value.

Values

SQL recognizes several kinds of values:

» Row values

» Literal values

» Variables

ATOMS AREN'T INDIVISIBLE EITHER

In the 19th century, scientists believed that an atom was the irreducible smallest possible piece of matter. That's why they named it *atom*, which comes from the Greek word *atomos*, which means *indivisible*. Now scientists know that atoms aren't indivisible — they're made up of protons, neutrons, and electrons. Protons and neutrons, in turn, are made up of quarks, gluons, and virtual quarks. Even these things may not be indivisible. Who knows?

The value of a field in a database table is called *atomic*, even though many fields aren't indivisible. A DATE value has components of year, month, and day. A TIMESTAMP value adds components of hour, minute, second, and so on. A REAL or FLOAT value has components of *exponent* and *mantissa*. A CHAR value has components that you can access by using SUBSTRING. Therefore, calling database field values *atomic* is true to the analogy of atoms of matter. Neither modern application of the term *atomic*, however, is true to the word's original meaning.

>> Special variables

>> Column references

Row values

The most visible values in a database are table *row values.* These are the values that each row of a database table contains. A row value is typically made up of multiple components because each column in a row contains a value. A *field* is the intersection of a single column with a single row. A field contains a *scalar*, or *atomic*, value. A value that's scalar or atomic has only a single component.

Literal values

In SQL, either a variable or a constant may represent a *value.* Logically enough, the value of a *variable* may change from time to time, but the value of a *constant* never changes. An important kind of constant is the *literal value.* The representation is itself the value.

Just as SQL has many data types, it also has many types of literals. Table 8-1 shows some examples of literals of the various data types.

Notice that single quotes enclose the literals of the non-numeric types. These marks help to prevent confusion; they can, however, also cause problems, as you can see in Table 8-1.

TABLE 8-1   **Example Literals of Various Data Types**

Data Type	Example Literal
BIGINT	8589934592
INTEGER	186282
SMALLINT	186
NUMERIC	186282.42
DECIMAL	186282.42
DECFLOAT	186282.42
REAL	6.02257E23
DOUBLE PRECISION	3.1415926535897E00
FLOAT	6.02257E23
CHARACTER(15)	'GREECE '
Note: Fifteen total characters and spaces are between the quote marks above.	
VARCHAR (CHARACTER VARYING)	'lepton'
NATIONAL CHARACTER(15)	'ΕΛΛΑΣ '[1]
Note: Fifteen total characters and spaces are between the quote marks above.	
NATIONAL CHARACTER VARYING(15)	'λεπτον'[2]
CHARACTER LARGE OBJECT(512) (CLOB(512))	(A really long character string)
BINARY(4)	'01001100011100001111000111001010'
VARBINARY(4) (BINARY VARYING(4))	'0100110001110000'
BINARY LARGE OBJECT(512) (BLOB(512))	(A really long string of ones and zeros)
DATE	DATE '1969-07-20'
TIME(2)	TIME '13.41.32.50'
TIMESTAMP(0)	TIMESTAMP '2018-02-25-13.03.16.000000'
TIME WITH TIMEZONE(4)	TIME '13.41.32.5000-08.00'
TIMESTAMP WITH TIMEZONE(0)	TIMESTAMP '2018-02-25-13.03.16.0000+02.00'
INTERVAL DAY	INTERVAL '7' DAY

[1]This term is the word that Greeks use to name their own country in their own language. (The English equivalent is Hellas.)

[2]This term is the word lepton in Greek national characters.

What if a literal is a character string that itself contains a phrase in single quotes? In that case, you must type two single quotes to show that one of the quote marks that you're typing is a part of the character string and not an indicator of the end of the string. You'd type `'Earth"s atmosphere'`, for example, to represent the character literal `'Earth's atmosphere'`.

Variables

Although being able to manipulate literals and other kinds of constants while dealing with a database gives you great power, having variables is helpful, too. In many cases, you'd need to do much more work if you didn't have variables. A *variable*, by the way, is a quantity that has a value that can change. Look at the following example to see why variables are valuable.

Suppose that you're a retailer who has several classes of customers. You give your high-volume customers the best price, your medium-volume customers the next best price, and your low-volume customers the highest price. You want to index all prices to your cost of goods. For your F-35 product, you decide to charge your high-volume customers (Class C) 1.4 times your cost of goods. You charge your medium-volume customers (Class B) 1.5 times your cost of goods, and you charge your low-volume customers (Class A) 1.6 times your cost of goods.

You store the cost of goods and the prices that you charge in a table named PRICING. To implement your new pricing structure, you issue the following SQL commands:

```
UPDATE PRICING
    SET Price = Cost * 1.4
    WHERE Product = 'F-35'
        AND Class = 'C' ;
UPDATE PRICING
    SET Price = Cost * 1.5
    WHERE Product = 'F-35'
        AND Class = 'B' ;
UPDATE PRICING
    SET Price = Cost * 1.6
    WHERE Product = 'F-35'
        AND Class = 'A' ;
```

This code is fine and meets your needs — for now. But if aggressive competition begins to eat into your market share, you may need to reduce your margins to remain competitive. To change your margins, you need to enter code something like this:

```
UPDATE PRICING
   SET Price = Cost * 1.25
   WHERE Product = 'F-35'
      AND Class = 'C' ;
UPDATE PRICING
   SET Price = Cost * 1.35
   WHERE Product = 'F-35'
      AND Class = 'B' ;
UPDATE PRICING
   SET Price = Cost * 1.45
   WHERE Product = 'F-35'
      AND Class = 'A' ;
```

If you're in a volatile market, you may need to rewrite your SQL code repeatedly. This task can become tedious, particularly if prices appear in multiple places in your code. You can minimize your work by replacing literals (such as 1.45) with variables (such as :multiplierA). Then you can perform your updates as follows:

```
UPDATE PRICING
   SET Price = Cost * :multiplierC
   WHERE Product = 'F-35'
      AND Class = 'C' ;
UPDATE PRICING
   SET Price = Cost * :multiplierB
   WHERE Product = 'F-35'
      AND Class = 'B' ;
UPDATE PRICING
   SET Price = Cost * :multiplierA
   WHERE Product = 'F-35'
      AND Class = 'A' ;
```

Now whenever market conditions force you to change your pricing, you need to change only the values of the variables :multiplierC, :multiplierB, and :multiplierA. These variables are parameters that pass to the SQL code, which then uses the variables to compute new prices.

TECHNICAL STUFF

Sometimes variables used in this way are called *parameters* or *host variables*. Variables are called *parameters* if they appear in applications written in SQL module language. They're called *host variables* when they're used in embedded SQL.

REMEMBER

Embedded SQL means that SQL statements are embedded into the code of an application written in a host language. Alternatively, you can use SQL module language to create an entire module of SQL code. The host language application then calls the module. Either method can give you the capabilities that you want. The approach that you use depends on your SQL implementation.

Special variables

If a user on a client machine connects to a database on a server, this connection establishes a *session.* If the user connects to several databases, the session associated with the most recent connection is considered the *current session; previous sessions* are considered *dormant.* SQL defines several *special variables* that are valuable on multiuser systems. These variables keep track of the different users. Here's a list of the special variables:

>> SESSION_USER: The special variable SESSION_USER holds a value that's equal to the user authorization identifier of the current SQL session. If you write a program that performs a monitoring function, you can interrogate SESSION_USER to find out who is executing SQL statements.

>> CURRENT_USER: An SQL module may have a user-specified authorization identifier associated with it. The CURRENT_USER variable stores this value. If a module has no such identifier, CURRENT_USER has the same value as SESSION_USER.

>> SYSTEM_USER: The SYSTEM_USER variable contains the operating system's user identifier. This identifier may differ from that same user's identifier in an SQL module. A user may log on to the system as LARRY, for example, but identify himself to a module as PLANT_MGR. The value in SESSION_USER is PLANT_MGR. If he makes no explicit specification of the module identifier, and CURRENT_USER also contains PLANT_MGR, SYSTEM_USER holds the value LARRY.

TIP

The SYSTEM_USER, SESSION_USER, and CURRENT_USER special variables track who is using the system. You can maintain a log table and periodically insert into that table the values that SYSTEM_USER, SESSION_USER, and CURRENT_USER contain. The following example shows how:

```
INSERT INTO USAGELOG (SNAPSHOT)
    VALUES ('User ' || SYSTEM_USER ||
        ' with ID ' || SESSION_USER ||
        ' active at ' || CURRENT_TIMESTAMP) ;
```

This statement produces log entries similar to the following example:

```
User LARRY with ID PLANT_MGR active at 2018-04-07-23.50.00
```

Column references

Every column contains one value for each row of a table. SQL statements often refer to such values. A fully qualified column reference consists of the table name, a period, and then the column name (for example, PRICING.Product). Consider the following statement:

```
SELECT PRICING.Cost
    FROM PRICING
    WHERE PRICING.Product = 'F-35' ;
```

Here PRICING.Product is a column reference. This reference contains the value 'F-35'. PRICING.Cost is also a column reference, but you don't know its value until the preceding SELECT statement executes.

TIP

Because it only makes sense to reference columns in the current table, you don't generally need to use fully qualified column references. The following statement, for example, is equivalent to the previous one:

```
SELECT Cost
    FROM PRICING
    WHERE Product = 'F-35' ;
```

Sometimes you may be dealing with more than one table — say, when two tables in a database contain one or more columns with the same name. In such a case, you must fully qualify column references for those columns to guarantee that you get the column you want.

For example, suppose that your company maintains facilities in both Kingston and Jefferson, and you maintain separate employee records for each site. You name the Kingston employee table EMP_KINGSTON, and you name the Jefferson employee table EMP_JEFFERSON. You want a list of employees who work at both sites, so you need to find the employees whose names appear in both tables. The following SELECT statement gives you what you want:

```
SELECT EMP_KINGSTON.FirstName, EMP_KINGSTON.LastName
    FROM EMP_KINGSTON, EMP_JEFFERSON
    WHERE EMP_KINGSTON.EmpID = EMP_JEFFERSON.EmpID ;
```

Because each employee's ID number is unique and remains the same regardless of the work site, you can use this ID as a link between the two tables. This retrieval returns only the names of employees who appear in both tables.

Value Expressions

An expression may be simple or complex. The expression can contain literal values, column names, parameters, host variables, subqueries, logical connectives, and arithmetic operators. Regardless of its complexity, an expression must reduce to a single value.

For this reason, SQL expressions are commonly known as *value expressions*. Combining multiple value expressions into a single expression is possible, as long as the component value expressions reduce to values that have compatible data types.

SQL has five kinds of value expressions:

>> String value expressions

>> Numeric value expressions

>> Datetime value expressions

>> Interval value expressions

>> Conditional value expressions

String value expressions

The simplest *string value expression* specifies a single string value. Other possibilities include a column reference, a set function, a scalar subquery, a CASE expression, a CAST expression, or a complex string value expression. (I discuss CASE and CAST value expressions in Chapter 9; I get into subqueries in Chapter 12.)

Only one operator is possible in a string value expression: the *concatenation operator*. You may concatenate any of the value expressions I mention in the bulleted list in the previous section with another expression to create a more complex string value expression. A pair of vertical lines (||) represents the concatenation operator. The following table shows some examples of string value expressions.

Expression	Produces
'Peanut ' || 'brittle'	'Peanut brittle'
'Jelly' || ' ' || 'beans'	'Jelly beans'
FIRST_NAME || ' ' || LAST_NAME	'Joe Smith'

Expression	Produces
`B'1100111' || B'01010011'`	`'110011101010011'`
`'' || 'Asparagus'`	`'Asparagus'`
`'Asparagus' || ''`	`'Asparagus'`
`'As' || '' || 'par' || '' || 'agus'`	`'Asparagus'`

As the table shows, if you concatenate a string to a zero-length string, the result is the same as the original string.

Numeric value expressions

In *numeric value expressions,* you can apply the addition, subtraction, multiplication, and division operators to numeric-type data. The expression must reduce to a numeric value. The components of a numeric value expression may be of different data types as long as *all* the data types are numeric. The data type of the result depends on the data types of the components from which you derive the result. Even so, the SQL standard doesn't rigidly specify the type that results from any specific combination of source-expression components. That's because of the differences among hardware platforms. Check the documentation for your specific platform when you're mixing numeric data types.

Here are some examples of numeric value expressions:

» `-27`

» `49 + 83`

» `5 * (12 - 3)`

» `PROTEIN + FAT + CARBOHYDRATE`

» `FEET/5280`

» `COST * :multiplierA`

Datetime value expressions

Datetime value expressions perform operations on data that deal with dates and times. These value expressions can contain components that are of the types `DATE`, `TIME`, `TIMESTAMP`, or `INTERVAL`. The result of a datetime value expression is always a datetime type (DATE, TIME, or TIMESTAMP). The following expression, for example, gives the date one week from today:

```
CURRENT_DATE + INTERVAL '7' DAY
```

Times are maintained in Universal Time Coordinated (UTC) — known in the UK as Greenwich Mean Time — but you can specify an offset to make the time correct for any particular time zone. For your system's local time zone, you can use the simple syntax given in the following example:

```
TIME '22:55:00' AT LOCAL
```

Alternatively, you can specify this value the long way:

```
TIME '22:55:00' AT TIME ZONE INTERVAL '-08.00' HOUR TO MINUTE
```

This expression defines the local time as the time zone for Portland, Oregon, which is eight hours earlier than that of Greenwich, England.

Interval value expressions

If you subtract one datetime from another, you get an *interval.* Adding one datetime to another makes no sense, so SQL doesn't permit you to do so. If you add two intervals together or subtract one interval from another interval, the result is an interval. You can also either multiply or divide an interval by a numeric constant.

SQL has two types of intervals: *year-month* and *day-time.* To avoid ambiguities, you must specify which to use in an interval expression. The following expression, for example, gives the interval in years and months until you reach retirement age:

```
(BIRTHDAY_65 - CURRENT_DATE) YEAR TO MONTH
```

The following example gives an interval of 40 days:

```
INTERVAL '17' DAY + INTERVAL '23' DAY
```

The example that follows approximates the total number of months that a mother of five has been pregnant (assuming that she's not currently expecting number six!):

```
INTERVAL '9' MONTH * 5
```

Intervals can be negative as well as positive and may consist of any value expression or combination of value expressions that evaluates to an interval.

Conditional value expressions

The value of a *conditional value expression* depends on a condition. The conditional value expressions CASE, NULLIF, and COALESCE are significantly more complex than the other kinds of value expressions. In fact, these three conditional value expressions are so complex that I don't have enough room to talk about them here. (I give conditional value expressions extensive coverage in Chapter 9.)

Functions

A *function* is a simple (okay, no more than moderately complex) operation that the usual SQL commands don't perform but that comes up often in practice. SQL provides functions that perform tasks that the application code in the host language (within which you embed your SQL statements) would otherwise need to perform. SQL has two main categories of functions: *set* (or *aggregate*) *functions* and *value functions.*

Set functions

Set functions apply to *sets* of rows in a table rather than to a single row. These functions summarize some characteristic of the current set of rows. The set may include all the rows in the table or a subset of rows that are specified by a WHERE clause. (I discuss WHERE clauses extensively in Chapter 10.) Programmers sometimes call set functions *aggregate functions* because these functions take information from multiple rows, process that information in some way, and deliver a single-row answer. That answer is an *aggregation* of the information in the rows making up the set.

To illustrate the use of the set functions, consider Table 8-2, a list of nutrition facts for 100 grams of selected foods.

A database table named FOODS stores the information in Table 8-2. Blank fields contain the value NULL. The set functions COUNT, AVG, MAX, MIN, and SUM can tell you important facts about the data in this table.

COUNT

The COUNT function tells you how many rows are in the table or how many rows in the table meet certain conditions. The simplest usage of this function is as follows:

```
SELECT COUNT (*)
   FROM FOODS ;
```

TABLE 8-2 **Nutrition Facts for 100 Grams of Selected Foods**

Food	Calories	Protein (grams)	Fat (grams)	Carbohydrate (grams)
Almonds, roasted	627	18.6	57.7	19.6
Asparagus	20	2.2	0.2	3.6
Bananas, raw	85	1.1	0.2	22.2
Beef, lean hamburger	219	27.4	11.3	
Chicken, light meat	166	31.6	3.4	
Opossum, roasted	221	30.2	10.2	
Pork, ham	394	21.9	33.3	
Beans, lima	111	7.6	0.5	19.8
Cola	39			10.0
Bread, white	269	8.7	3.2	50.4
Bread, whole wheat	243	10.5	3.0	47.7
Broccoli	26	3.1	0.3	4.5
Butter	716	0.6	81.0	0.4
Jelly beans	367		0.5	93.1
Peanut brittle	421	5.7	10.4	81.0

This function yields a result of 15, because it counts all rows in the FOODS table. The following statement produces the same result:

```
SELECT COUNT (Calories)
    FROM FOODS ;
```

Because the `Calories` column in every row of the table has an entry, the count is the same. If a column contains nulls, however, the function doesn't count the rows corresponding to those nulls.

The following statement returns a value of 11 because 4 of the 15 rows in the table contain nulls in the `Carbohydrate` column.

```
SELECT COUNT (Carbohydrate)
    FROM FOODS ;
```

TIP

A field in a database table may contain a null value for a variety of reasons. One common reason is that the actual value is not known (or not *yet* known). Or the value may be known but not yet entered. Sometimes, if a value is known to be zero, the data-entry operator doesn't bother entering anything in a field — leaving that field a null. This is not a good practice because zero is a definite value, and you can include it in computations. Null is *not* a definite value, and SQL doesn't include null values in computations.

You can also use the COUNT function, in combination with DISTINCT, to determine how many distinct values exist in a column. Consider the following statement:

```
SELECT COUNT (DISTINCT Fat)
    FROM FOODS ;
```

The answer that this statement returns is 12. You can see that a 100-gram serving of asparagus has the same fat content as 100 grams of bananas (0.2 grams) and that a 100-gram serving of lima beans has the same fat content as 100 grams of jelly beans (0.5 grams). Thus the table has a total of only 12 distinct fat values.

AVG

The AVG function calculates and returns the average of the values in the specified column. Of course, you can use the AVG function only on columns that contain numeric data, as in the following example:

```
SELECT AVG (Fat)
    FROM FOODS ;
```

The result is 15.37. This number is so high primarily because of the presence of butter in the database. You may wonder what the average fat content may be if you didn't include butter. To find out, you can add a WHERE clause to your statement, as follows:

```
SELECT AVG (Fat)
    FROM FOODS
    WHERE Food <> 'Butter' ;
```

The average fat value drops down to 10.32 grams per 100 grams of food.

MAX

The MAX function returns the maximum value found in the specified column. The following statement returns a value of 81 (the fat content in 100 grams of butter):

```
SELECT MAX (Fat)
   FROM FOODS ;
```

MIN

The MIN function returns the minimum value found in the specified column. The following statement returns a value of 0.4, because the function doesn't treat the nulls as zeros:

```
SELECT MIN (Carbohydrate)
   FROM FOODS ;
```

SUM

The SUM function returns the sum of all the values found in the specified column. The following statement returns 3,924, which is the total caloric content of all 15 foods:

```
SELECT SUM (Calories)
   FROM FOODS ;
```

LISTAGG

SQL:2016 introduced a new set function, LISTAGG, which aggregates the values of a group of table rows into a list of values separated by a delimiter, such as a comma, that you can specify. A common use of this capability is to transform the aggregation of table values into a string of comma-separated values (as in a CSV file). Syntax for the LISTAGG function follows this model:

```
LISTAGG (<expression>, <delimiter>) WITHIN GROUP (ORDER BY fieldname, ...)
```

As an example, suppose your database has an EMPLOYEE table that records the EmployeeID, FirstName, LastName, and DepartmentID of each of your employees. Suppose further that you want a listing of all your employees, grouped by department and listed in alphabetical order of each employee's last name. You could build such a listing with the following query:

```
SELECT DepartmentID,
       LISTAGG(LastName, ',') WITHIN GROUP (ORDER BY LastName)
       AS Employees
```

```
FROM EMPLOYEE
GROUP BY DepartmentID ;
```

The result will be a tabular result set with a `DepartmentID` column and an `Employees` column. Each row of the result set will hold the `DepartmentID` of a department followed by a comma-separated list of the employees in that department. The rows will be in alphanumeric order by `DepartmentID`, and the employee names in each row will be ordered alphabetically.

Value functions

A number of operations apply in a variety of contexts. Because you need to use these operations so often, incorporating them into SQL as value functions makes good sense. ISO/IEC standard SQL offers relatively few value functions compared with specific database management system implementations such as Access, Oracle, or SQL Server, but the few that standard SQL does have are probably the ones that you'll use most often. SQL uses the following four types of value functions:

>> String value functions

>> Numeric value functions

>> Datetime value functions

>> Interval value functions

String value functions

String value functions take one character string as an input and produce another character string as an output. SQL has ten such functions:

>> SUBSTRING

>> SUBSTRING SIMILAR

>> SUBSTRING_REGEX

>> TRANSLATE_REGEX

>> OVERLAY

>> UPPER

>> LOWER

>> TRIM

>> TRANSLATE

>> CONVERT

SUBSTRING

Use the SUBSTRING function to extract a substring from a source string. The extracted substring is of the same type as the source string. If the source string is a CHARACTER VARYING string, for example, the substring is also a CHARACTER VARYING string. Following is the syntax of the SUBSTRING function:

```
SUBSTRING (string_value FROM start [FOR length])
```

The clause in square brackets ([ ]) is optional. The substring extracted from string_value begins with the character that start represents and continues for length characters. If the FOR clause is absent, the substring extracted extends from the start character to the end of the string. Consider the following example:

```
SUBSTRING ('Bread, whole wheat' FROM 8 FOR 7)
```

The substring extracted is 'whole w'. This substring starts with the eighth character of the source string and has a length of seven characters. On the surface, SUBSTRING doesn't seem like a very valuable function; if you have a literal like 'Bread, whole wheat', you don't need a function to figure out characters 8 through 14. SUBSTRING really is a valuable function, however, because the string value doesn't need to be a literal. The value can be any expression that evaluates to a character string. Thus, you could have a variable named fooditem that takes on different values at different times. The following expression would extract the desired substring regardless of what character string the fooditem variable currently represents:

```
SUBSTRING (:fooditem FROM 8 FOR 7)
```

All the value functions are similar in that these functions can operate on expressions that evaluate to values as well as on the literal values themselves.

WARNING

You need to watch out for a couple of things if you use the SUBSTRING function. Make sure that the substring that you specify actually falls within the source string. If you ask for a substring that starts at (say) character eight but the source string is only four characters long, you get a null result. You must therefore have some idea of the form of your data before you specify a substring function. You also don't want to specify a negative substring length, because the end of a string can't precede the beginning.

If a column is of the VARCHAR type, you may not know how far the field extends for a particular row. This lack of knowledge doesn't present a problem for the SUBSTRING function. If the length that you specify goes beyond the right edge of the field, SUBSTRING returns whatever it finds. It doesn't return an error.

Say that you have the following statement:

```
SELECT * FROM FOODS
    WHERE SUBSTRING (Food FROM 8 FOR 7) = 'white' ;
```

This statement returns the row for white bread from the FOODS table, even though the value in the Food column ('Bread, white') is less than 14 characters long.

TIP

If any *operand* (value from which an operator derives another value) in the substring function has a null value, SUBSTRING returns a null result.

SUBSTRING SIMILAR

The regular expression substring function is a triadic function (meaning it operates on three parameters). The three parameters are a source character string, a pattern string, and an escape character. It then uses pattern matching (based on POSIX-based regular expressions) to extract and return a result string from the source character string.

Two instances of the escape character, each followed by the double-quote character, are used to partition the pattern string into three parts. Here's an example:

Suppose the source character string S is 'Four score and seven years ago, our fathers brought forth upon this continent, a new nation'. Suppose further that the pattern string R is 'and '/"'seven'/"' years', where the forward slash is the escape character.

Then

```
SUBSTRING S SIMILAR TO R ;
```

returns a result that is the middle piece of the pattern string, 'seven' in this case.

SUBSTRING_REGEX

SUBSTRING_REGEX searches a string for an XQuery regular expression pattern and returns one occurrence of the matching substring.

According to the ISO/IEC international standard JTC 1/SC 32, the syntax of a substring regular expression is as follows:

```
SUBSTRING_REGEX <left paren>
    <XQuery pattern> [ FLAG <XQuery option flag> ]
    IN <regex subject string>
```

```
          [ FROM <start position> ]
          [ USING <char length units> ]
          [ OCCURRENCE <regex occurrence> ]
          [ GROUP <regex capture group> ] <right paren>
```

<XQuery pattern> is a character string expression whose value is an XQuery regular expression.

<XQuery option flag> is an optional character string, corresponding to the $flags argument of the [XQuery F&O] function fn:match.

<regex subject string> is the character string to be searched for matches to the <XQuery pattern>.

<start position> is an optional exact numeric value with scale 0, indicating the character position at which to start the search. (The default is 1.)

<char length units> is CHARACTERS or OCTETS, indicating the unit in which <start position> is measured. (The default is CHARACTERS.)

<regex occurrence> is an optional exact numeric value with scale 0, indicating which occurrence of a match is desired. (The default is 1.)

<regex capture group> is an optional exact numeric value with scale 0 indicating which capture group of a match is desired. (The default is 0, indicating the entire occurrence.)

Here are some examples of the use of SUBSTRING_REGEX:

```
SUBSTRING_REGEX ('\p{L}*' IN 'Just do it.')='Just'
SUBSTRING_REGEX ('\p{L}*' IN 'Just do it.' FROM 2)= 'ust'
SUBSTRING_REGEX ('\p{L}*' IN 'Just do it.' OCCURRENCE 2) = 'do'
SUBSTRING_REGEX ( '(do) (\p{L}*' IN 'Just do it.' GROUP 2) = 'it'
```

TRANSLATE_REGEX

TRANSLATE_REGEX searches a string for an XQuery regular expression pattern and returns the string with either one or every occurrence of the XQuery regular expression replaced by an XQuery replacement string.

According to the ISO/IEC international standard JTC 1/SC 32, the syntax of a regex transliteration is as follows:

```
TRANSLATE_REGEX <left paren>
<XQuery pattern> [ FLAG <XQuery option flag> ]
IN <regex subject string>
[ WITH <regex replacement string> ]
[ FROM <start position> ]
[ USING <char length units> ]
[ OCCURRENCE <regex transliteration occurrence> ] <right paren>
<regex transliteration occurrence> ::=
<regex occurrence>
| ALL
```

where:

» <regex replacement string> is a character string whose value is suitable for use as the $replacement argument of the [XQuery F&O] function fn:replace. Default is the zero-length string.

» <regex transliteration occurrence> is either the keyword ALL, or an exact numeric value with scale 0, indicating which occurrence of a match is desired (default is ALL).

Here are some examples with no replacement string:

```
TRANSLATE_REGEX ('i' IN 'Bill did sit.') = 'Bll dd st.'
TRANSLATE_REGEX ('i' IN 'Bill did sit.' OCCURRENCE ALL) = 'Bll dd st.'
TRANSLATE_REGEX ('i' IN 'Bill did sit.' FROM 5) = 'Bill dd st.'
TRANSLATE_REGEX ('i' IN 'Bill did sit.' Occurrence 2) = 'Bill dd sit.'
```

Here are a few examples with replacement strings:

```
TRANSLATE_REGEX ('i' IN 'Bill did sit.' WITH 'a') = 'Ball dad sat. '
TRANSLATE_REGEX ('i' IN 'Bill did sit.' WITH 'a' OCCURRENCE ALL)= 'Ball dad sat.'
TRANSLATE_REGEX ('i' IN 'Bill did sit.' WITH 'a' OCCURRENCE 2) = 'Bill dad sit.'
TRANSLATE_REGEX ('i' IN 'Bill did sit.' WITH 'a' FROM 5) = 'Bill dad sat.'
```

OVERLAY

OVERLAY replaces a given substring of a string (specified by a given numeric starting position and a given length) with a replacement string. When the length specified for the substring is zero, nothing is removed from the original string, but the replacement string is inserted into the original string, starting at the specified starting position.

UPPER

The UPPER value function converts a character string to all-uppercase characters, as in the examples shown in the following table.

This Statement	Returns
UPPER ('e. e. cummings')	'E. E. CUMMINGS'
UPPER ('Isaac Newton, Ph.D.')	'ISAAC NEWTON, PH.D.'

The UPPER function doesn't affect a string that's already in all-uppercase characters.

LOWER

The LOWER value function converts a character string to all-lowercase characters, as in the examples in the following table.

This Statement	Returns
LOWER ('TAXES')	'taxes'
LOWER ('E. E. Cummings')	'e. e. cummings'

The LOWER function doesn't affect a string that's already in all-lowercase characters.

TRIM

Use the TRIM function to trim off leading or trailing blanks (or other characters) from a character string. The following examples show how to use TRIM.

This Statement	Returns
TRIM (LEADING ' ' FROM ' treat ')	'treat '
TRIM (TRAILING ' ' FROM ' treat ')	' treat'
TRIM (BOTH ' ' FROM ' treat ')	'treat'
TRIM (BOTH 't' from 'treat')	'rea'

The default trim character is the blank, so the following syntax also is legal:

```
TRIM (BOTH FROM ' treat ')
```

This syntax gives you the same result as the third example in the table — 'treat'.

TRANSLATE AND CONVERT

The TRANSLATE and CONVERT functions take a source string in one character set and transform the original string into a string in another character set. Examples might be English to Kanji or Hebrew to French. The conversion functions that specify these transformations are implementation-specific. Consult the documentation of your implementation for details.

REMEMBER

If translating from one language to another were as easy as invoking an SQL TRANSLATE function, that would be great. Unfortunately, it's not that easy. All TRANSLATE does is translate a character in the first character set to the corresponding character in the second character set. The function can, for example, translate 'Ελλασ' to 'Ellas'. But it can't translate 'Ελλασ' to 'Greece'.

Numeric value functions

Numeric value functions can take a variety of data types as input, but the output is always a numeric value. SQL has 15 types of numeric value functions:

>> Position expression (POSITION)

>> Regex occurrences function (OCCURRENCES_REGEX)

>> Regex position expression (POSITION_REGEX)

>> Extract expression (EXTRACT)

>> Length expression (CHAR_LENGTH, CHARACTER_LENGTH, OCTET_LENGTH)

>> Cardinality expression (CARDINALITY)

>> Absolute value expression (ABS)

>> Modulus expression (MOD)

>> Natural logarithm (LN)

>> Exponential function (EXP)

>> Power function (POWER)

>> Square root (SQRT)

>> Floor function (FLOOR)

>> Ceiling function (CEIL, CEILING)

>> Width bucket function (WIDTH_BUCKET)

POSITION

POSITION searches for a specified target string within a specified source string and returns the character position where the target string begins. For a character string, the syntax looks like this:

```
POSITION (target IN source [USING char length units])
```

You can optionally specify a character length unit other than CHARACTER, but this is rare. If Unicode characters are in use, depending on the type, a character could be 8, 16, or 32 bits long. In cases where a character is 16 or 32 bits long, you can explicitly specify 8 bits with USING OCTETS.

For a binary string, the syntax looks like this:

```
POSITION (target IN source)
```

If the value of the target is equal to an identical-length substring of contiguous octets in the source string, then the result is one greater than the number of octets preceding the start of the first such substring.

The following table shows a few examples.

This Statement	Returns
POSITION ('B' IN 'Bread, whole wheat')	1
POSITION ('Bre' IN 'Bread, whole wheat')	1
POSITION ('wh' IN 'Bread, whole wheat')	8
POSITION ('whi' IN 'Bread, whole wheat')	0
POSITION ('' IN 'Bread, whole wheat')	1
POSITION ('01001001' IN '0011000101001001001000110'	2

For both character strings and binary strings, if the function doesn't find the target string, the POSITION function returns a zero value. Also for both string types, if the target string has zero length (as in the last character example), the POSITION function always returns a value of one. If any operand in the function has a null value, the result is a null value.

OCCURRENCES_REGEX

OCCURRENCES_REGEX is a numeric function that returns the number of matches for a regular expression in a string. The syntax is as follows:

```
OCCURRENCES_REGEX <left paren>
<XQuery pattern> [ FLAG <XQuery option flag> ]
IN <regex subject string>
[ FROM <start position> ]
[ USING <char length units> ] <right paren>
```

Here are some examples:

```
OCCURRENCES_REGEX ( 'i' IN 'Bill did sit.' ) = 3
OCCURRENCES_REGEX ( 'i' IN 'Bill did sit.' FROM 5) = 2
OCCURRENCES_REGEX ( 'I' IN 'Bill did sit.' ) = 0
```

POSITION_REGEX

POSITION_REGEX is a numeric function that returns the position of the start of a match, or one plus the end of a match, for a regular expression in a string. Here's the syntax:

```
POSITION_REGEX <left paren> [ <regex position start or after> ]
<XQuery pattern> [ FLAG <XQuery option flag> ]
IN <regex subject string>
[ FROM <start position> ]
[ USING <char length units> ]
[ OCCURRENCE <regex occurrence> ]
[ GROUP <regex capture group> ] <right paren>

<regex position start or after> ::= START | AFTER
```

Perhaps some examples would make this clearer:

```
POSITION_REGEX ( 'i' IN 'Bill did sit.' ) = 2
POSITION_REGEX ( START 'i' IN 'Bill did sit.' ) = 2
POSITION_REGEX ( AFTER 'i' IN 'Bill did sit.' ) = 3
POSITION_REGEX ( 'i' IN 'Bill did sit.' FROM 5) = 7
POSITION_REGEX ( 'i' IN 'Bill did sit.' OCCURRENCE 2 ) = 7
POSITION_REGEX ( 'I' IN 'Bill did sit.' ) = 0
```

EXTRACT

The EXTRACT function extracts a single field from a datetime or an interval. The following statement, for example, returns 08:

```
EXTRACT (MONTH FROM DATE '2013-08-20')
```

CHARACTER_LENGTH

The CHARACTER_LENGTH function returns the number of characters in a character string. The following statement, for example, returns 16:

```
CHARACTER_LENGTH ('Opossum, roasted')
```

REMEMBER

As I note in regard to the SUBSTRING function (in the "SUBSTRING" section, earlier in the chapter), this function is not particularly useful if its argument is a literal such as 'Opossum, roasted'. I can just as easily write 16 as I can CHARACTER_LENGTH ('Opossum, roasted'). In fact, writing 16 is easier. This function is more useful if its argument is an expression rather than a literal value.

OCTET_LENGTH

In music, a vocal ensemble made up of eight singers is called an *octet*. Typically, the parts that the ensemble represents are first and second soprano, first and second alto, first and second tenor, and first and second bass. In computer terminology, an ensemble of eight data bits is called a *byte*. The word *byte* is clever in that the term clearly relates to *bit* but implies something larger than a bit. A nice wordplay — but (unfortunately) nothing in the word *byte* conveys the concept of "eightness." By borrowing the musical term, a more apt description of a collection of eight bits becomes possible.

Practically all modern computers use eight bits to represent a single alphanumeric character. More complex character sets (such as Chinese) require 16 bits to represent a single character. The OCTET_LENGTH function counts and returns the number of octets (bytes) in a string. If the string is a bit string, OCTET_LENGTH returns the number of octets you need to hold that number of bits. If the string is an English-language character string (with one octet per character), the function returns the number of characters in the string. If the string is a Chinese character string, the function returns a number that is twice the number of Chinese characters. The following string is an example:

```
OCTET_LENGTH ('Beans, lima')
```

This function returns 11 because each character takes up one octet.

TECHNICAL STUFF

Some character sets use a variable number of octets for different characters. In particular, some character sets that support mixtures of Kanji and Latin characters use *escape* characters to switch between the two character sets. A string that contains both Latin and Kanji (for example) may have 30 characters and require 30 octets if all the characters are Latin; 62 characters if all the characters are Kanji (60 characters plus a leading and trailing shift character); and 150 characters if the characters alternate between Latin and Kanji (because each Kanji character needs two octets for the character and one octet each for the leading and trailing shift characters). The OCTET_LENGTH function returns the number of octets you need for the current value of the string.

CARDINALITY

Cardinality deals with collections of elements such as arrays or multisets, where each element is a value of some data type. The cardinality of the collection is the number of elements that it contains. One use of the CARDINALITY function might be this:

```
CARDINALITY (TeamRoster)
```

This function would return 12, for example, if there were 12 team members on the roster. TeamRoster, a column in the TEAMS table, can be either an array or a multiset. An *array* is an ordered collection of elements, and a *multiset* is an unordered collection of elements. For a team roster, which changes frequently, multiset makes more sense.

ARRAY_MAX_CARDINALITY

The CARDINALITY function returns the number of elements in the array or multiset that you specify. What it does not tell you is the maximum cardinality that was assigned to that array. There are occasions when you might want to know that.

As a result, SQL:2011 added a new function ARRAY_MAX_CARDINALITY. As you might guess, it returns the maximum cardinality of the array that you specify. There is no declared maximum cardinality for a multiset.

TRIM_ARRAY

Whereas the TRIM function trims off the first or last character in a string, the TRIM_ARRAY function trims off the last elements of an array.

To trim off the last three elements of the TeamRoster array, use the following syntax:

```
TRIM_ARRAY (TeamRoster, 3)
```

ABS

The ABS function returns the absolute value of a numeric value expression.

```
ABS (-273)
```

In this case, the function returns 273.

MOD

The MOD function returns the *modulus* of two numeric value expressions.

```
MOD (3,2)
```

In this case, the function returns 1, the modulus of three divided by two.

SIN

The SIN function returns the sine of a numeric value expression.

```
SIN (numeric value expression)
```

COS

The COS function returns the cosine of a numeric value expression.

```
COS (numeric value expression)
```

TAN

The TAN function returns the tangent of a numeric value expression.

```
TAN (numeric value expression)
```

ASIN

The ASIN function returns the arcsine of a numeric value expression.

```
ASIN (numeric value expression)
```

ACOS

The ACOS function returns the arccosine of a numeric value expression.

```
ACOS (numeric value expression)
```

ATAN

The ATAN function returns the arctangent of a numeric value expression.

```
ATAN (numeric value expression)
```

SINH

The SINH function returns the hyperbolic sine of a numeric value expression.

```
SINH (numeric value expression)
```

COSH

The COSH function returns the hyperbolic cosine of a numeric value expression.

```
COSH (numeric value expression)
```

TANH

The TANH function returns the hyperbolic tangent of a numeric value expression.

```
TANH (numeric value expression)
```

LOG

The LOG function returns the logarithm to a specified base of a numeric value expression.

```
LOG (base, numeric value expression)
```

LOG10

The LOG10 function returns the base-ten logarithm of a numeric value expression.

```
Log10 (numeric value expression)
```

LN

The LN function returns the natural logarithm of a numeric value expression.

```
LN (numeric value expression)
```

For LN (9), this function returns something like 2.197224577. The number of digits beyond the decimal point depends on the SQL implementation.

EXP

The EXP function raises the base of the natural logarithms *e* to the power specified by a numeric value expression.

```
EXP (2)
```

Here the function returns something like 7.389056. The number of digits beyond the decimal point depends on the SQL implementation.

POWER

The POWER function raises the value of the first numeric value expression to the power of the second numeric value expression.

```
POWER (2,8)
```

Here this function returns 256, which is 2 raised to the eighth power.

SQRT

The SQRT function returns the square root of the value of the numeric value expression.

```
SQRT (4)
```

In this case, the function returns 2, the square root of 4.

FLOOR

The FLOOR function truncates the numeric value expression to the largest integer not greater than the expression.

```
FLOOR (3.141592)
```

This function returns 3.

CEIL OR CEILING

The CEIL or CEILING function augments the numeric value expression to the smallest integer not less than the expression.

```
CEIL (3.141592)
```

This function returns 4.

WIDTH_BUCKET

The WIDTH_BUCKET function, used in *online application processing* (OLAP), is a function of four arguments, returning an integer between 0 (zero) and the value of the fourth argument plus 1 (one). It assigns the first argument to an *equiwidth partitioning* of the range of numbers between the second and third arguments. Values outside this range are assigned to either 0 (zero) or the value of the fourth argument plus 1 (one).

For example:

```
WIDTH_BUCKET (PI, 0, 10, 5)
```

Suppose PI is a numeric value expression with a value of 3.141592. The example partitions the interval from zero to 9.999999 . . . into five equal *buckets,* each with a width of two. The function returns a value of 2, because 3.141592 falls into the second bucket, which covers the range from 2 to 3.999999.

Datetime value functions

SQL includes three functions that return information about the current date, current time, or both. CURRENT_DATE returns the current date; CURRENT_TIME returns the current time; and CURRENT_TIMESTAMP returns (surprise!) both the current date and the current time. CURRENT_DATE doesn't take an argument, but CURRENT_TIME and CURRENT_TIMESTAMP both take a single argument. The argument specifies the precision for the "seconds" part of the time value that the function returns. (Datetime data types and the precision concept are described in Chapter 2.)

The following table offers some examples of these datetime value functions.

This Statement	Returns
CURRENT_DATE	2017–12–31
CURRENT_TIME (1)	08:36:57.3
CURRENT_TIMESTAMP (2)	2017–12–31 08:36:57.38

The date that CURRENT_DATE returns is DATE type data. The time that CURRENT_TIME (p) returns is TIME type data, and the timestamp that CURRENT_TIMESTAMP(p) returns is TIMESTAMP type data. Because SQL retrieves date and time information from your computer's system clock, the information is correct for the time zone in which the computer resides.

In some applications, you may want to take advantage of functions that operate on character-type data; to do so, you convert dates, times, or timestamps to character strings. You can perform such a type conversion by using the CAST expression, which I describe in Chapter 9.

Interval value functions

An interval value function named ABS was introduced in SQL:1999. It's similar to the ABS numeric value function, but operates on interval-type data rather than numeric-type data. ABS takes a single operand and returns an interval of the identical precision that is guaranteed not to have a negative value. Here's an example:

```
ABS ( TIME '11:31:00' - TIME '12:31:00' )
```

The result is

```
INTERVAL +'1:00:00' HOUR TO SECOND
```

Table functions

Table functions return entire tables rather than just values. There are two types of table functions: ordinary table functions, and as of SQL:2016, polymorphic table functions.

Ordinary table functions

An ordinary table function takes one or more tables as input, operates on them in some manner, and then outputs a result table. These functions must specify the names and types of the columns they return (the row-type) at the time of creation.

Polymorphic table functions

A polymorphic table function (PTF) returns a table whose row type is *not* declared when the function is created. The row type may depend on the arguments in the invocation of the PTF. A PTF may have generic table parameters, meaning that no row type is declared when the PTF is created. Furthermore, the row type of the result may depend on the row types of the input tables. At the time of this writing, polymorphic table functions are not yet fully supported by any popular DBMS.

Chapter **9**

Using Advanced SQL Value Expressions

SQL is described in Chapter 2 as a *data sublanguage.* In fact, the sole function of SQL is to operate on data in a database. SQL lacks many of the features of a conventional procedural language. As a result, developers who use SQL must switch back and forth between SQL and its host language to control the flow of execution. This repeated switching complicates matters at development time and negatively affects performance at run time.

The performance penalty exacted by SQL's limitations prompts the addition of new features to SQL every time a new version of the international specification is released. One of those added features, the CASE expression, provides a long-sought conditional structure. A second feature, the CAST expression, facilitates data conversion in a table from one type of data to another. A third feature, the row value expression, enables you to operate on a list of values where previously you could operate only on a single value. For example, if your list of values is a list of columns in a table, you can now perform an operation on all those columns by using a very simple syntax.

CASE Conditional Expressions

Every complete computer language has some sort of conditional statement or command. In fact, most have several. Probably the most common conditional statement or command is the IF...THEN...ELSE...ENDIF structure. If the condition following the IF keyword evaluates to True, the block of commands following the THEN keyword executes. If the condition doesn't evaluate to True, the block of commands after the ELSE keyword executes. The ENDIF keyword signals the end of the structure. This structure is great for any decision that goes one of two ways. The structure doesn't work as well for decisions that can have more than two possible outcomes.

REMEMBER

Most complete languages have a CASE statement that handles situations in which you may want to perform more than two tasks based on more than two possible values of a condition.

SQL has a CASE statement and a CASE *expression.* A CASE expression is only part of a statement — not a statement in its own right. In SQL, you can place a CASE expression almost anywhere a value is legal. At run time, a CASE expression evaluates to a value. SQL's CASE *statement* doesn't evaluate to a value; rather, it causes a block of statements to be executed.

The CASE expression searches a table, one row at a time, taking on the value of a specified result whenever one of a list of conditions is True. If the first condition is not satisfied for a row, the second condition is tested — and if it is True, the result specified for it is given to the expression, and so on until all conditions are processed. If no match is found, the expression takes on a NULL value. Processing then moves to the next row.

You can use the CASE expression in the following two ways:

>> **Use the expression with search conditions.** CASE searches for rows in a table where specified conditions are True. If CASE finds a search condition to be True for a table row, the statement containing the CASE expression makes a specified change to that row.

>> **Use the expression to compare a table field to a specified value.** The outcome of the statement containing the CASE expression depends on which of several specified values in the table field is equal to each table row.

The next two sections, "Using CASE with search conditions" and "Using CASE with values," help clarify these concepts. In the first section, two examples use CASE with search conditions. One example searches a table and makes changes to table values, based on a condition. The second section explores two examples of the value form of CASE.

Using CASE with search conditions

One powerful way to use the CASE expression is to search a table for rows in which a specified search condition is True. If you use CASE this way, the expression uses the following syntax:

```
CASE
    WHEN condition1 THEN result1
    WHEN condition2 THEN result2
    ...
    WHEN conditionn THEN resultn
    ELSE resultx
END
```

CASE examines the first *qualifying row* (the first row that meets the conditions of the enclosing WHERE clause, if any) to see whether condition1 is True. If it is, the CASE expression receives a value of result1. If condition1 is not True, CASE evaluates the row for condition2. If condition2 is True, the CASE expression receives the value of result2, and so on. If none of the stated conditions are True, the CASE expression receives the value of resultx. The ELSE clause is optional. If the expression has no ELSE clause and none of the specified conditions are True, the expression receives a null value. After the SQL statement containing the CASE expression applies itself to the first qualifying row in a table and takes the appropriate action, it processes the next row. This sequence continues until the SQL statement finishes processing the entire table.

Updating values based on a condition

Because you can embed a CASE expression within an SQL statement almost anywhere a value is possible, this expression gives you tremendous flexibility. You can use CASE within an UPDATE statement, for example, to make changes to table values — based on certain conditions. Consider the following example:

```
UPDATE FOODS
    SET RATING = CASE
                    WHEN FAT < 1
                        THEN 'very low fat'
                    WHEN FAT < 5
                        THEN 'low fat'
                    WHEN FAT < 20
                        THEN 'moderate fat'
                    WHEN FAT < 50
                        THEN 'high fat'
                    ELSE 'heart attack city'
                END ;
```

This statement evaluates the WHEN conditions in order until the first True value is returned, after which the statement ignores the rest of the conditions.

Table 8-2 in Chapter 8 shows the fat content of 100 grams of certain foods. A database table holding this information can contain a RATING column that gives a quick assessment of the fat content's meaning. If you run the preceding UPDATE on the FOODS table in Chapter 8, the statement assigns asparagus a value of very low fat, gives chicken a value of low fat, and puts butter in the heart attack city category.

Avoiding conditions that cause errors

Another valuable use of CASE is *exception avoidance* — checking for conditions that cause errors.

Consider a case that determines compensation for salespeople. Companies that compensate their salespeople by straight commission often pay their new employees by giving them a *draw* against the future commissions they're expected to earn. In the following example, new salespeople receive a draw against commission; the draw is phased out gradually as their commissions rise:

```
UPDATE SALES_COMP
    SET COMP = COMMISSION + CASE
                        WHEN COMMISSION > DRAW
                            THEN 0
                        WHEN COMMISSION < DRAW
                            THEN DRAW
                    END ;
```

If the salesperson's commission is zero, the structure in this example avoids a division-by-zero operation, which would cause an error if allowed to happen. If the salesperson has a nonzero commission, the total compensation is the commission plus a draw that's reduced in proportion to the size of the commission.

All the THEN expressions in a CASE expression must be of the same type — all numeric, all character, or all date. The result of the CASE expression is also of the same type.

Using CASE with values

You can use a more compact form of the CASE expression if you're comparing a test value for equality with a series of other values. This form is useful within a SELECT or UPDATE statement if a table contains a limited number of values in a column and you want to associate a corresponding result value to each of those column values. If you use CASE in this way, the expression has the following syntax:

```
CASE test_value
    WHEN value1 THEN result1
    WHEN value2 THEN result2
    ...
    WHEN valuen THEN resultn
    ELSE resultx
END
```

If the test value (test_value) is equal to value1, then the expression takes on the value result1. If test_value is not equal to value1 but is equal to value2, then the expression takes on the value result2. The expression tries each comparison value in turn, all the way down to valuen, until it achieves a match. If none of the comparison values equal the test value, then the expression takes on the value resultx. Again, if the optional ELSE clause isn't present and none of the comparison values match the test value, the expression receives a null value.

To understand how the value form works, consider a case in which you have a table containing the names and ranks of various military officers. You want to list the names preceded by the correct abbreviation for each rank. The following statement does the job:

```
SELECT CASE RANK
            WHEN 'general'           THEN 'Gen.'
            WHEN 'colonel'           THEN 'Col.'
            WHEN 'lieutenant colonel' THEN 'Lt. Col.'
            WHEN 'major'             THEN 'Maj.'
            WHEN 'captain'           THEN 'Capt.'
            WHEN 'first lieutenant'  THEN '1st. Lt.'
            WHEN 'second lieutenant' THEN '2nd. Lt.'
            ELSE NULL
        END,
        LAST_NAME
    FROM OFFICERS ;
```

The result is a list similar to the following example:

```
Capt. Midnight
Col.  Sanders
Gen.  Washington
Maj.  Disaster
      Nimitz
```

Chester Nimitz was an admiral in the United States Navy during World War II. Because his rank isn't listed in the CASE expression, the ELSE clause doesn't give him a title.

For another example, suppose Captain Midnight gets a promotion to major and you want to update the OFFICERS database accordingly. Assume that the variable officer_last_name contains the value 'Midnight' and that the variable new_rank contains an integer (4) that corresponds to Midnight's new rank, according to the following table.

new_rank	Rank
1	general
2	colonel
3	lieutenant colonel
4	major
5	captain
6	first lieutenant
7	second lieutenant
8	NULL

You can record the promotion by using the following SQL code:

```
UPDATE OFFICERS
    SET RANK = CASE :new_rank
                    WHEN 1 THEN 'general'
                    WHEN 2 THEN 'colonel'
                    WHEN 3 THEN 'lieutenant colonel'
                    WHEN 4 THEN 'major'
                    WHEN 5 THEN 'captain'
                    WHEN 6 THEN 'first lieutenant'
                    WHEN 7 THEN 'second lieutenant'
                    WHEN 8 THEN NULL
                END
    WHERE LAST_NAME = :officer_last_name ;
```

An alternative syntax for the CASE expression with values is:

```
CASE
    WHEN test_value = value1 THEN result1
    WHEN test_value = value2 THEN result2
    ...
```

```
      WHEN test_value = valuen THEN resultn
      ELSE resultx
END
```

A special CASE — NULLIF

The one thing you can be sure of in this world is change. Sometimes things change from one known state to another. Other times, you think you know something but later you find out you didn't know it after all. Classical thermodynamics and modern chaos theory both tell us that systems naturally migrate from a well-known, ordered state into a disordered state that no one can predict. Anyone who has ever monitored the status of a teenager's room for a one-week period after the room is cleaned can vouch for the accuracy of these theories.

Database tables have definite values in fields containing known contents. Usually, if the value of a field is unknown, the field contains the null value. In SQL, you can use a CASE expression to change the contents of a table field from a definite value to a null value. The null value indicates that you no longer know the field's value. Consider the following example.

Imagine that you own a small airline that offers flights between Southern California and Washington state. Until recently, some of your flights stopped at San Jose International Airport to refuel before continuing. Unfortunately, you just lost your right to fly into San Jose. From now on, you must make your refueling stop at either San Francisco International Airport or Oakland International Airport. At this point, you don't know which flights stop at which airport, but you do know that none of the flights are stopping at San Jose. You have a FLIGHT database that contains important information about your routes, and now you want to update the database to remove all references to San Jose. The following example shows one way to do this:

```
UPDATE FLIGHT
    SET RefuelStop = CASE
                          WHEN RefuelStop = 'San Jose'
                          THEN NULL
                          ELSE RefuelStop
                     END ;
```

TIP

Because occasions like this one — in which you want to replace a known value with a null value — frequently arise, SQL offers a shorthand notation to accomplish this task. The preceding example, expressed in this shorthand form, looks like this:

```
UPDATE FLIGHT
    SET RefuelStop = NULLIF(RefuelStop, 'San Jose') ;
```

You can translate this expression to English as, "Update the FLIGHT table by setting the RefuelStop column to null if the existing value of RefuelStop is 'San Jose'. Otherwise make no change."

NULLIF is even handier if you're converting data that you originally accumulated for use with a program written in a standard programming language such as C++ or Java. Standard programming languages don't have nulls, so a common practice is to use special values to represent the concept of "not known" or "not applicable". A numeric –1 may represent a not-known value for SALARY, for example, and a character string "∗∗∗" may represent a not-known or not-applicable value for JOBCODE. If you want to represent these not-known and not-applicable states in an SQL-compatible database by using nulls, you must convert the special values to nulls. The following example makes this conversion for an employee table, in which some salary values are unknown:

```
UPDATE EMP
   SET Salary = CASE Salary
                   WHEN -1 THEN NULL
                   ELSE Salary
                END ;
```

You can perform this conversion more conveniently by using NULLIF, as follows:

```
UPDATE EMP
   SET Salary = NULLIF(Salary, -1) ;
```

Another special CASE — COALESCE

COALESCE, like NULLIF, is a shorthand form of a particular CASE expression. COALESCE deals with a list of values that may or may not be null. Here's how it works:

>> **If one of the values in the list is not null:** The COALESCE expression takes on that value.

>> **If more than one value in the list is not null:** The expression takes on the value of the first non-null item in the list.

>> **If all the values in the list are null:** The expression takes on the null value.

A CASE expression with this function has the following form:

```
CASE
   WHEN value1 IS NOT NULL
      THEN value1
```

```
    WHEN value2 IS NOT NULL
       THEN value2
    ...
    WHEN valuen IS NOT NULL
       THEN valuen
    ELSE NULL
END
```

The corresponding COALESCE shorthand looks like this:

```
COALESCE(value1, value2, ..., valuen)
```

You may want to use a COALESCE expression after you perform an OUTER JOIN operation (discussed in Chapter 11). In such cases, COALESCE can save you a lot of typing.

CAST Data-Type Conversions

Chapter 2 covers the data types that SQL recognizes and supports. Ideally, each column in a database table has a perfect choice of data type. In this non-ideal world, however, exactly what that perfect choice may be isn't always clear. In defining a database table, suppose you assign a data type to a column that works perfectly for your current application. Suppose that later on you want to expand your application's scope — or write an entirely new application that uses the data differently. This new use could require a data type different from the one you originally chose.

You may want to compare a column of one type in one table with a column of a different type in a different table. For example, you could have dates stored as character data in one table and as date data in another table. Even if both columns contain the same sort of information (dates, for example), the fact that the types are different may prevent you from making the comparison. In the earliest SQL standards, SQL-86 and SQL-89, type incompatibility posed a big problem. SQL-92, however, introduced an easy-to-use solution in the CAST expression.

The CAST expression converts table data or host variables of one type to another type. After you make the conversion, you can proceed with the operation or analysis that you originally envisioned.

REMEMBER

Naturally, you face some restrictions when using the CAST expression. You can't just indiscriminately convert data of any type into any other type. The data that you're converting must be compatible with the new data type. You can, for example, use CAST to convert the CHAR(10) character string '201 7-04-26' to the DATE type. But you can't use CAST to convert the CHAR(10) character string 'rhinoceros' to the DATE type. You can't convert an INTEGER to the SMALLINT type if the former exceeds the maximum size of a SMALLINT.

You can convert an item of any character type to any other type (such as numeric or date) provided the item's value has the form of a literal of the new type. Conversely, you can convert an item of any type to any of the character types, provided the value of the item has the form of a literal of the original type.

The following list describes some additional conversions you can make:

>> Any numeric type to any other numeric type. If converting to a less fractionally precise type, the system rounds or truncates the result.

>> Any exact numeric type to a single component interval, such as INTERVAL DAY or INTERVAL SECOND.

>> Any DATE to a TIMESTAMP. The time part of the TIMESTAMP fills in with zeros.

>> Any TIME to a TIME with a different fractional-seconds precision or a TIMESTAMP. The date part of the TIMESTAMP fills in with the current date.

>> Any TIMESTAMP to a DATE, a TIME, or a TIMESTAMP with a different fractional-seconds precision.

>> Any year-month INTERVAL to an exact numeric type or another year-month INTERVAL with different leading-field precision.

>> Any day-time INTERVAL to an exact numeric type or another day-time INTERVAL with different leading-field precision.

One of the conversions that comes up quite often is the conversion from a datetime to a character string type, or the inverse, converting a character string to a datetime type. Amazingly enough, the SQL standard did not specify how to do this until SQL:2016. By that time, all the implementations had come up with their own way of doing it. As a consequence, at the time of this writing, none of the popular implementations complies completely with the standard syntax.

The template placeholders specified in Chapter 7 in the section on formatting and parsing dates and times give the elements that can be combined into a format template such as 'YYYY-MM-DD' for Year-Month-Day.

To convert a datetime to the character string type, use the following:

```
CAST (<datetime> AS <character string type> [FORMAT<template>])
```

An example of this might be:

```
CAST ('1969-07-20' AS CHAR)
```

This would not change the order of the components of the date, but would change its type.

Alternatively,

```
CAST ('1969-07-20' AS CHAR FORMAT 'MM-DD-YYYY')
```

would change both the order of the components and the type.

To convert a character string to the datetime type, the following syntax complies with SQL:2016:

```
CAST('1969-07-20' AS DATE FORMAT '07-20-1969')
```

This converts the string to a date and puts it into the data format most commonly used in the USA.

Using CAST within SQL

Suppose you work for a company that keeps track of prospective employees as well as the employees you've actually hired. You list the prospective employees in a table named PROSPECT, and you distinguish them by their Social Security numbers, which you happen to store as a CHAR(9) type. You list the employees in a table named EMPLOYEE, and you distinguish them by their Social Security numbers, which are of the INTEGER type. You now want to generate a list of all people who appear in both tables. You can use CAST to perform the task:

```
SELECT * FROM EMPLOYEE
   WHERE EMPLOYEE.SSN =
      CAST(PROSPECT.SSN AS INTEGER) ;
```

Using CAST between SQL and the host language

The key use of CAST is to deal with data types that are available in SQL but not in the host language that you use. The following list offers some examples of these data types:

>> SQL has DECIMAL and NUMERIC, but FORTRAN and Pascal don't.

>> SQL has FLOAT and REAL, but standard COBOL doesn't.

>> SQL has DATETIME, which no other language has.

Suppose you want to use FORTRAN or Pascal to access tables with DECIMAL(5,3) columns, and you don't want any inaccuracies to result from converting those values to the REAL data type used by FORTRAN and Pascal. You can perform this task by using CAST to move the data to and from character-string host variables. You retrieve a numeric salary of 198.37 as a CHAR(10) value of '0000198.37'. Then, if you want to update that salary to 203.74, you can place that value in a CHAR(10) as '0000203.74'. First you use CAST to change the SQL DECIMAL(5,3) data type to the CHAR(10) type for the employee whose ID number you're storing in the host variable :emp_id_var, as follows:

```
SELECT CAST(Salary AS CHAR(10)) INTO :salary_var
       FROM EMP
       WHERE EmpID = :emp_id_var ;
```

The FORTRAN or Pascal application examines the resulting character-string value in :salary_var, possibly sets the string to a new value of '000203.74', and then updates the database by calling the following SQL code:

```
UPDATE EMP
   SET Salary = CAST(:salary_var AS DECIMAL(5,3))
      WHERE EmpID = :emp_id_var ;
```

Dealing with character-string values such as '000198.37' is awkward in FORTRAN or Pascal, but you can write a set of subroutines to do the necessary manipulations. You can then retrieve and update any SQL data from any host language, getting — and then setting — exact values.

The general idea is that CAST is most valuable for converting between host types and the database rather than for converting within the database.

Row Value Expressions

In the original SQL standards, SQL-86 and SQL-89, most operations dealt with a single value or a single column in a table row. To operate on multiple values, you had to build complex expressions by using logical *connectives* (which I discuss in Chapter 10).

SQL-92 introduced *row value expressions*, which operate on a list of values or columns rather than on a single value or column. A row value expression is a list of value expressions that you enclose in parentheses and separate by commas. You can code these expressions to operate on an entire row at once or on a selected subset of the row.

Chapter 6 covers how to use the INSERT statement to add a new row to an existing table. To do so, the statement uses a row value expression. Consider the following example:

```
INSERT INTO FOODS
    (FOODNAME, CALORIES, PROTEIN, FAT, CARBOHYDRATE)
    VALUES
    ('Cheese, cheddar', 398, 25, 32.2, 2.1) ;
```

In this example, ('Cheese, cheddar', 398, 25, 32.2, 2.1) is a row value expression. If you use a row value expression in an INSERT statement this way, it can contain null and default values. (A *default value* is the value that a table column assumes if you specify no other value.) The following line, for example, is a legal row value expression:

```
('Cheese, cheddar', 398, NULL, 32.2, DEFAULT)
```

You can add multiple rows to a table by putting multiple row value expressions in the VALUES clause, as follows:

```
INSERT INTO FOODS
    (FOODNAME, CALORIES, PROTEIN, FAT, CARBOHYDRATE)
    VALUES
    ('Lettuce', 14, 1.2, 0.2, 2.5),
    ('Butter', 720, 0.6, 81.0, 0.4),
    ('Mustard', 75, 4.7, 4.4, 6.4),
    ('Spaghetti', 148, 5.0, 0.5, 30.1) ;
```

You can use row value expressions to save yourself from having to enter comparisons manually. Suppose you have two tables of nutritional values, one compiled in English and the other in Spanish. You want to find those rows in the English language table that correspond exactly to the rows in the Spanish language table. Without a row value expression, you may need to formulate something like the following example:

```
SELECT * FROM FOODS
    WHERE FOODS.CALORIES = COMIDA.CALORIA
        AND FOODS.PROTEIN = COMIDA.PROTEINAS
        AND FOODS.FAT = COMIDA.GRASAS
        AND FOODS.CARBOHYDRATE = COMIDA.CARBOHIDRATO ;
```

Row value expressions enable you to code the same logic, as follows:

```
SELECT * FROM FOODS
    WHERE (FOODS.CALORIES, FOODS.PROTEIN, FOODS.FAT,
        FOODS.CARBOHYDRATE)
    =
        (COMIDA.CALORIA, COMIDA.PROTEINAS, COMIDA.GRASAS,
        COMIDA.CARBOHIDRATO) ;
```

TIP

In this example, you don't save much typing. You would benefit slightly more if you were comparing more columns. In cases of marginal benefit like this example, you may be better off sticking with the older syntax because its meaning is clearer.

You gain one benefit by using a row value expression instead of its coded equivalent — the row value expression is processed much faster. In principle, a clever implementation can analyze the coded version and implement it as the row value version. In practice, this operation is a difficult optimization that no DBMS that I am aware of can perform.

Chapter **10**

Zeroing In on the Data You Want

database management system has two main functions: storing data and providing easy access to that data. Storing data is nothing special; a file cabinet can perform that chore. The hard part of data management is providing easy access. For data to be useful, you must be able to separate the (usually) small amount you want from the huge amount you don't want.

SQL enables you to use some characteristics of the data to determine whether a specific table row is of interest to you. The SELECT, DELETE, and UPDATE statements convey to the database *engine* (the part of the DBMS that interacts directly with the data), which rows to select, delete, or update. You add modifying clauses to the SELECT, DELETE, and UPDATE statements to refine the search to your specifications.

Modifying Clauses

The modifying clauses available in SQL are FROM, WHERE, GROUP BY, HAVING, and ORDER BY. The FROM clause tells the database engine which table or tables to operate on. The WHERE and HAVING clauses specify a data characteristic that determines whether to include a specific row in the current operation. The GROUP BY and ORDER BY clauses specify how to display the retrieved rows. Table 10-1 provides a summary.

TABLE 10-1   **Modifying Clauses and Functions**

Modifying Clause	Function
FROM	Specifies from which tables data should be taken
WHERE	Filters out rows that don't satisfy the search condition
GROUP BY	Separates rows into groups based on the values in the grouping columns
HAVING	Filters out groups that don't satisfy the search condition
ORDER BY	Sorts the results of prior clauses to produce final output

REMEMBER

If you use more than one of these clauses, they must appear in the following order:

```
SELECT column_list
    FROM table_list
    [WHERE search_condition]
    [GROUP BY grouping_column]
    [HAVING search_condition]
    [ORDER BY ordering_condition] ;
```

Here's the lowdown on the execution of these clauses:

>> The WHERE clause is a filter that passes the rows that meet the search condition and rejects rows that don't meet the condition.

>> The GROUP BY clause rearranges the rows that the WHERE clause passes according to the value of the grouping column.

>> The HAVING clause is another filter that takes each group that the GROUP BY clause forms and passes those groups that meet the search condition, rejecting the rest.

>> The ORDER BY clause sorts whatever remains after all the preceding clauses process the table.

TIP

As the square brackets ([ ]) indicate, the WHERE, GROUP BY, HAVING, and ORDER BY clauses are optional.

SQL evaluates these clauses in the order FROM, WHERE, GROUP BY, HAVING, and finally SELECT. The clauses operate like a pipeline — each clause receives the result of the prior clause and produces an output that the next clause takes as input. In functional notation, this order of evaluation appears as follows:

```
SELECT(HAVING(GROUP BY(WHERE(FROM...)))))
```

ORDER BY operates after SELECT, which explains why ORDER BY can only reference columns in the SELECT list. ORDER BY can't reference other columns in the FROM table(s).

FROM Clauses

The FROM clause is easy to understand if you specify only one table, as in the following example:

```
SELECT * FROM SALES ;
```

This statement returns all the data in all the rows of every column in the SALES table. You can, however, specify more than one table in a FROM clause. Consider the following example:

```
SELECT *
    FROM CUSTOMER, SALES ;
```

This statement forms a virtual table that combines the data from the CUSTOMER table with the data from the SALES table. (For more about virtual tables, see Chapter 6.) Each row in the CUSTOMER table combines with every row in the SALES table to form the new table. The new virtual table that this combination forms contains the number of rows in the CUSTOMER table multiplied by the number of rows in the SALES table. If the CUSTOMER table has 10 rows and the SALES table has 100, then the new virtual table has 1,000 rows.

TIP

This operation is called the *Cartesian product* of the two source tables. The Cartesian product is a type of JOIN. (I cover JOIN operations in detail in Chapter 11.)

In most applications, when you take the Cartesian product of two tables, most of the rows that are formed in the new virtual table are meaningless. That's also true of the virtual table that forms from the CUSTOMER and SALES tables; only the rows where the CustomerID from the CUSTOMER table matches the CustomerID from the SALES table are of interest. You can filter out the rest of the rows by using a WHERE clause.

WHERE Clauses

I use the WHERE clause many times throughout this book without really explaining it because its meaning and use are obvious: A statement performs an operation (such as SELECT, DELETE, or UPDATE) only on table rows WHERE a stated condition is True. The syntax of the WHERE clause is as follows:

```
SELECT column_list
    FROM table_name
    WHERE condition ;

DELETE FROM table_name
    WHERE condition ;

UPDATE table_name
    SET column_1=value_1, column_2=value_2, ..., column_n=value_n
    WHERE condition ;
```

The condition in the WHERE clause may be simple or arbitrarily complex. You may join multiple conditions together by using the logical connectives AND, OR, and NOT (which I discuss later in this chapter) to create a single condition.

The following are some typical examples of WHERE clauses:

```
WHERE CUSTOMER.CustomerID = SALES.CustomerID
WHERE FOODS.Calories = COMIDA.Caloria
WHERE FOODS.Calories < 219
WHERE FOODS.Calories > 3 * base_value
WHERE FOODS.Calories < 219 AND FOODS.Protein > 27.4
```

The conditions that these WHERE clauses express are known as predicates. A *predicate* is an expression that asserts a fact about values.

The predicate FOODS.Calories < 219, for example, is True if the value for the current row of the column FOODS.Calories is less than 219. If the assertion is True, it satisfies the condition. An assertion may be True, False, or unknown. The unknown case arises if one or more elements in the assertion are null. The *comparison predicates* (=, ‹, ›, ‹›, ‹=, and ›=) are the most common, but SQL offers several others that greatly increase your capability to filter out a desired data item from others in the same column. These predicates give you that filtering capability:

>> Comparison predicates

>> BETWEEN

>> IN [NOT IN]

>> LIKE [NOT LIKE]

>> NULL

>> ALL, SOME, ANY

>> EXISTS

>> UNIQUE

>> OVERLAPS

>> MATCH

>> SIMILAR

>> DISTINCT

Comparison predicates

The examples in the preceding section show typical uses of comparison predicates in which you compare one value with another. For every row in which the comparison evaluates to a True value, that value satisfies the WHERE clause, and the operation (SELECT, UPDATE, DELETE, or whatever) executes upon that row. Rows that the comparison evaluates to FALSE are skipped. Consider the following SQL statement:

```
SELECT * FROM FOODS
    WHERE Calories <219 ;
```

This statement displays all rows from the FOODS table that have a value of less than 219 in the Calories column.

Six comparison predicates are listed in Table 10-2.

TABLE 10-2

SQL's Comparison Predicates

Comparison	Symbol
Equal	=
Not equal	<>
Less than	<
Less than or equal	<=
Greater than	>
Greater than or equal	>=

BETWEEN

Sometimes you want to select a row if the value in a column falls within a specified range. One way to make this selection is by using comparison predicates. For example, you can formulate a WHERE clause to select all the rows in the FOODS table that have a value in the Calories column greater than 100 and less than 300, as follows:

```
WHERE FOODS.Calories > 100 AND FOODS.Calories < 300
```

This comparison doesn't include foods with a calorie count of exactly 100 or 300. To include the end points (in this case, 100 and 300), you can write the statement as follows:

```
WHERE FOODS.Calories >= 100 AND FOODS.Calories <= 300
```

Another way of specifying a range that includes the end points is to use a BETWEEN predicate in the following manner:

```
WHERE FOODS.Calories BETWEEN 100 AND 300
```

TIP

This clause is functionally identical to the preceding example, which uses comparison predicates. This formulation saves some typing — and it's a little more intuitive than the one that uses two comparison predicates joined by the logical connective AND.

WARNING

The BETWEEN keyword may be confusing because it doesn't tell you *explicitly* whether the clause includes the end points. In fact, the clause *does* include these end points. When you use the BETWEEN keyword, a little birdy doesn't swoop down to remind you that the first term in the comparison must be equal to or less than the second. If, for example, FOODS.Calories contains a value of 200, the following clause returns a True value:

```
WHERE FOODS.Calories BETWEEN 100 AND 300
```

However, a clause that you may think is equivalent to the preceding example returns the opposite result, False:

```
WHERE FOODS.Calories BETWEEN 300 AND 100
```

If you use BETWEEN, you must be able to guarantee that the first term in your comparison is always equal to or less than the second term.

You can use the BETWEEN predicate with character, bit, and datetime data types as well as with the numeric types. You may see something like the following example:

```
SELECT FirstName, LastName
    FROM CUSTOMER
    WHERE CUSTOMER.LastName BETWEEN 'A' AND 'Mzzz' ;
```

This example returns all customers whose last names are in the first half of the alphabet.

IN and NOT IN

The IN and NOT IN predicates deal with whether specified values (such as OR, WA, and ID) are contained within a set of values (such as the states of the United States). You may, for example, have a table that lists suppliers of a commodity that your company purchases on a regular basis. You want to know the phone numbers of the suppliers located in the Pacific Northwest. You can find these numbers by using comparison predicates, such as those shown in the following example:

```
SELECT Company, Phone
    FROM SUPPLIER
    WHERE State = 'OR' OR State = 'WA' OR State = 'ID' ;
```

You can also use the IN predicate to perform the same task, as follows:

```
SELECT Company, Phone
    FROM SUPPLIER
    WHERE State IN ('OR', 'WA', 'ID') ;
```

This formulation is a bit more compact than the one using comparison predicates and logical OR. It also eliminates any possible confusion between the logical OR operator and the abbreviation for the state of Oregon.

The NOT IN version of this predicate works the same way. Say that you have locations in California, Arizona, and New Mexico, and to avoid paying sales tax, you want to consider using suppliers located anywhere except in those states. Use the following construction:

```
SELECT Company, Phone
    FROM SUPPLIER
    WHERE State NOT IN ('CA', 'AZ', 'NM') ;
```

Using the IN keyword this way saves you a little typing — though (frankly) that isn't much of an advantage. You can do the same job by using comparison predicates as shown in this section's first example.

TIP

You may have another good reason to use the IN predicate rather than comparison predicates, even if using IN doesn't save much typing: Your DBMS probably implements the two methods differently, and one of the methods may be significantly faster than the other on your system. You may want to run a performance comparison on the two ways of expressing inclusion in (or exclusion from) a group and then use the technique that produces the quicker result. A DBMS with a good optimizer will probably choose the more efficient method, regardless of which predicate you use.

The IN keyword is valuable in another area, too. If IN is part of a subquery, the keyword enables you to pull information from two tables to obtain results that you can't derive from a single table. I cover subqueries in detail in Chapter 12, but here's an example that shows how a subquery uses the IN keyword.

Suppose you want to display the names of all customers who've bought the F-35 product in the last 30 days. Customer names are in the CUSTOMER table, and sales transaction data is in the TRANSACT table. You can use the following query:

```
SELECT FirstName, LastName
    FROM CUSTOMER
    WHERE CustomerID IN
        (SELECT CustomerID
            FROM TRANSACT
            WHERE ProductID = 'F-35'
            AND TransDate >= (CurrentDate - 30)) ;
```

The inner SELECT of the TRANSACT table nests within the outer SELECT of the CUSTOMER table. The inner SELECT finds the CustomerID numbers of all customers who bought the F-35 product in the last 30 days. The outer SELECT displays the first and last names of all customers whose CustomerID is retrieved by the inner SELECT.

LIKE and NOT LIKE

You can use the LIKE predicate to compare two character strings for a partial match. Partial matches are valuable if you don't know the exact form of the string for which you're searching. You can also use partial matches to retrieve multiple rows that contain similar strings in one of the table's columns.

To identify partial matches, SQL uses two wildcard characters. The percent sign (%) can stand for any string of characters that have zero or more characters. The underscore (_) stands for any single character. Table 10-3 provides some examples that show how to use LIKE.

TABLE 10-3 **SQL's LIKE Predicate**

Statement	Values Returned
WHERE Word LIKE 'intern%'	intern
	internal
	international
	internet
	interns
WHERE Word LIKE '%Peace%'	Justice of the Peace
	Peaceful Warrior
WHERE Word LIKE 'T_p_'	Tape
	Taps
	Tipi
	Tips
	Tops
	Type

The NOT LIKE predicate retrieves all rows that don't satisfy a partial match, including one or more wildcard characters, as in the following example:

```
WHERE Phone NOT LIKE '503%'
```

This example returns all the rows in the table for which the phone number starts with something other than 503.

TIP

You may want to search for a string that includes an actual percent sign or under-score. In that case, you want SQL to interpret the percent sign as a percent sign and not as a wildcard character. You can conduct such a search by typing an escape character just prior to the character you want SQL to take literally. You can choose any character as the escape character, as long as that character doesn't appear in the string that you're testing, as shown in the following example:

```
SELECT Quote
    FROM BARTLETTS
    WHERE Quote LIKE '20#%'
        ESCAPE '#' ;
```

The % character is escaped by the preceding # sign, so the statement interprets this symbol as a percent sign rather than as a wildcard. You can "escape" an underscore — or the escape character itself — in the same way. The preceding query, for example, would find the following quotation in *Bartlett's Familiar Quotations:*

```
20% of the salespeople produce 80% of the results.
```

The query would also find the following:

```
20%
```

SIMILAR

SQL:1999 added the SIMILAR predicate, but it was deprecated in SQL:2011. It should not be used in any new development projects. When a feature is depre-cated, that means that a time will come when the feature is no longer a part of the SQL standard. It would be wise to remove it from existing application programs where it has been used.

NULL

The NULL predicate finds all rows where the value in the selected column is null. In the FOODS table in Chapter 8, several rows have null values in the Carbohy-drate column. You can retrieve their names by using a statement such as the following:

```
SELECT (Food)
    FROM FOODS
    WHERE Carbohydrate IS NULL ;
```

This query returns the following values:

```
Beef, lean hamburger
Chicken, light meat
Opossum, roasted
Pork, ham
```

As you might expect, including the NOT keyword reverses the result, as in the following example:

```
SELECT (Food)
    FROM FOODS
    WHERE Carbohydrate IS NOT NULL ;
```

This query returns all the rows in the table except the four that the preceding query returns.

WARNING

The statement Carbohydrate IS NULL is *not* the same as Carbohydrate = NULL. To illustrate this point, assume that, in the current row of the FOODS table, both Carbohydrate and Protein are null. From this fact, you can draw the following conclusions:

>> Carbohydrate IS NULL is True.

>> Protein IS NULL is True.

>> Carbohydrate IS NULL AND Protein IS NULL is True.

>> Carbohydrate = Protein is unknown.

>> Carbohydrate = NULL is an illegal expression.

Using the keyword NULL in a comparison is meaningless because the answer always returns as *unknown.*

Why is Carbohydrate = Protein defined as unknown even though Carbohydrate and Protein have the same (null) value? Because NULL simply means "I don't know." You don't know what the Carbohydrate value is, and you don't know what the Protein value is; therefore, you don't know whether those (unknown) values are the same. Maybe Carbohydrate is 37, and Protein is 14, or maybe Carbohydrate is 93, and Protein is 93. If you don't know both the carbohydrate value *and* the protein value, you can't say whether the two are the same.

ALL, SOME, ANY

Thousands of years ago, the Greek philosopher Aristotle formulated a system of logic that became the basis for much of Western thought. The essence of this logic is to start with a set of premises that you know to be true, apply valid operations to these premises, and, thereby, arrive at new truths. An example of this procedure is as follows:

Premise 1: All Greeks are human.

Premise 2: All humans are mortal.

Conclusion: All Greeks are mortal.

Another example:

Premise 1: Some Greeks are women.

Premise 2: All women are human.

Conclusion: Some Greeks are human.

By way of presenting a third example, let me state the same logical idea of the second example in a slightly different way:

If any Greeks are women and all women are human, then some Greeks are human.

The first example uses the universal quantifier ALL in both premises, enabling you to make a sound deduction about all Greeks in the conclusion. The second example uses the existential quantifier SOME in one premise, enabling you to make a deduction about some, but not all, Greeks in the conclusion. The third example uses the existential quantifier ANY, which is a synonym for SOME, to reach the same conclusion you reach in the second example.

Look at how SOME, ANY, and ALL apply in SQL.

Consider an example in baseball statistics. Baseball is a physically demanding sport, especially for pitchers. A starting pitcher must throw the baseball from the pitcher's mound to home plate between 90 and 150 times to record a complete game. This effort can be exhausting, and if (as is often the case) the pitcher becomes ineffective before the game ends, a relief pitcher must replace him. Pitching an entire game is an outstanding achievement, regardless of whether the effort results in a victory.

ANY CAN BE AMBIGUOUS

The original SQL used the word ANY for existential quantification. This usage turned out to be confusing and error-prone because the English language connotations of *any* are sometimes universal and sometimes existential:

- "Do any of you know where Baker Street is?"

- "I can eat more hot dogs than any of you."

The first sentence is probably asking whether at least one person knows where Baker Street is; here *any* is used as an existential quantifier. The second sentence, however, is a boast that's stating that I can eat more hot dogs than the biggest eater among all of you people can eat. In this case, *any* is used as a universal quantifier.

Thus, for the SQL-92 standard, the developers retained the word ANY for compatibility with early products, but they also added the word SOME as a less confusing synonym. SQL continues to support both existential quantifiers.

Suppose you're keeping track of the number of complete games that all major-league pitchers pitch. In one table, you list all the American League pitchers, and in another table, you list all the National League pitchers. Both tables contain the players' first names, last names, and number of complete games pitched.

The American League permits a designated hitter (DH) (who isn't required to play a defensive position) to bat in place of any of the nine players who play defense. The National League doesn't allow designated hitters, but does allow pinch-hitters. When the pinch-hitter comes into the game for the pitcher, the pitcher can't play for the remainder of the game. In the American League, usually the DH bats for the pitcher, because pitchers are notoriously poor hitters. Pitchers must spend so much time and effort on perfecting their pitching that they don't have as much time to practice batting as the other players do.

Suppose you have a theory that, on average, American League starting pitchers throw more complete games than do National League starting pitchers. This idea is based on your observation that designated hitters enable hard-throwing, weak-hitting, American League pitchers to keep pitching as long as they're effective, even in a close game. Because a DH is already batting for these pitchers, their poor hitting isn't a liability. In the National League, however, under everyday circumstances the pitcher would go to bat. When trailing in the late innings, most managers would call for a pinch hitter to bat for the pitcher, judging that getting a base hit in this situation is more important than keeping an effective pitcher in the game. To test your theory, you formulate the following query:

```
SELECT FirstName, LastName
   FROM AMERICAN_LEAGUER
   WHERE CompleteGames > ALL
      (SELECT CompleteGames
         FROM NATIONAL_LEAGUER) ;
```

The subquery (the inner SELECT) returns a list showing, for every National League pitcher, the number of complete games he pitched. The outer query returns the first and last names of all American Leaguers who pitched more complete games than ALL of the National Leaguers. The entire query returns the names of those American League pitchers who pitched more complete games than the pitcher who has thrown the most complete games in the National League.

Consider the following similar statement:

```
SELECT FirstName, LastName
   FROM AMERICAN_LEAGUER
   WHERE CompleteGames > ANY
      (SELECT CompleteGames
         FROM NATIONAL_LEAGUER) ;
```

In this case, you use the existential quantifier ANY instead of the universal quantifier ALL. The subquery (the inner, nested query) is identical to the subquery in the previous example. This subquery retrieves a complete list of the complete game statistics for all the National League pitchers. The outer query returns the first and last names of all American League pitchers who pitched more complete games than ANY National League pitcher. Because you can be virtually certain that at least one National League pitcher hasn't pitched a complete game, the result probably includes all American League pitchers who've pitched at least one complete game.

If you replace the keyword ANY with the equivalent keyword SOME, the result is the same. If the statement that at least one National League pitcher hasn't pitched a complete game is a true statement, you can then say that SOME National League pitcher hasn't pitched a complete game.

EXISTS

You can use the EXISTS predicate in conjunction with a subquery to determine whether the subquery returns any rows. If the subquery returns at least one row, that result satisfies the EXISTS condition, and the outer query executes. Consider the following example:

```
SELECT FirstName, LastName
  FROM CUSTOMER
  WHERE EXISTS
    (SELECT DISTINCT CustomerID
      FROM SALES
      WHERE SALES.CustomerID = CUSTOMER.CustomerID);
```

Here the SALES table contains all your company's sales transactions. The table includes the CustomerID of the customer who makes each purchase, as well as other pertinent information. The CUSTOMER table contains each customer's first and last names, but no information about specific transactions.

The subquery in the preceding example returns a row for every customer who has made at least one purchase. The outer query returns the first and last names of the customers who made the purchases that the SALES table records.

EXISTS is equivalent to a comparison of COUNT with zero, as the following query shows:

```
SELECT FirstName, LastName
  FROM CUSTOMER
  WHERE 0 <>
    (SELECT COUNT(*)
      FROM SALES
      WHERE SALES.CustomerID = CUSTOMER.CustomerID);
```

For every row in the SALES table that contains a CustomerID that's equal to a CustomerID in the CUSTOMER table, this statement displays the FirstName and LastName columns in the CUSTOMER table. For every sale in the SALES table, therefore, the statement displays the name of the customer who made the purchase.

UNIQUE

As you do with the EXISTS predicate, you use the UNIQUE predicate with a subquery. Although the EXISTS predicate evaluates to True only if the subquery returns at least one row, the UNIQUE predicate evaluates to True only if no two rows returned by the subquery are identical. In other words, the UNIQUE predicate evaluates to True only if all the rows that its subquery returns are unique. Consider the following example:

```
SELECT FirstName, LastName
  FROM CUSTOMER
  WHERE UNIQUE
```

```
      (SELECT CustomerID FROM SALES
          WHERE SALES.CustomerID = CUSTOMER.CustomerID);
```

This statement retrieves the names of all new customers for whom the SALES table records only one sale. Because a null value is an unknown value, two null values aren't considered equal to each other; when the UNIQUE keyword is applied to a result table that contains only two null rows, the UNIQUE predicate evaluates to True.

DISTINCT

The DISTINCT predicate is like the UNIQUE predicate, except in the way it treats nulls. If all the values in a result table are UNIQUE, then they're also DISTINCT from each other. However, unlike the result for the UNIQUE predicate, if the DISTINCT keyword is applied to a result table that contains only two null rows, the DISTINCT predicate evaluates to False. Two null values are *not* considered distinct from each other, while at the same time they are considered to be unique.

REMEMBER

This strange situation seems contradictory, but there's a reason for it. In some situations, you may want to treat two null values as different from each other — in which case, use the UNIQUE predicate. When you want to treat the two nulls as if they're the same, use the DISTINCT predicate.

OVERLAPS

You use the OVERLAPS predicate to determine whether two time intervals overlap each other. This predicate is useful for avoiding scheduling conflicts. If the two intervals overlap, the predicate returns a True value. If they don't overlap, the predicate returns a False value.

You can specify an interval in two ways: either as a start time and an end time or as a start time and a duration. Here are some examples:

```
(TIME '2:55:00', INTERVAL '1' HOUR)
OVERLAPS
(TIME '3:30:00', INTERVAL '2' HOUR)
```

This first example returns a True because 3:30 is less than one hour after 2:55.

```
(TIME '9:00:00', TIME '9:30:00')
OVERLAPS
(TIME '9:29:00', TIME '9:31:00')
```

This example returns a True because you have a one-minute overlap between the two intervals.

```
(TIME '9:00:00', TIME '10:00:00')
OVERLAPS
(TIME '10:15:00', INTERVAL '3' HOUR)
```

This example returns a False because the two intervals don't overlap.

```
(TIME '9:00:00', TIME '9:30:00')
OVERLAPS
(TIME '9:30:00', TIME '9:35:00')
```

This example returns a False because even though the two intervals are contiguous, they don't overlap.

MATCH

In Chapter 5, I discuss referential integrity, which involves maintaining consistency in a multi-table database. You can lose integrity by adding a row to a child table that doesn't have a corresponding row in the child's parent table. You can cause similar problems by deleting a row from a parent table if rows corresponding to that row exist in a child table.

Suppose your business has a CUSTOMER table that keeps track of all your customers and a SALES table that records all sales transactions. You don't want to add a row to SALES until after you enter the customer making the purchase into the CUSTOMER table. You also don't want to delete a customer from the CUSTOMER table if that customer made purchases that exist in the SALES table.

REMEMBER

Before you perform an insertion or a deletion, you may want to check the candidate row to make sure that inserting or deleting that row doesn't cause integrity problems. The MATCH predicate can perform such a check.

Say you have a CUSTOMER table and a SALES table. CustomerID is the primary key of the CUSTOMER table and acts as a foreign key in the SALES table. Every row in the CUSTOMER table must have a unique CustomerID that isn't null. CustomerID isn't unique in the SALES table, because repeat customers buy more than once. This situation is fine; it doesn't threaten integrity because CustomerID is a foreign key rather than a primary key in that table.

TIP

Seemingly, `CustomerID` can be null in the SALES table, because someone can walk in off the street, buy something, and walk out before you get a chance to enter his or her name and address into the CUSTOMER table. This situation can create trouble — a row in the child table with no corresponding row in the parent table. To overcome this problem, you can create a generic customer in the CUSTOMER table and assign all such anonymous sales to that customer.

Say that a customer steps up to the cash register and claims that she bought an F-35 stealth technology strike fighter on December 18, 2017. Although she has lost her receipt, she now wants to return the plane because it shows up like an aircraft carrier on opponents' radar screens. You can verify whether she bought an F-35 by searching your SALES database for a match. First, you must retrieve her `CustomerID` into the variable `vcustid`; then you can use the following syntax:

```
... WHERE (:vcustid, 'F-35', '2017-12-18')
        MATCH
        (SELECT CustomerID, ProductID, SaleDate
            FROM SALES)
```

If the MATCH predicate returns a True value, the database contains a sale of the F-35 on December 18, 2017, to this client's `CustomerID`. Take back the defective product and refund the customer's money. (*Note:* If any values in the first argument of the MATCH predicate are null, a True value always returns.)

SQL's developers added the MATCH predicate and the UNIQUE predicate for the same reason — they provide a way to explicitly perform the tests defined for the implicit referential integrity (RI) and UNIQUE constraints.

The general form of the MATCH predicate is as follows:

```
Row_value MATCH [UNIQUE] [SIMPLE| PARTIAL | FULL ]
        Subquery
```

The UNIQUE, SIMPLE, PARTIAL, and FULL options relate to rules that come into play if the row value expression *R* has one or more columns that are null. (For more about using row value expressions, see Chapter 9.) The rules for the MATCH predicate are a copy of corresponding referential integrity rules.

Referential integrity rules and the MATCH predicate

Referential integrity rules require that the values of a column or columns in one table match the values of a column or columns in another table. You refer to the columns in the first table as the *foreign key* and the columns in the second table as the *primary key* or *unique key*. For example, you may declare the column `EmpDeptNo` in an EMPLOYEE table as a foreign key that references the `DeptNo` column of a DEPT table. This matchup ensures that if you record an employee in the EMPLOYEE table as working in department 123, a row appears in the DEPT table where `DeptNo` is 123.

If the members of the foreign key/primary key pair both consist of a single column, the situation is pretty straightforward. However, the two keys can consist of multiple columns. The `DeptNo` value, for example, may be unique only within a `Location`; therefore, to uniquely identify a DEPT row, you must specify both a `Location` and a `DeptNo`. If both the Boston and Tampa offices have a department 123, you need to identify the departments as (`'Boston'`, `'123'`) and (`'Tampa'`, `'123'`). In this case, the EMPLOYEE table needs two columns to identify a DEPT. Call those columns `EmpLoc` and `EmpDeptNo`. If an employee works in department 123 in Boston, the `EmpLoc` and `EmpDeptNo` values are `'Boston'` and `'123'`. And the foreign-key declaration in the EMPLOYEE table looks like this:

```
FOREIGN KEY (EmpLoc, EmpDeptNo)
    REFERENCES DEPT (Location, DeptNo)
```

Drawing valid conclusions from your data becomes immensely complicated if the data contains nulls. That's because sometimes you want to treat such data one way, and sometimes you want to treat it another way. The UNIQUE, SIMPLE, PARTIAL, and FULL keywords specify different ways of treating data that contains nulls. If your data does not contain any null values, you can save yourself a lot of head-scratching by merely skipping from here to the next section of this chapter, "Logical Connectives." If your data *does* contain null values, drop out of speed-reading mode now and read the following list slowly and carefully. Each entry in the list given here presents a different situation with respect to null values — and tells how the MATCH predicate handles it.

Here are scenarios that illustrate the rules for dealing with null values and the MATCH predicate:

>> **The values are both one way or the other.** If neither of the values of `EmpLoc` and `EmpDeptNo` are null (or both are null), then the referential integrity rules are the same as for single-column keys with values that are null or not null.

>> **One value is null and one isn't.** If, for example, `EmpLoc` is null and `EmpDeptNo` is not null — or `EmpLoc` is not null and `EmpDeptNo` is null — you need new rules. When implementing rules, if you insert or update the EMPLOYEE table with `EmpLoc` and `EmpDeptNo` values of (`NULL`, `'123'`) or (`'Boston'`, `NULL`), you have six main alternatives: SIMPLE, PARTIAL, and FULL, each either with or without the UNIQUE keyword.

» **The UNIQUE keyword is present.** A matching row in the subquery result table must be unique for the predicate to evaluate to a True value.

» **Both components of the row value expression R are null.** The MATCH predicate returns a True value regardless of the contents of the subquery result table being compared.

» **Neither component of the row value expression R is null, SIMPLE is specified, UNIQUE is not specified, and at least one row in the subquery result table matches R.** The MATCH predicate returns a True value. Otherwise it returns a False value.

» **Neither component of the row value expression R is null, SIMPLE is specified, UNIQUE is specified, and at least one row in the subquery result table is both unique and matches R.** The MATCH predicate returns a True value. Otherwise it returns a False value.

» **Any component of the row value expression R is null and SIMPLE is specified.** The MATCH predicate returns a True value.

» **Any component of the row value expression R isn't null, PARTIAL is specified, UNIQUE isn't specified, and the non-null part of at least one row in the subquery result table matches R.** The MATCH predicate returns a True value. Otherwise it returns a False value.

» **Any component of the row value expression R is non-null, PARTIAL is specified, UNIQUE is specified, and the non-null parts of R match the non-null parts of at least one unique row in the subquery result table.** The MATCH predicate returns a True value. Otherwise it returns a False value.

» **Neither component of the row value expression R is null, FULL is specified, UNIQUE is not specified, and at least one row in the subquery result table matches R.** The MATCH predicate returns a True value. Otherwise it returns a False value.

» **Neither component of the row value expression R is null, FULL is specified, UNIQUE is specified, and at least one row in the subquery result table is both unique and matches R.** The MATCH predicate returns a True value. Otherwise it returns a False value.

» **Any component of the row value expression R is null, and FULL is specified.** The MATCH predicate returns a False value.

Logical Connectives

Often (as several previous examples show) applying only one condition in a query isn't enough to return the rows you want from a table. In some cases, the rows must satisfy two or more conditions. In other cases, if a row satisfies any of two or more conditions, it qualifies for retrieval. On still other occasions, you want to retrieve only rows that don't satisfy a specified condition. To meet these needs, SQL offers the logical connectives AND, OR, and NOT.

AND

If multiple conditions must all be True before you can retrieve a row, use the AND logical connective. Consider the following example:

```
SELECT InvoiceNo, SaleDate, Salesperson, TotalSale
    FROM SALES
    WHERE SaleDate>= '2017-12-10'
        AND SaleDate<= '2017-12-16' ;
```

The WHERE clause must meet the following two conditions:

» SaleDate must be greater than or equal to December 10, 2017.

» SaleDate must be less than or equal to December 16, 2017.

Only rows that record sales occurring during the week of December 10 meet both conditions. The query returns only these rows.

WARNING

Notice that the AND connective is strictly logical. This restriction can sometimes be confusing because people commonly use the word *and* with a looser meaning. Suppose, for example, that your boss says to you, "I'd like to retrieve the sales data for Ferguson and Ford." He said, "Ferguson and Ford," so you may write the following SQL query:

```
SELECT *
   FROM SALES
   WHERE Salesperson = 'Ferguson'
      AND Salesperson = 'Ford';
```

Well, don't take that answer back to your boss. The following query is more like what the big kahuna had in mind:

```
SELECT *
   FROM SALES
   WHERE Salesperson IN ('Ferguson', 'Ford') ;
```

The first query won't return anything, because none of the sales in the SALES table were made by *both* Ferguson and Ford. The second query will return the information on all sales made by *either* Ferguson *or* Ford, which is probably what the boss wanted.

OR

If any one of two or more conditions must be True to qualify a row for retrieval, use the OR logical connective, as in the following example:

```
SELECT InvoiceNo, SaleDate, Salesperson, TotalSale
   FROM SALES
      WHERE Salesperson = 'Ford'
         OR TotalSale > 200 ;
```

This query retrieves all of Ford's sales, regardless of how large, as well as all sales of more than $200, regardless of who made the sales.

NOT

The NOT connective negates a condition. If the condition normally returns a True value, adding NOT causes the same condition to return a False value. If a condition normally returns a False value, adding NOT causes the condition to return a True value. Consider the following example:

```
SELECT InvoiceNo, SaleDate, Salesperson, TotalSale
   FROM SALES
      WHERE NOT (Salesperson = 'Ford') ;
```

This query returns rows for all sales transactions completed by salespeople other than Ford.

WARNING

When you use AND, OR, or NOT, sometimes the scope of the connective isn't clear. To be safe, use parentheses to make sure that SQL applies the connective to the predicate you want. In the preceding example, the NOT connective applies to the entire predicate (Salesperson = 'Ford').

GROUP BY Clauses

Sometimes, rather than retrieving individual records, you want to know something about a group of records. The GROUP BY clause is the tool you need.

Suppose you're the sales manager of another location, and you want to look at the performance of your sales force. If you do a simple SELECT, such as the following query:

```
SELECT InvoiceNo, SaleDate, Salesperson, TotalSale
   FROM SALES;
```

you receive a result similar to that shown in Figure 10-1.

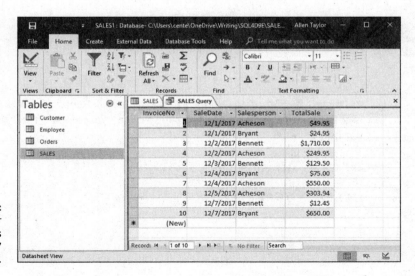

FIGURE 10-1:
A result set for retrieval of sales from 12/01/2017 to 12/07/2017.

This result gives you some idea of how well your salespeople are doing, because so few total sales are involved. However, in real life, a company would have many more sales — and it wouldn't be so easy to tell whether sales objectives were being met. To do the real analysis, you can combine the GROUP BY clause with one of the *aggregate* functions (also called *set functions*) to get a quantitative picture of sales performance. For example, you can see which salesperson is selling more of the profitable high-ticket items by using the average (AVG) function as follows:

```
SELECT Salesperson, AVG(TotalSale)
    FROM SALES
    GROUP BY Salesperson;
```

The result of this query, when run on Microsoft Access 2016, is shown in Figure 10-2. Running the query with a different database management system would retrieve the same result, but might appear a little different.

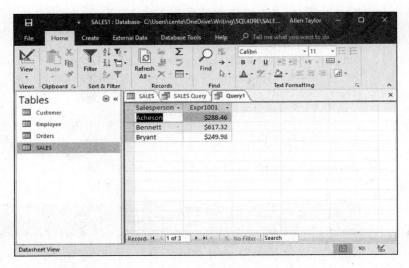

FIGURE 10-2:
Average sales for each salesperson.

As shown in Figure 10-2, the average value of Bennett's sales is considerably higher than that of the other two salespeople. You compare total sales with a similar query:

```
SELECT Salesperson, SUM(TotalSale)
    FROM SALES
    GROUP BY Salesperson;
```

This query gives the result shown in Figure 10-3.

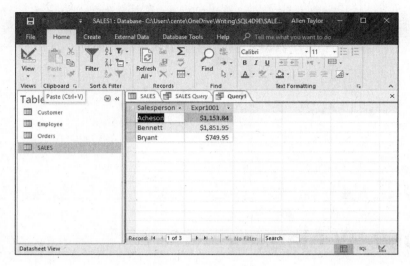

FIGURE 10-3:
Total sales for each salesperson.

Bennett also has the highest total sales, which is consistent with having the highest average sales.

HAVING Clauses

You can analyze the grouped data further by using the HAVING clause. The HAVING clause is a filter that acts like a WHERE clause, but on groups of rows rather than on individual rows. To illustrate the function of the HAVING clause, suppose the sales manager considers Bennett to be in a class by himself. His performance distorts the overall data for the other salespeople. (Aha — a curve-wrecker.) You can exclude Bennett's sales from the grouped data by using a HAVING clause as follows:

```
SELECT Salesperson, SUM(TotalSale)
    FROM SALES
    GROUP BY Salesperson
    HAVING Salesperson <>'Bennett';
```

This query gives you the result shown in Figure 10-4. Only rows where the salesperson is not Bennett are considered.

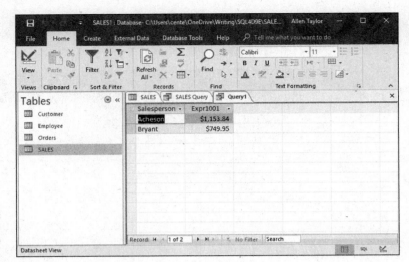

FIGURE 10-4:
Total sales for all salespeople except Bennett.

ORDER BY Clauses

Use the ORDER BY clause to display the output table of a query in either ascending or descending alphabetical order. Whereas the GROUP BY clause gathers rows into groups and sorts the groups into alphabetical order, ORDER BY sorts individual rows. The ORDER BY clause must be the last clause that you specify in a query. If the query also contains a GROUP BY clause, the clause first arranges the output rows into groups. The ORDER BY clause then sorts the rows within each group. If you have no GROUP BY clause, then the statement considers the entire table as a group, and the ORDER BY clause sorts all its rows according to the column (or columns) that the ORDER BY clause specifies.

To illustrate this point, consider the data in the SALES table. The SALES table contains columns for InvoiceNo, SaleDate, Salesperson, and TotalSale. If you use the following example, you see all the data in the SALES table — but in an arbitrary order:

```
SELECT * FROM SALES ;
```

In one implementation, this may be the order in which you inserted the rows in the table; in another implementation, the order may be that of the most recent updates. The order can also change unexpectedly if anyone physically reorganizes the database. That's one reason it's usually a good idea to specify the order in which you want the rows. You may, for example, want to see the rows in order by the SaleDate like this:

```
SELECT * FROM SALES ORDER BY SaleDate ;
```

This example returns all the rows in the SALES table in order by SaleDate.

TIP

For rows with the same SaleDate, the default order depends on the implementation. You can, however, specify how to sort the rows that share the same SaleDate. You may want to see the sales for each SaleDate in order by InvoiceNo, as follows:

```
SELECT * FROM SALES ORDER BY SaleDate, InvoiceNo ;
```

This example first orders the sales by SaleDate; then for each SaleDate, it orders the sales by InvoiceNo. But don't confuse that example with the following query:

```
SELECT * FROM SALES ORDER BY InvoiceNo, SaleDate ;
```

This query first orders the sales by INVOICE_NO. Then for each different InvoiceNo, the query orders the sales by SaleDate. This probably won't yield the result you want, because it's unlikely that multiple sale dates will exist for a single invoice number.

The following query is another example of how SQL can return data:

```
SELECT * FROM SALES ORDER BY Salesperson, SaleDate ;
```

This example first orders by Salesperson and then by SaleDate. After you look at the data in that order, you may want to invert it, as follows:

```
SELECT * FROM SALES ORDER BY SaleDate, Salesperson ;
```

This example orders the rows first by SaleDate and then by Salesperson.

All these ordering examples are in ascending (ASC) order, which is the default sort order. The last SELECT shows earlier sales first — and, within a given date, shows sales for 'Adams' before 'Baker'. If you prefer descending (DESC) order, you can specify this order for one or more of the order columns, as follows:

```
SELECT * FROM SALES
ORDER BY SaleDate DESC, Salesperson ASC ;
```

This example specifies a descending order for sale dates, showing the more recent sales first, and an ascending order for salespeople, putting them in alphabetical order. That should give you a better picture of how Bennett's performance stacks up against that of the other salespeople.

Limited FETCH

Whenever the ISO/IEC SQL standard is changed, it is usually to expand the capabilities of the language. This is a good thing. However, sometimes when you make such a change you cannot anticipate all the possible consequences. This happened with the addition of limited FETCH capability in SQL:2008.

The idea of the limited FETCH is that although a SELECT statement may return an indeterminate number of rows, perhaps you care only about the top three or perhaps the top ten. Pursuant to this idea, SQL:2008 added syntax shown in the following example:

```
SELECT Salesperson, AVG(TotalSale)
    FROM SALES
    GROUP BY Salesperson
    ORDER BY AVG(TotalSale) DESC
    FETCH FIRST 3 ROWS ONLY;
```

That looks fine. You want to see who your top three salespeople are in terms of those who are selling mostly high-priced products. However, there is a small problem with this. What if three people are tied with the same average total sale, below the top two salespeople? Only one of those three will be returned. Which one? It is indeterminate.

Indeterminacy is intolerable to any self-respecting database professional, so this situation was corrected in SQL:2011. New syntax was added to include ties, in this manner:

```
SELECT Salesperson, AVG(TotalSale)
    FROM SALES
    GROUP BY Salesperson
    ORDER BY AVG(TotalSale) DESC
    FETCH FIRST 3 ROWS WITH TIES;
```

Now the result is completely determined: If there is a tie, you get all the tied rows. As before, if you leave off the WITH TIES modifier, the result is indeterminate.

A couple of additional enhancements were made to the limited FETCH capability in SQL:2011.

First, percentages are handled, as well as just a specific number of rows. Consider the following example:

```
SELECT Salesperson, AVG(TotalSale)
   FROM SALES
   GROUP BY Salesperson
   ORDER BY AVG(TotalSale) DESC
   FETCH FIRST 10 PERCENT ROWS ONLY;
```

It's conceivable that there might be a problem with ties when dealing with percentages, just as there is with a simple number of records, so the WITH TIES syntax may also be used here. You can include ties or not, depending on what you want in any given situation.

Second, suppose you don't want the top three or the top ten percent, but instead want the second three or second ten percent? Perhaps you want to skip directly to some point deep in the result set. SQL:2011 covers this situation also. The code would be similar to this:

```
SELECT Salesperson, AVG(TotalSale)
   FROM SALES
   GROUP BY Salesperson
   ORDER BY AVG(TotalSale) DESC
      OFFSET 3 ROWS
   FETCH NEXT 3 ROWS ONLY;
```

The OFFSET keyword tells how many rows to skip before fetching. The NEXT keyword specifies that the rows to be fetched are the ones immediately following the offset. Now the salespeople with the fourth, fifth, and sixth highest average sale total are returned. As you can see, without the WITH TIES syntax, there is still an indeterminacy problem. If the third, fourth, and fifth salespeople are tied, it is indeterminate which two will be included in this second batch and which one will have been included in the first batch.

WARNING

It may be best to avoid using the limited FETCH capability. It's too likely to deliver misleading results.

Peering through a Window to Create a Result Set

Windows and window functions were first introduced in SQL:1999. With a window, a user can optionally partition a data set, optionally order the rows in each partition, and specify a collection of rows (the window frame) that is associated with a given row.

The window frame of a row R is some subset of the partition containing R. For example, the window frame may consist of all the rows from the beginning of the partition up to and including R, based on the way rows are ordered in the partition.

A window function computes a value for a row R, based on the rows in the window frame of R.

For example, suppose you have a SALES table that has columns of CustID, InvoiceNo, and TotalSale. Your sales manager may want to know what the total sales were to each customer over a specified range of invoice numbers. You can obtain what she wants with the following SQL code:

```
SELECT CustID, InvoiceNo,
    SUM (TotalSale) OVER
    ( PARTITION BY CustID
      ORDER BY InvoiceNo
      ROWS BETWEEN
      UNBOUNDED PRECEDING
      AND CURRENT ROW )
    FROM SALES;
```

The OVER clause determines how the rows of the query are partitioned before being processed, in this case by the SUM function. A partition is assigned to each customer. Within each partition will be a list of invoice numbers, and associated with each of them will be the sum of all the TotalSale values over the specified range of rows, for each customer.

SQL:2011 has added several major enhancements to the original window functionality, incorporating new keywords.

Partitioning a window into buckets with NTILE

The NTILE window function apportions an ordered window partition into some positive integer number n of buckets, numbering the buckets from 1 to n. If the number of rows in a partition m is not evenly divisible by n, then after the NTILE function fills the buckets evenly, the remainder of m/n, called r, is apportioned to the first r buckets, making them larger than the other buckets.

Suppose you want to classify your employees by salary, partitioning them into five buckets, from highest to lowest. You can do it with the following code:

```
SELECT FirstName, LastName, NTILE (5)
   OVER (ORDER BY Salary DESC)
   AS BUCKET
   FROM Employee;
```

If there are, for example, 11 employees, each bucket is filled with two except for the first bucket, which is filled with three. The first bucket will contain the three highest paid employees, and the fifth bucket will contain the two lowest paid employees.

Navigating within a window

Added in SQL:2011 are five window functions that evaluate an expression in a row R2 that is somewhere in the window frame of the current row R1. The functions are LAG, LEAD, NTH_VALUE, FIRST_VALUE, and LAST_VALUE.

These functions enable you to pull information from specified rows that are within the window frame of the current row.

Looking back with the LAG function

The LAG function enables you to retrieve information from the current row in the window you're examining as well as information from another row that you specify that precedes the current row.

Suppose, for example, that you have a table that records the total sales for each day of the current year. One thing you might want to know is how today's sales compare to yesterday's. You could do this with the LAG function, as follows:

```
SELECT TotalSale AS TodaySale,
   LAG (TotalSale) OVER
   (ORDER BY SaleDate) AS PrevDaySale
   FROM DailyTotals;
```

For each row in DailyTotals, this query would return a row listing that row's total sales figure and the previous day's total sales figure. The default offset is 1, which is why the previous day's result is returned rather than any other.

To compare the current day's sales to those of a week prior, you could use the following:

```
SELECT TotalSale AS TodaySale,
   LAG (TotalSale, 7) OVER
```

```
    (ORDER BY SaleDate) AS PrevDaySale
    FROM DailyTotals;
```

The first seven rows in a window frame will not have a predecessor that is a week older. The default response to this situation is to return a null result for `PrevDaySale`. If you would prefer some other result to a null result, for example zero, you can specify what you want returned in this situation instead of the default null value, for example, 0 (zero), as shown here:

```
SELECT TotalSale AS TodaySale,
    LAG (TotalSale, 7, 0) OVER
    (ORDER BY SaleDate) AS PrevDaySale
    FROM DailyTotals;
```

The default behavior is to count rows that have a lag extent, which in this case is `TotalSale`, which contains a null value. If you want to skip over such rows and count only rows that have an actual value in the lag extent, you can do so by adding the keywords `IGNORE NULLS` as shown in the following variant of the example:

```
SELECT TotalSale AS TodaySale,
    LAG (TotalSale, 7, 0) IGNORE NULLS
    OVER (ORDER BY SaleDate) AS PrevDaySale
    FROM DailyTotals;
```

Looking ahead with the LEAD function

The `LEAD` window function operates the same way the `LAG` function operates except that, instead of looking back to a preceding row, it looks ahead to a row following the current row in the window frame. An example might be:

```
SELECT TotalSale AS TodaySale,
    LEAD (TotalSale, 7, 0) IGNORE NULLS
    OVER (ORDER BY SaleDate) AS NextDaySale
    FROM DailyTotals;
```

Looking to a specified row with the NTH_VALUE function

The `NTH_VALUE` function is similar to the `LAG` and `LEAD` functions, except that instead of evaluating an expression in a row preceding or following the current row, it evaluates an expression in a row that is at a specified offset from the first or the last row in the window frame.

Here's an example:

```
SELECT TotalSale AS ChosenSale,
    NTH_VALUE (TotalSale, 2)
    FROM FIRST
    IGNORE NULLS
    OVER (ORDER BY SaleDate)
    ROWS BETWEEN 10 PRECEDING AND 10 FOLLOWING )
        AS EarlierSale
    FROM DailyTotals;
```

In this example, EarlierSale is evaluated as follows:

>> The window frame associated with the current row is formed. It includes the ten preceding and the ten following rows.

>> TotalSale is evaluated in each row of the window frame.

>> IGNORE NULLS is specified, so any rows containing a null value for TotalSale are skipped.

>> Starting from the first value remaining after the exclusion of rows containing a null value for TotalSale, move forward by two rows (forward because FROM FIRST was specified).

The value of EarlierSale is the value of TotalSale from the specified row.

If you don't want to skip rows that have a null value for TotalSale, specify RESPECT NULLS rather than IGNORE NULLS. The NTH_VALUE function works similarly if you specify FROM LAST rather than FROM FIRST, except instead of counting forward from the first record in the window frame, you count backward from the last record in the window frame. The number specifying the number of rows to count is still positive, even though you're counting backward rather than forward.

Looking to a very specific value with FIRST_VALUE and LAST_VALUE

The FIRST_VALUE and LAST_VALUE functions are special cases of the NTH_VALUE function. FIRST_VALUE is equivalent to NTH_VALUE where FROM FIRST is specified and the offset is 0 (zero). LAST_VALUE is equivalent to NTH_VALUE where FROM LAST is specified and the offset is 0. With both, you can choose to either ignore or respect nulls.

Nesting window functions

Sometimes to get the result you need, the easiest way is to nest one function within another. SQL:2011 added the capability to do such nesting with window functions.

As an example, consider a case where a stock investor is trying to determine whether it is a good time to buy a particular stock. To get a handle on this, she decides to compare the current stock price to the price it sold for on the immediately previous 100 trades. She wonders, how many times in the previous 100 trades it sold for less than the current price. To reach an answer, she makes the following query:

```
SELECT SaleTime,
    SUM ( CASE WHEN SalePrice <
    VALUE OF (SalePrice AT CURRENT ROW)
    THEN 1 ELSE 0 )
    OVER (ORDER BY SaleTime
    ROWS BETWEEN 100 PRECEDING AND CURRENT ROW )
    FROM StockSales;
```

The window encompasses the 100 rows preceding the current row, which correspond to the 100 sales immediately prior to the current moment. Every time a row is evaluated where the value of SalePrice is less than the most recent price, 1 is added to the sum. The result is a number that tells you the number of sales out of the previous hundred that were made at a lower price than the current price.

Evaluating groups of rows

Sometimes the sort key you have chosen to place a partition in order will have duplicates. You may want to evaluate all rows that have the same sort key as a group. In such cases you can use the GROUPS option. With it you can count groups of rows where the sort keys are identical.

Here's an example:

```
SELECT CustomerID, SaleDate,
    SUM (InvoiceTotal) OVER
    (PARTITION BY CustomerID
     ORDER BY SaleDate
    GROUPS BETWEEN 2 PRECEDING AND 2 FOLLOWING)
    FROM Customers;
```

The window frame in this example consists of up to five groups of rows: two groups before the group containing the current row, the group containing the current row, and two groups following the group containing the current row. The rows in each group have the same SaleDate, and the SaleDate associated with each group is different from the SaleDate values for the other groups.

Row pattern recognition

A worthwhile feature would be to be able to recognize a pattern in a table. This need was recognized in SQL:2016 with the inclusion of the MATCH_RECOGNIZE function. As its name implies, this function recognizes matches between the data in a table column and a pattern.

For example, as you work through the rows of a table, you may want to know if there is a pattern or perhaps a trend in the values of a column. If there is a pattern that you deem significant, it would be good to be able to recognize that pattern when it appears. The MATCH_RECOGNIZE function does this. It is very flexible, but the flexibility brings with it a great amount of complexity.

The MATCH_RECOGNIZE function resides within the FROM clause of a SELECT statement. It processes rows from an input table, and as part of that process creates an output table that contains rows produced whenever the target pattern is recognized.

The syntax is:

```
SELECT <columns> FROM <input table>
MATCH_RECOGNIZE (
    [PARTITION BY <columns>]
    [ORDER BY <columns>]
    MEASURES MATCH_NUMBER () AS <number>,
        <attribute> AS <start of pattern value>,
        LAST <attribute> AS <trend reversal value>,
        LAST <attribute> AS <end of pattern value>,
        [<other functions>]
    ONE ROW PER MATCH/ALL ROWS PER MATCH
    AFTER MATCH SKIP <where to skip to after a match>
    PATTERN <the row pattern being sought>
    [SUBSET <the union of the row pattern variables>]
    DEFINE <a Boolean condition>
) ;
```

As you can see, I was not kidding when I said MATCH_RECOGNIZE is complex. However, considering how important it can be to be able to find patterns in data, putting in the effort to learn how to use it could be a good use of your time. There is an eighty-page ISO/IEC technical report that gives explanation and examples of use that make MATCH_RECOGNIZE clearer. Access it here:

```
http://standards.iso.org/ittf/PubliclyAvailableStandards/
c065143_ISO_IEC_TR_19075-5_2016.zip
```

Chapter **11**

Using Relational Operators

You probably know by now that SQL is a query language for relational databases. In previous chapters, I present simple databases, and in most cases, my examples deal with only one table. In this chapter, I put the *relational* in "relational database." After all, the name means "a database that consists of multiple related tables." Here's where you finally see those relationships.

Because the data in a relational database is distributed across multiple tables, a query usually draws data from more than one table. SQL has operators that combine data from multiple sources into a single result set. These are the UNION, INTERSECTION, and EXCEPT operators, as well as a family of JOIN operators. Each operator combines data from multiple tables in a different way.

UNION

The UNION operator is the SQL implementation of relational algebra's union operator. The UNION operator enables you to draw information from two or more tables that have the same structure. *Same structure* means

» The tables must all have the same number of columns.

» Corresponding columns must all have identical data types and lengths.

When these criteria are met, the tables are *union-compatible:* The union of the two tables returns all the rows that appear in either table and eliminates duplicates.

Suppose you create a baseball-statistics database (like the one in Chapter 12). It contains two union-compatible tables named AMERICAN and NATIONAL. Both tables have three columns, and corresponding columns are all the same type. In fact, corresponding columns have identical column names (although this condition isn't required for union compatibility).

NATIONAL lists the players' names and the number of complete games pitched by National League pitchers. AMERICAN lists the same information about pitchers in the American League. The UNION of the two tables gives you a virtual result table containing all the rows in the first table plus all the rows in the second table. For this example, I put just a few rows in each table to illustrate the operation:

```
SELECT * FROM NATIONAL ;
FirstName    LastName     CompleteGames
----------   --------     -------------
Sal          Maglie                  11
Don          Newcombe                 9
Sandy        Koufax                  13
Don          Drysdale                12

SELECT * FROM AMERICAN ;

FirstName    LastName    CompleteGames
----------   --------    -------------
Whitey       Ford                  12
Don          Larson                10
Bob          Turley                 8
Allie        Reynolds              14

SELECT * FROM NATIONAL
UNION
SELECT * FROM AMERICAN ;

FirstName    LastName     CompleteGames
----------   --------     -------------
Allie        Reynolds              14
Bob          Turley                 8
Don          Drysdale              12
Don          Larson                10
```

Don	Newcombe	9
Sal	Maglie	11
Sandy	Koufax	13
Whitey	Ford	12

The UNION DISTINCT operator functions identically to the UNION operator without the DISTINCT keyword. In both cases, duplicate rows are eliminated from the result set.

WARNING

I've been using the asterisk (*) as shorthand for all the columns in a table. This shortcut is fine most of the time, but it can get you into trouble when you use relational operators in embedded or module-language SQL. If you add one or more new columns to one table and not to another, or you add different columns to the two tables, the two tables are no longer union-compatible — and your program will be invalid the next time it's recompiled. Even if the same new columns are added to both tables so they're still union-compatible, your program is probably not prepared to deal with the additional data. You should explicitly list the columns you want, instead of relying on the * shorthand. When you're entering ad hoc SQL queries from the console, the asterisk probably works fine, because you can quickly display a table structure to verify union compatibility if your query isn't successful.

The UNION ALL operation

As I mention previously, the UNION operation usually eliminates any duplicate rows that result from its operation, which is the desired result most of the time. Sometimes, however, you may want to preserve duplicate rows. On those occasions, use UNION ALL.

Referring to the example, suppose that "Bullet" Bob Turley had been traded in midseason from the New York Yankees in the American League to the Brooklyn Dodgers in the National League. Now suppose that during the season, he pitched eight complete games for each team. The ordinary UNION displayed in the example throws away one of the two lines containing Turley's data. Although he seemed to pitch only 8 complete games in the season, he actually hurled a remarkable 16 complete games. The following query gives you the true facts:

```
SELECT * FROM NATIONAL
UNION ALL
SELECT * FROM AMERICAN ;
```

TIP

You can sometimes form a UNION of two tables even if they're not union-compatible. If the columns you want in your result table are present *and compatible* in both tables, you can perform a UNION CORRESPONDING operation. Only the specified columns are considered — and they are the only columns displayed in the result table.

The CORRESPONDING operation

Baseball statisticians keep different statistics on pitchers than they keep on out-fielders. In both cases, first names, last names, putouts, errors, and fielding per-centages are recorded. Outfielders, of course, don't have a won/lost record, a saves record, or several other stats that pertain only to pitching. You can still perform a UNION that takes data from the OUTFIELDER table and from the PITCHER table to give you some overall information about defensive skill:

```
SELECT *
    FROM OUTFIELDER
UNION CORRESPONDING
    (FirstName, LastName, Putouts, Errors, FieldPct)
SELECT *
    FROM PITCHER ;
```

The result table holds the first and last names of all the outfielders and pitchers, along with the putouts, errors, and fielding percentage of each player. As with the simple UNION, duplicates are eliminated. Thus, if a player spent some time in the outfield and he also pitched in one or more games, the UNION CORRESPONDING operation loses some of his statistics. To avoid this problem, use UNION ALL CORRESPONDING.

TIP

Each column name in the list following the CORRESPONDING keyword must be a name that exists in both union-joined tables. If you omit this list of names, an implicit list of all names that appear in both tables is used. But this implicit list of names may change when new columns are added to one or both tables. Therefore you're better off explicitly listing the column names than you are if you omit them.

INTERSECT

The UNION operation produces a result table containing all rows that appear in *any* of the source tables. If you want only rows that appear in *all* the source tables, you can use the INTERSECT operation, which is the SQL implementation of relational algebra's intersect operation. I illustrate INTERSECT by returning to the fantasy world in which Bob Turley was traded to the Dodgers in midseason:

```
SELECT * FROM NATIONAL;
FirstName     LastName      CompleteGames

---------     ---------     -------------
Sal           Maglie                   11
Don           Newcombe                  9
Sandy         Koufax                   13
```

```
Don            Drysdale              12
Bob            Turley                 8

SELECT * FROM AMERICAN;
FIRST_NAME  LAST_NAME  COMPLETE_GAMES
----------  ---------  --------------
Whitey      Ford                   12
Don         Larson                 10
Bob         Turley                  8
Allie       Reynolds               14
```

Only rows that appear in all source tables show up in the INTERSECT operation's result table:

```
SELECT *
    FROM NATIONAL
INTERSECT
SELECT *
    FROM AMERICAN;

FirstName   LastName    CompleteGames
----------  ---------   --------------
Bob         Turley                  8
```

The result table tells you that Bob Turley was the only pitcher to throw the same number of complete games in both leagues (a rather obscure distinction for old Bullet Bob). *Note:* As was the case with UNION, INTERSECT DISTINCT produces the same result as the INTERSECT operator used alone. In this example, only one of the identical rows featuring Bob Turley is returned.

TIP

The ALL and CORRESPONDING keywords function in an INTERSECT operation the same way they do in a UNION operation. If you use ALL, duplicates are retained in the result table. If you use CORRESPONDING, the intersected tables don't need to be union-compatible, although the corresponding columns must have matching types and lengths.

Here's what you get with INTERSECT ALL:

```
SELECT *
    FROM NATIONAL
INTERSECT ALL
SELECT *
    FROM AMERICAN;
```

FirstName	LastName	CompleteGames
Bob	Turley	8
Bob	Turley	8

Consider another example: A municipality keeps track of the cell phones carried by police officers, firefighters, street sweepers, and other city employees. A database table called PHONES contains data on all phones in active use. Another table named OUT, with an identical structure, contains data on all phones that have been taken out of service. No phones should ever exist in both tables. With an INTERSECT operation, you can test to see whether such an unwanted duplication has occurred:

```
SELECT *
    FROM PHONES
INTERSECT CORRESPONDING (PhoneID)
SELECT *
    FROM OUT ;
```

REMEMBER

If this operation gives you a result table containing any rows at all, you know you have a problem. You should investigate any PhoneID entries that appear in the result table. The corresponding phone is either active or out of service; it can't be both. After you detect the problem, you can perform a DELETE operation on one of the two tables to restore database integrity.

EXCEPT

The UNION operation acts on two source tables and returns all rows that appear in either table. The INTERSECT operation returns all rows that appear in both the first and the second tables. In contrast, the EXCEPT (or EXCEPT DISTINCT) operation returns all rows that appear in the first table but that *do not* also appear in the second table.

Returning to the municipal phone database example (see the "INTERSECT" section, earlier in this chapter), say that a group of phones that had been declared out of service and returned to the vendor for repairs have now been fixed and placed back into service. The PHONES table was updated to reflect the returned phones, but the returned phones were not removed from the OUT table as they should have been. You can display the PhoneID numbers of the phones in the OUT table, with the reactivated ones eliminated, using an EXCEPT operation:

```
SELECT *
    FROM OUT
EXCEPT CORRESPONDING (PhoneID)
SELECT *
    FROM PHONES;
```

This query returns all the rows in the OUT table whose PhoneID is not also present in the PHONES table.

Join Operators

The UNION, INTERSECT, and EXCEPT operators are valuable in multi-table databases that contain union-compatible tables. In many cases, however, you want to draw data from multiple tables that have very little in common. Joins are powerful relational operators that combine data from multiple tables into a single result table. The source tables may have little (or even nothing) in common with each other.

SQL supports several types of joins. The best one to choose in a given situation depends on the result you're trying to achieve. The following sections give you the details.

Basic join

Any multi-table query is a type of join. The source tables are joined in the sense that the result table includes information taken from all the source tables. The simplest join is a two-table SELECT that has no WHERE clause qualifiers: Every row of the first table is joined to every row of the second table. The result table is the Cartesian product of the two source tables. The number of rows in the result table is equal to the number of rows in the first source table multiplied by the number of rows in the second source table.

For example, imagine that you're the personnel manager for a company and that part of your job is to maintain employee records. Most employee data, such as home address and telephone number, is not particularly sensitive. But some data, such as current salary, should be available only to authorized personnel. To maintain security of the sensitive information, keep it in a separate table that is password protected. Consider the following pair of tables:

```
EMPLOYEE                        COMPENSATION
--------                        ------------

EmpID                           Employ
FName                           Salary
LName                           Bonus
City
Phone
```

Fill the tables with some sample data:

```
EmpID    FName    LName     City      Phone
-----    -----    -----     ----      -----
    1    Whitey   Ford      Orange    555-1001
    2    Don      Larson    Newark    555-3221
    3    Sal      Maglie    Nutley    555-6905
    4    Bob      Turley    Passaic   555-8908


Employ   Salary   Bonus
------   ------   -----
    1    33000    10000
    2    18000    2000
    3    24000    5000
    4    22000    7000
```

Create a virtual result table with the following query:

```
SELECT *
   FROM EMPLOYEE, COMPENSATION ;
```

Here's what the query produces:

```
EmpID FName   LName   City     Phone      Employ Salary Bonus
----- -----   -----   ----     -----      ------ ------ -----
    1 Whitey  Ford    Orange   555-1001        1 33000  10000
    1 Whitey  Ford    Orange   555-1001        2 18000  2000
    1 Whitey  Ford    Orange   555-1001        3 24000  5000
    1 Whitey  Ford    Orange   555-1001        4 22000  7000
    2 Don     Larson  Newark   555-3221        1 33000  10000
    2 Don     Larson  Newark   555-3221        2 18000  2000
    2 Don     Larson  Newark   555-3221        3 24000  5000
    2 Don     Larson  Newark   555-3221        4 22000  7000
    3 Sal     Maglie  Nutley   555-6905        1 33000  10000
```

3	Sal	Maglie	Nutley	555-6905	2	18000	2000
3	Sal	Maglie	Nutley	555-6905	3	24000	5000
3	Sal	Maglie	Nutley	555-6905	4	22000	7000
4	Bob	Turley	Passaic	555-8908	1	33000	10000
4	Bob	Turley	Passaic	555-8908	2	18000	2000
4	Bob	Turley	Passaic	555-8908	3	24000	5000
4	Bob	Turley	Passaic	555-8908	4	22000	7000

The result table, which is the Cartesian product of the EMPLOYEE and COMPEN-SATION tables, contains considerable redundancy. Furthermore, it doesn't make much sense. It combines every row of EMPLOYEE with every row of COMPENSA-TION. The only rows that convey meaningful information are those in which the EmpID number that came from EMPLOYEE matches the Employ number that came from COMPENSATION. In those rows, an employee's name and address are associated with his or her own compensation.

When you're trying to get useful information out of a multi-table database, the Cartesian product produced by a basic join is almost *never* what you want, but it's almost *always* the first step toward what you want. By applying constraints to the JOIN with a WHERE clause, you can filter out the unwanted rows. The following section explains how to filter the stuff you don't need to see.

Equi-join

The most common join that uses the WHERE clause filter is the equi-join. An *equi-join* is a basic join with a WHERE clause that contains a condition specifying that the value in one column in the first table must be equal to the value of a corresponding column in the second table. Applying an equi-join to the example tables from the previous section brings a more meaningful result:

```
SELECT *
    FROM EMPLOYEE, COMPENSATION
    WHERE EMPLOYEE.EmpID = COMPENSATION.Employ ;
```

This query produces the following results:

EmpID	FName	LName	City	Phone	Employ	Salary	Bonus
1	Whitey	Ford	Orange	555-1001	1	33000	10000
2	Don	Larson	Newark	555-3221	2	18000	2000
3	Sal	Maglie	Nutley	555-6905	3	24000	5000
4	Bob	Turley	Passaic	555-8908	4	22000	7000

In this result table, the salaries and bonuses on the right apply to the employees named on the left. The table still has some redundancy because the EmpID column duplicates the Employ column. You can fix this problem by slightly reformulating the query, like this:

```
SELECT EMPLOYEE.*,COMPENSATION.Salary,COMPENSATION.Bonus
    FROM EMPLOYEE, COMPENSATION
    WHERE EMPLOYEE.EmpID = COMPENSATION.Employ ;
```

This query produces the following result table:

EmpID	FName	LName	City	Phone	Salary	Bonus
1	Whitey	Ford	Orange	555-1001	33000	10000
2	Don	Larson	Newark	555-3221	18000	2000
3	Sal	Maglie	Nutley	555-6905	24000	5000
4	Bob	Turley	Passaic	555-8908	22000	7000

This table tells you what you want to know but doesn't burden you with any extraneous data. The query is somewhat tedious to write, however. To avoid ambiguity, you can qualify the column names with the names of the tables they came from. Typing those table names repeatedly provides good exercise for the fingers but has no other merit.

You can cut down on the amount of typing by using aliases (or *correlation names*). An *alias* is a short name that stands for a table name. If you use aliases in recasting the preceding query, it comes out like this:

```
SELECT E.*, C.Salary, C.Bonus
    FROM EMPLOYEE E, COMPENSATION C
    WHERE E.EmpID = C.Employ ;
```

In this example, E is the alias for EMPLOYEE, and C is the alias for COMPENSATION. The alias is local to the statement it's in. After you declare an alias (in the FROM clause), you must use it throughout the statement. You can't use both the alias and the long form of the table name in the same statement.

TIP

Even if you could mix the long form of table names with aliases, you wouldn't want to, because doing so creates major confusion. Consider the following example:

```
SELECT T1.C, T2.C
    FROM T1 T2, T2 T1
    WHERE T1.C > T2.C ;
```

In this example, the alias for T1 is T2, and the alias for T2 is T1. Admittedly, this isn't a smart selection of aliases, but it isn't forbidden by the rules. If you mix aliases with long-form table names, you can't tell which table is which.

The preceding example with aliases is equivalent to the following SELECT statement with no aliases:

```
SELECT T2.C, T1.C
   FROM T1 , T2
   WHERE T2.C > T1.C ;
```

SQL enables you to join more than two tables. The maximum number varies from one implementation to another. The syntax is analogous to the two-table case; here's what it looks like:

```
SELECT E.*, C.Salary, C.Bonus, Y.TotalSales
   FROM EMPLOYEE E, COMPENSATION C, YTD_SALES Y
   WHERE E.EmpID = C.Employ
      AND C.Employ = Y.EmpNo ;
```

This statement performs an equi-join on three tables, pulling data from corresponding rows of each one to produce a result table that shows the salespeople's names, the amount of sales they are responsible for, and their compensation. The sales manager can quickly see whether compensation is in line with production.

TIP

Storing a salesperson's year-to-date sales in a separate YTD_SALES table ensures better computer performance and data reliability than keeping that data in the EMPLOYEE table. The data in the EMPLOYEE table is relatively static. A person's name, address, and telephone number don't change very often. In contrast, the year-to-date sales change frequently (you hope). Because the YTD_SALES table has fewer columns than the EMPLOYEE table, you may be able to update it more quickly. If, in the course of updating sales totals, you don't touch the EMPLOYEE table, you decrease the risk of accidentally modifying employee information that should stay the same.

Cross join

CROSS JOIN is the keyword for the basic join without a WHERE clause. Therefore

```
SELECT *
FROM EMPLOYEE, COMPENSATION ;
```

can also be written as

```
SELECT *
FROM EMPLOYEE CROSS JOIN COMPENSATION ;
```

The result is the Cartesian product (also called the *cross product*) of the two source tables. CROSS JOIN rarely gives you the final result you want, but it can be useful as the first step in a chain of data-manipulation operations that ultimately produce the desired result.

Natural join

The *natural join* is a special case of an equi-join. In the WHERE clause of an equi-join, a column from one source table is compared with a column of a second source table for equality. The two columns must be the same type and length and must have the same name. In fact, in a natural join, all columns in one table that have the same names, types, and lengths as corresponding columns in the second table are compared for equality.

Imagine that the COMPENSATION table from the preceding example has columns EmpID, Salary, and Bonus rather than Employ, Salary, and Bonus. In that case, you can perform a natural join of the COMPENSATION table with the EMPLOYEE table. The traditional JOIN syntax would look like this:

```
SELECT E.*, C.Salary, C.Bonus
   FROM EMPLOYEE E, COMPENSATION C
   WHERE E.EmpID = C.EmpID ;
```

This query is a special case of a natural join. The SELECT statement will return joined rows where E.EmpID = C.EmpID. Consider the following:

```
SELECT E.*, C.Salary, C.Bonus
   FROM EMPLOYEE E NATURAL JOIN COMPENSATION C ;
```

This query will join rows where E.EmpID = C.EmpID, where E.Salary = C.Salary, and where E.Bonus = C.Bonus. The result table will contain only rows where *all* corresponding columns match. In this example, the results of both queries will be the same because the EMPLOYEE table does not contain either a Salary or a Bonus column.

Condition join

A *condition join* is like an equi-join, except the condition being tested doesn't have to be an equality (although it can be). It can be any well-formed predicate. If the condition is satisfied, then the corresponding row becomes part of the result table. The syntax is a little different from what you have seen so far: The condition is contained in an ON clause rather than in a WHERE clause.

Say that a baseball statistician wants to know which National League pitchers have pitched the same number of complete games as one or more American League pitchers. This question is a job for an equi-join, which can also be expressed with condition-join syntax:

```
SELECT *
   FROM NATIONAL JOIN AMERICAN
   ON NATIONAL.CompleteGames = AMERICAN.CompleteGames ;
```

Column-name join

The *column-name join* is like a natural join, but it's more flexible. In a natural join, all the source table columns that have the same name are compared with each other for equality. With the column-name join, you select which same-name columns to compare. You can choose them all if you want, making the column-name join (effectively) a natural join. Or you may choose fewer than all same-name columns. In this way, you have a great degree of control over which cross-product rows qualify to be placed into your result table.

Suppose you're a chess-set manufacturer and have one inventory table that keeps track of your stock of white pieces and another that keeps track of black pieces. The tables contain data as follows:

```
WHITE                              BLACK
-----                              -----

Piece  Quant  Wood                 Piece   Quant  Wood
-----  -----  ----                 -----   -----  ----

King    502   Oak                  King     502   Ebony
Queen   398   Oak                  Queen    397   Ebony
Rook   1020   Oak                  Rook    1020   Ebony
Bishop  985   Oak                  Bishop   985   Ebony
Knight  950   Oak                  Knight   950   Ebony
Pawn    431   Oak                  Pawn     453   Ebony
```

For each piece type, the number of white pieces should match the number of black pieces. If they don't match, some chessmen are being lost or stolen, and you need to tighten security measures.

A natural join compares all columns with the same name for equality. In this case, a result table with no rows is produced because no rows in the WOOD column in the WHITE table match any rows in the WOOD column in the BLACK table. This result table doesn't help you determine whether any merchandise is missing. Instead, do a column-name join that excludes the WOOD column from consideration. It can take the following form:

```
SELECT *
   FROM WHITE JOIN BLACK
   USING (Piece, Quant) ;
```

The result table shows only the rows for which the number of white pieces in stock equals the number of black pieces:

```
Piece Quant Wood Piece  Quant Wood
_____ _____ ____ _____  _____ ____
King    502 Oak  King     502 Ebony
Rook   1020 Oak  Rook    1020 Ebony
Bishop  985 Oak  Bishop   985 Ebony
Knight  950 Oak  Knight   950 Ebony
```

The shrewd person can deduce that Queen and Pawn are missing from the list, indicating a shortage somewhere for those piece types.

Inner join

By now, you're probably getting the idea that joins are pretty esoteric and that it takes an uncommon level of spiritual discernment to deal with them adequately. You may have even heard of the mysterious *inner join* and speculated that it probably represents the core or essence of relational operations. Well, ha! The joke's on you: There's nothing mysterious about inner joins. In fact, all the joins covered so far in this chapter are inner joins. I could have formulated the column-name join in the last example as an inner join by using the following syntax:

```
SELECT *
   FROM WHITE INNER JOIN BLACK
   USING (Piece, Quant) ;
```

The result is the same.

The inner join is so named to distinguish it from the outer join. An inner join discards all rows from the result table that don't have corresponding rows in both source tables. An outer join preserves unmatched rows. That's the difference. Nothing metaphysical about it.

Outer join

When you're joining two tables, the first one (call it the one on the left) may have rows that don't have matching counterparts in the second table (the one on the right). Conversely, the table on the right may have rows that don't have matching counterparts in the table on the left. If you perform an inner join on those tables, all the unmatched rows are excluded from the output. *Outer joins*, however, don't exclude the unmatched rows. Outer joins come in three types: the left outer join, the right outer join, and the full outer join.

Left outer join

In a query that includes a join, the left table is the one that precedes the keyword JOIN, and the right table is the one that follows it. The *left outer join* preserves unmatched rows from the left table but discards unmatched rows from the right table.

To understand outer joins, consider a corporate database that maintains records of the company's employees, departments, and locations. Tables 11-1, 11-2, and 11-3 contain the database's example data.

TABLE 11-1

LOCATION

LOCATION_ID	CITY
1	Boston
3	Tampa
5	Chicago

TABLE 11-2

DEPT

DEPT_ID	LOCATION_ID	NAME
21	1	Sales
24	1	Admin
27	5	Repair
29	5	Stock

TABLE 11-3

EMPLOYEE

EMP_ID	DEPT_ID	NAME
61	24	Kirk
63	27	McCoy

Now suppose you want to see all the data for all employees, including department and location. You get this with an equi-join:

```
SELECT *
    FROM LOCATION L, DEPT D, EMPLOYEE E
    WHERE L.LocationID = D.LocationID
        AND D.DeptID = E.DeptID ;
```

This statement produces the following result:

| 1 | Boston | 24 | 1 | Admin | 61 | 24 | Kirk |
| 5 | Chicago | 27 | 5 | Repair | 63 | 27 | McCoy |

This result table gives all the data for all the employees, including location and department. The equi-join works because every employee has a location and a department.

Next, suppose you want the data on the locations, with the related department and employee data. This is a different problem because a location without any associated departments may exist. To get what you want, you must use an outer join, as in the following example:

```
SELECT *
    FROM LOCATION L LEFT OUTER JOIN DEPT D
        ON (L.LocationID = D.LocationID)
    LEFT OUTER JOIN EMPLOYEE E
        ON (D.DeptID = E.DeptID);
```

This join pulls data from three tables. First, the LOCATION table is joined to the DEPT table. The result set is then joined to the EMPLOYEE table. Rows from the table on the left of the LEFT OUTER JOIN operator that have no corresponding row in the table on the right are included in the result. Thus, in the first join, all locations are included, even if no department associated with them exists. In the second join, all departments are included, even if no employee associated with them exists. The result is as follows:

1	Boston	24	1	Admin	61	24	Kirk
5	Chicago	27	5	Repair	63	27	McCoy
3	Tampa	NULL	NULL	NULL	NULL	NULL	NULL
5	Chicago	29	5	Stock	NULL	NULL	NULL
1	Boston	21	1	Sales	NULL	NULL	NULL

The first two rows are the same as the two result rows in the previous example. The third row (3 Tampa) has nulls in the department and employee columns because no departments are defined for Tampa and no employees are stationed there. The fourth and fifth rows (5 Chicago and 1 Boston) contain data about the Stock and the Sales departments, but the Employee columns for these rows contain nulls because these two departments have no employees. This outer join tells you everything that the equi-join told you — plus the following:

>> All the company's locations, whether they have any departments or not

>> All the company's departments, whether they have any employees or not

The rows returned in the preceding example aren't guaranteed to be in the order you want. The order may vary from one implementation to the next. To make sure that the rows returned are in the order you want, add an ORDER BY clause to your SELECT statement, like this:

```
SELECT *
    FROM LOCATION L LEFT OUTER JOIN DEPT D
        ON (L.LocationID = D.LocationID)
    LEFT OUTER JOIN EMPLOYEE E
        ON (D.DeptID = E.DeptID)
    ORDER BY L.LocationID, D.DeptID, E.EmpID;
```

TIP

You can abbreviate the left outer join language as LEFT JOIN because there's no such thing as a left *inner* join.

Right outer join

I bet you figured out how the right outer join behaves. Right! The *right outer join* preserves unmatched rows from the right table but discards unmatched rows from the left table. You can use it on the same tables and get the same result by reversing the order in which you present tables to the join:

```
SELECT *
    FROM EMPLOYEE E RIGHT OUTER JOIN DEPT D
        ON (D.DeptID = E.DeptID)
    RIGHT OUTER JOIN LOCATION L
        ON (L.LocationID = D.LocationID) ;
```

In this formulation, the first join produces a table that contains all departments, whether they have an associated employee or not. The second join produces a table that contains all locations, whether they have an associated department or not.

TIP

You can abbreviate the right outer join language as RIGHT JOIN because there's no such thing as a right *inner* join.

Full outer join

The *full outer join* combines the functions of the left outer join and the right outer join. It retains the unmatched rows from both the left and the right tables. Consider the most general case of the company database used in the preceding examples. It could have

» Locations with no departments

» Departments with no locations

>> Departments with no employees

>> Employees with no departments

To show all locations, departments, and employees, regardless of whether they have corresponding rows in the other tables, use a full outer join in the following form:

```
SELECT *
    FROM LOCATION L FULL OUTER JOIN DEPT D
        ON (L.LocationID = D.LocationID)
    FULL OUTER JOIN EMPLOYEE E
        ON (D.DeptID = E.DeptID) ;
```

TIP

You can abbreviate the full-outer-join language as FULL JOIN because (this may sound hauntingly familiar) there's no such thing as a full *inner* join.

Union join

Unlike the other kinds of join, the *union join* makes no attempt to match a row from the left source table with any rows in the right source table. It creates a new virtual table that contains the union of all the columns in both source tables. In the virtual result table, the columns that came from the left source table contain all the rows that were in the left source table. For those rows, the columns that came from the right source table all have the null value. Similarly, the columns that came from the right source table contain all the rows that were in the right source table. For those rows, the columns that came from the left source table all have the null value. Thus, the table resulting from a union join contains all the columns of both source tables — and the number of rows it contains is the sum of the number of rows in the two source tables.

The result of a union join by itself is not immediately useful in most cases; it produces a result table with many nulls in it. But you can get useful information from a union join when you use it in conjunction with the COALESCE expression discussed in Chapter 9. Look at an example.

Suppose that you work for a company that designs and builds experimental rockets. You have several projects in the works. You also have several design engineers who have skills in multiple areas. As a manager, you want to know which employees, having which skills, have worked on which projects. Currently, this data is scattered among the EMPLOYEE table, the PROJECTS table, and the SKILLS table.

The EMPLOYEE table carries data about employees, and EMPLOYEE.EmpID is its primary key. The PROJECTS table has a row for each project that an employee has worked on. PROJECTS.EmpID is a foreign key that references the EMPLOYEE table.

The SKILLS table shows the expertise of each employee. `SKILLS.EmpID` is a foreign key that references the EMPLOYEE table.

The EMPLOYEE table has one row for each employee; the PROJECTS table and the SKILLS table have zero or more rows.

Tables 11-4, 11-5, and 11-6 show example data in the three tables.

TABLE 11-4

EMPLOYEE Table

EmpID	Name
1	Ferguson
2	Frost
3	Toyon

TABLE 11-5

PROJECTS Table

ProjectName	EmpID
X-63 Structure	1
X-64 Structure	1
X-63 Guidance	2
X-64 Guidance	2
X-63 Telemetry	3
X-64 Telemetry	3

TABLE 11-6

SKILLS Table

Skill	EmpID
Mechanical Design	1
Aerodynamic Loading	1
Analog Design	2
Gyroscope Design	2
Digital Design	3
R/F Design	3

From the tables, you can see that Ferguson has worked on X-63 and X-64 structure design and has expertise in mechanical design and aerodynamic loading.

Now suppose that, as a manager, you want to see all the information about all the employees. You decide to apply an equi-join to the EMPLOYEE, PROJECTS, and SKILLS tables:

```
SELECT *
    FROM EMPLOYEE E, PROJECTS P, SKILLS S
    WHERE E.EmpID = P.EmpID
        AND E.EmpID = S.EmpID ;
```

You can express this same operation as an inner join by using the following syntax:

```
SELECT *
    FROM EMPLOYEE E INNER JOIN PROJECTS P
        ON (E.EmpID = P.EmpID)
    INNER JOIN SKILLS S
        ON (E.EmpID = S.EmpID) ;
```

Both formulations give the same result, as shown in Table 11-7.

TABLE 11-7   ## Result of Inner Join

E.EmpID	Name	P.EmpID	ProjectName	S.EmpID	Skill
1	Ferguson	1	X-63 Structure	1	Mechanical Design
1	Ferguson	1	X-63 Structure	1	Aerodynamic Loading
1	Ferguson	1	X-64 Structure	1	Mechanical Design
1	Ferguson	1	X-64 Structure	1	Aerodynamic Loading
2	Frost	2	X-63 Guidance	2	Analog Design
2	Frost	2	X-63 Guidance	2	Gyroscope Design
2	Frost	2	X-64 Guidance	2	Analog Design
2	Frost	2	X-64 Guidance	2	Gyroscope Design
3	Toyon	3	X-63 Telemetry	3	Digital Design
3	Toyon	3	X-63 Telemetry	3	R/F Design
3	Toyon	3	X-64 Telemetry	3	Digital Design
3	Toyon	3	X-64 Telemetry	3	R/F Design

This data arrangement is not particularly enlightening. The employee ID numbers appear three times, and the projects and skills are duplicated for each employee. Bottom line: The inner joins are not well suited to answering this type of question. You can put the union join to work here, along with some strategically chosen SELECT statements, to produce a more suitable result. You begin with the basic union join:

```
SELECT *
    FROM EMPLOYEE E UNION JOIN PROJECTS P
        UNION JOIN SKILLS S ;
```

Notice that the union join has no ON clause. It doesn't filter the data, so an ON clause isn't needed. This statement produces the result shown in Table 11-8.

TABLE 11-8   ## Result of Union Join

E.EmpID	Name	P.EmpID	ProjectName	S.EmpID	Skill
1	Ferguson	NULL	NULL	NULL	NULL
NULL	NULL	1	X-63 Structure	NULL	NULL
NULL	NULL	1	X-64 Structure	NULL	NULL
NULL	NULL	NULL	NULL	1	Mechanical Design
NULL	NULL	NULL	NULL	1	Aerodynamic Loading
2	Frost	NULL	NULL	NULL	NULL
NULL	NULL	2	X-63 Guidance	NULL	NULL
NULL	NULL	2	X-64 Guidance	NULL	NULL
NULL	NULL	NULL	NULL	2	Analog Design
NULL	NULL	NULL	NULL	2	Gyroscope Design
3	Toyon	NULL	NULL	NULL	NULL
NULL	NULL	3	X-63 Telemetry	NULL	NULL
NULL	NULL	3	X-64 Telemetry	NULL	NULL
NULL	NULL	NULL	NULL	3	Digital Design
NULL	NULL	NULL	NULL	3	R/F Design

Each table has been extended to the right or left with nulls, and those null-extended rows have been union joined. The order of the rows is arbitrary and depends on the implementation. Now you can massage the data to put it in a more useful form.

Notice that the table has three ID columns, two of which are null in any row. You can improve the display by coalescing the ID columns. As I note in Chapter 9, the COALESCE expression takes on the value of the first non-null value in a list of values. In the present case, it takes on the value of the only non-null value in a column list:

```
SELECT COALESCE (E.EmpID, P.EmpID, S.EmpID) AS ID,
     E.Name, P.ProjectName, S.Skill
   FROM EMPLOYEE E UNION JOIN PROJECTS P
     UNION JOIN SKILLS S
   ORDER BY ID ;
```

The FROM clause is the same as in the previous example, but now the three EMP_ID columns are coalesced into a single column named ID. You're also ordering the result by ID. Table 11-9 shows the result.

TABLE 11-9   **Result of Union Join with COALESCE Expression**

ID	Name	ProjectName	Skill
1	Ferguson	X-63 Structure	NULL
1	Ferguson	X-64 Structure	NULL
1	Ferguson	NULL	Mechanical Design
1	Ferguson	NULL	Aerodynamic Loading
2	Frost	X-63 Guidance	NULL
2	Frost	X-64 Guidance	NULL
2	Frost	NULL	Analog Design
2	Frost	NULL	Gyroscope Design
3	Toyon	X-63 Telemetry	NULL
3	Toyon	X-64 Telemetry	NULL
3	Toyon	NULL	Digital Design
3	Toyon	NULL	R/F Design

Each row in this result has data about a project or a skill, but not both. When you read the result, you first must determine what type of information is in each row (project or skill). If the ProjectName column has a non-null value, the row names a project on which the employee has worked. If the Skill column is not null, the row names one of the employee's skills.

TIP

You can make the result a little clearer by adding another COALESCE to the SELECT statement, as follows:

```
SELECT COALESCE (E.EmpID, P.EmpID, S.EmpID) AS ID,
      E.Name, COALESCE (P.Type, S.Type) AS Type,
      P.ProjectName, S.Skill
   FROM EMPLOYEE E
      UNION JOIN (SELECT "Project" AS Type, P.*
                      FROM PROJECTS) P
      UNION JOIN (SELECT "Skill" AS Type, S.*
                      FROM SKILLS) S
   ORDER BY ID, Type ;
```

In this union join, the PROJECTS table in the previous example is replaced with a nested SELECT that appends a column named P.Type with a constant value "Project" to the columns coming from the PROJECTS table. Similarly, the SKILLS table is replaced with a nested SELECT that appends a column named S.Type with a constant value "Skill" to the columns coming from the SKILLS table. In each row, P.Type is either null or "Project", and S.Type is either null or "Skill".

The outer SELECT list specifies a COALESCE of those two Type columns into a single column named Type. You then specify Type in the ORDER BY clause, which sorts the rows that all have the same ID in an order that puts all projects first, followed by all skills. The result is shown in Table 11-10.

TABLE 11-10 **Refined Result of Union Join with COALESCE Expressions**

ID	Name	Type	ProjectName	Skill
1	Ferguson	Project	X-63 Structure	NULL
1	Ferguson	Project	X-64 Structure	NULL
1	Ferguson	Skill	NULL	Mechanical Design
1	Ferguson	Skill	NULL	Aerodynamic Loading
2	Frost	Project	X-63 Guidance	NULL
2	Frost	Project	X-64 Guidance	NULL
2	Frost	Skill	NULL	Analog Design
2	Frost	Skill	NULL	Gyroscope Design
3	Toyon	Project	X-63 Telemetry	NULL
3	Toyon	Project	X-64 Telemetry	NULL
3	Toyon	Skill	NULL	Digital Design
3	Toyon	Skill	NULL	R/F Design

The result table now presents a very readable account of the project experience and skill sets of all employees in the EMPLOYEE table.

Considering the number of JOIN operations available, relating data from different tables shouldn't be a problem, regardless of the tables' structure. You can trust that if the raw data exists in your database, SQL has the means to get it out and display it in a meaningful form.

ON versus WHERE

The function of the ON and WHERE clauses in the various types of joins is potentially confusing. These facts may help you keep things straight:

» The ON clause is part of the inner, left, right, and full joins. The cross join and union join don't have an ON clause because neither of them does any filtering of the data.

» The ON clause in an inner join is logically equivalent to a WHERE clause; the same condition could be specified either in an ON clause or a WHERE clause.

» The ON clauses in outer joins (left, right, and full joins) are different from WHERE clauses. The WHERE clause simply filters the rows returned by the FROM clause. Rows rejected by the filter are not included in the result. The ON clause in an outer join first filters the rows of a cross product and then includes the rejected rows, extended with nulls.

Chapter **12**

Delving Deep with Nested Queries

O ne of the best ways to protect your data's integrity is to avoid modification anomalies (see Chapter 5 for the gory details of those) by normalizing your database. *Normalization* involves breaking up a single table into multiple tables, each of which has a single theme. You don't want product information in the same table with customer information, for example, even if the customers have bought products.

If you normalize a database properly, the data is scattered across multiple tables. Most queries that you want to make need to pull data from two or more tables. One way to do this is to use a join operator or one of the other relational operators

(UNION, INTERSECT, or EXCEPT). The relational operators take information from multiple tables and combine it all into a single result set. Different operators combine the data in different ways.

REMEMBER

Another way to pull data from two or more tables is to use a nested query. In SQL, a *nested query* is one in which an outer enclosing statement contains within it a subquery. That subquery may serve as an enclosing statement for a lower-level subquery that is nested within it. There are no theoretical limits to the number of nesting levels a nested query may have, but you do face some practical limits that depend on your SQL implementation.

Subqueries are invariably SELECT statements, but the outermost enclosing statement may also be an INSERT, UPDATE, or DELETE statement.

TIP

A subquery can operate on a table other than the table that its enclosing statement operates on, so nested queries give you another way to extract information from multiple tables.

For example, suppose that you want to query your corporate database to find all department managers who are more than 50 years old. With the joins I discuss in Chapter 11, you can use a query like this:

```
SELECT D.Deptno, D.Name, E.Name, E.Age
    FROM DEPT D, EMPLOYEE E
    WHERE D.ManagerID = E.ID AND E.Age >50 ;
```

D is the alias for the DEPT table, and E is the alias for the EMPLOYEE table. The EMPLOYEE table has an ID column that is the primary key, and the DEPT table has a ManagerID column that is the ID value of the employee who is the department's manager. A simple join (the list of tables in the FROM clause) pairs the related tables, and a WHERE clause filters out all rows except those that meet the criteria. Note that the SELECT statement's parameter list includes the Deptno and Name columns from the DEPT table and the Name and Age columns from the EMPLOYEE table.

Next, suppose that you're interested in the same set of rows but you want only the columns from the DEPT table. In other words, you're interested in the departments whose managers are 50 or older, but you don't care who those managers are or exactly how old they are. You could then write the query with a *subquery* rather than a join:

```
SELECT D.Deptno, D.Name
    FROM DEPT D
    WHERE EXISTS (SELECT * FROM EMPLOYEE E
      WHERE E.ID = D.ManagerID AND E.Age > 50) ;
```

This query has two new elements: the EXISTS keyword and the SELECT * in the WHERE clause of the inner SELECT. The inner SELECT is a subquery (or *subselect*), and the EXISTS keyword is one of several tools for use with a subquery that is described in this chapter.

What Subqueries Do

Subqueries are located within the WHERE clause of their enclosing statement. Their function is to set the search conditions for the WHERE clause. Each kind of subquery produces a different result. Some subqueries produce a list of values that is then used as input by the enclosing statement. Other subqueries produce a single value that the enclosing statement then evaluates with a comparison operator. A third kind of subquery returns a value of True or False.

Nested queries that return sets of rows

To illustrate how a nested query returns a set of rows, imagine that you work for a systems integrator of computer equipment. Your company, Zetec Corporation, assembles systems from components that you buy, and then it sells them to companies and government agencies. You keep track of your business with a relational database. The database consists of many tables, but right now you're concerned with only three of them: the PRODUCT table, the COMP_USED table, and the COMPONENT table. The PRODUCT table (shown in Table 12-1) contains a list of all your standard products. The COMPONENT table (shown in Table 12-2) lists components that go into your products, and the COMP_USED table (shown in Table 12-3) tracks which components go into each product.

TABLE 12-1

PRODUCT Table

Column	Type	Constraints
Model	CHAR (6)	PRIMARY KEY
ProdName	CHAR (35)	
ProdDesc	CHAR (31)	
ListPrice	NUMERIC (9,2)	

TABLE 12-2

COMPONENT Table

Column	Type	Constraints
CompID	CHAR (6)	PRIMARY KEY
CompType	CHAR (10)	
CompDesc	CHAR (31)	

TABLE 12-3

COMP_USED Table

Column	Type	Constraints
Model	CHAR (6)	FOREIGN KEY (for PRODUCT)
CompID	CHAR (6)	FOREIGN KEY (for COMPONENT)

A component may be used in multiple products, and a product can contain multiple components (a many-to-many relationship). This situation can cause integrity problems. To circumvent the problems, create the linking table COMP_USED to relate COMPONENT to PRODUCT. A component may appear in many rows in the COMP_USED table, but each of those rows will reference only one component (a one-to-many relationship). Similarly, a product may appear in many rows in COMP_USED, but each row references only one product (another one-to-many relationship). Adding the linking table transforms a troublesome many-to-many relationship into two relatively simple one-to-many relationships. This process of reducing the complexity of relationships is one example of normalization.

Subqueries introduced by the keyword IN

One form of a nested query compares a single value with the set of values returned by a SELECT statement. It uses the IN predicate with the following syntax:

```
SELECT column_list
    FROM table
    WHERE expression IN (subquery) ;
```

The expression in the WHERE clause evaluates to a value. If that value is IN the list returned by the subquery, then the WHERE clause returns a True value. The specified columns from the table row being processed are added to the result table. The subquery may reference the same table referenced by the outer query, or it may reference a different table.

In the following example, I use Zetec's database to demonstrate this type of query. Assume that there's a shortage of computer monitors in the computer industry, so that when you run out of monitors, you can no longer deliver products that include them. You want to know which products are affected. Glancing gratefully at your own monitor, enter the following query:

```
SELECT Model
    FROM COMP_USED
    WHERE CompID IN
        (SELECT CompID
            FROM COMPONENT
            WHERE CompType = 'Monitor') ;
```

SQL processes the innermost query first, so it processes the COMPONENT table, returning the value of CompID for every row where CompType is 'Monitor'. The result is a list of the ID numbers of all monitors. The outer query then compares the value of CompID in every row in the COMP_USED table against the list. If the comparison is successful, the value of the Model column for that row is added to the outer SELECT's result table. The result is a list of all product models that include a monitor. The following example shows what happens when you run the query:

```
Model
-----
CX3000
CX3010
CX3020
MB3030
MX3020
MX3030
```

You now know which products will soon be out of stock. It's time to go to the sales force and tell them to slow down on promoting these products.

When you use this form of nested query, the subquery must specify a single column, and that column's data type must match the data type of the argument preceding the IN keyword.

TIP

I'm sure you remember the KISS principle. *Keeping things simple* is important when you're dealing with software of any kind, but it is especially important when dealing with database software. Statements that include nested SELECTs can be difficult to get right. One way to get them working the way they should is to run the inner SELECT all by itself first and then verify that the result you get is the result you expect. When you're sure the inner SELECT is functioning properly, you can enclose it in the outer part of the statement and have a better chance that the whole thing will work as advertised.

Subqueries introduced by the keyword NOT IN

Just as you can introduce a subquery with the IN keyword, you can do the opposite and introduce it with the NOT IN keywords. In fact, now is a great time for Zetec management to make such a query. By using the query in the preceding section, Zetec management found out what products not to sell. That is valuable information, but it doesn't pay the rent. What Zetec management really wants to know is what products *to* sell. Management wants to emphasize the sale of products that *don't* contain monitors. A nested query featuring a subquery introduced by the NOT IN keywords provides the requested information:

```
SELECT Model
    FROM COMP_USED
    WHERE CompID NOT IN
        (SELECT CompID
            FROM COMPONENT
            WHERE CompType = 'Monitor')) ;
```

This query produces the following result:

```
Model
-----
PX3040
PB3050
PX3040
PB3050
```

REMEMBER

Worth noting is the fact that the result set contains duplicates. The duplication occurs because a product containing several components that are not monitors has a row in the COMP_USED table for each component. The query creates an entry in the result table for each of those rows.

In the example, the number of rows does not create a problem because the result table is short. In the real world, however, such a result table may have hundreds or thousands of rows. To avoid confusion, it's best to eliminate the duplicates. You can do so easily by adding the DISTINCT keyword to the query. Only rows that are distinct (different) from all previously retrieved rows are added to the result table:

```
SELECT DISTINCT Model
    FROM COMP_USED
```

```
WHERE CompID NOT IN
    (SELECT CompID
        FROM COMPONENT
        WHERE CompType = 'Monitor')) ;
```

As expected, the result is as follows:

```
Model
-----
PX3040
PB3050
```

Nested queries that return a single value

Introducing a subquery with one of the six comparison operators (=, <>, <, <=, >, >=) is often useful. In such a case, the expression preceding the operator evaluates to a single value, and the subquery following the operator must also evaluate to a single value. An exception is the case of the *quantified comparison operator*, which is a comparison operator followed by a quantifier (ANY, SOME, or ALL).

To illustrate a case in which a subquery returns a single value, look at another piece of Zetec Corporation's database. It contains a CUSTOMER table that holds information about the companies that buy Zetec products. It also contains a CONTACT table that holds personal data about individuals at each of Zetec's customer organizations. The tables are structured as shown in Tables 12-4 and 12-5.

TABLE 12-4

CUSTOMER Table

Column	Type	Constraints
CustID	INTEGER	PRIMARY KEY
Company	CHAR (40)	UNIQUE
CustAddress	CHAR (30)	
CustCity	CHAR (20)	
CustState	CHAR (2)	
CustZip	CHAR (10)	
CustPhone	CHAR (12)	
ModLevel	INTEGER	

TABLE 12-5 CONTACT Table

Column	Type	Constraints
CustID	INTEGER	PRIMARY KEY
ContFName	CHAR (10)	
ContLName	CHAR (16)	
ContPhone	CHAR (12)	
ContInfo	CHAR (50)	

Say that you want to look at the contact information for Olympic Sales, but you don't remember that company's CustID. Use a nested query like this one to recover the information you want:

```
SELECT *
    FROM CONTACT
        WHERE CustID =
            (SELECT CustID
                FROM CUSTOMER
                    WHERE Company = 'Olympic Sales') ;
```

The result looks something like this:

```
CustID ContFName  ContLName   ContPhone    ContInfo
------ ---------  ---------   ----------   ---------
   118 Jerry      Attwater    505-876-3456 Will play
                                           major role in
                                           additive
                                           manufacturing.
```

You can now call Jerry at Olympic and tell him about this month's special sale on 3D printers.

When you use a subquery in an "=" comparison, the subquery's SELECT list must specify a single column (CustID in the example). When the subquery is executed, it must return a single row in order to have a single value for the comparison.

In this example, I assume that the CUSTOMER table has only one row with a Company value of 'Olympic Sales'. The CREATE TABLE statement for CUSTOMER specifies a UNIQUE constraint for Company, and this statement guarantees that the subquery in the preceding example returns a single value (or no value). Subqueries like the one in this example, however, are commonly used on columns that are not specified to be UNIQUE. In such cases, you must rely on prior knowledge of the database contents for believing that the column has no duplicates.

If more than one customer has a value of 'Olympic Sales' in the Company column (perhaps in different states), the subquery raises an error.

If no customer with such a company name exists, the subquery is treated as if it was null, and the comparison becomes *unknown.* In this case, the WHERE clause returns no row (because it returns only rows with the condition True and filters rows with the condition False or unknown). This would probably happen, for example, if someone misspelled the Company as 'Olumpic Sales'.

Although the equal operator (=) is the most common, you can use any of the other five comparison operators in a similar structure. For every row in the table specified in the enclosing statement's FROM clause, the single value returned by the subquery is compared with the expression in the enclosing statement's WHERE clause. If the comparison gives a True value, a row is added to the result table.

You can guarantee that a subquery will return a single value if you include an aggregate function in it. *Aggregate functions* always return a single value. (Aggregate functions are described in Chapter 3.) Of course, this way of returning a single value is helpful only if you want the result of an aggregate function.

Suppose you are a Zetec salesperson and you need to earn a big commission check to pay for some unexpected bills. You decide to concentrate on selling Zetec's most expensive product. You can find out what that product is with a nested query:

```
SELECT Model, ProdName, ListPrice
    FROM PRODUCT
        WHERE ListPrice =
            (SELECT MAX(ListPrice)
                FROM PRODUCT) ;
```

In the preceding nested query, both the subquery and the enclosing statement operate on the same table. The subquery returns a single value: the maximum list price in the PRODUCT table. The outer query retrieves all rows from the PRODUCT table that have that list price.

The next example shows a comparison subquery that uses a comparison operator other than =:

```
SELECT Model, ProdName, ListPrice
    FROM PRODUCT
        WHERE ListPrice <
```

```
      (SELECT AVG(ListPrice)
          FROM PRODUCT) ;
```

The subquery returns a single value: the average list price in the PRODUCT table. The outer query retrieves all rows from the PRODUCT table that have a lower list price than the average list price.

In the original SQL standard, a comparison could have only one subquery, and it had to be on the right side of the comparison. SQL:1999 allowed either or both operands of the comparison to be subqueries, and later versions of SQL retain that expansion of capability.

The ALL, SOME, and ANY quantifiers

Another way to make sure that a subquery returns a single value is to introduce it with a quantified comparison operator. The universal quantifier ALL, and the existential quantifiers SOME and ANY, when combined with a comparison operator, process the list returned by a subquery, reducing it to a single value.

You'll see how these quantifiers affect a comparison by looking at the baseball pitchers' complete game database from Chapter 11, which is listed next.

The contents of the two tables are given by the following two queries:

```
SELECT * FROM NATIONAL

FirstName    LastName    CompleteGames
---------    --------    -------------
Sal          Maglie               11
Don          Newcombe              9
Sandy        Koufax               13
Don          Drysdale             12
Bob          Turley                8

SELECT * FROM AMERICAN

FirstName    LastName    CompleteGames
---------    --------    -------------
Whitey       Ford                 12
Don          Larson               10
Bob          Turley                8
Allie        Reynolds             14
```

The presumption is that the pitchers with the most complete games should be in the American League because of the presence of designated hitters in that league. One way to verify this presumption is to build a query that returns all American League pitchers who have thrown more complete games than all the National League pitchers. The query can be formulated as follows:

```
SELECT *
   FROM AMERICAN
   WHERE CompleteGames > ALL
      (SELECT CompleteGames FROM NATIONAL) ;
```

This is the result:

```
FirstName   LastName   CompleteGames
----------  --------   -------------
Allie       Reynolds   14
```

The subquery (`SELECT CompleteGames FROM NATIONAL`) returns the values in the `CompleteGames` column for all National League pitchers. The `> ALL` quantifier says to return only those values of `CompleteGames` in the AMERICAN table that are greater than each of the values returned by the subquery. This condition translates into "greater than the highest value returned by the subquery." In this case, the highest value returned by the subquery is 13 (Sandy Koufax). The only row in the AMERICAN table higher than that is Allie Reynolds's record, with 14 complete games.

What if your initial presumption was wrong? What if the major-league leader in complete games was a National League pitcher, in spite of the fact that the National League has no designated hitter? If that was the case, the query

```
SELECT *
   FROM AMERICAN
   WHERE CompleteGames > ALL
      (SELECT CompleteGames FROM NATIONAL) ;
```

would return a warning that no rows satisfy the query's conditions — meaning that no American League pitcher has thrown more complete games than the pitcher who has thrown the most complete games in the National League.

Nested queries that are an existence test

A query returns data from all table rows that satisfy the query's conditions. Sometimes many rows are returned; sometimes only one comes back. Sometimes none of the rows in the table satisfy the conditions, and no rows are returned. You can use the `EXISTS` and `NOT EXISTS` predicates to introduce a subquery. That structure tells you whether any rows in the table located in the subquery's FROM clause meet the conditions in its WHERE clause.

REMEMBER

Subqueries introduced with EXISTS and NOT EXISTS are fundamentally different from the other subqueries in this chapter so far. In all the previous cases, SQL first executes the subquery and then applies that operation's result to the enclosing statement. EXISTS and NOT EXISTS subqueries, on the other hand, are examples of correlated subqueries.

A *correlated subquery* first finds the table and row specified by the enclosing statement and then executes the subquery on the row in the subquery's table that correlates with the current row of the enclosing statement's table.

The subquery either returns one or more rows or it returns none. If it returns at least one row, the EXISTS predicate succeeds (see the following section), and the enclosing statement performs its action. In the same circumstances, the NOT EXISTS predicate fails (see the section after that), and the enclosing statement does not perform its action. After one row of the enclosing statement's table is processed, the same operation is performed on the next row. This action is repeated until every row in the enclosing statement's table has been processed.

EXISTS

Suppose you are a salesperson for Zetec Corporation and you want to call your primary contact people at all of Zetec's customer organizations in California. Try the following query:

```
SELECT *
    FROM CONTACT
    WHERE EXISTS
        (SELECT *
            FROM CUSTOMER
            WHERE CustState = 'CA'
                AND CONTACT.CustID = CUSTOMER.CustID) ;
```

Notice the reference to CONTACT.CustID, which is referencing a column from the outer query and comparing it with another column, CUSTOMER.CustID, from the inner query. For each candidate row of the outer query, you evaluate the inner query, using the CustID value from the current CONTACT row of the outer query in the WHERE clause of the inner query.

Here's what happens:

1. The CustID column links the CONTACT table to the CUSTOMER table.

2. SQL looks at the first record in the CONTACT table, finds the row in the CUSTOMER table that has the same CustID, and checks that row's CustState field.

3. If CUSTOMER.CustState = 'CA', the current CONTACT row is added to the result table.

4. The next CONTACT record is then processed in the same way, and so on, until the entire CONTACT table has been processed.

5. Because the query specifies SELECT * FROM CONTACT, all the contact table's fields are returned, including the contact's name and phone number.

NOT EXISTS

In the previous example, the Zetec salesperson wants to know the names and numbers of the contact people of all the customers in California. Imagine that a second salesperson is responsible for all of the United States except California. She can retrieve her contact people by using NOT EXISTS in a query similar to the preceding one:

```
SELECT *
    FROM CONTACT
    WHERE NOT EXISTS
        (SELECT *
            FROM CUSTOMER
            WHERE CustState = 'CA'
                AND CONTACT.CustID = CUSTOMER.CustID) ;
```

Every row in CONTACT for which the subquery does not return a row is added to the result table.

Other correlated subqueries

As noted in a previous section of this chapter, subqueries introduced by IN or by a comparison operator need not be correlated queries, but they can be.

Correlated subqueries introduced with IN

In the earlier section "Subqueries introduced by the keyword IN," I discuss how a noncorrelated subquery can be used with the IN predicate. To show how a correlated subquery may use the IN predicate, ask the same question that came up with the EXISTS predicate: What are the names and phone numbers of the contacts at all of Zetec's customers in California? You can answer this question with a correlated IN subquery:

```
SELECT *
   .FROM CONTACT
    WHERE 'CA' IN
        (SELECT CustState
            FROM CUSTOMER
            WHERE CONTACT.CustID = CUSTOMER.CustID) ;
```

The statement is evaluated for each record in the CONTACT table. If, for that record, the CustID numbers in CONTACT and CUSTOMER match, then the value of CUSTOMER.CustState is compared to 'CA'. The result of the subquery is a list that contains, at most, one element. If that one element is 'CA', the WHERE clause of the enclosing statement is satisfied, and a row is added to the query's result table.

Subqueries introduced with comparison operators

A correlated subquery can also be introduced by one of the six comparison operators, as shown in the next example.

Zetec pays bonuses to its salespeople based on their total monthly sales volume. The higher the volume is, the higher the bonus percentage is. The bonus percentage list is kept in the BONUSRATE table:

MinAmount	MaxAmount	BonusPct
0.00	24999.99	0.
25000.00	49999.99	0.1
50000.00	99999.99	0.2
100000.00	249999.99	0.3
250000.00	499999.99	0.4
500000.00	749999.99	0.5
750000.00	999999.99	0.6

If a person's monthly sales are between $100,000.00 and $249,999.99, the bonus is 0.3 percent of sales.

Sales are recorded in a transaction master table named TRANSMASTER:

TRANSMASTER		
Column	Type	Constraints

```
------            ----            -----------
TransID           INTEGER         PRIMARY KEY
CustID            INTEGER         FOREIGN KEY
EmpID             INTEGER         FOREIGN KEY
TransDate         DATE
NetAmount         NUMERIC
Freight           NUMERIC
Tax               NUMERIC
InvoiceTotal      NUMERIC
```

Sales bonuses are based on the sum of the NetAmount field for all of a person's transactions in the month. You can find any person's bonus rate with a correlated subquery that uses comparison operators:

```
SELECT BonusPct
    FROM BONUSRATE
        WHERE MinAmount <=
            (SELECT SUM (NetAmount)
                FROM TRANSMASTER
                    WHERE EmpID = 133)
            AND MaxAmount >=
                (SELECT SUM (NetAmount)
                    FROM TRANSMASTER
                        WHERE EmpID = 133) ;
```

This query is interesting in that it contains two subqueries, making use of the logical connective AND. The subqueries use the SUM aggregate operator, which returns a single value: the total monthly sales of employee number 133. That value is then compared against the MinAmount and the MaxAmount columns in the BONUSRATE table, producing the bonus rate for that employee.

If you had not known the EmpID but had known the EmplName, you could arrive at the same answer with a more complex query:

```
SELECT BonusPct
    FROM BONUSRATE
        WHERE MinAmount <=
            (SELECT SUM (NetAmount)
                FROM TRANSMASTER
                    WHERE EmpID =
                        (SELECT EmpID
                            FROM EMPLOYEE
                                WHERE EmplName = 'Coffin'))
            AND MaxAmount >=
```

```
            (SELECT SUM (NetAmount)
          FROM TRANSMASTER
            WHERE EmpID =
                (SELECT EmpID
                  FROM EMPLOYEE
                    WHERE EmplName = 'Coffin'));
```

This example uses subqueries nested within subqueries, which, in turn, are nested within an enclosing query to arrive at the bonus rate for the employee named Coffin. This structure works only if you know for sure that the company has one, and only one, employee whose last name is Coffin. If you know that more than one employee has the same last name, you can add terms to the WHERE clause of the innermost subquery until you're sure that only one row of the EMPLOYEE table is selected.

Subqueries in a HAVING clause

You can have a correlated subquery in a HAVING clause just as you can in a WHERE clause. As I mention in Chapter 10, a HAVING clause is usually preceded by a GROUP BY clause. The HAVING clause acts as a filter to restrict the groups created by the GROUP BY clause. Groups that don't satisfy the condition of the HAVING clause are not included in the result. When used this way, the HAVING clause is evaluated for each group created by the GROUP BY clause.

TIP

In the absence of a GROUP BY clause, the HAVING clause is evaluated for the set of rows passed by the WHERE clause — which is considered to be a single group. If neither a WHERE clause nor a GROUP BY clause is present, the HAVING clause is evaluated for the entire table:

```
SELECT TM1.EmpID
   FROM TRANSMASTER TM1
      GROUP BY TM1.Department
      HAVING MAX (TM1.NetAmount) >= ALL
         (SELECT 2 * AVG (TM2.NetAmount)
            FROM TRANSMASTER TM2
            WHERE TM1.EmpID <> TM2.EmpID) ;
```

This query uses two aliases for the same table, enabling you to retrieve the EmpID number of all salespeople who had a sale of at least twice the average sale of all the other salespeople. The query works as follows:

1. The outer query groups TRANSMASTER rows by the employees' department. This is done with the SELECT, FROM, and GROUP BY clauses.

2. The HAVING clause filters these groups. For each group, it calculates the MAX of the NetAmount column for the rows in that group.

3. The inner query evaluates twice the average NetAmount from all rows of TRANSMASTER whose EmpID is different from the EmpID of the current group of the outer query.

REMEMBER

In the last line, you have to reference two different EmpID values — so you use different aliases for TRANSMASTER in the FROM clauses of the outer and inner queries.

4. You use those aliases in the comparison of the query's last line to indicate that you're referencing both the EmpID from the current row of the inner subquery (TM2.EmpID) *and* the EmpID from the current group of the outer subquery (TM1.EmpID).

UPDATE, DELETE, and INSERT

In addition to SELECT statements, UPDATE, DELETE, and INSERT statements can also include WHERE clauses. Those WHERE clauses can contain subqueries in the same way that SELECT statements' WHERE clauses do.

For example, Zetec has just made a volume purchase deal with Olympic Sales and wants to provide Olympic with a retroactive 10 percent credit for all its purchases in the last month. You can give this credit with an UPDATE statement:

```
UPDATE TRANSMASTER
    SET NetAmount = NetAmount * 0.9
    WHERE SaleDate > (CurrentDate - 30) DAY AND CustID =
        (SELECT CustID
            FROM CUSTOMER
            WHERE Company = 'Olympic Sales') ;
```

You can also have a correlated subquery in an UPDATE statement. Suppose the CUSTOMER table has a column LastMonthsMax, and Zetec wants to give such a credit for purchases that exceed LastMonthsMax for the customer:

```
UPDATE TRANSMASTER TM
    SET NetAmount = NetAmount * 0.9
    WHERE NetAmount>
        (SELECT LastMonthsMax
            FROM CUSTOMER C
            WHERE C.CustID = TM.CustID) ;
```

Note that this subquery is correlated: The WHERE clause in the last line references both the CustID of the CUSTOMER row from the subquery and the CustID of the current TRANSMASTER row that is a candidate for updating.

A subquery in an UPDATE statement can also reference the table that is being updated. Suppose that Zetec wants to give a 10 percent credit to customers whose purchases have exceeded $10,000:

```
UPDATE TRANSMASTER TM1
    SET NetAmount = NetAmount * 0.9
    WHERE 10000 < (SELECT SUM(NetAmount)
              FROM TRANSMASTER TM2
                    WHERE TM1.CustID = TM2.CustID);
```

The inner subquery calculates the SUM of the NetAmount column for all TRANS-MASTER rows for the same customer. What does this mean? Suppose the customer with CustID = 37 has four rows in TRANSMASTER with values for NetAmount: 3000, 5000, 2000, and 1000. The SUM of NetAmount for this CustID is 11000.

The order in which the UPDATE statement processes the rows is defined by your implementation and is generally not predictable. The order may differ depending on how the rows are arranged on the disk. Assume that the implementation processes the rows for this CustID in this order: first the TRANSMASTER with a NetAmount of 3000, then the one with NetAmount = 5000, and so on. After the first three rows for CustID 37 have been updated, their NetAmount values are 2700 (90 percent of $3,000), 4500 (90 percent of $5,000), and 1800 (90 percent of $2,000). Then, when you process the last TRANSMASTER row for CustID 37 (whose NetAmount is 1000), the SUM returned by the subquery would *seem* to be 10000 — that is, the SUM of the new NetAmount values of the first three rows for CustID 37, and the old NetAmount value of the last row for CustID 37. Thus it would seem that the last row for CustID 37 isn't updated, because the comparison with that SUM is not True — after all, 10000 is not less than 10000. But that is not how the UPDATE statement is defined when a subquery references the table that is being updated.

REMEMBER

All evaluations of subqueries in an UPDATE statement reference the old values of the table — the ones that are being updated. In the preceding UPDATE for CustID 37, the subquery returns 11000 — the original SUM.

The subquery in a WHERE clause operates the same as a SELECT statement or an UPDATE statement. The same is true for DELETE and INSERT. To delete all of Olympic's transactions, use this statement:

```
DELETE FROM TRANSMASTER
    WHERE CustID =
      (SELECT CustID
          FROM CUSTOMER
          WHERE Company = 'Olympic Sales') ;
```

As with UPDATE, DELETE subqueries can also be correlated and can also reference
the table being deleted. The rules are similar to the rules for UPDATE subqueries.
Suppose you want to delete all rows from TRANSMASTER for customers whose
total NetAmount is larger than $10,000:

```
DELETE FROM TRANSMASTER TM1
    WHERE 10000 < (SELECT SUM(NetAmount)
       FROM TRANSMASTER TM2
          WHERE TM1.CustID = TM2.CustID) ;
```

This query deletes all rows from TRANSMASTER that have CustID 37, as well as
any other customers with purchases exceeding $10,000. All references to TRANS-
MASTER in the subquery denote the contents of TRANSMASTER before any deletions by the current statement. So even when you're deleting the last TRANSMASTER
row for CustID 37, the subquery is evaluated on the original TRANSMASTER table
and returns 11000.

REMEMBER

When you update, delete, or insert database records, you risk making a table's
data inconsistent with other tables in the database. Such an inconsistency is called
a *modification anomaly,* discussed in Chapter 5. If you delete TRANSMASTER
records and a TRANSDETAIL table depends on TRANSMASTER, you must delete
the corresponding records from TRANSDETAIL, too. This operation is called a *cascading delete,* because the deletion of a parent record must cascade to its associated
child records. Otherwise the undeleted child records become orphans. In this case,
they would be invoice detail lines that are in limbo because they are no longer
connected to an invoice record.

If your implementation of SQL doesn't support cascading deletes, you must do the
deletions yourself. In this case, delete the appropriate records from the child table
before deleting the corresponding record from the parent. That way, you don't
have orphan records in the child table, even for a second.

Retrieving changes with pipelined DML

In the preceding section, I show how an UPDATE, DELETE, or INSERT statement can
include a nested SELECT statement within a WHERE clause. SQL:2011 introduced a
related capability, in which a data manipulation command (such as UPDATE,

INSERT, DELETE, or MERGE statements) can be nested within a SELECT statement. This capability is called *pipelined DML*.

One way to look at a data change operation is to envision a table before it is changed with a DELETE, INSERT, or UPDATE operation. You could call the table before the change the old table and the table after the change, the new table. During the data change operation, auxiliary tables, called *delta tables,* are created. A DELETE operation creates an old delta table, which contains the rows to be deleted. An INSERT operation creates a new delta table, which contains the rows to be inserted. An UPDATE operation would create both an old and a new delta table, the old for the rows being replaced and the new for the rows replacing them.

With pipelined DML, you can retrieve the information in the delta tables. Suppose you want to delete from your product line all products with ProductIDs between 1000 and 1399, and you want a record of exactly which products in that range are deleted. You could use the following code:

```
SELECT Oldtable.ProductID
    FROM OLD TABLE (DELETE FROM Product
                    WHERE ProductID BETWEEN 1000 AND 1399)
        AS Oldtable ;
```

In this example, the keywords OLD TABLE specify that the result of the SELECT is coming from the old delta table. The result is the list of ProductID numbers for the products that are being deleted.

Similarly, you could retrieve a list from the new delta table by using the NEW TABLE keywords, which displays the Product ID numbers of rows inserted by an INSERT operation or updated by an UPDATE operation. Because an UPDATE operation created both an old delta table and a new delta table, you can retrieve the contents of either or both by using pipelined DML.

Chapter **13**

Recursive Queries

One of the major criticisms of SQL, up through and including SQL-92, was its inability to implement *recursive processing*. Many important problems that are difficult to solve by other means yield readily to recursive solutions. Extensions included in SQL:1999 allow recursive queries — which greatly expand the language's power. If your SQL implementation includes the recursion extensions, you can efficiently solve a large new class of problems. However, because recursion is not a part of core SQL, many implementations currently available do not include it.

What Is Recursion?

Recursion is a feature that's been around for years in programming languages such as Logo, LISP, and C++. In these languages, you can define a *function* (a set of one or more commands) that performs a specific operation. The main program invokes the function by issuing a command called a *function call.* If the function calls itself as a part of its operation, you have the simplest form of recursion.

A simple program that uses recursion in one of its functions provides an illustration of the joys and pitfalls of recursion. The following program, written in C++, draws a spiral on the computer screen. It assumes that the drawing tool is initially pointing toward the top of the screen, and it includes three functions:

>> The function line(*n*) draws a line *n* units long.

>> The function left_turn(*d*) rotates the drawing tool *d* degrees counterclockwise.

>> You can define the function spiral(segment) as follows:

```
void spiral(int segment)
{
    line(segment)
    left_turn(90)
    spiral(segment + 1)
} ;
```

If you call spiral(1) from the main program, the following actions take place:

spiral(1) draws a line one unit long toward the top of the screen.

spiral(1) turns left 90 degrees.

spiral(1) calls spiral(2).

spiral(2) draws a line two units long toward the left side of the screen.

spiral(2) turns left 90 degrees.

spiral(2) calls spiral(3).

And so on. . . .

Eventually the program generates the spiral shown in Figure 13-1.

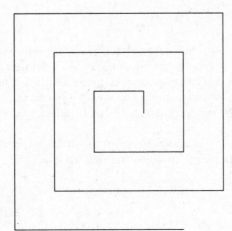

FIGURE 13-1:
Result of calling
spiral(1).

Houston, we have a problem

Well, okay, the situation here is not as serious as it was for Apollo 13 when the main oxygen tank exploded while the spacecraft was en route to the moon. Your problem is that the spiral-drawing program keeps calling itself and drawing longer and longer lines. It will continue to do that until the computer executing it runs out of resources and (if you're lucky) puts an obnoxious error message on the screen. If you're unlucky, the computer just crashes.

Failure is not an option

The scenario described in the previous section shows one of the dangers of using recursion. A program written to call itself invokes a new instance of itself — which in turn calls yet another instance, *ad infinitum*. This is generally not what you want. (Think of a certain cartoon mouse in a wizard's hat trying to stop all those marching broomsticks. . . .)

To address this problem, programmers include a *termination condition* within the recursive function — a limit on how deep the recursion can go — so the program performs the desired action and then terminates gracefully. You can include a termination condition in your spiral-drawing program to save computer resources and prevent dizziness in programmers:

```
void spiral2(int segment)
{
    if (segment <= 10)
    {
        line(segment)
        left_turn(90)
        spiral2(segment + 1)
    }
} ;
```

When you call `spiral2(1)`, it executes and then (recursively) calls itself until the value of `segment` exceeds 10. At the point where `segment` equals 11, the `if (segment <=10)` construct returns a False value, and the code within the interior braces is skipped. Control returns to the previous invocation of `spiral2` and, from there, returns all the way up to the first invocation, after which the program terminates. Figure 13-2 shows the sequence of calls and returns that occur.

Every time a function calls itself, it takes you one level farther away from the main program that was the starting point of the operation. For the main program to continue, the deepest iteration must return control to the iteration that called it. That iteration will have to do likewise, returning all the way back to the main program that made the first call to the recursive function.

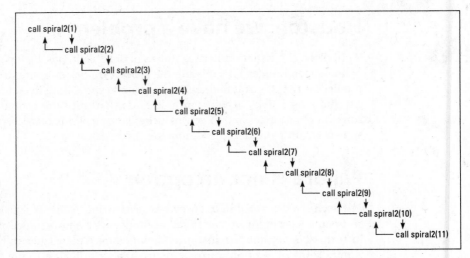

FIGURE 13-2:
Descending
through recursive
calls, and then
climbing back up
to terminate.

TIP

Recursion is a powerful tool for repeatedly executing code when you don't know at the outset how many times the code should be repeated. It's ideal for searching through tree-shaped structures such as family trees, complex electronic circuits, or multilevel distribution networks.

What Is a Recursive Query?

A *recursive query* is a query that is functionally dependent upon itself. The simplest form of such functional dependence works like this: Query Q1 invokes itself in the body of the query expression. A more complex case is where query Q1 depends on query Q2, which in turn depends on query Q1. There is still a functional dependency, and recursion is still involved, no matter how many queries lie between the first and the second invocation of the same query. If that sounds weird, don't worry: Here's how it works . . .

Where Might You Use a Recursive Query?

Recursive queries may help save you time and frustration in dealing with various kinds of problems. Suppose, for example, that you have a pass that gives you free air travel on any flight of the (fictional) Vannevar Airlines. Way cool. The next question you ask is, "Where can I go for free?" The FLIGHT table contains all the flights that Vannevar runs. Table 13-1 shows the flight number and the source and destination of each flight.

TABLE 13-1

Flights Offered by Vannevar Airlines

Flight No.	Source	Destination
3141	Portland	Orange County
2173	Portland	Charlotte
623	Portland	Daytona Beach
5440	Orange County	Montgomery
221	Charlotte	Memphis
32	Memphis	Champaign
981	Montgomery	Memphis

Figure 13-3 illustrates the routes on a map of the United States.

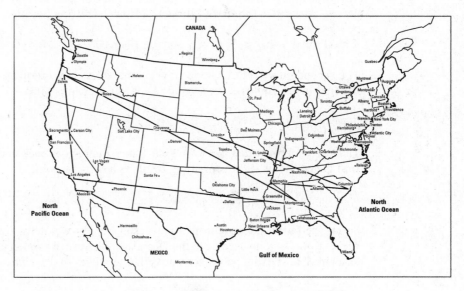

FIGURE 13-3:
Route map for
Vannevar Airlines.

To get started on your vacation plan, create a database table for FLIGHT by using SQL as follows:

```
CREATE TABLE FLIGHT (
    FlightNo        INTEGER        NOT NULL,
    Source          CHAR (30),
    Destination     CHAR (30) );
```

After the table is created, you can populate it with the data shown in Table 13-1.

Suppose you're starting from Portland and you want to visit a friend in Montgomery. Naturally you wonder, "What cities can I reach via Vannevar if I start from Portland?" and "What cities can I reach via the same airline if I start from Montgomery?" Some cities are reachable in one hop; others are not. Some might require two or more hops. You can find all the cities that you can get to via Vannevar, starting from any given city on its route map — but if you do it one query at a time, you're . . .

Querying the hard way

To find out what you want to know — provided you have the time and patience — you can make a series of queries, first using Portland as the starting city:

```
SELECT Destination FROM FLIGHT WHERE Source = 'Portland';
```

The first query returns Orange County, Charlotte, and Daytona Beach. Your second query uses the first of these results as a starting point:

```
SELECT Destination FROM FLIGHT WHERE Source = 'Orange County';
```

The second query returns Montgomery. Your third query returns to the results of the first query and uses the second result as a starting point:

```
SELECT Destination FROM FLIGHT WHERE Source = 'Charlotte';
```

The third query returns Memphis. Your fourth query goes back to the results of the first query and uses the remaining result as a starting point:

```
SELECT Destination FROM FLIGHT WHERE Source = 'Daytona Beach';
```

Sorry, the fourth query returns a null result because Vannevar offers no outgoing flights from Daytona Beach. But the second query returned another city (Montgomery) as a possible starting point, so your fifth query uses that result:

```
SELECT Destination FROM FLIGHT WHERE Source = 'Montgomery';
```

This query returns Memphis, but you already know it's among the cities you can get to (in this case, via Charlotte). But you go ahead and try this latest result as a starting point for another query:

```
SELECT Destination FROM FLIGHT WHERE Source = 'Memphis';
```

The query returns Champaign — which you can add to the list of reachable cities (even if you have to get there in two hops). As long as you're considering multiple hops, you plug in Champaign as a starting point:

```
SELECT Destination FROM FLIGHT WHERE Source = 'Champaign';
```

Oops. This query returns a null value; Vannevar offers no outgoing flights from Champaign. (Seven queries so far. Are you fidgeting yet?)

Vannevar doesn't offer a flight out of Daytona Beach, either, so if you go there, you're stuck — which might not be a hardship if it's Spring Break week. (Of course, if you use up a week running individual queries to find out where to go next, you might get a worse headache than you'd get from a week of partying.) Or you might get stuck in Champaign — in which case, you could enroll in the University of Illinois and take a few database courses.

Granted, this method will (eventually) answer the question, "What cities are reachable from Portland?" But running one query after another, making each one dependent on the results of a previous query, is complicated, time-consuming, and fidgety.

Saving time with a recursive query

A simpler way to get the info you need is to craft a single recursive query that does the entire job in one operation. Here's the syntax for such a query:

```
WITH RECURSIVE
    REACHABLEFROM (Source, Destination)
      AS (SELECT Source, Destination
            FROM FLIGHT
          UNION
          SELECT in.Source, out.Destination
            FROM REACHABLEFROM in, FLIGHT out
            WHERE in.Destination = out.Source
         )
    SELECT * FROM REACHABLEFROM
    WHERE Source = 'Portland';
```

The first time through the recursion, FLIGHT has seven rows and REACHABLE-FROM has none. The UNION takes the seven rows from FLIGHT and copies them into REACHABLEFROM. At this point, REACHABLEFROM has the data shown in Table 13-2.

TABLE 13-2

REACHABLEFROM After One Pass through Recursion

Source	Destination
Portland	Orange County
Portland	Charlotte
Portland	Daytona Beach
Orange County	Montgomery
Charlotte	Memphis
Memphis	Champaign
Montgomery	Memphis

WARNING

As I mention earlier, recursion is not a part of core SQL, and thus some implementations may not include it.

The second time through the recursion, things start to get interesting. The WHERE clause (WHERE in.Destination = out.Source) means that you're looking only at rows where the Destination field of the REACHABLEFROM table equals the Source field of the FLIGHT table. For those rows, you're taking two fields — the Source field from REACHABLEFROM and the Destination field from FLIGHT — and adding them to REACHABLEFROM as a new row. Table 13-3 shows the result of this iteration of the recursion.

TABLE 13-3

REACHABLEFROM After Two Passes through the Recursion

Source	Destination
Portland	Orange County
Portland	Charlotte
Portland	Daytona Beach
Orange County	Montgomery
Charlotte	Memphis
Memphis	Champaign
Montgomery	Memphis
Portland	Montgomery
Portland	Memphis
Orange County	Memphis
Charlotte	Champaign

The results are looking more useful. REACHABLEFROM now contains all the Destination cities that are reachable from any Source city in two hops or less. Next, the recursion processes three-hop trips, and so on, until all possible destination cities have been reached.

After the recursion is complete, the third and final SELECT statement (which is outside the recursion) extracts from REACHABLEFROM only those cities you can reach from Portland by flying Vannevar. In this example, all six other cities are reachable from Portland — in few enough hops that you won't feel like you're traveling by pogo stick.

REMEMBER

If you scrutinize the code in the recursive query, it doesn't *look* any simpler than the seven individual queries it replaces. It does, however, have two advantages:

>> When you set it in motion, it completes the entire operation without any further intervention.

>> It can do the job fast.

Imagine a real-world airline with many more cities on its route map. The more possible destinations that are available, the greater the advantage of using the recursive method.

What makes this query recursive? The fact that you're defining REACHABLEFROM in terms of itself. The recursive part of the definition is the second SELECT statement, the one just after the UNION. REACHABLEFROM is a temporary table that fills with data progressively as the recursion proceeds. Processing continues until all possible destinations have been added to REACHABLEFROM. Any duplicates are eliminated, because the UNION operator doesn't add duplicates to the result table. After the recursion has finished running, REACHABLEFROM contains all the cities that are reachable from any starting city. The third and final SELECT statement returns only those destination cities that you can reach from Portland. Bon voyage.

Where Else Might You Use a Recursive Query?

Any problem that you can lay out as a treelike structure can potentially be solved by using a recursive query. The classic industrial application is *materials processing* (the process of turning raw materials into finished goods). Suppose your company is building a new gasoline-electric hybrid car. Such a machine is built of subassemblies (engine, batteries, and so on), which are constructed from smaller subassemblies (crankshaft, electrodes, and so on), which are made of even smaller parts.

Keeping track of all the various parts can be difficult in a relational database that does not use recursion. Recursion enables you to start with the complete machine and ferret your way along any path to get to the smallest part. Want to find out the specs for the fastening screw that holds the clamp to the negative electrode of the auxiliary battery? The WITH RECURSIVE structure gives SQL the capability to address such a brass-tacks-level problem.

TIP

Recursion is also a natural for *what-if* processing. In the Vannevar Airlines example, what if management discontinues service from Portland to Charlotte? How does that affect the cities that are reachable from Portland? A recursive query quickly gives you the answer.

4
Controlling Operations

IN THIS PART . . .

Controlling access

Protecting data from corruption

Applying procedural languages

Chapter **14**

Providing Database Security

A system administrator must have special knowledge of how a database works. That's why, in preceding chapters, I discuss the parts of SQL that create databases and manipulate data — and (in Chapter 3) introduce SQL's facilities for protecting databases from harm or misuse. In this chapter, I go into more depth on the subject of misuse — and preventing it by the savvy use of SQL features.

The person in charge of a database can determine who has access to the database — and can set users' access levels, granting or revoking access to aspects of the system. The system administrator can even grant or revoke the right to grant and revoke access privileges. If you use them correctly, the security tools that SQL provides are powerful protectors of important data. Used incorrectly, these same tools can tie up the efforts of legitimate users in a big knot of red tape when they're just trying to do their jobs.

Because databases often contain sensitive information that you shouldn't make available to everyone, SQL provides different levels of access — from complete to none, with several levels in between. By controlling which operations each authorized user can perform, the database administrator can make available all the data that the users need to do their jobs — but restrict access to parts of the database that not everyone should see or change.

The SQL Data Control Language

The SQL statements that you use to create databases form a group known as the *Data Definition Language* (DDL). After you create a database, you can use another set of SQL statements — known collectively as the *Data Manipulation Language* (DML) — to add, change, and remove data from the database. SQL includes additional statements that don't fall into either of these categories. Programmers sometimes refer to these statements collectively as the *Data Control Language* (DCL). DCL statements primarily protect the database from unauthorized access, from harmful interaction among multiple database users, and from power failures and equipment malfunctions. In this chapter, I discuss protection from unauthorized access.

User Access Levels

SQL provides controlled access to nine database-management functions:

>> **Creating, seeing, modifying, and deleting:** These functions correspond to the INSERT, SELECT, UPDATE, and DELETE operations that I discuss in Chapter 6.

>> **Referencing:** Using the REFERENCES keyword (which I discuss in Chapters 3 and 5) involves applying referential integrity constraints to a table that depends on another table in the database.

>> **Using:** The USAGE keyword pertains to domains, character sets, collations, and translations. (I define domains, character sets, collations, and translations in Chapter 5.)

>> **Defining new data types:** You deal with user-defined type names with the UNDER keyword.

>> **Responding to an event:** The use of the TRIGGER keyword causes an SQL statement or statement block to be executed whenever a predetermined event occurs.

>> **Executing:** Using the EXECUTE keyword causes a routine to be executed.

The database administrator

In most installations with more than a few users, the supreme database authority is the *database administrator* (DBA). The DBA has all rights and privileges to all aspects of the database. Being a DBA can give you a feeling of power — and responsibility. With all that power at your disposal, you can easily mess up your database and destroy thousands of hours of work. DBAs must think clearly and carefully about the consequences of every action they perform.

The DBA not only has all rights to the database, but also controls the rights that other users have. Thus, highly trusted individuals can access more functions — and, perhaps, more tables — than can the majority of users.

A surefire way to become a DBA is to install the database management system. The person that installs a database is automatically a DBA. The installation manual gives you an account, or *login*, and a password. That login identifies you as a specially privileged user. Sometimes, the system calls this privileged user the DBA, sometimes the *system administrator,* and sometimes the *super user* (sorry, no cape and boots provided). As your first official act after logging in, you should change your password from the default to a secret one of your own.

REMEMBER

If you don't change the password, then anyone who reads the manual *can also log in with full DBA privileges.* After you change the password, only people who know the new password can log in as DBA. I suggest that you share the new DBA password with only a small number of highly trusted people. After all, a falling meteor could strike you tomorrow; you could win the lottery; or you may become unavailable to the company in some other way. Your colleagues must be able to carry on in your absence. Anyone who knows the DBA login and password becomes the DBA after using that information to access the system.

TIP

If you have DBA privileges, log in as DBA only if you need to perform a specific task that requires DBA privileges. After you finish, log out. For routine work, log in by using your own personal login ID and password. This approach may prevent you from making mistakes that have serious consequences for other users' tables (as well as for your own).

Database object owners

Another class of privileged user, along with the DBA, is the *database object owner.* Tables and views, for example, are *database objects.* Any user who creates such an object can specify its owner. A table owner enjoys every possible privilege associated with that table, including the privilege to grant access to the table to other people. Because you can base views on underlying tables, someone other than a table's owner can create a view based on that table. However, the view owner only receives privileges that he or she has for the underlying table. Bottom line: A user can't circumvent the protection on another user's table simply by creating a view based on that table.

The public

In network terms, "the public" consists of all users who are not specially privileged users (that is, either DBAs or object owners) and to whom a privileged user hasn't specifically granted access rights. If a privileged user grants certain access rights to PUBLIC, then everyone who can access the system gains those rights.

In most installations, a hierarchy of user privilege exists, in which the DBA stands at the highest level and the public at the lowest. Figure 14-1 illustrates the privilege hierarchy.

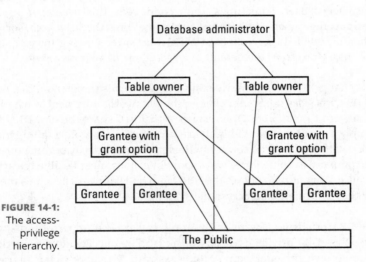

FIGURE 14-1:
The access-privilege hierarchy.

Granting Privileges to Users

The DBA, by virtue of his or her position, has all privileges on all objects in the database. After all, the owner of an object has all privileges with respect to that object — and the database itself is an object. No one else has any privileges with respect to any object — unless someone who already has those privileges (and the authority to pass them on) specifically grants the privileges. You grant privileges to someone by using the GRANT statement, which has the following syntax:

```
GRANT privilege-list
    ON object
    TO user-list
    [WITH HIERARCHY OPTION]
    [WITH GRANT OPTION]
    [GRANTED BY grantor] ;
```

In this statement, *privilege-list* is defined as follows:

```
privilege [, privilege] ...
```

or

```
ALL PRIVILEGES
```

Here *privilege* is defined as follows:

```
SELECT
| DELETE
| INSERT [(column-name [, column-name]...)]
| UPDATE [(column-name [, column-name]...)]
| REFERENCES [(column-name [, column-name]...)]
| USAGE
| UNDER
| TRIGGER
| EXECUTE
```

In the original statement, *object* is defined as follows:

```
[ TABLE ] <table name>
| DOMAIN <domain name>
| COLLATION <collation name>
| CHARACTER SET <character set name>
| TRANSLATION <transliteration name>
| TYPE <schema-resolved user-defined type name>
| SEQUENCE <sequence generator name>
| <specific routine designator>
```

And *user-list* in the statement is defined as follows:

```
login-ID [, login-ID]...
| PUBLIC
```

The *grantor* is either the CURRENT_USER or the CURRENT_ROLE.

The preceding syntax considers a view to be a table. The SELECT, DELETE, INSERT, UPDATE, TRIGGER, and REFERENCES privileges apply to tables and views only. The USAGE privilege applies to domains, character sets, collations, and translations. The UNDER privilege applies only to types, and the EXECUTE privilege applies only to routines. The following sections give examples of the various ways you can use the GRANT statement — and the results of those uses.

Roles

A *user name* is one type of authorization identifier, but it's not the only one. It identifies a person (or a program) authorized to perform one or more functions on a database. In a large organization with many users, granting privileges to every individual employee can be tedious and time-consuming. SQL addresses this problem by introducing the notion of roles.

A *role*, identified by a role name, is a set of zero or more privileges that can be granted to multiple people who all require the same level of access to the database. For example, everyone who performs the role SecurityGuard has the same privileges. These privileges are different from those granted to the people who have the role SalesClerk.

As always, not every feature mentioned in the latest version of the SQL specification is available in every implementation. Check your DBMS documentation before you try to use roles.

You can create roles by using syntax similar to the following:

```
CREATE ROLE SalesClerk ;
```

After you've created a role, you can assign people to the role with the GRANT statement, similar to the following:

```
GRANT SalesClerk to Becky ;
```

You can grant privileges to a role in exactly the same way that you grant privileges to users, with one exception: It won't argue or complain.

Inserting data

To grant a role the privilege of adding data to a table, follow this example:

```
GRANT INSERT
    ON CUSTOMER
    TO SalesClerk ;
```

This privilege enables any clerk in the sales department to add new customer records to the CUSTOMER table.

Looking at data

To enable people to view the data in a table, use the following example:

```
GRANT SELECT
    ON PRODUCT
    TO PUBLIC ;
```

This privilege enables anyone with access to the system (PUBLIC) to view the contents of the PRODUCT table.

WARNING

This statement can be dangerous. Columns in the PRODUCT table may contain information that not everyone should see, such as CostOfGoods. To provide access to most information while withholding access to sensitive information, define a view on the table that doesn't include the sensitive columns. Then grant SELECT privileges on the view rather than the underlying table. The following example shows the syntax for this procedure:

```
CREATE VIEW MERCHANDISE AS
    SELECT Model, ProdName, ProdDesc, ListPrice
        FROM PRODUCT ;
GRANT SELECT
    ON MERCHANDISE
    TO PUBLIC ;
```

Using the MERCHANDISE view, the public doesn't get to see the PRODUCT table's CostOfGoods column or any other column. The public sees only the four columns listed in the CREATE VIEW statement.

Modifying table data

In any active organization, table data changes over time. You need to grant to some people the right and power to make changes — and also prevent everyone else from doing so. To grant change privileges such as updating, follow this example:

```
GRANT UPDATE (BonusPct)
    ON BONUSRATE
    TO SalesMgr ;
```

The sales manager can adjust the bonus rate that salespeople receive for sales (the `BonusPct` column), based on changes in market conditions. However, the sales manager can't modify the values in the `MinAmount` and `MaxAmount` columns that define the ranges for each step in the bonus schedule. To enable updates to all columns, you must specify either all column names or no column names, as shown in the following example:

```
GRANT UPDATE
    ON BONUSRATE
    TO VPSales ;
```

Deleting obsolete rows from a table

Customers go out of business or stop buying products for some other reason. Employees quit, retire, are laid off, or die. Products become obsolete. Life goes on, and things that you tracked in the past may no longer be of interest. Someone needs to remove obsolete records from your tables. You want to carefully control who can remove which records. Regulating such privileges is another job for the `GRANT` statement, as shown in the following example:

```
GRANT DELETE
    ON EMPLOYEE
    TO PersonnelMgr ;
```

The personnel manager can remove records from the EMPLOYEE table. So can the DBA and the EMPLOYEE table owner (who's probably also the DBA). No one else can remove personnel records (unless another `GRANT` statement gives that person the power to do so).

Referencing related tables

If one table includes a second table's primary key as a foreign key, information in the second table becomes available to users of the first table. This situation potentially creates a dangerous back door through which unauthorized users can extract confidential information. In such a case, a user doesn't need access rights to a table to discover something about its contents. If the user has access rights to a table that references the target table, those rights often enable the user to access the target table as well.

Suppose, for example, that the table LAYOFF_LIST contains the names of the employees who will be laid off next month. Only authorized management has `SELECT` access to the table. An unauthorized employee, however, deduces that the table's primary key is `EmpID`. The employee then creates a new table SNOOP, which has `EmpID` as a foreign key, enabling him to sneak a peek at LAYOFF_LIST.

(I describe how to create a foreign key with a REFERENCES clause in Chapter 5. It's high on the list of techniques every system administrator should know how to use — and how to spot.) Here's the code that creates the sneaky table:

```
CREATE TABLE SNOOP
    (EmpID INTEGER REFERENCES LAYOFF_LIST) ;
```

Now all that the employee needs to do is try to INSERT rows corresponding to all employee ID numbers into SNOOP. The table accepts the inserts for only the employees on the layoff list. All rejected inserts are for employees not on the list.

TIP

All is not lost. You aren't at risk of exposing all private data you want to keep to yourself. Recent versions of SQL prevent this security breach by requiring privileged users to grant *explicitly* any reference rights to other users, as shown in the following example:

```
GRANT REFERENCES (EmpID)
    ON LAYOFF_LIST
    TO PERSONNEL_CLERK ;
```

You might want to check that your DBMS has this updated feature.

Using domains

Domains, character sets, collations, and translations also have an effect on security issues. You must keep a close watch on all of these — on created domains, in particular — to avoid having them be used to undermine your security measures.

You can define a domain that encompasses a set of columns. In doing so, you want all these columns to have the same type and to share the same constraints. The columns you create in your CREATE DOMAIN statement inherit the type and constraints of the domain. You can override these characteristics for specific columns, if you want, but domains provide a convenient way to apply numerous characteristics to multiple columns with a single declaration.

Domains come in handy if you have multiple tables that contain columns with similar characteristics. Your business database, for example, may consist of several tables, each of which contains a Price column that should have a type of DECIMAL(10,2) and values that aren't negative and are no greater than 10,000. Before you create tables that hold these columns, create a domain that specifies the columns' characteristics, like this:

```
CREATE DOMAIN PriceTypeDomain  DECIMAL (10,2)
    CHECK (Price >= 0 AND Price <= 10000) ;
```

Perhaps you identify your products in multiple tables by ProductCode, which is always of type CHAR (5), with a first character of X, C, or H and a last character of either 9 or 0. You can create a domain for these columns, too, as in the following example:

```
CREATE DOMAIN ProductCodeDomain CHAR (5)
    CHECK (SUBSTR (VALUE, 1,1) IN ('X', 'C', 'H')
    AND SUBSTR (VALUE, 5, 1) IN (9, 0) ) ;
```

With the domains in place, you can now proceed to create tables, as follows:

```
CREATE TABLE PRODUCT (
    ProductCode         ProductCodeDomain,
    ProductName         CHAR (30),
    Price               PriceTypeDomain) ;
```

WARNING

As I have mentioned previously for other ISO/IEC standard SQL features, no DBMS product supports them all. CREATE DOMAIN is one that is not universally supported. Sybase's iAnywhere DBMS supports it, as do Firebird and PostgreSQL, but Oracle and SQL Server do not.

In the table definition, instead of giving the data type for ProductCode and Price, specify the appropriate domain. This action gives those columns the correct type and also applies the constraints you specify in your CREATE DOMAIN statements.

When you use domains, you open up your database to certain security implications. What if someone else wants to use the domains you create — can this cause problems? Yes. What if someone creates a table with a column that has a domain of PriceTypeDomain? That person can assign progressively larger values to that column until it rejects a value. By doing so, the user can determine the upper bound on PriceType that you specify in the CHECK clause of your CREATE DOMAIN statement. If you consider that upper bound to be private information, you don't want others to access the PriceType domain. To protect tables in such situations, SQL allows only those to whom the domain owner explicitly grants permission to use domains. Thus, only the domain owner (as well as the DBA) can grant such permission. After you deem that it's safe to do so, you can grant users permission by using a statement such as the one shown in the following example:

```
GRANT USAGE ON DOMAIN PriceType TO SalesMgr ;
```

WARNING

Different security problems may arise if you DROP domains. Tables that contain columns that you define in terms of a domain cause problems if you try to DROP the domain. You may need to DROP all such tables first. Or you may find yourself unable to DROP the domain. How a domain DROP is handled may vary from one implementation to another. iAnywhere may do it one way, whereas PostgreSQL may do it another way. At any rate, you may want to restrict who can DROP domains. The same applies to character sets, collations, and translations.

Causing SQL statements to be executed

Sometimes the execution of one SQL statement triggers the execution of another SQL statement, or even a block of statements. SQL supports triggers. A *trigger* specifies a trigger event, a trigger action time, and one or more triggered actions:

>> The **trigger event** causes the trigger to execute, or fire.

>> The **trigger action time** determines when the triggered action occurs, either just before or just after the trigger event.

>> The **triggered action** is the execution of one or more SQL statements.

If more than one SQL statement is triggered, the statements must all be contained within a BEGIN ATOMIC...END structure. The trigger action can be an INSERT, UPDATE, or DELETE statement.

For example, you can use a trigger to execute a statement that checks the validity of a new value before an UPDATE is allowed. If the new value is found to be invalid, the update can be aborted.

A user or role must have the TRIGGER privilege in order to create a trigger. Here's an example:

```
CREATE TRIGGER CustomerDelete BEFORE DELETE
    ON CUSTOMER FOR EACH ROW
    WHEN State = 'NY'
    INSERT INTO CUSTLOG VALUES ('deleted a NY customer') ;
```

Whenever a New York customer is deleted from the CUSTOMER table, an entry in the log table CUSTLOG records the deletion.

Granting Privileges across Levels

In Chapter 2, I describe structured types as one kind of user-defined type (UDT). Much of the architecture of structured types is derived from the ideas of object-oriented programming. One of the ideas that comes out of that is the idea of a *hierarchy*, in which a type can have *subtypes* that derive some of their attributes from the type they come from (their *supertype*). In addition to those inherited attributes, they can also have attributes that are exclusively their own. There can be multiple levels of such a hierarchy, with the type at the bottom being called a *leaf type*.

A typed table is a table in which each row stored in the table is an instance of the associated structured type. A typed table has one column for each attribute of its associated structured type. The name and data type of the column are the same as the name and data type of the attribute.

As an example, suppose you are a creator of paintings that you sell through galleries. In addition to original works of art, you also sell signed, numbered, limited editions, unsigned unnumbered open editions, and posters. You can create a structured type for your artwork as follows:

```
CREATE TYPE artwork (
    artist          CHARACTER VARYING (30),
    title           CHARACTER VARYING (50),
    description     CHARACTER VARYING (256),
    medium          CHARACTER VARYING (20),
    creationDate    DATE )
    NOT FINAL
```

WARNING

Here's another case of a feature that is not present on all DBMS products. However, PostgreSQL has the CREATE TYPE statement, as do Oracle and SQL Server.

As an artist trying to keep track of your inventory, you want to distinguish between originals and reproductions. You might further want to distinguish between different kinds of reproductions. Figure 14-2 shows one possible use of a hierarchy to facilitate the needed distinctions. The artwork type can have subtypes, which in turn can have subtypes of their own.

There is a one-to-one correspondence between the types in the type hierarchy and the tables in the typed table hierarchy. Standard tables, as discussed in Chapters 4 and 5, cannot be placed into a hierarchy similar to the one discussed here for typed tables.

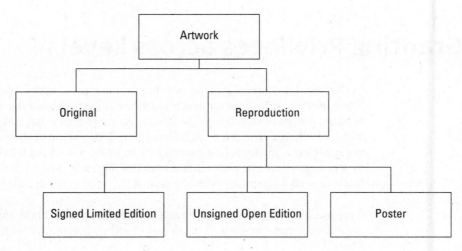

FIGURE 14-2:
Artwork table hierarchy.

Instead of a primary key, a typed table has a self-referencing column that guarantees uniqueness, not only for the maximal supertable of a hierarchy, but also for all its subtables. The self-referencing column is specified by a REF IS clause in the maximal supertable's CREATE statement. When the reference is system generated, uniqueness across the board is guaranteed.

Granting the Power to Grant Privileges

The DBA can grant any privileges to anyone. An object owner can grant any privileges on that object to anyone. But users who receive privileges this way can't in turn grant those privileges to someone else. This restriction helps the DBA or table owner to retain control. Only users that the DBA or object owner empowers to do so can perform the operation in question.

From a security standpoint, putting limits on the capability to delegate access privileges makes a lot of sense. Many occasions arise, however, in which users need the power to delegate their authority. Work can't come to a screeching halt every time someone is ill, on vacation, or out to lunch.

REMEMBER

You can trust *some* users with the power to delegate their access rights to reliable designated alternates. To pass such a right of delegation to a user, the GRANT statement uses the WITH GRANT OPTION clause. The following statement shows one example of how you can use this clause:

```
GRANT UPDATE (BonusPct)
    ON BONUSRATE
    TO SalesMgr
    WITH GRANT OPTION ;
```

Now the sales manager can delegate the UPDATE privilege by issuing the following statement:

```
GRANT UPDATE (BonusPct)
    ON BONUSRATE
    TO AsstSalesMgr ;
```

After the execution of this statement, anyone with the role of assistant sales manager can make changes to the BonusPct column in the BONUSRATE table.

WARNING

Of course, you make a tradeoff between security and convenience when you delegate access rights to a designated alternate. The owner of the BONUSRATE table relinquishes considerable control in granting the UPDATE privilege to the sales manager by using the WITH GRANT OPTION. The table owner hopes that the sales manager takes this responsibility seriously and is careful about passing on the privilege.

Taking Privileges Away

If you have a way to give access privileges to people, you should also have a way of taking those privileges away. People's job functions change, and with these changes their data access needs change. Say an employee leaves the organization to join a competitor. You should probably revoke all access privileges to that person — immediately.

SQL allows you to remove access privileges by using the REVOKE statement. This statement acts like the GRANT statement does, except that it has the reverse effect. The syntax for this statement is as follows:

```
REVOKE [GRANT OPTION FOR] privilege-list
    ON object
    FROM user-list [RESTRICT|CASCADE] ;
```

You can use this structure to revoke specified privileges while leaving others intact. The principal difference between the REVOKE statement and the GRANT statement is the presence of the optional RESTRICT or CASCADE keyword in the REVOKE statement.

For example, suppose you used WITH GRANT OPTION when you granted certain privileges to a user. Eventually, when you want to revoke those privileges, you can use CASCADE in the REVOKE statement. When you revoke a user's privileges in this way, you also yank privileges from anyone to whom that person had granted privileges.

On the other hand, the REVOKE statement with the RESTRICT option works only if the grantee *hasn't* delegated the specified privileges. In that case, the REVOKE statement revokes the grantee's privileges just fine. But if the grantee passed on the specified privileges, the REVOKE statement with the RESTRICT option doesn't revoke anything — and instead returns an error code. This is a clear warning to you that you need to find out who was granted privileges by the person whose privileges you are trying to revoke. You may or may not want to revoke that person's privileges.

You can use a REVOKE statement with the optional GRANT OPTION FOR clause to revoke only the grant option for specified privileges while enabling the grantee to retain those privileges for himself. If the GRANT OPTION FOR clause and the CASCADE keyword are both present, you revoke all privileges that the grantee granted, along with the grantee's right to bestow such privileges — as if you'd never granted the grant option in the first place. If the GRANT OPTION FOR clause and the RESTRICT clause are both present, one of two things happens:

>> If the grantee didn't grant to anyone else any of the privileges you're revoking, then the REVOKE statement executes and removes the grantee's ability to grant privileges.

>> If the grantee has already granted at least one of the privileges you're revoking, the REVOKE statement doesn't execute and returns an error code instead.

WARNING

The fact that you can grant privileges by using WITH GRANT OPTION, combined with the fact that you can also selectively revoke privileges, makes system security much more complex than it appears at first glance. Multiple grantors, for example, can conceivably grant a privilege to any single user. If one of those grantors then revokes the privilege, the user still retains that privilege because of the still-existing grant from another grantor. If a privilege passes from one user to another by way of the WITH GRANT OPTION, this situation creates a *chain of dependency,* in which one user's privileges depend on those of another user. If you're a DBA or an object owner, always be aware that after you grant a privilege by using the WITH GRANT OPTION clause, that privilege may show up in unexpected places. Revoking the privilege from unwanted users while letting legitimate users retain the same privilege may prove challenging. In general, the GRANT OPTION and CASCADE clauses encompass numerous subtleties. If you use these clauses, check both the SQL standard and your product documentation — carefully — to ensure that you understand how the clauses work.

Using GRANT and REVOKE Together to Save Time and Effort

Enabling multiple privileges for multiple users on selected table columns may require a lot of typing. Consider this example: The vice president of sales wants everyone in the sales department to see everything in the CUSTOMER table, but only sales managers should update, delete, or insert rows. *Nobody* should update the CustID field. The sales managers' names are Tyson, Keith, and David. You can grant appropriate privileges to these managers with GRANT statements, as follows:

```
GRANT SELECT, INSERT, DELETE
   ON CUSTOMER
   TO Tyson, Keith, David ;
GRANT UPDATE
   ON CUSTOMER (Company, CustAddress, CustCity,
      CustState, CustZip, CustPhone, ModLevel)
   TO Tyson, Keith, David ;
GRANT SELECT
```

```
    ON CUSTOMER
    TO Jen, Val, Mel, Neil, Rob, Sam, Walker, Ford,
       Brandon, Cliff, Joss, MichelleT, Allison, Andrew,
       Scott, MichelleB, Jaime, Lynleigh, Matthew, Amanda;
```

That should do the trick. Everyone has SELECT rights on the CUSTOMER table. The sales managers have full INSERT and DELETE rights on the table, and they can update any column but the CustID column.

TIP

Here's an easier way to get the same result:

```
GRANT SELECT
    ON CUSTOMER
    TO SalesReps ;
GRANT INSERT, DELETE, UPDATE
    ON CUSTOMER
    TO Managers ;
REVOKE UPDATE
    ON CUSTOMER (CustID)
    FROM Managers ;
```

Assuming you've assigned roles appropriately, it still takes three statements in this example for the same protection as was given by the three statements in the preceding example. No one may change data in the CustID column; only Tyson, Keith, and David have INSERT, DELETE, and UPDATE privileges. These latter three statements are significantly shorter than those in the preceding example because you don't name all the users in the sales department, all the managers, or all the columns in the table.

Chapter **15**

Protecting Data

Everyone has heard of Murphy's Law — usually stated, "If anything *can* go wrong, it *will*." People joke about this pseudo-law because most of the time things go fine. At times, you may feel lucky because you're untouched by what purports to be one of the basic laws of the universe. When unexpected problems arise, you probably just recognize what has happened and deal with it.

In a complex structure, the potential for unanticipated problems shoots way up. (A mathematician might say it "increases approximately as the square of the complexity.") Thus large software projects are almost always delivered late and are often loaded with bugs. A nontrivial, multiuser DBMS application is a large, complex structure. In the course of operation, many things can go wrong. Methods have been developed for minimizing the impact of these problems, but the problems can never be eliminated completely. This is good news for professional people who do database maintenance and repair — automating them out of a job will probably never be possible. This chapter discusses the major things that can go wrong with a database and the tools that SQL provides for you to deal with the problems that arise.

Threats to Data Integrity

Cyberspace (including your network) is a nice place to visit, but for the data living there, it's no picnic. Data can be damaged or corrupted in a variety of ways. Chapter 5 discusses problems resulting from bad input data, operator error, and deliberate destruction. Poorly formulated SQL statements and improperly designed applications can also damage your data — and figuring out how doesn't take much imagination. Two relatively obvious threats — platform instability and equipment failure — can also trash your data. Both hazards are detailed in the following sections, as well as problems that can be caused by concurrent access.

Platform instability

Platform instability is a category of problem that shouldn't even exist, but alas, it does. It is most prevalent when you're running one or more new and relatively untried components in your system. Problems can lurk in a new DBMS release, a new operating system version, or new hardware. Conditions or situations that have never appeared before can show up while you're running a critical job. Your system locks up, and your data is damaged. Beyond directing a few choice words at your computer and the people who built it, you can't do much except hope your latest backup was a good one.

WARNING

Never put important production work on a system that has *any* unproven components. Resist the temptation to put your bread-and-butter work on an untried beta release of the newest, most function-laden version of your DBMS or operating system. If you must gain some hands-on experience with a new software product, do so on a machine that's completely isolated from your production network.

Equipment failure

Even well-proven, highly reliable equipment fails sometimes, sending your data to the great beyond. Everything physical wears out eventually — even modern, solid-state computers. If such a failure happens while your database is open and active, you can lose data — and sometimes (even worse) not realize it. Such a failure will happen sooner or later. If Murphy's Law is in operation that day, the failure will happen at the worst possible time.

TIP

One way to protect data against equipment failure is *redundancy*. Keep extra copies of everything. For maximum safety (provided your organization can swing it financially), have duplicate hardware configured exactly like your production system. Have database and application backups that can be loaded and run on your backup hardware when needed. If cost constraints keep you from duplicating everything (which effectively doubles your costs), at least be sure to back up your database and applications frequently enough that an unexpected failure doesn't require you to reenter a large amount of data. Many DBMS products include replication capabilities. That is all well and good, but it won't help unless you configure your system to actually use them.

Another way to avoid the worst consequences of equipment failure is to use *transaction processing* — a topic that takes center stage later in this chapter. A *transaction* is an indivisible unit of work, so when you use transaction processing, either an entire transaction is executed or none of it is. This all-or-nothing approach may seem drastic, but the worst problems arise when a series of database operations is only partially processed. Thus you're much less likely to lose or corrupt your data, even if the machine on which the database resides is crashing.

Concurrent access

Assume that you're running proven hardware and software, your data are good, your application is bug-free, and your equipment is inherently reliable. Data utopia, right? Not quite. Problems can still arise when multiple people try to use the same database table at the same time *(concurrent access)*, and their computers argue about who gets to go first *(contention)*. Multiple-user database systems must be able to handle the ruckus efficiently.

Transaction interaction trouble

Contention troubles can lurk even in applications that seem straightforward. Consider this example. You're writing an order-processing application that involves four tables: ORDER_MASTER, CUSTOMER, LINE_ITEM, and INVENTORY. The following conditions apply:

>> The ORDER_MASTER table has OrderNumber as a primary key and CustomerNumber as a foreign key that references the CUSTOMER table.

>> The LINE_ITEM table has LineNumber as a primary key, ItemNumber as a foreign key that references the INVENTORY table, and Quantity as one of its columns.

>> The INVENTORY table has ItemNumber as a primary key; it also has a field named QuantityOnHand.

>> All three tables have other columns, but they don't enter into this example.

Your company policy is to ship each order completely or not at all. No partial ship-ments or back orders are allowed. (Relax. It's a hypothetical situation.) You write the ORDER_PROCESSING application to process each incoming order in the ORDER_MASTER table as follows: It first determines whether your company can ship *all* the line items. If so, it writes the order and then decrements the QuantityOnHand column of the INVENTORY table as required. (This action deletes the affected entries from the ORDER_MASTER and LINE_ITEM tables.) So far, so good. You set up the application to process orders in one of two ways when users access the database concurrently:

>> Method 1 processes the INVENTORY row that corresponds to each row in the LINE_ITEM table. If QuantityOnHand is large enough, the application decre-ments that field. If QuantityOnHand is not large enough, it rolls back the transaction to restore all inventory reductions made to other LINE_ITEMs in this order.

>> Method 2 checks every INVENTORY row that corresponds to a row in the order's LINE_ITEMs. If they are *all* big enough, then it processes those items by decrementing them.

Usually, Method 1 is more efficient when you succeed in processing the order; Method 2 is more efficient when you fail. Thus, if most orders can be filled most of the time, you're better off using Method 1. If most orders can't be filled most of the time, you're better off with Method 2. Suppose this hypothetical application is up and running on a multiuser system that doesn't have adequate concurrency control. Yep. Trouble is brewing, all right. Consider this scenario:

1. **A customer contacts an order processor at your company (User 1) to order ten bolt cutters and five wide adjustable wrenches.**

2. **User 1 uses Method 1 to process the order. The first item in the order is ten pieces of Item 1 (bolt cutters).**

   As it happens, your company has ten bolt cutters in stock, and User 1's order takes them all.

   The order-processing function chugs along, decrementing the quantity of bolt cutters to zero. Then things get (as the Chinese proverb says) *interesting*. Another customer contacts your company to process an order and talks to User 2.

3. **User 2 attempts to process the customer's small order for one bolt-cutter — and finds that there are no bolt cutters in stock.**

   User 2's order is rolled back because it can't be filled.

4. **Meanwhile, User 1 tries to complete his customer's order and checks the system for five pieces of Item 37 (wide adjustable wrenches).**

Unfortunately, your company only has four wide adjustable wrenches in stock. User 1's complete order (including the bolt cutters) is rolled back because it can't be completely filled.

The INVENTORY table is now back to the state it was in before either user started operating. Neither order has been filled, even though User 2's order could have been.

In a slightly different scenario, Method 2 fares little better, although for a different reason. User 1 checks all the items ordered and decides that all the items ordered *are* available. Then User 2 comes in and processes an order for one of those items *before* User 1 performs the decrement operation; User 1's transaction fails.

Serialization eliminates harmful interactions

No conflict occurs if transactions are executed *serially* rather than concurrently. (Taking turns — what a concept.) In the first example, if User 1's unsuccessful transaction was completed before User 2's transaction started, the ROLLBACK function would have made the single bolt cutter ordered by User 2 available. (The ROLLBACK function rolls back, or undoes the entire transaction.) If the transactions had run serially in the second example, User 2 would have had no opportunity to change the quantity of any item until User 1's transaction was complete. User 1's transaction completes, either successfully or unsuccessfully, and User 2 then sees how many bolt cutters are left in stock.

If transactions are executed serially (one after the other), they have no chance of interacting destructively. Execution of concurrent transactions is *serializable* if the result is the same as it would be if the transactions were executed serially.

WARNING

Serializing concurrent transactions isn't a cure-all. You have to make a tradeoff between performance and protection from harmful interactions. The more you isolate transactions from each other, the more time it takes to perform each function. (In cyberspace, as in real life, waiting in line takes time.) Be aware of the tradeoffs so you can configure your system for adequate protection — but not more protection than you need. Controlling concurrent access too tightly can kill overall system performance.

Reducing Vulnerability to Data Corruption

You can take precautions at several levels to reduce the chances of losing data through some mishap or unanticipated interaction. You can set up your DBMS to take some of these precautions for you. When you configure your DBMS appropriately, it acts like a guardian angel to protect you from harm, operating behind the scenes; you don't even know that the DBMS is helping you out. Your database administrator (DBA) can take other precautions at his or her discretion that you may not be aware of. As the developer, you can take precautions as you write your code.

TIP

To avoid a lot of grief, get into the habit of adhering to a few simple principles automatically so they're always included in your code or in your interactions with your database:

>> Use SQL transactions.

>> Tailor the level of isolation to balance performance and protection.

>> Know when and how to set transactions, lock database objects, and perform backups.

Details coming right up.

Using SQL transactions

The transaction is one of SQL's main tools for maintaining database integrity. An *SQL transaction* encapsulates all the SQL statements that can have an effect on the database. An SQL transaction is completed with either a COMMIT or ROLLBACK statement:

>> If the transaction finishes with a COMMIT, the effects of all the statements in the transaction are applied to the database in one rapid-fire sequence.

>> If the transaction finishes with a ROLLBACK, the effects of all the statements are *rolled back* (that is, undone), and the database returns to the state it was in before the transaction began.

REMEMBER

In this discussion, the term *application* means either an execution of a program (whether in Java, C++, or some other programming language) or a series of actions performed at a terminal during a single logon.

An application can include a series of SQL transactions. The first SQL transaction begins when the application begins; the last SQL transaction ends when the application ends. Each COMMIT or ROLLBACK that the application performs ends one SQL transaction and begins the next. For example, an application with three SQL transactions has the following form:

```
Start of the application
    Various SQL statements (SQL transaction-1)
COMMIT or ROLLBACK
    Various SQL statements (SQL transaction-2)
COMMIT or ROLLBACK
    Various SQL statements (SQL transaction-3)
COMMIT or ROLLBACK
End of the application
```

REMEMBER

I use the phrase *SQL transaction* because the application may be using other capabilities (such as for network access) that do other sorts of transactions. In the following discussion, I use *transaction* to mean *SQL transaction* specifically.

A normal SQL transaction has an access mode that is either READ-WRITE or READ-ONLY; it has an isolation level that is SERIALIZABLE, REPEATABLE READ, READ COMMITTED, or READ UNCOMMITTED. (You can find transaction characteristics in the "Isolation levels" section, later in this chapter.) The default characteristics are READ-WRITE and SERIALIZABLE. If you want any other characteristics, you have to specify them with a SET TRANSACTION statement such as the following:

```
SET TRANSACTION READ ONLY ;
```

or

```
SET TRANSACTION READ ONLY REPEATABLE READ ;
```

or

```
SET TRANSACTION READ COMMITTED ;
```

You can have multiple SET TRANSACTION statements in an application, but you can specify only one in each transaction, and it must be the first SQL statement executed in the transaction. If you want to use a SET TRANSACTION statement, execute it either at the beginning of the application or after a COMMIT or ROLLBACK.

REMEMBER

You must perform a SET TRANSACTION at the beginning of every transaction for which you want nondefault properties, because each new transaction after a COMMIT or ROLLBACK is given the default properties automatically.

TECHNICAL STUFF

A SET TRANSACTION statement can also specify a DIAGNOSTICS SIZE, which determines the number of error conditions for which the implementation should be prepared to save information. (Such a numerical limit is necessary because an implementation can detect more than one error during a statement.) The SQL default for this limit is implementation-defined, and that default is almost always adequate.

The default transaction

The default SQL transaction has characteristics that are satisfactory for most users most of the time. If necessary, you can specify different transaction characteristics with a SET TRANSACTION statement, as described in the previous section. (SET TRANSACTION gets its own spotlight treatment later in the chapter.)

The default transaction makes a couple of other implicit assumptions:

>> The database will change over time.

>> It's always better to be safe than sorry.

It sets the mode to READ-WRITE, which, as you may expect, enables you to issue statements that change the database. It also sets the isolation level to SERIALIZABLE, which is the highest level of isolation possible (thus the safest). The default diagnostics size is implementation-dependent. Look at your SQL documentation to see what that size is for your system.

Isolation levels

Ideally, the system handles your transactions independently from every other transaction, even if those transactions happen concurrently with yours. This concept is referred to as *isolation*. In the real world of networked multiuser systems with real-time access requirements, however, complete isolation is not always feasible. Isolation may exact too large a performance penalty. A tradeoff question arises: "How much isolation do you really want, and how much are you willing to pay for it in terms of performance?"

Getting mucked up by a dirty read

The weakest level of isolation is called READ UNCOMMITTED, which allows the sometimes-problematic dirty read. A *dirty read* is a situation in which a change made by one user can be read by a second user before the first user completes her transaction with a COMMIT statement.

The problem arises if the first user aborts and rolls back her transaction. The second user's operations are now based on an incorrect value. The classic example of this foul-up can appear in an inventory application. In "Transaction interaction trouble," earlier in this chapter, I outline one possible scenario of this type, but here's another example: One user decrements inventory; a second user reads the new (lower) value. The first user rolls back her transaction (restoring the inventory to its initial value), but the second user, thinking inventory is low, orders more stock and possibly creates a severe overstock. And that's if you're lucky.

Don't use the READ UNCOMMITTED isolation level unless you don't care about accurate results.

You *can* use READ UNCOMMITTED if you want to generate approximate statistical data, such as these examples:

>> Maximum delay in filling orders

>> Average age of salespeople who don't make quota

>> Average age of new employees

In many such cases, approximate information is sufficient; the extra cost of the concurrency control required to give an exact result — mainly a performance slowdown — may not be worthwhile.

Getting bamboozled by a nonrepeatable read

The next highest level of isolation is READ COMMITTED: A change made by another transaction isn't visible to your transaction until the other user has finalized the other transaction with the COMMIT statement. This level gives you a better result than you can get from READ UNCOMMITTED, but it's still subject to a *nonrepeatable read* — serious problem that happens like a comedy of errors.

Consider the classic inventory example:

1. User 1 queries the database to see how many items of a particular product are in stock. The number is ten.

2. At almost the same time, User 2 starts, and then finalizes, a transaction with the COMMIT statement that records an order for ten units of that same product, decrementing the inventory to zero.

3. Now User 1, having seen that ten are available, tries to order five of them. Five are no longer left, however, because User 2 has raided the pantry.

User 1's initial read of the quantity available is not repeatable. Because the quantity has changed out from under User 1, any assumptions made on the basis of the initial read are not valid.

Risking the phantom read

An isolation level of REPEATABLE READ guarantees that the nonrepeatable-read problem doesn't happen. This isolation level, however, is still haunted by the *phantom read* — a problem that arises when the data a user is reading changes in response to another transaction (and does not show the change onscreen) *while the user is reading it.*

Suppose, for example, that User 1 issues a command whose search condition (the WHERE clause or HAVING clause) selects a set of rows — and, immediately afterward, User 2 performs and commits an operation that changes the data in *some* of those rows. Those data items met User 1's search condition at the start of this snafu, but now they no longer do. Maybe some other rows that first did *not* meet the original search condition now *do* meet it. User 1, whose transaction is still active, has no inkling of these changes; the application behaves as if nothing has happened. The hapless User 1 issues another SQL statement with the same search conditions as the original one, expecting to retrieve the same rows. Instead, the second operation is performed on rows other than those used in the first operation. Reliable results go out the window, spirited away by the phantom read.

Getting a reliable (if slower) read

An isolation level of SERIALIZABLE is not subject to any of the problems that beset the other three levels. At this level, concurrent transactions can be run without interfering with each other, and results are the same as they'd be if the transactions had been run serially — one after the other — rather than in parallel. If you're running at this isolation level, hardware or software problems can still cause your transaction to fail, but at least you don't have to worry about the validity of your results if you know your system is functioning properly.

Of course, superior reliability may come at the price of slower performance, so you're back in Tradeoff City. Table 15-1 shows how the different isolation levels stack up.

TABLE 15-1

Isolation Levels and Problems Solved

Isolation Level	Problems Solved Dirty Read	Nonrepeatable Read	Phantom Read
READ UNCOMMITTED	No	No	No
READ COMMITTED	Yes	No	No
REPEATABLE READ	Yes	Yes	No
SERIALIZABLE	Yes	Yes	Yes

The implicit transaction-starting statement

Some SQL implementations require that you signal the beginning of a transaction with an explicit statement, such as BEGIN or BEGIN TRAN. Standard SQL does not. If you don't have an active transaction and you issue a statement that calls for one, standard SQL starts a default transaction for you. CREATE TABLE, SELECT, and UPDATE are examples of statements that require the context of a transaction. Issue one of these statements, and standard SQL starts a transaction for you.

SET TRANSACTION

On occasion, you may want to use transaction characteristics that are different from those set by default. You can specify different characteristics with a SET TRANSACTION statement before you issue your first statement that actually requires a transaction. The SET TRANSACTION statement enables you to specify mode, isolation level, and diagnostics size.

To change all three, for example, you may issue the following statement:

```
SET TRANSACTION
    READ ONLY,
    ISOLATION LEVEL READ UNCOMMITTED,
    DIAGNOSTICS SIZE 4 ;
```

With these settings, you can't issue any statements that change the database (READ ONLY), and you have set the lowest and most hazardous isolation level (READ UNCOMMITTED). The diagnostics area has a size of 4. You are making minimal demands on system resources.

In contrast, you may issue this statement:

```
SET TRANSACTION
    READ WRITE,
    ISOLATION LEVEL SERIALIZABLE,
    DIAGNOSTICS SIZE 8 ;
```

These settings enable you to change the database; they also give you the highest level of isolation — and a larger diagnostics area. The tradeoff is that they also make larger demands on system resources. Depending on your implementation, these settings may turn out to be the same as those used by the default transaction. Naturally, you can issue SET TRANSACTION statements with other choices for isolation level and diagnostics size.

TIP

Set your transaction isolation level as high as you need to, but no higher. Always setting your isolation level to SERIALIZABLE just to be on the safe side may seem reasonable, but it isn't so for all systems. Depending on your implementation (and on what you're doing), you may not need to do so — and performance can suffer significantly if you do. If you don't intend to change the database in your transaction, for example, set the mode to READ ONLY. Bottom line: Don't tie up any system resources that you don't need.

COMMIT

Although SQL doesn't require an explicit transaction-starting keyword, it has two that terminate a transaction: COMMIT and ROLLBACK. Use COMMIT when you've come to the end of the transaction and you want to make permanent the changes (if any) that you made to the database. You may include the optional keyword WORK (COMMIT WORK) if you want. If the database encounters an error or the system crashes while a COMMIT is in progress, you may have to roll the transaction back and try it again.

ROLLBACK

When you come to the end of a transaction, you may decide that you don't want to make permanent the changes that have occurred during the transaction. In such a case, you should restore the database to the state it was in before the transaction began. To do this, issue a ROLLBACK statement. ROLLBACK is a fail-safe mechanism.

TIP

Even if the system crashes while a ROLLBACK is in progress, you can restart the ROLLBACK after you restore the system; the rollback will continue its work, restoring the database to its pre-transaction state.

Locking database objects

The isolation level — set either by default or by a `SET TRANSACTION` statement — tells the DBMS how zealous to be in protecting your work from interaction with the work of other users. The main protection from harmful transactions that the DBMS gives to you is its application of locks to the database objects you're using. Here are a few examples:

>> The table row you're accessing is locked, preventing others from accessing that record while you're using it.

>> An entire table is locked, if you're performing an operation that could affect the whole table.

>> Reading, but not writing, is allowed. Sometimes writing is allowed but not reading.

Each implementation handles locking in its own way. Some implementations are more bulletproof than others, but most up-to-date systems protect you from the worst problems that can arise in a concurrent-access situation.

Backing up your data

Backing up data is a protective action that your DBA should perform on a regular basis. All system elements should be backed up at intervals that depend on how frequently they're updated. If your database is updated daily, it should be backed up daily. Your applications, forms, and reports may change, too, though less frequently. Whenever you make changes to them, your DBA should back up the new versions.

TIP

Keep several generations of backups. Sometimes, database damage doesn't become evident until some time has passed. To return to the last good version, you may have to go back several backup versions.

You can perform a backup in one of several different ways:

>> Use SQL to create backup tables and copy data into them.

>> Use an implementation-defined mechanism that backs up the whole database or portions of it. Using such a mechanism is generally more convenient and efficient than using SQL.

>> Your installation may have a mechanism in place for backing up everything, including databases, programs, documents, spreadsheets, utilities, and computer games. If so, you may not have to do anything beyond assuring yourself that the backups are performed frequently enough to protect you.

HAVING AN ACID DATABASE

You may hear database designers say they want their databases to have ACID. Well, no, they're not planning to zonk their creations with a 1960s psychedelic or dissolve the data they contain into a bubbly mess. ACID is simply an acronym for Atomicity, Consistency, Isolation, and Durability. These four characteristics are necessary to protect a database from corruption:

- **Atomicity:** Database transactions should be *atomic* in the classic sense of the word: The entire transaction is treated as an indivisible unit. Either it is executed in its entirety (committed), or the database is restored (rolled back) to the state it would have been in if the transaction had not been executed.

- **Consistency:** Oddly enough, the meaning of *consistency* is not consistent; it varies from one application to another. When you transfer funds from one account to another in a banking application, for example, you want the total amount of money from both accounts at the end of the transaction to be the same as it was at the beginning of the transaction. In a different application, your criterion for consistency might be different.

- **Isolation:** Ideally, database transactions should be totally isolated from other transactions that execute at the same time. If the transactions are serializable, then total isolation is achieved. If the system has to process transactions at top speed, sometimes lower levels of isolation can enhance performance.

- **Durability:** After a transaction has committed or rolled back, you should be able to count on the database being in the proper state: well stocked with uncorrupted, reliable, up-to-date data. Even if your system suffers a hard crash after a commit — but before the transaction is stored to disk — a durable DBMS can guarantee that upon recovery from the crash, the database can be restored to its proper state.

Savepoints and subtransactions

Ideally, transactions should be atomic — as indivisible as the ancient Greeks thought atoms were. However, atoms are not really indivisible — and, starting with SQL:1999, database transactions are not really atomic. A transaction is divisible into multiple *subtransactions.* Each subtransaction is terminated by a SAVEPOINT statement. The SAVEPOINT statement is used in conjunction with the ROLLBACK statement. Before the introduction of *savepoints* (the point in the program where the SAVEPOINT statement takes effect), the ROLLBACK statement could be used only to cancel an entire transaction. Now it can be used to roll back a transaction to a savepoint within the transaction. What good is this, you might ask?

Granted, the primary use of the ROLLBACK statement is to prevent data corruption if a transaction is interrupted by an error condition. And no, rolling back to a savepoint does not make sense if an error occurred while a transaction was in progress; you'd want to roll back the *entire* transaction to bring the database back to the state it was in before the transaction started. But you might have other reasons for rolling back part of a transaction.

Suppose you're performing a complex series of operations on your data. Partway through the process, you receive results that lead you to conclude that you're going down an unproductive path. If you were thinking ahead enough to put a SAVEPOINT statement just before you started on that path, you can roll back to the savepoint and try another option. Provided the rest of your code was in good shape before you set the savepoint, this approach works better than aborting the current transaction and starting a new one just to try a new path.

To insert a savepoint into your SQL code, use the following syntax:

```
SAVEPOINT savepoint_name ;
```

You can cause execution to roll back to that savepoint with code such as the following:

```
ROLLBACK TO SAVEPOINT savepoint_name ;
```

Some SQL implementations may not include the SAVEPOINT statement. If your implementation is one of those, you won't be able to use it.

Constraints Within Transactions

Ensuring the validity of the data in your database means doing more than just making sure the data is of the right type. Perhaps some columns, for example, should never hold a null value — and maybe others should hold only values that fall within a certain range. Such restrictions are *constraints*, as discussed in Chapter 5.

Constraints are relevant to transactions because they can conceivably prevent you from doing what you want. For example, suppose that you want to add data to a table that contains a column with a NOT NULL constraint. One common method of adding a record is to append a blank row to your table and then insert values into it later. The NOT NULL constraint on one column, however, causes the append operation to fail. SQL doesn't allow you to add a row that has a null value in a column with a NOT NULL constraint, even though you plan to add data to that column before your transaction ends. To address this problem, SQL enables you to designate constraints as either DEFERRABLE or NOT DEFERRABLE.

Constraints that are NOT DEFERRABLE are applied immediately. You can set DEFERRABLE constraints to be either initially DEFERRED or IMMEDIATE. If a DEFERRABLE constraint is set to IMMEDIATE, it acts like a NOT DEFERRABLE constraint — it is applied immediately. If a DEFERRABLE constraint is set to DEFERRED, it is not enforced. (No, your code doesn't have an attitude problem; it's simply following orders.)

To append blank records or perform other operations that may violate DEFERRABLE constraints, you can use a statement similar to the following:

```
SET CONSTRAINTS ALL DEFERRED ;
```

This statement puts all DEFERRABLE constraints in the DEFERRED condition. It does not affect the NOT DEFERRABLE constraints. After you've performed all operations that could violate your constraints — and the table reaches a state that doesn't violate them — you can reapply them. The statement that reapplies your constraints looks like this:

```
SET CONSTRAINTS ALL IMMEDIATE ;
```

If you made a mistake and any of your constraints are still being violated, you find out as soon as this statement takes effect.

If you do not explicitly set your DEFERRED constraints to IMMEDIATE, SQL does it for you when you attempt to COMMIT your transaction. If a violation is still present at that time, the transaction does not COMMIT; instead, SQL gives you an error message.

SQL's handling of constraints protects you from entering invalid data (or an invalid *absence* of data, which is just as important), at the same time giving you the flexibility to violate constraints temporarily while a transaction is still active.

Consider a payroll example to see why being able to defer the application of constraints is important.

Assume that an EMPLOYEE table has columns EmpNo, EmpName, DeptNo, and Salary. EMPLOYEE.DeptNo is a foreign key that references the DEPT table. Assume also that the DEPT table has columns DeptNo and DeptName. DeptNo is the primary key.

In addition, you want to have a table like DEPT that also contains a `Payroll` column which (in turn) holds the sum of the `Salary` values for employees in each department.

Assuming you are using a DBMS that supports this SQL standard functionality, you can create the equivalent of this table with the following view:

```
CREATE VIEW DEPT2 AS
    SELECT D.*, SUM(E.Salary) AS Payroll
        FROM DEPT D, EMPLOYEE E
        WHERE D.DeptNo = E.DeptNo
        GROUP BY D.DeptNo ;
```

You can also define this same view as follows:

```
CREATE VIEW DEPT3 AS
    SELECT D.*,
        (SELECT SUM(E.Salary)
            FROM EMPLOYEE E
            WHERE D.DeptNo = E.DeptNo) AS Payroll
    FROM DEPT D ;
```

But suppose that, for efficiency, you don't want to calculate the `SUM` every time you reference `DEPT3.Payroll`. Instead, you want to store an actual `Payroll` column in the DEPT table. You will then update that column every time you change a `Salary`.

To make sure that the `Salary` column is accurate, you can include a `CONSTRAINT` in the table definition:

```
CREATE TABLE DEPT
    (DeptNo CHAR(5),
    DeptNameCHAR(20),
    Payroll DECIMAL(15,2),
    CHECK (Payroll = (SELECT SUM(Salary)
                        FROM EMPLOYEE E
                        WHERE E.DeptNo= DEPT.DeptNo)));
```

Now, suppose you want to increase the `Salary` of employee 123 by 100. You can do it with the following update:

```
UPDATE EMPLOYEE
    SET Salary = Salary + 100
    WHERE EmpNo = '123' ;
```

With this approach, you must remember to do the following as well:

```
UPDATE DEPT D
   SET Payroll = Payroll + 100
   WHERE D.DeptNo = (SELECT E.DeptNo
           FROM EMPLOYEE E
           WHERE E.EmpNo = '123') ;
```

(You use the subquery to reference the DeptNo of employee 123.)

But there's a problem: Constraints are checked after each statement. In principle, *all* constraints are checked. In practice, implementations check only the constraints that reference the values modified by the statement.

After the first preceding UPDATE statement, the implementation checks all constraints that reference any values that the statement modifies. This includes the constraint defined in the DEPT table, because that constraint references the Salary column of the EMPLOYEE table and the UPDATE statement is modifying that column. After the first UPDATE statement, that constraint is violated. You assume that before you execute the UPDATE statement the database is correct, and each Payroll value in the DEPT table equals the sum of the Salary values in the corresponding columns of the EMPLOYEE table. When the first UPDATE statement increases a Salary value, this equality is no longer true. The second UPDATE statement corrects this — and again leaves the database values in a state for which the constraint is True. Between the two updates, the constraint is False.

The SET CONSTRAINTS DEFERRED statement lets you temporarily disable or *suspend* all constraints, or only specified constraints. The constraints are deferred until either you execute a SET CONSTRAINTS IMMEDIATE statement or you execute a COMMIT or ROLLBACK statement. So you surround the previous two UPDATE statements with SET CONSTRAINTS statements. The code looks like this:

```
SET CONSTRAINTS DEFERRED ;
UPDATE EMPLOYEE
   SET Salary = Salary + 100
   WHERE EmpNo = '123' ;
UPDATE DEPT D
   SET Payroll = Payroll + 100
   WHERE D.DeptNo = (SELECT E.DeptNo
           FROM EMPLOYEE E
     WHERE E.EmpNo = '123') ;
SET CONSTRAINTS IMMEDIATE ;
```

This procedure defers all constraints. If you insert new rows into DEPT, the primary keys won't be checked; you've removed protection that you may want to keep. Instead, you should specify the constraints that you want to defer. To do this, name the constraints when you create them:

```
CREATE TABLE DEPT
    (DeptNo CHAR(5),
     DeptName CHAR(20),
     Payroll DECIMAL(15,2),
     CONSTRAINT PayEqSumsal
     CHECK (Payroll = SELECT SUM(Salary)
     FROM EMPLOYEE E
     WHERE E.DeptNo = DEPT.DeptNo)) ;
```

With constraint names in place, you can then reference your constraints individually:

```
SET CONSTRAINTS PayEqSumsal DEFERRED;
UPDATE EMPLOYEE
    SET Salary = Salary + 100
    WHERE EmpNo = '123' ;
UPDATE DEPT D
    SET Payroll = Payroll + 100
    WHERE D.DeptNo = (SELECT E.DeptNo
                        FROM EMPLOYEE E
                        WHERE E.EmpNo = '123') ;
SET CONSTRAINTS PayEqSumsal IMMEDIATE;
```

Without a constraint name in the CREATE statement, SQL generates one implicitly. That implicit name is in the schema information (catalog) tables. But specifying the names explicitly is more straightforward.

Now suppose that you mistakenly specified an increment value of 1000 in the second UPDATE statement. This value is allowed in the UPDATE statement because the constraint has been deferred. But when you execute SET CONSTRAINTS ... IMMEDIATE, the specified constraints are checked. If they fail, SET CONSTRAINTS raises an exception. If, instead of a SET CONSTRAINTS ... IMMEDIATE statement, you execute COMMIT and the constraints are found to be False, COMMIT instead performs a ROLLBACK.

REMEMBER

Bottom line: You can defer the constraints only *within* a transaction. When the transaction is terminated by a ROLLBACK or a COMMIT, the constraints are both enabled and checked. The SQL capability of deferring constraints is meant to be used within a transaction. If used properly, the terminated transaction doesn't create any data that violates a constraint available to other transactions.

Avoiding SQL Injection Attacks

It's hard enough to keep your data safe from platform instability, equipment failure, and concurrent access. What if someone is *deliberately* trying to steal or corrupt your data, or harm you in some other way? That can cause far more serious problems. There are many ways that a malicious actor could attack a computer system, but the one most connected to database applications is the SQL injection attack.

The name is very descriptive. In an SQL injection attack, a malicious actor attempts to inject malicious code into a database application. Such code could transfer control of the database to the attacker. At that point the attacker could surreptitiously alter the data to the detriment of the owner or the users, or she could just delete entire tables.

A weak point of any application is any solicitation of input from the user, including asking for login credentials. As an application developer, when you code text boxes for the user to enter a username and a password into, you expect the user to enter a username and a password. A hacker, on the other hand, will enter something that you don't expect, something that will cause the application to react in a way that tells the attacker something that she did not already know. That knowledge enables her to penetrate a little farther. When she attains system administrator privileges, the game is over and your data is at her mercy.

SQL injection attacks take advantage of dynamic SQL in an application's code. There are two kinds of SQL: static SQL and dynamic SQL. *Static SQL* is hard-coded into an application program and becomes fixed at compile time. It cannot be easily hacked. *Dynamic SQL*, on the other hand, is assembled and executed at runtime. An SQL injection attack makes use of this by tacking some extra code onto a legal data entry. This extra code gets incorporated into the dynamic SQL statement that was designed to accept and act upon the input that was supposed to be entered into that text box. The attacking code could cause sensitive information to be revealed to the hacker, or it could even destroy the database.

There are defenses against SQL injection attacks. Primarily, these involve carefully validating any user input before incorporating it into a dynamic SQL statement. I cover SQL injection in detail, as well as other threats to a database in my *SQL All-In-One For Dummies* (Wiley Publishing, Inc.).

Chapter **16**

Using SQL within Applications

Previous chapters address SQL statements mostly in isolation. For example, questions are asked about data, and SQL queries are developed that retrieve answers to the questions. This mode of operation, *interactive SQL*, is fine for discovering what SQL can do — but it's not how SQL is typically used.

Even though SQL syntax can be described as similar to that of English, it isn't an easy language to master. The overwhelming majority of computer users are not fluent in SQL — and you can reasonably assume that they never will be, even if this book is wildly successful. When a database question comes up, Joe User probably won't sit down at his terminal and enter an SQL SELECT statement to find the answer. Systems analysts and application developers are the people who are likely to be comfortable with SQL, and they typically don't make a career out of entering ad hoc queries into databases. Instead, they develop applications to make those queries.

TIP

If you plan to perform the same operation repeatedly, you shouldn't have to rebuild it every time from your keyboard. Write an application to do the job and then run it as often as you like. SQL can be a part of an application, but when it is, it works a little differently than it does in an interactive mode.

SQL in an Application

In Chapter 2, SQL is presented to you as an incomplete programming language. To use SQL in an application, you have to combine it with a *procedural* language such as Visual Basic, C, C++, C#, Java, COBOL, or Python. Because of the way it's structured, SQL has some strengths and weaknesses. Procedural languages are structured differently from SQL, and consequently have *different* strengths and weaknesses.

Happily, the strengths of SQL tend to make up for the weaknesses of procedural languages, and the strengths of the procedural languages are in those areas where SQL is weak. By combining the two, you can build powerful applications with a broad range of capabilities. Recently, *object-oriented rapid application development* (RAD) tools, such as Microsoft's Visual Studio and the open-source Eclipse environment, have appeared, which incorporate SQL code into applications developed by manipulating onscreen objects instead of writing procedural code.

Keeping an eye out for the asterisk

In the interactive SQL discussions in previous chapters, the asterisk (*) serves as a shorthand substitute for "all columns in the table." If the table has numerous columns, the asterisk can save a lot of typing. However, using the asterisk this way is problematic when you use SQL in an application program. After your application is written, you or someone else may add new columns to a table or delete old ones. Doing so changes the meaning of "all columns." When your application specifies "all columns" with an asterisk, it may retrieve columns other than those it thinks it's getting.

Such a change to a table doesn't affect existing programs until they have to be recompiled to fix a bug or make some change, perhaps months after the change was made. Then the effect of the * wildcard expands to include all the now-current columns. This change may cause the application to fail in a way unrelated to the bug fix (or other change made), creating your own personal debugging nightmare.

TIP

To be safe, specify all column names explicitly in an application instead of using the asterisk wildcard. (For more about wildcard characters, see Chapter 6.)

SQL strengths and weaknesses

SQL is strong in data retrieval. If important information is buried somewhere in a single-table or multi-table database, SQL gives you the tools you need to retrieve it. You don't need to know the order of the table's rows or columns because SQL doesn't deal with rows or columns individually. The SQL transaction-processing facilities ensure that your database operations are unaffected by any other users who may be simultaneously accessing the same tables that you are.

A major weakness of SQL is its rudimentary user interface. It has no provision for formatting screens or reports. It accepts command lines from the keyboard and sends retrieved values to the monitor screen, one row at a time.

Sometimes a strength in one context is a weakness in another. One strength of SQL is that it can operate on an entire table at once. Whether the table has one row, a hundred rows, or a hundred thousand rows, a single SELECT statement can extract the data you want. SQL can't easily operate on one row at a time, however — and sometimes you do want to deal with each row individually. In such cases, you can use SQL's cursor facility (described in Chapter 19) or you can use a procedural host language.

Procedural languages' strengths and weaknesses

In contrast to SQL, procedural languages are designed for one-row-at-a-time operations, which give the application developer precise control over the way a table is processed. This detailed control is a great strength of procedural languages. But a corresponding weakness is that the application developer must have detailed knowledge about how the data is stored in the database tables. The order of the database's columns and rows is significant and must be taken into account.

REMEMBER

Because of the step-by-step nature of procedural languages, they have the flexibility to produce user-friendly screens for data entry and viewing. You can also produce sophisticated printed reports with any desired layout.

Problems in combining SQL with a procedural language

It makes sense to try to combine SQL and procedural languages in such a way that you can benefit from their mutual strengths and not be penalized by their combined weaknesses. As valuable as such a combination may be, you must overcome some challenges before you can achieve this perfect marriage in a practical way.

Contrasting operating modes

A big problem in combining SQL with a procedural language is that SQL operates on tables a set at a time, whereas procedural languages work on them a row at a time. Sometimes this issue isn't a big deal. You can separate set operations from row operations, doing each with the appropriate tool.

But if you want to search a table for records meeting certain conditions and perform different operations on the records depending on whether they meet the conditions, you may have a problem. Such a process requires both the retrieval power of SQL and the branching capability of a procedural language. Embedded SQL gives you this combination of capabilities. You can simply *embed* SQL statements at strategic locations within a program that you have written in a conventional procedural language. (See "Embedded SQL," later in this chapter, for more information.)

Data type incompatibilities

Another hurdle to the smooth integration of SQL with any procedural language is that SQL's data types differ from the data types of all the major procedural languages. This circumstance shouldn't be surprising, because the data types defined for any one procedural language are different from the types for the other procedural languages.

You can look high and low, but you won't find any standardization of data types across languages. In SQL releases before SQL-92, data-type incompatibility was a major concern. In SQL-92 (and also in subsequent releases of the SQL standard), the CAST statement addresses the problem. Chapter 9 explains how you can use CAST to convert a data item from the procedural language's data type to one recognized by SQL, as long as the data item itself is compatible with the new data type.

Hooking SQL into Procedural Languages

Although you face some potential hurdles when you integrate SQL with procedural languages, mark my words — the integration can be done successfully. In fact, in many instances, you *must* integrate SQL with procedural languages if you intend to produce the desired result in the allotted time — or produce it at all. Luckily, you can use any of several methods for combining SQL with procedural languages. Three of the methods — embedded SQL, module language, and RAD tools — are outlined in the next few sections.

Embedded SQL

The most common method of mixing SQL with procedural languages is called *embedded SQL*. Wondering how embedded SQL works? Take one look at the name and you have the basics down: Drop SQL statements into the middle of a procedural program, wherever you need them.

Of course, as you may expect, an SQL statement that suddenly appears in the middle of a C program can present a challenge for a compiler that isn't expecting it. For that reason, programs containing embedded SQL are usually passed through a *preprocessor* before being compiled or interpreted. The EXEC SQL directive warns the preprocessor of the imminent appearance of SQL code.

As an example of embedded SQL, look at a program written in Oracle's Pro*C version of the C language. The program, which accesses a company's EMPLOYEE table, prompts the user for an employee name and then displays that employee's salary and commission. It then prompts the user for new salary and commission data — and updates the employee table with it:

```
EXEC SQL BEGIN DECLARE SECTION;
    VARCHAR uid[20];
    VARCHAR pwd[20];
    VARCHAR ename[10];
    FLOAT salary, comm;
    SHORT salary_ind, comm_ind;
EXEC SQL END DECLARE SECTION;
main()
{
    int sret;            /* scanf return code */
    /* Log in */
    strcpy(uid.arr,"FRED");     /* copy the user name */
    uid.len=strlen(uid.arr);
    strcpy(pwd.arr,"TOWER");    /* copy the password */
    pwd.len=strlen(pwd.arr);
    EXEC SQL WHENEVER SQLERROR STOP;
    EXEC SQL WHENEVER NOT FOUND STOP;
    EXEC SQL CONNECT :uid;
    printf("Connected to user: percents \n",uid.arr);
    printf("Enter employee name to update:  ");
    scanf("percents",ename.arr);
    ename.len=strlen(ename.arr);
    EXEC SQL SELECT SALARY,COMM INTO :salary,:comm
            FROM EMPLOY
            WHERE ENAME=:ename;
```

```
        printf("Employee: percents salary: percent6.2f comm:
                percent6.2f \n",
                ename.arr, salary, comm);
        printf("Enter new salary:  ");
        sret=scanf("percentf",&salary);
        salary_ind = 0;
        if (sret == EOF !! sret == 0)     /* set indicator */
              salary_ind =-1;     /* Set indicator for NULL */
        printf("Enter new commission:  ");
        sret=scanf("percentf",&comm);
        comm_ind = 0;     /* set indicator */
        if (sret == EOF !! sret == 0)
              comm_ind=-1;              /* Set indicator for NULL */
        EXEC SQL UPDATE EMPLOY
                   SET SALARY=:salary:salary_ind
                   SET COMM=:comm:comm_ind
                   WHERE ENAME=:ename;
        printf("Employee percents updated. \n",ename.arr);
        EXEC SQL COMMIT WORK;
        exit(0);
}
```

You don't have to be an expert in C to understand the essence of what this program is doing (and how it intends to do it). Here's a rundown of the order in which the statements execute:

1. SQL declares host variables.

2. C code controls the user login procedure.

3. SQL sets up error handling and connects to the database.

4. C code solicits an employee name from the user and places it in a variable.

5. An SQL SELECT statement retrieves the data for the named employee's salary and commission, and the statement stores the data in the host variables :salary and :comm.

6. C then takes over again and displays the employee's name, salary, and commission and then solicits new values for salary and commission. It also checks to see whether an entry has been made, and if one has not, it sets an indicator.

7. SQL updates the database with the new values.

8. C then displays an Operation complete message.

9. SQL commits the transaction, and C finally exits the program.

You can mix the commands of two languages like this because of the preprocessor. The preprocessor separates the SQL statements from the host language commands, placing the SQL statements in a separate external routine. Each SQL statement is replaced with a host-language CALL of the corresponding external routine. The language compiler can now do its job.

The way the SQL part is passed to the database depends on the implementation. You, as the application developer, don't have to worry about any of this. The preprocessor takes care of it. You *should* be concerned about a few things, however, that do not appear in interactive SQL — things such as host variables and incompatible data types.

Declaring host variables

Some information must be passed between the host language program and the SQL segments. You pass this data with *host variables*. In order for SQL to recognize the host variables, you must declare them before you use them. Declarations are included in a declaration segment that precedes the program segment. The declaration segment is announced by the following directive:

```
EXEC SQL BEGIN DECLARE SECTION ;
```

The end of the declaration segment is signaled by this line:

```
EXEC SQL END DECLARE SECTION ;
```

Every SQL statement must be preceded by an EXEC SQL directive. The end of an SQL segment may or may not be signaled by a terminator directive. In COBOL, the terminator directive is "END-EXEC", and in C, it's a semicolon.

Converting data types

Depending on the compatibility of the data types supported by the host language and those supported by SQL, you may have to use CAST to convert certain types. You can use host variables that have been declared in the DECLARE SECTION. Remember to prefix host variable names with a colon (:) when you use them in SQL statements, as in the following example:

```
INSERT INTO FOODS
    (FOODNAME, CALORIES, PROTEIN, FAT, CARBOHYDRATE)
    VALUES
    (:foodname, :calories, :protein, :fat, :carbo) ;
```

Module language

Module language provides another method for using SQL with a procedural programming language. With module language, you explicitly put all the SQL statements into a separate SQL module.

REMEMBER

An SQL *module* is simply a list of SQL statements. Each SQL statement is included in an SQL *procedure* and is preceded by a specification of the procedure's name and the number and types of parameters.

Each SQL procedure contains only one SQL statement. In the host program, you explicitly call an SQL procedure at whatever point in the host program you want to execute the SQL statement in that procedure. You call the SQL procedure as if it were a subprogram in the host language.

Thus you can use an SQL module and the associated host program to explicitly hand-code the result of the SQL preprocessor for embedded syntax.

TIP

Embedded SQL is much more common than module language. Most vendors offer some form of module language, but few emphasize it in their documentation. Module language does have several advantages:

>> **SQL programmers don't have to be experts in the procedural language.** Because the SQL is completely separated from the procedural language, you can hire the best SQL programmers available to write your SQL modules, whether or not they have any experience with your procedural language. In fact, you can even defer deciding which procedural language to use until after your SQL modules are written and debugged.

>> **You can hire the best programmers who work in your procedural language, even if they know nothing about SQL.** It stands to reason that if your SQL experts don't have to be procedural language experts, certainly the procedural language experts don't have to worry themselves over learning SQL.

>> **No SQL is mixed in with the procedural code, so your procedural language debugger works.** This can save you considerable development time.

REMEMBER

Once again, what can be looked at as an advantage from one perspective may be a disadvantage from another. Because the SQL modules are separated from the procedural code, following the flow of the logic isn't as easy as it is in embedded SQL when you're trying to understand how the program works.

Module declarations

The syntax for the declarations in a module is as follows:

```
MODULE [module-name]
    [NAMES ARE character-set-name]
    LANGUAGE {ADA|C|COBOL|FORTRAN|MUMPS|PASCAL|PLI|SQL}
    [SCHEMA schema-name]
    [AUTHORIZATION authorization-id]
    [temporary-table-declarations...]
    [cursor-declarations...]
    [dynamic-cursor-declarations...]
    procedures...
```

The square brackets indicate that the module name is optional. Naming it anyway is a good idea if you want to keep things from getting too confusing.

TIP

The optional NAMES ARE clause specifies a character set. If you don't include a NAMES ARE clause, the default set of SQL characters for your implementation is used. The LANGUAGE clause tells the module which language it will be called from. The compiler must know what the calling language is, because it will make the SQL statements appear to the calling program as if they are subprograms in that program's language.

Although the SCHEMA clause and the AUTHORIZATION clause are both optional, you must specify at least one of them. Or you can specify both. The SCHEMA clause specifies the default schema, and the AUTHORIZATION clause specifies the authorization identifier. The *authorization identifier* establishes the privileges you have. If you don't specify an authorization ID, the DBMS uses the authorization ID associated with your session to determine the privileges that your module is allowed. If you don't have the privileges needed to perform the operation your procedure calls for, your procedure isn't executed.

TIP

If your procedure requires temporary tables, declare them with the temporary-table declaration clause. Declare cursors and dynamic cursors before you declare any procedures that use them. Declaring a cursor after a procedure starts executing is permissible as long as that procedure doesn't use the cursor. Declaring cursors to be used by later procedures may make sense. (You can find more in-depth information on cursors in Chapter 19.)

Module procedures

Following all the declarations I discuss in the previous section, the functional parts of the module are the procedures. An SQL module language procedure has a name, parameter declarations, and executable SQL statements. The procedural language program calls the procedure by its name and passes values to it through the declared parameters. Procedure syntax looks like this:

```
PROCEDURE procedure-name
    (parameter-declaration [, parameter-declaration]...
    SQL statement ;
    [SQL statements] ;
```

The parameter declaration should take the following form:

```
parameter-name data-type
```

or

```
SQLSTATE
```

The parameters you declare may be input parameters, output parameters, or both. SQLSTATE is a status parameter through which errors are reported. (You can delve deeper into parameters by heading to Chapter 21.)

Object-oriented RAD tools

By using state-of-the-art RAD tools, you can develop sophisticated applications without knowing how to write a single line of code in C++, C#, Python, Java, or any procedural language, for that matter. Instead, you choose objects from a library and place them in appropriate spots on the screen.

REMEMBER

Objects of different standard types have characteristic properties, and selected events are appropriate for each object type. You can also associate a method with an object. The *method* is a procedure written in (well, yeah) a procedural language. Building useful applications without writing any methods is possible, however.

TIP

Although you can build complex applications without using a procedural language, sooner or later you'll probably need SQL. SQL has a richness of expression that is difficult, if not impossible, to duplicate with object-oriented programming. As a result, full-featured RAD tools offer you a mechanism for injecting SQL statements into your object-oriented applications. Microsoft's Visual Studio is an example of an object-oriented development environment that offers SQL capability. Microsoft Access is another application development environment that enables you to use SQL in conjunction with its procedural language, VBA.

Chapter 4 shows you how to create database tables with Access. That operation represents only a small fraction of Access's capabilities. Access is a tool, and its primary purpose is to develop applications that process the data in database tables. Using Access, you can place objects on forms and then customize the objects by giving them properties, events, and methods. You can manipulate the forms and objects with VBA code, which can contain embedded SQL.

WARNING

Although RAD tools such as Access can deliver high-quality applications in less time, they usually don't work across all platforms. Access, for example, runs only with the Microsoft Windows operating system. You may get lucky and discover that the RAD tool you chose works on a few platforms, but if building platform-independent functionality is important to you — or if you think you may want to migrate your application to a different platform eventually — beware.

RAD tools such as Access represent the beginning of the eventual merger of relational and object-oriented database design. The structural strengths of relational design and SQL will both survive. They will be augmented by the rapid — and comparatively bug-free — development that comes from object-oriented programming.

Using SQL with Microsoft Access

The primary audience for Microsoft Access is people who want to develop relatively simple applications without programming. If that describes you, you might want to put my *Access 2013 All-In-One For Dummies* on your shelf as a reference book. The procedural language VBA (Visual Basic for Applications) and SQL are both built into Access, but are not emphasized in either advertising or documentation. If you want to use VBA and SQL to develop more sophisticated applications, try my book, *Access 2003 Power Programming with VBA*, also published by Wiley. The programming aspect of Access hasn't changed much over the past decade. Be aware though, that the SQL in Access is not a full implementation — and you almost need the detective skills of Sherlock Holmes to even find it.

REMEMBER

I mention the three components of SQL — Data Definition Language, Data Manipulation Language, and Data Control Language — in Chapter 3. The subset of SQL contained in Access primarily implements the Data Manipulation Language. You can do table creation operations with Access SQL, but they are a lot easier to do with the RAD tool I describe in Chapter 4. The same goes for implementing security features, which I cover in Chapter 14.

To get a look at some Access SQL, you need to sneak up on it from behind. Consider an example taken from the database of the fictitious Oregon Lunar Society, a nonprofit research organization. The Society has several research teams, one of which is the Moon Base Research Team (MBRT). A question has arisen as to which scholarly papers have been written by members of the team. A query was formulated using Access's Query By Example (QBE) facility to retrieve the desired data. The query, shown in Figure 16-1, pulls data from the RESEARCHTEAMS, AUTHORS, and PAPERS tables with the help of the AUTH-RES and AUTH-PAP intersection tables that were added to break up many-to-many relationships.

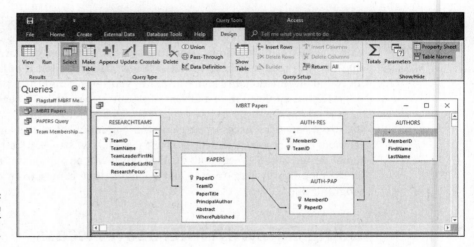

FIGURE 16-1:
The Design View of MBRT Papers query.

After clicking on the Home tab to access the toolbar, you can click the View icon drop-down menu in the upper left corner of the window to reveal the other available views of the database. One of the choices is SQL View. (See Figure 16-2.)

FIGURE 16-2:
One of your View menu options is SQL View.

When you click SQL View, the SQL editing window appears, showing the SQL statement that Access has generated, based on the choices you made using QBE.

TIP

This SQL statement, shown in Figure 16-3, is what actually gets sent to the database engine. The database engine, which interfaces directly with the database itself, understands only SQL. Any information entered into the QBE environment must be translated into SQL before it is sent on to the database engine for processing.

FIGURE 16-3:
An SQL statement that retrieves the names of all the papers written by members of the MBRT.

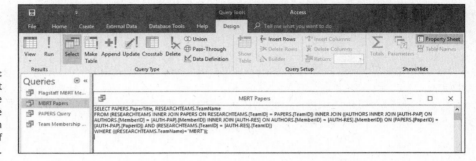

WARNING

You may notice that the syntax of the SQL statement shown in Figure 16-3 differs somewhat from the syntax of ANSI/ISO-standard SQL. Take the old adage, "When in Rome, do as the Romans do," to heart here. When working with Access, use the Access dialect of SQL. That advice also goes for any other environment that you may be working in. All implementations of SQL differ from the standard in one respect or another.

If you want to write a new query in Access SQL — one that has not already been created using QBE, that is — you can simply erase some existing query from the SQL editing window and type in a new SQL `SELECT` statement. Click the DESIGN tab and then the red Exclamation Point (Run) icon on the toolbar at the top of the screen to run your new query. The result appears onscreen in Datasheet View.

5
Taking SQL to the Real World

Chapter **17**

Accessing Data with ODBC and JDBC

I n recent years, computers have become increasingly interconnected, both within and between organizations. With this connection comes the need for sharing database information across networks. The major obstacle to the free sharing of information across networks is the incompatibility of the operating software and applications running on different machines. SQL's creation and its ongoing evolution have been major steps toward overcoming hardware and software incompatibility.

Unfortunately, "standard" SQL is not all that standard. Even DBMS vendors who claim to comply with the international SQL standard have included proprietary extensions in their SQL implementations — which make them incompatible with the proprietary extensions in *other* vendors' implementations. The vendors are loath to give up their extensions because their customers have designed them into their applications and have become dependent on them. User organizations, particularly large ones, need another way to make cross-DBMS communication possible — a tool that doesn't require vendors to dumb down their implementations to the lowest common denominator. This other way is ODBC (Open DataBase Connectivity).

ODBC

ODBC is a standard interface between a database and an application that accesses the data in the database. Having a standard enables any application front end to access any database back end by using SQL. The only requirement is that the front end and the back end both adhere to the ODBC standard. ODBC 4.0 is the current version of the standard.

An application accesses a database by using a *driver* (in this case, the ODBC driver), which is specifically designed to interface with that particular database. The driver's front end, the side that goes to the application, rigidly adheres to the ODBC standard. It looks the same to the application, regardless of what database engine is on the back end. The driver's back end is customized to the specific database engine that it's addressing. With this architecture, applications don't have to be customized to — or even be aware of — which back-end database engine actually controls the data they're using. The driver masks the differences between back ends.

The ODBC interface

The *ODBC interface* is essentially a set of definitions, each of which is accepted as standard. The definitions cover everything needed to establish communication between an application and a database. The ODBC interface defines the following:

>> A function-call library

>> Standard SQL syntax

>> Standard SQL data types

>> A standard protocol for connecting to a database engine

>> Standard error codes

The ODBC *function calls* make the connection to a back-end database engine possible; they execute SQL statements and pass results back to the application.

TIP

To perform an operation on a database, include the appropriate SQL statement as an argument of an ODBC function call. As long as you use the ODBC-specified standard SQL syntax, the operation works — regardless of what database engine is on the back end.

Components of ODBC

The ODBC interface consists of four functional components, referred to as ODBC layers. Each component plays a role in making ODBC flexible enough to provide transparent communication from any compatible front end to any compatible back end. The four layers of the ODBC interface are between the user and the data that the user wants, as follows:

» **Application:** The application is the part of the ODBC interface that's closest to the user. Of course, even systems that don't use ODBC include an application. Nonetheless, including the application as a part of the ODBC interface makes sense. The application has to know that it's communicating with its data source through ODBC. It must connect smoothly with the ODBC driver manager, in strict accordance with the ODBC standard.

» **Driver manager:** The driver manager is a *dynamic link library* (DLL), which is generally supplied by Microsoft. It loads appropriate drivers for the system's (possibly multiple) data sources and directs function calls coming in from the application to the appropriate data sources via their drivers. The driver manager also handles some ODBC function calls directly and detects and handles some types of errors. Although Microsoft originated the ODBC standard, it is now universally accepted, even by open-source hardliners.

» **Driver DLL:** Because data sources can be different from each other (in some cases, *very* different), you need a way to translate standard ODBC function calls into the native language of each data source. Translation is the job of the driver DLL. Each driver DLL accepts function calls through the standard ODBC interface and then translates them into code that is understandable to its associated *data source*. When the data source responds with a result set, the driver reformats it in the reverse direction into a standard ODBC result set. The driver is the crucial element that enables any ODBC-compatible application to manipulate the structure and the contents of an ODBC-compatible data source.

» **Data source:** The data source may be one of many different things. It may be a relational DBMS and an associated database residing on the same computer as the application. It may be such a database on a remote computer. It may be an *indexed sequential access method* (ISAM) file with no DBMS, either on the local or a remote computer. It may or may not include a network. The myriad different forms that the data source can take require that a custom driver be available for each one.

ODBC in a Client/Server Environment

In a client/server system, the interface between the client part and the server part is called the *application programming interface* (API). An ODBC driver, for example, includes an API. APIs can be either proprietary or standard. A *proprietary* API is one in which the client part of the interface has been specifically designed to work with one specific back end on the server. The actual code that forms this interface is a driver — and in a proprietary system, it's called a *native driver.* A native driver is optimized for use with a specific front-end client and its associated back-end data source. Because native drivers are optimized for both the specific front-end application and the specific DBMS back end that they're working with, the drivers tend to pass commands and information back and forth quickly, with a minimum of delay.

TIP

If your client/server system always accesses the same type of data source, and you're sure you'll never need to access data on another type of data source, then you may want to use the native driver supplied with your DBMS. However, if you may need to access data that's stored in a different form sometime in the future, then using an ODBC API now could save you a great deal of rework later.

ODBC drivers are also optimized to work with specific back-end data sources, but they all have the same front-end interface to the driver manager. Any driver that hasn't been optimized for a particular front end, therefore, is probably not as fast as a *native* driver that's specifically designed for that front end. A major complaint about the first generation of ODBC drivers was their poor performance when compared with native drivers. Recent benchmarks, however, have shown that ODBC 4.0 drivers are quite competitive in performance to native drivers. The technology is mature enough that it's no longer necessary to sacrifice performance to gain the advantages of standardization.

ODBC and the Internet

Database operations over the Internet differ in several important ways from database operations on a client/server system, although the user may not notice any difference. The most visible difference from the user's point of view is the client portion of the system, which includes the user interface. In a client/server system, the user interface is the part of an application that communicates with the data source on the server — using ODBC-compatible SQL statements. Over the web, the client portion of the system is still on the local computer, but it communicates with the data source on the server using the HTTP standard protocol.

Anyone with the appropriate client-end software (and the appropriate authorization) can access the data that is stored out on the web. This means that you can create an application at your work computer and then access it later with your mobile device. Figure 17-1 compares client/server systems with web-based systems.

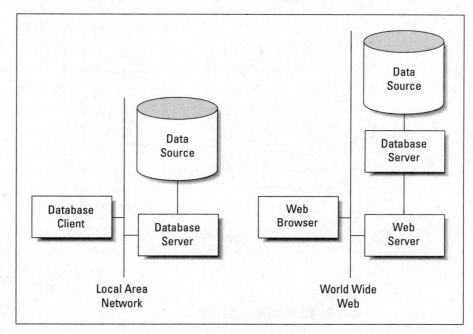

FIGURE 17-1: A client/server system versus a web-based database system.

Server extensions

In the web-based system, communication between the application front end on the client machine and the web server on the server machine takes place using HTTP. A system component called a *server extension* translates the commands coming over the network into ODBC-compatible SQL. Then the database server acts on the SQL, which in turn deals directly with the data source. In the reverse direction, the data source sends the result set that is generated by a query through the database server to the server extension, which then translates it into a form that the web server can handle. The results are then sent over the web to the application front end on the client machine, where they're displayed to the user. Figure 17-2 shows the anatomy of this type of system.

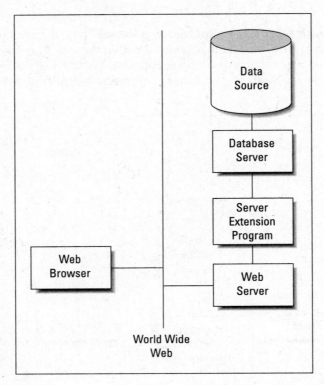

FIGURE 17-2:
A web-based
database system
with a server
extension.

Client extensions

Applications such as Microsoft Access 2019 are designed to operate either on data that is stored locally on the user's machine, on a server located on a local or wide area network (LAN or WAN), or out on the Internet in the cloud. Microsoft's cloud repository is called OneDrive. It's also possible to access an application in the cloud using nothing more than a web browser. Web browsers were designed — and are now optimized — to provide easy-to-understand and easy-to-use interfaces to web sites of all kinds. The most popular browsers, Google Chrome, Mozilla Firefox, Microsoft Internet Explorer, and Apple Safari, were not designed or optimized to be database front ends. For meaningful interaction with a database to occur over the Internet, the client side of the system needs functionality that the browser does not provide. To fill this need, several types of *client extensions* have been developed. These extensions include ActiveX controls, Java applets, and scripts. The extensions communicate with the server via HTTP, using HTML, which is the language of the web. Any HTML code that deals with database access is translated into ODBC-compatible SQL by the server extension before being forwarded to the data source.

ActiveX controls

Microsoft's ActiveX controls work with Microsoft's Internet Explorer, which is a very popular browser. However, it has recently lost market share to Google Chrome and Mozilla's Firefox.

Scripts

Scripts are the most flexible tools for creating client extensions. Using a scripting language, such as the ubiquitous JavaScript or Microsoft's VBScript, gives you maximum control over what happens at the client end. You can put validation checks on data-entry fields, thus enabling the rejection or correction of invalid entries without ever going out onto the web. This can save you time as well as reduce traffic on the web, thus benefiting other users as well. Of course, validation checks can also be made at the server end by applying constraints to the values that data items can take. As with Java applets, scripts are embedded in an HTML page and execute as the user interacts with that page.

ODBC and an Intranet

An *intranet* is a local- or wide-area network that operates like a simpler version of the Internet. Because an intranet is contained within a single organization, you don't need complex security measures such as firewalls. All the tools that are designed for application development on the web operate equally well as development tools for intranet applications. ODBC works on an intranet in the same way that it does on the Internet. If you have multiple data sources, clients using web browsers (and the appropriate client and server extensions) can communicate with them with SQL that passes through HTML and ODBC stages. At the driver, the ODBC-compliant SQL is translated into the database's native command language and executed.

JDBC

JDBC (Java DataBase Connectivity) is similar to ODBC, but it differs in a few important respects. One such difference is hinted at by its name. JDBC is a database interface that always looks the same to the client program — regardless of what data source is sitting on the server (back end). The difference is that JDBC expects the client application to be written in the Java language rather than another language such as C++ or Visual Basic. Another difference is that Java and JDBC were both specifically designed to run on the web or on an intranet.

Java is a C++-like language that was developed by Sun Microsystems specifically for the development of web-client programs. When a connection is established between a server and a client over the web, the appropriate Java applet is downloaded to the client, where the applet commences to run. The applet, which is embedded in an HTML page, provides the database-specific functionality that the client needs to provide flexible access to server data. Figure 17-3 is a schematic representation of a web database application with a Java applet running on the client machine.

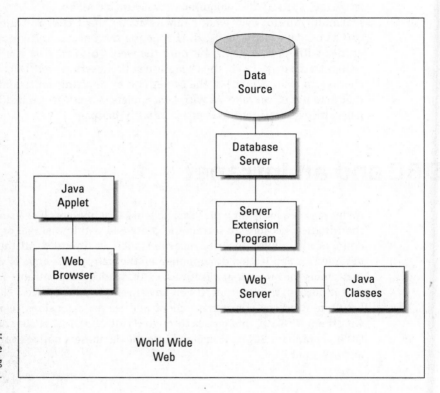

FIGURE 17-3: A web database application, using a Java applet.

An *applet* is a small application that resides on a server. When a client connects to that server over the web, the applet is downloaded and starts running in the client computer. Java applets are specially designed so they can run in a *sandbox* — a well-defined (and isolated) area in the client computer's memory set aside for running applets. The applet is not allowed to affect anything outside the sandbox. This architecture is designed to protect the client machine from potentially hostile applets that may try to extract sensitive information or cause malicious damage.

A major advantage to using Java applets is that they're always up to date. Because the applets are downloaded from the server every time they're used (as opposed to being retained on the client), the client is always guaranteed to have the latest version whenever it runs a Java applet.

TIP

If you're responsible for maintaining your organization's server, you never have to worry about losing compatibility with some of your clients when you upgrade the server software. Just make sure that your downloadable Java applet is compatible with the new server configuration — because, as long as their web browsers have been configured to enable Java applets, all your clients automatically become compatible too. Java is a full-featured programming language, and it is entirely possible to write robust applications with Java that can access databases in some kind of client/server system. When used this way, a Java application that accesses a database via JDBC is similar to a C++ application that accesses a database via ODBC. But a Java application acts quite different from a C++ application when it comes to the Internet (or an intranet).

When the system that you're interested in is on the Net, the operating conditions are different from the conditions in a client/server system. The client side of an application that operates over the Internet is a browser, with minimal computational capabilities. These capabilities must be augmented in order for significant database processing to be done; Java applets provide these capabilities.

WARNING

You face a certain amount of danger when you download anything from a server that you don't know to be trustworthy. If you download a Java applet, that danger is greatly reduced but not completely eliminated. Be wary about letting executable code enter your machine from a questionable server.

Like ODBC, JDBC passes SQL statements from the front-end application (applet) running on the client to the data source on the back end. It also serves to pass result sets or error messages from the data source back to the application. The value of using JDBC is that the applet writer can write to the standard JDBC interface without needing to know or care what database is located at the back end. JDBC performs whatever conversion is necessary for accurate two-way communication to take place. Although designed to work over the web, JDBC also works in client/server environments where an application written in Java communicates with a database back end through the JDBC interface.

Chapter 18

Operating on XML Data with SQL

S tarting with SQL:2008, ISO/IEC standard SQL supports XML. XML (eXtensible Markup Language) files have become a universally accepted standard for exchanging data between dissimilar platforms. With XML, it doesn't matter if the person you're sharing data with has a different application environment, a different operating system, or even different hardware. XML can form a data bridge between the two of you.

How XML Relates to SQL

XML, like HTML, is a markup language, which means that it's not a full-function language such as C++ or Java. It's not even a data sublanguage such as SQL. However, unlike those languages, it is cognizant of the content of the data it transports. Where HTML deals only with formatting the text and graphics in a document, XML gives structure to the document's content. XML itself does not deal with formatting. To do that, you have to augment XML with a *style sheet*. As it does with HTML, a style sheet applies formatting to an XML document.

The structure of an XML document is provided by its XML schema, which is an example of *metadata* (data that describes data). An XML schema describes where elements may occur in a document and in what order. It may also describe the data type of an element and constrain the values that a type may include.

SQL and XML provide two different ways of structuring data so that you can save it and retrieve selected information from it:

>> SQL is an excellent tool for dealing with numeric and text data that can be categorized by data type and have a well-defined size.

SQL was created as a standard way to maintain and operate on data kept in relational databases.

>> XML is better at dealing with free-form data that cannot be easily categorized.

The driving motivations for the creation of XML were to provide a universal standard for transferring data between dissimilar computers and for displaying it on the web.

The strengths and goals of SQL and XML are complementary. Each reigns supreme in its own domain and forms alliances with the other to give users the information they want, when they want it, and where they want it.

The XML Data Type

The XML type was introduced with SQL:2003. This means that conforming implementations can store and operate on XML-formatted data directly, without first converting it to XML from one of the other SQL data types.

The XML data type, including its subtypes, although intrinsic to any implementation that supports it, acts like a user-defined type (UDT). The subtypes are:

>> XML(DOCUMENT(UNTYPED))

>> XML(DOCUMENT(ANY))

>> XML(DOCUMENT(XMLSCHEMA))

>> XML(CONTENT(UNTYPED))

>> XML(CONTENT(ANY))

>> XML(CONTENT(XMLSCHEMA))

>> XML(SEQUENCE)

The XML type brings SQL and XML into close contact because it enables applications to perform SQL operations on XML content, and XML operations on SQL content. You can include a column of the XML type with columns of any of the other predefined types covered in Chapter 2 in a join operation in the WHERE clause of a query. In true relational database fashion, your DBMS will determine the optimal way to execute the query and then will do it.

When to use the XML type

Whether or not you should store data in XML format depends on what you plan to do with that data. Here are some instances where it makes sense to store data in XML format:

» When you want to store an entire block of data and retrieve the whole block later.

» When you want to be able to query the whole XML document. Some implementations have expanded the scope of the EXTRACT operator to enable extracting desired content from an XML document.

» When you need strong typing of data inside SQL statements. Using the XML type guarantees that data values are valid XML values and not just arbitrary text strings.

» To ensure compatibility with future, as yet unspecified, storage systems that might not support existing types such as CHARACTER LARGE OBJECT, or CLOB. (See Chapter 2 for more information on CLOB.)

» To take advantage of future optimizations that will support only the XML type.

Here's an example of how you might use the XML type:

```
CREATE TABLE CLIENT (
     ClientName          CHAR (30)       NOT NULL,
     Address1            CHAR (30),
     Address2            CHAR (30),
     City                CHAR (25),
     State               CHAR (2),
     PostalCode          CHAR (10),
     Phone               CHAR (13),
     Fax                 CHAR (13),
     ContactPerson       CHAR (30),
     Comments            XML(SEQUENCE) ) ;
```

This SQL statement will store an XML document in the `Comments` column of the CLIENT table. The resulting document might look something like the following:

```
<Comments>
    <Comment>
        <CommentNo>1</CommentNo>
        <MessageText>Is VetLab equipped to analyze penguin
            blood?</MessageText>
        <ResponseRequested>Yes</ResponseRequested>
    </Comment>
    <Comment>
        <CommentNo>2</CommentNo>
        <MessageText>Thanks for the fast turnaround on the
            leopard seal sputum sample.</MessageText>
        <ResponseRequested>No</ResponseRequested>
    </Comment>
</Comments>
```

When not to use the XML type

Just because the SQL standard allows you to use the XML type doesn't mean that you always should. In fact, on many occasions, it doesn't make sense to use the XML type. Most data in relational databases today is better off in its current format than it is in XML format. Here are a couple of examples of when not to use the XML type:

>> When the data breaks down naturally into a relational structure with tables, rows, and columns

>> When you will need to update pieces of the document rather than deal with the document as a whole

Mapping SQL to XML and XML to SQL

To exchange data between SQL databases and XML documents, the various elements of an SQL database must be translatable into equivalent elements of an XML document, and vice versa. I describe which elements need to be translated in the following sections.

Mapping character sets

In SQL, the character sets supported depend on which implementation you're using. This means that IBM's DB2 may support character sets that are not supported by Microsoft's SQL Server. SQL Server may support character sets not supported by Oracle. Although the most common character sets are almost universally supported, if you use a less common character set, migrating your database and application from one RDBMS platform to another may be difficult.

XML has no compatibility issue with character sets — it supports only one, Unicode. This is a good thing from the point of view of exchanging data between any given SQL implementation and XML. All the RDBMS vendors have to define a mapping between strings of each of their character sets and Unicode, as well as a reverse mapping from Unicode to each of their character sets. Luckily, XML doesn't also support multiple character sets. If it did, vendors would have a many-to-many problem that would require several more mappings and reverse mappings to resolve.

Mapping identifiers

XML is much stricter than SQL in the characters it allows in identifiers. Characters that are legal in SQL but illegal in XML must be mapped to something legal before they can become part of an XML document. SQL supports delimited identifiers. This means that all sorts of odd characters such as %, $, and & are legal, as long as they're enclosed within double quotes. Such characters are not legal in XML. Furthermore, XML Names that begin with the characters *XML* in any combination of cases are reserved and thus cannot be used with impunity. If you have any SQL identifiers that begin with those letters, you have to change them.

An agreed-upon mapping bridges the identifier gap between SQL and XML. In moving from SQL to XML, all SQL identifiers are converted to Unicode. From there, any SQL identifiers that are also legal XML Names are left unchanged. SQL identifier characters that are not legal XML Names are replaced with a hexadecimal code that either takes the form "_xNNNN_" or "_xNNNNNNNN_", where N represents an uppercase hexadecimal digit. For example, the underscore will be represented by "_x005F_". The colon will be represented by "_x003A_". These representations are the codes for the Unicode characters for the underscore and colon. The case where an SQL identifier starts with the characters *x, m,* and *l* is handled by prefixing all such instances with a code in the form "_xFFFF_".

Conversion from XML to SQL is much easier. All you need to do is scan the characters of an XML Name for a sequence of "_xNNNN_" or "_xNNNNNNNN_". Whenever you find such a sequence, replace it with the character that the Unicode corresponds to. If an XML Name begins with the characters "_xFFFF_", ignore them.

By following these simple rules, you can map an SQL identifier to an XML Name and then back to an SQL identifier again. However, this happy situation does not hold for a mapping from XML Name to SQL identifier and back to XML Name.

Mapping data types

The SQL standard specifies that an SQL data type must be mapped to the closest possible XML Schema data type. The designation *closest possible* means that all values allowed by the SQL type will be allowed by the XML Schema type, and the fewest possible values not allowed by the SQL type will be allowed by the XML Schema type. XML facets, such as maxInclusive and minInclusive, can restrict the values allowed by the XML Schema type to the values allowed by the corresponding SQL type. For example, if the SQL data type restricts values of the INTEGER type to the range –2157483648<value<2157483647, in XML the maxInclusive value can be set to 2157483647, and the minInclusive value can be set to –2157483648. Here's an example of such a mapping:

```
<xsd:simpleType>
    <xsd:restriction base="xsd:integer"/>
        <xsd:maxInclusive value="2157483647"/>
        <xsd:minInclusive value="-2157483648"/>
        <xsd:annotation>
            <sqlxml:sqltype name="INTEGER"/>
        </xsd:annotation>
    </xsd:restriction>
</xsd:simpleType>
```

The annotation section retains information from the SQL type definition that is not used by XML, but you may find it valuable later if the document is mapped back to SQL.

Mapping tables

You can map a table to an XML document. Similarly, you can map all the tables in a schema or all the tables in a catalog. Privileges are maintained by the mapping. A person who has the SELECT privilege on only some table columns will be able to map only those columns to the XML document. The mapping actually produces two documents, one that contains the data in the table and the other that contains the XML Schema that describes the first document. Here's an example of the mapping of an SQL table to an XML data-containing document:

```
<CUSTOMER>
    <row>
        <FirstName>Abe</FirstName>
        <LastName>Abelson</LastName>
        <City>Springfield</City>
        <AreaCode>714</AreaCode>
        <Telephone>555-1111</Telephone>
    </row>
    <row>
        <FirstName>Bill</FirstName>
        <LastName>Bailey</LastName>
        <City>Decatur</City>
        <AreaCode>714</AreaCode>
        <Telephone>555-2222</Telephone>
    </row>
    .
    .
    .
</CUSTOMER>
```

The root element of the document has been given the name of the table. Each table row is contained within a `<row>` element, and each row element contains a sequence of column elements, each named after the corresponding column in the source table. Each column element contains a data value.

Handling null values

Because SQL data might include null values, you must decide how to represent them in an XML document. You can represent a null value either as nil or absent. If you choose the nil option, then the attribute `xsi:nil="true"` marks the column elements that represent null values. It might be used in the following way:

```
<row>
        <FirstName>Bill</FirstName>
        <LastName>Bailey</LastName>
        <City xsi:nil="true"/>
        <AreaCode>714</AreaCode>
        <Telephone>555-2222</Telephone>
</row>
```

If you choose the absent option, you could implement it as follows:

```
<row>
        <FirstName>Bill</FirstName>
        <LastName>Bailey</LastName>
```

```
        <AreaCode>714</AreaCode>
        <Telephone>555-2222</Telephone>
</row>
```

In this case, the row containing the null value is absent. There is no reference to it.

Generating the XML Schema

When mapping from SQL to XML, the first document generated is the one that contains the data. The second contains the schema information. As an example, consider the schema for the CUSTOMER document shown in the "Mapping tables" section, earlier in this chapter:

```
<xsd:schema>
    <xsd:simpleType name="CHAR_15">
        <xsd:restriction base="xsd:string">
            <xsd:length value = "15"/>
        </xsd:restriction>
    </xsd:simpleType>

    <xsd:simpleType name="CHAR_25">
        <xsd:restriction base="xsd:string">
            <xsd:length value = "25"/>
        </xsd:restriction>
    </xsd:simpleType>

    <xsd:simpleType name="CHAR_3">
        <xsd:restriction base="xsd:string">
            <xsd:length value = "3"/>
        </xsd:restriction>
    </xsd:simpleType>

    <xsd:simpleType name="CHAR_8">
        <xsd:restriction base="xsd:string">
            <xsd:length value = "8"/>
        </xsd:restriction>
    </xsd:simpleType>

    <xsd:sequence>
        <xsd:element name="FirstName" type="CHAR_15"/>
        <xsd:element name="LastName" type="CHAR_25"/>
        <xsd:element
          name="City" type="CHAR_25 nillable="true"/>
        <xsd:element
```

```
          name="AreaCode" type="CHAR_3" nillable="true"/>
       <xsd:element
          name="Telephone" type="CHAR_8" nillable="true"/>
     </xsd:sequence>

  </xsd:schema>
```

This schema is appropriate if the nil approach to handling nulls is used. The absent approach requires a slightly different element definition. For example:

```
<xsd:element name="City" type="CHAR_25" minOccurs="0"/>
```

SQL Functions That Operate on XML Data

The SQL standard defines a number of operators, functions, and pseudo-functions that, when applied to an SQL database, produce an XML result, or when applied to XML data produce a result in standard SQL form. The functions include XMLELEMENT, XMLFOREST, XMLCONCAT, and XMLAGG. In the following sections, I give brief descriptions of these functions, as well as several others that are frequently used when publishing to the web. Some of the functions rely heavily on XQuery, a standard query language designed specifically for querying XML data. XQuery is a huge topic in itself and is beyond the scope of this book. To find out more about XQuery, a good source of information is Jim Melton and Stephen Buxton's *Querying XML*, published by Morgan Kaufmann.

XMLDOCUMENT

The XMLDOCUMENT operator takes an XML value as input and returns another XML value as output. The new XML value is a document node that is constructed according to the rules of the computed document constructor in XQuery.

XMLELEMENT

The XMLELEMENT operator translates a relational value into an XML element. You can use the operator in a SELECT statement to pull data in XML format from an SQL database and publish it on the web. Here's an example:

```
SELECT c.LastName
    XMLELEMENT ( NAME"City", c.City ) AS "Result"
FROM CUSTOMER c
WHERE LastName="Abelson" ;
```

Here is the result returned:

LastName	Result
Abelson	`<City>Springfield</City>`

XMLFOREST

The XMLFOREST operator produces a list, or *forest*, of XML elements from a list of relational values. Each of the operator's values produces a new element. Here's an example of this operator:

```
SELECT c.LastName
    XMLFOREST (c.City,
               c.AreaCode,
               c.Telephone ) AS "Result"
FROM CUSTOMER c
WHERE LastName="Abelson" OR LastName="Bailey" ;
```

This snippet produces the following output:

LastName	Result
Abelson	`<City>Springfield</City>`
	`<AreaCode>714</AreaCode>`
	`<Telephone>555-1111</Telephone>`
Bailey	`<City>Decatur</City>`
	`<AreaCode>714</AreaCode>`
	`<Telephone>555-2222</Telephone>`

XMLCONCAT

XMLCONCAT provides an alternate way to produce a forest of elements by concatenating its XML arguments. For example, the following code:

```
SELECT c.LastName,
    XMLCONCAT(
        XMLELEMENT ( NAME"first", c.FirstName,
        XMLELEMENT ( NAME"last", c.LastName)
        ) AS "Result"
FROM CUSTOMER c ;
```

produces these results:

LastName	Result
Abelson	`<first>Abe</first>`
	`<last>Abelson</last>`
Bailey	`<first>Bill</first>`
	`<last>Bailey</last>`

XMLAGG

XMLAGG, the aggregate function, takes XML documents or fragments of XML documents as input and produces a single XML document as output in GROUP BY queries. The aggregation contains a forest of elements. Here's an example to illustrate the concept:

```
SELECT XMLELEMENT
    ( NAME "City",
        XMLATTRIBUTES ( c.City AS "name" ) ,
        XMLAGG (XMLELEMENT ( NAME "last" c.LastName )
                )
    ) AS "CityList"
FROM CUSTOMER c
GROUP BY City ;
```

When run against the CUSTOMER table, this query produces the following results:

CityList

```
<City name="Decatur">
    <last>Bailey</last>
</City>
<City name="Philo">
    <last>Stetson</last>
    <last>Stetson</last>
    <last>Wood</last>
</City>
<City name="Springfield">
    <last>Abelson</last>
</City>
```

XMLCOMMENT

The `XMLCOMMENT` function enables an application to create an XML comment. Its syntax is:

```
XMLCOMMENT ( 'comment content'
    [RETURNING
        { CONTENT | SEQUENCE } ] )
```

For example:

```
XMLCOMMENT ('Back up database at 2 am every night.')
```

would create an XML comment that looks like this:

```
<!--Back up database at 2 am every night. -->
```

XMLPARSE

The `XMLPARSE` function produces an XML value by performing a nonvalidating parse of a string. You might use it like this:

```
XMLPARSE (DOCUMENT '   GREAT JOB!'
        PRESERVE WHITESPACE )
```

The preceding code would produce an XML value that is either `XML(UNTYPED DOCUMENT)` or `XML(ANY DOCUMENT)`. Which of the two subtypes is chosen depends on the implementation you're using.

XMLPI

The `XMLPI` function allows applications to create XML processing instructions. The syntax for this function is:

```
XMLPI NAME target
    [ , string-expression ]
    [RETURNING
        { CONTENT | SEQUENCE } ] )
```

The `target` placeholder represents the identifier of the target of the processing instruction. The `string-expression` placeholder represents the content of the PI. This function creates an XML comment of the form:

```
<? target string-expression ?>
```

XMLQUERY

The XMLQUERY function evaluates an XQuery expression and returns the result to the SQL application. The syntax of XMLQUERY is:

```
XMLQUERY ( XQuery-expression
    [ PASSING { By REF | BY VALUE }
        argument-list ]
      RETURNING { CONTENT | SEQUENCE }
    { BY REF | BY VALUE } )
```

Here's an example of the use of XMLQUERY:

```
SELECT max_average,
     XMLQUERY (
        'for $batting_average in
                /player/batting_average
           where /player/lastname = $var1
           return $batting_average'
         PASSING BY VALUE
             'Mantle' AS var1,
         RETURNING SEQUENCE BY VALUE )
FROM offensive_stats
```

XMLCAST

The XMLCAST function is similar to an ordinary SQL CAST function, but it has some additional restrictions. The XMLCAST function enables an application to cast a value from an XML type to either another XML type or an SQL type. Similarly, you can use it to cast a value from an SQL type to an XML type. Here are a few restrictions:

>> At least one of the types involved, either the source type or the destination type, must be an XML type.

>> Neither of the types involved may be an SQL collection type, row type, structured type, or reference type.

>> Only values of one of the XML types or the SQL null type may be cast to XML(UNTYPED DOCUMENT) or to XML(ANY DOCUMENT).

Here's an example:

```
XMLCAST ( CLIENT.ClientName AS XML(UNTYPED CONTENT))
```

The XMLCAST function is transformed into an ordinary SQL CAST. The only reason for using a separate keyword is to enforce the restrictions listed here.

Predicates

Predicates return a value of True or False. Some predicates specifically relate to XML.

DOCUMENT

The purpose of the DOCUMENT predicate is to determine whether an XML value is an XML document. It tests to see whether an XML value is an instance of either XML(ANY DOCUMENT) or XML(UNTYPED DOCUMENT). The syntax is:

```
XML-value IS [NOT]
    [ANY | UNTYPED] DOCUMENT
```

If the expression evaluates to True, the predicate returns TRUE; otherwise, it returns FALSE. If the XML value is null, the predicate returns an UNKNOWN value. If you don't specify either ANY or UNTYPED, the default assumption is ANY.

CONTENT

You use the CONTENT predicate to determine whether an XML value is an instance of XML(ANY CONTENT) or XML(UNTYPED CONTENT). Here's the syntax:

```
XML-value IS [NOT]
    [ANY | UNTYPED] CONTENT
```

If you don't specify either ANY or UNTYPED, ANY is the default.

XMLEXISTS

As the name implies, you can use the XMLEXISTS predicate to determine whether a value exists. Here's the syntax:

```
XMLEXISTS ( XQuery-expression
    [ argument-list ])
```

The XQuery expression is evaluated using the values provided in the argument list. If the value queried by the XQuery expression is the SQL NULL value, the predicate's result is unknown. If the evaluation returns an empty XQuery sequence, the predicate's result is FALSE; otherwise, it is TRUE. You can use this predicate to determine whether an XML document contains some particular content before you use a portion of that content in an expression.

VALID

The VALID predicate is used to evaluate an XML value to see whether it is valid in the context of a registered XML Schema. The syntax of the VALID predicate is more complex than is the case for most predicates:

```
xml-value IS [NOT] VALID
    [XML valid identity constraint option]
    [XML valid according-to clause]
```

This predicate checks to see whether the XML value is one of the five XML subtypes: XML(SEQUENCE), XML(ANY CONTENT), XML(UNTYPED CONTENT), XML(ANY DOCUMENT), or XML(UNTYPED DOCUMENT). Additionally, it might optionally check to see whether the validity of the XML value depends on identity constraints, and whether it is valid with respect to a particular XML Schema (the validity target).

There are four possibilities for the identity-constraint-option component of the syntax:

>> WITHOUT IDENTITY CONSTRAINTS: If the identity-constraint-option syntax component isn't specified, WITHOUT IDENTITY CONSTRAINTS is assumed. If DOCUMENT is specified, then it acts like a combination of the DOCUMENT predicate and the VALID predicate WITH IDENTITY CONSTRAINTS GLOBAL.

>> WITH IDENTITY CONSTRAINTS GLOBAL: This component of the syntax means the value is checked not only against the XML Schema, but also against the XML rules for ID/IDREF relationships.

ID and IDREF are XML attribute types that identify elements of a document.

>> WITH IDENTITY CONSTRAINTS LOCAL: This component of the syntax means the value is checked against the XML Schema but not against the XML rules for ID/IDREF or the XML Schema rules for identity constraints.

>> DOCUMENT: This component of the syntax means the XML value expression is a document and is valid WITH IDENTITY CONSTRAINTS GLOBAL syntax with an XML valid according to clause. The XML valid according to clause identifies the schema that the value will be validated against.

REMEMBER

Transforming XML Data into SQL Tables

Until recently, when thinking about the relationship between SQL and XML, the emphasis has been on converting SQL table data into XML to make it accessible on the Internet. SQL:2008 addressed the complementary problem of converting XML data into SQL tables so that it can be easily queried using standard SQL statements. The XMLTABLE pseudo-function performs this operation. The syntax for XMLTABLE is:

```
XMLTABLE ( [namespace-declaration,]
XQuery-expression
[PASSING argument-list]
COLUMNS XMLtbl-column-definitions
```

where the argument-list is:

```
value-expression AS identifier
```

and XMLtbl-column-definitions is a comma-separated list of column definitions, which may contain:

```
column-name FOR ORDINALITY
```

and/or:

```
column-name data-type
[BY REF | BY VALUE]
[default-clause]
[PATH XQuery-expression]
```

Here's an example of how you might use XMLTABLE to extract data from an XML document into an SQL pseudo-table. A pseudo-table isn't persistent, but in every other respect, it behaves like a regular SQL table. If you want to make it persistent, you can create a table with a CREATE TABLE statement and then insert the XML data into the newly created table.

```
SELECT clientphone.*
FROM
    clients_xml ,
    XMLTABLE(
        'for $m in
            $col/client
        return
            $m'
```

```
      PASSING clients_xml.client AS "col"
      COLUMNS
        "ClientName" CHARACTER (30) PATH 'ClientName' ,
        "Phone" CHARACTER (13) PATH 'phone'
      ) AS clientphone
```

When you run this statement, you see the following result:

```
ClientName                              Phone

-----------------------------------     --------------
Abe Abelson                             (714)555-1111
Bill Bailey                             (714)555-2222
Chuck Wood                              (714)555-3333


(3 rows in clientphone)
```

Mapping Non-Predefined Data Types to XML

In the SQL standard, the non-predefined data types include domain, distinct UDT, row, array, and multiset. You can map each of these to XML-formatted data, using appropriate XML code. The next few sections show examples of how to map these types.

Domain

To map an SQL domain to XML, you must first have a domain. For this example, create one by using a CREATE DOMAIN statement:

```
CREATE DOMAIN WestCoast AS CHAR (2)
    CHECK (State IN ('CA', 'OR', 'WA', 'AK')) ;
```

Now, create a table that uses that domain:

```
CREATE TABLE WestRegion (
    ClientName          Character (20)      NOT NULL,
    State               WestCoast           NOT NULL
    ) ;
```

Here's the XML Schema to map the domain into XML:

```
<xsd:simpleType>
    Name='DOMAIN.Sales.WestCoast'>

    <xsd:annotation>
        <xsd:appinfo>
            <sqlxml:sqltype kind='DOMAIN'
                schemaName='Sales'
                typeName='WestCoast'
                mappedType='CHAR_2'
                final='true'/>
        <xsd:appinfo>
    </xsd:annotation>

    <xsd:restriction base='CHAR_2'/>

</xsd:simpleType>
```

When this mapping is applied, it results in an XML document that contains something like the following:

```
<WestRegion>
<row>
    .

    .

    <State>AK</State>
    .

    .

    .
    </row>
    .

    .
</WestRegion>
```

Distinct UDT

With a distinct UDT, you can do much the same as what you can do with a domain, but with stronger typing. Here's how:

```
CREATE TYPE WestCoast AS Character (2) FINAL ;
```

The XML Schema to map this type to XML is as follows:

```
<xsd:simpleType>
    Name='UDT.Sales.WestCoast'>

    <xsd:annotation>
        <xsd:appinfo>
            <sqlxml:sqltype kind='DISTINCT'
                schemaName='Sales'
                typeName='WestCoast'
                mappedType='CHAR_2'
                final='true'/>
        <xsd:appinfo>
        </xsd:annotation>

    <xsd:restriction base='CHAR_2'/>

</xsd:simpleType>
```

This creates an element that is the same as the one created for the preceding domain.

Row

The ROW type enables you to cram multiple items, or even a whole row's worth of information, into a single field of a table row. You can create a ROW type as part of the table definition, in the following manner:

```
CREATE TABLE CONTACTINFO (
    Name          CHARACTER (30)
    Phone         ROW (Home CHAR (13), Work CHAR (13))
) ;
```

You can now map this type to XML with the following schema:

```
<xsd:complexType Name='ROW.1'>

    <xsd:annotation>
        <xsd:appinfo>
            <sqlxml:sqltype kind='ROW'>
                <sqlxml:field name='Home'
                    mappedType='CHAR_13'/>
                <sqlxml:field name='Work'
```

```
                mappedType='CHAR_13'/>
            </sqlxml:sqltype>
    <xsd:appinfo>
  </xsd:annotation>

    <xsd:sequence>
      <xsd:element Name='Home' nillable='true'
          Type='CHAR_13'/>
      <xsd:element Name='Work' nillable='true'
          Type='CHAR_13'/>
    </xsd:sequence>

  </xsd:complexType>
```

This mapping could generate the following XML for a column:

```
<Phone>
    <Home>(888)555-1111</Home>
    <Work>(888)555-1212</Work>
</Phone>
```

Array

You can put more than one element in a single field by using an Array rather than the ROW type. For example, in the CONTACTINFO table, declare Phone as an array and then generate the XML Schema that will map the array to XML.

```
CREATE TABLE CONTACTINFO (
    Name        CHARACTER (30),
    Phone       CHARACTER (13) ARRAY [4]
) ;
```

You can now map this type to XML with the following schema:

```
<xsd:complexType Name='ARRAY_4.CHAR_13'>

    <xsd:annotation>
      <xsd:appinfo>
        <sqlxml:sqltype kind='ARRAY'
                        maxElements='4'
                        mappedElementType='CHAR_13'/>
      </xsd:appinfo>
    </xsd:annotation>
```

```
    <xsd:sequence>
        <xsd:element Name='element'
        minOccurs='0' maxOccurs='4'
        nillable='true' type='CHAR_13'/>
    </xsd:sequence>

</xsd:complexType>
```

This schema would generate something like this:

```
<Phone>
    <element>(888)555-1111</element>
    <element>xsi:nil='true'/>
    <element>(888)555-3434</element>
</Phone>
```

REMEMBER

The element in the array containing xsi:nil='true' reflects the fact that the second phone number in the source table contains a null value.

Multiset

The phone numbers in the preceding example could just as well be stored in a multiset as in an array. To map a multiset, use something akin to the following:

```
CREATE TABLE CONTACTINFO (
    Name        CHARACTER (30),
    Phone       CHARACTER (13) MULTISET
) ;
```

You can now map this type to XML with the following schema:

```
<xsd:complexType Name='MULTISET.CHAR_13'>

    <xsd:annotation>
        <xsd:appinfo>
            <sqlxml:sqltype kind='MULTISET'
                            mappedElementType='CHAR_13'/>
        </xsd:appinfo>
    </xsd:annotation>

    <xsd:sequence>
        <xsd:element Name='element'
        minOccurs='0' maxOccurs='unbounded'
```

```
                nillable='true' type='CHAR_13'/>
    </xsd:sequence>

</xsd:complexType>
```

This schema would generate something like this:

```
<Phone>
    <element>(888)555-1111</element>
    <element>xsi:nil='true'/>
    <element>(888)555-3434</element>
</Phone>
```

The Marriage of SQL and XML

SQL provides the worldwide standard method for storing data in a highly structured fashion. The structure enables users to maintain data stores of a wide range of sizes and to efficiently extract from those data stores the information they want. XML has risen from a de facto standard to an official standard vehicle for transporting data between incompatible systems, particularly over the Internet. By bringing these two powerful methods together, the value of both is greatly increased. SQL can now handle data that doesn't fit nicely into the strict relational paradigm that was originally defined by Dr. Codd. XML can now efficiently take data from SQL databases or send data to them. The result is more readily available information that is easier to share. After all, at its core, sharing is what marriage is all about.

Chapter **19**

SQL and JSON

I n the early days of computing, there were no databases. Data was kept in flat files, with no organizing structure. Clearly, there had to be a better way, and database architectures were devised in the 1950s and 1960s, primarily the hierarchical architecture and the network architecture. These early architectures were largely superseded by the relational architecture, which became dominant in the 1980s and the decades since. Relational databases are based on that relational architecture, and SQL is the universally used language for operating on relational databases.

In recent years, primarily with the advent of "big data," a variety of non-relational architectures have taken hold in different application areas. Collectively known as NoSQL database architectures, each one has its own way of organizing and storing data.

It became clear that there was much to be gained if data stored in one kind of NoSQL database could be sent to and used by a different kind of NoSQL database. To get around the problem of different file formats in different NoSQL databases, a data interchange format was developed that all the NoSQL databases could use to share data with each other. That data interchange format is named *JSON*, which is an acronym for *JavaScript Object Notation*.

Although derived from JavaScript, JSON can be used with any programming language that supports it. The Object part of the name refers to the fact that data can be transferred in the form of JSON objects. Don't get too hung up on that, however. Data can also be transferred in the form of arrays, numbers, and strings, as well as true, false, and null values.

Using JSON with SQL

Now, as NoSQL databases have become increasingly popular, the value of exchanging data with relational databases has become clear. There are decades worth of data stored in relational databases that could be of value to applications designed to operate on NoSQL databases. The reverse is also true. Huge quantities of data are being stored in NoSQL databases that could be used by applications designed to operate on relational databases. To meet this need, functionality has been added to the ISO/IEC SQL specification to enable the translation of JSON data into a form that can be handled by SQL, and conversely, the translation of SQL-compatible relational data into JSON data. The tool for making these translations is the SQL/JSON data model, which defines a variety of data items, as well as a set of built-in functions to operate on those items.

Ingesting and storing JSON data into a relational database

To store JSON data in a relational database, it is ingested into a relational database as either a character string or a binary string. That string is stored as an ordinary database column. Once stored, it can be retrieved and operated on by the SQL/JSON built-in functions, described later in this chapter.

Generating JSON data from relational data

In response to an SQL query, built-in functions can generate JSON objects or arrays regardless of whether the source of the data was originally JSON data that had been parsed into an SQL table column or ordinary SQL data that had not originally been JSON data.

Querying JSON data stored in relational tables

A new language, SQL/JSON path language, is embedded in SQL operators to enable the querying of JSON data stored in SQL-compatible relational database tables.

The SQL/JSON Data Model

Because SQL and JSON store data in fundamentally different ways, if data is to be shared across those two environments, a way of bridging that gap must exist. That bridge is the SQL/JSON data model.

JSON data comes in a variety of forms, including JSON arrays, JSON objects, JSON members, JSON literal null values, JSON literal true values, JSON literal false values, JSON numbers, and JSON strings. SQL has no counterpart for JSON arrays, JSON objects, or JSON members. In addition, JSON nulls, numbers, and strings are not exactly the same as SQL nulls, numbers, and strings. Going the other way, JSON has no counterpart for SQL datetime data. To bridge these gaps, a set of SQL/JSON items have been defined. They reside within the SQL environment, but are able to communicate with JSON data stored outside that environment.

SQL/JSON items

JSON data, stored in the form of character or binary strings, can be parsed into SQL/JSON items. An SQL/JSON item can be

» An SQL/JSON scalar

» An SQL/JSON null

» An SQL/JSON array

» An SQL/JSON object

SQL/JSON scalar

The SQL/JSON scalar is defined as a non-null value of any of the following SQL types:

» Character string, using the Unicode character set

» Numeric

» Boolean

» Datetime

SQL/JSON null

The SQL/JSON null is defined as a value distinct from any value of any SQL type. It is even distinct from any SQL null value.

SQL/JSON array

The SQL/JSON array is defined as an ordered list of zero or more SQL/JSON items. These items are called the SQL/JSON elements of the SQL/JSON array. Elements in the array are separated by commas and enclosed in square brackets. For example:

```
[ 3.1415927, "string theory", false]
```

SQL arrays are 1-relative, meaning that the first element is called element 1. SQL/JSON, however, follows the JavaScript standard of being 0-relative. The first element of a SQL/JSON array is called element 0.

SQL/JSON object

The SQL/JSON object is defined as an unordered collection of zero or more SQL/JSON members, where a member is a pair whose first value is a character string with character set Unicode and whose second value is an SQL/JSON item. The first value of an SQL/JSON member is called the key, and the second value is called the bound value. Members are sometimes called key/value pairs, and sometimes name/value pairs. SQL/JSON objects can be serialized by separating the members with commas and enclosing the entire object in curly braces. An example might be

```
{ "name" : "Joe Friday",  "badge" : 714, "objective" : "the facts" }
```

SQL/JSON sequences

An SQL/JSON sequence is defined as an ordered list of zero or more SQL/JSON items. It can be thought of as a *container* of zero or more SQL/JSON items.

Parsing JSON

Parsing is the importing of data in some storage format into the SQL/JSON data model. Normally the format would be a Unicode character string, although other, implementation-dependent formats are possible.

Serializing JSON

Serializing JSON is the reverse of the parsing operation. It is the exporting of a value from the SQL/JSON data model back to some storage format. One thing to note is that SQL/JSON datetimes cannot be serialized, and another is that SQL/JSON sequences of length greater than one also cannot be serialized.

SQL/JSON Functions

Operations on JSON data are performed by built-in functions. These SQL/JSON functions belong to two groups: query functions and constructor functions. Query functions evaluate SQL/JSON path language expressions against JSON values, producing values of SQL/JSON types, which are then converted to SQL types. SQL/JSON path language is described later in this chapter.

Constructor functions use values of SQL types to produce JSON values (either JSON objects or JSON arrays), which are represented in SQL character or binary string types.

JSON API common syntax

There are several query functions, all of which share a common syntax. They all require a path expression, the JSON value to be input to that path expression for querying and processing, and possibly optional parameter values passed to the path expression.

The syntax is

```
<JSON API common syntax> ::=
  <JSON context item> <comma>
    <JSON path specification>
      [ AS <JSON table path name> ]
        [ <JSON passing clause> ]
<JSON context item> ::= <JSON value expression>
<JSON path specification> ::=
  <character string literal>
<JSON passing clause> ::=
  PASSING <JSON argument>
    [ { <comma> <JSON argument> } ]
<JSON argument> ::=
  <JSON value expression> AS <identifier>
```

The type of the value expression contained in the <JSON value expression> immediately contained in the <JSON context item> (second line above) is a string type.

JSON value expression

As noted in the previous BNF syntax definition, a JSON context item is just a JSON value expression. A JSON value expression can be defined as

```
<JSON value expression> ::=
   <value expression> [ <JSON input clause> ]

<JSON input clause> ::= FORMAT <JSON representation>

<JSON representation> ::=
  JSON [ ENCODING { UTF8 | UTF16 | UTF32 } ]
  | Implementation-defined JSON representation option>
```

This shows that a JSON value expression is a value expression with an optional input clause. The input clause specifies the format of the JSON representation, which specifies the encoding as being either one of three Unicode formats or an implementation-defined alternative.

Path expression

Following the JSON context item and a comma is the JSON path specification, which must be a character string literal. The table path name and passing clause are optional parts of the JSON path specification.

PASSING clause

The PASSING clause is used to pass parameters to the SQL/JSON path expression.

JSON OUTPUT clause

When JSON data comes back to an application as the result of the operation of a function, the application author can specify the data type, format, and encoding of the JSON text created by the function. The syntax for the output clause is

```
<JSON output clause> ::=
  RETURNING ,data type>
  [ FORMAT <JSON representation> ]

<JSON representation> ::=
  JSON [ ENCODING { UTF8 | UTF16 | UTF32 } ]
  | Implementation-defined JSON representation option>
```

If FORMAT is not specified, then FORMAT JSON is the default.

Query functions

The SQL/JSON query functions are JSON_EXISTS, JSON_VALUE, JSON_QUERY, and JSON_TABLE. These functions evaluate path language expressions against JSON values. The results returned are values of SQL/JSON types, which are then converted to SQL types. Path language is described later in this chapter.

JSON_EXISTS

JSON_EXISTS determines whether a JSON value satisfies a search condition in the path specification. The syntax is

```
<JSON exists predicate> ::=
    JSON_EXISTS <left paren>
        <JSON API common syntax>
        [ <JSON exists error behavior> ON ERROR ]
    <right paren>
<JSON exists error behavior> ::=
    TRUE | FALSE | UNKNOWN | ERROR
```

If the optional ON ERROR clause is not included, the default assumption is FALSE ON ERROR. JSON_EXISTS evaluates the SQL/JSON path expression, returning a True result if the path expression finds one or more SQL/JSON items.

Sample data that can be used to learn how to use the query functions, including JSON_EXISTS, can be found on pages 24 and 25 of Section 6 of the SQL Technical Report ISO/IEC TR 19075-6:2017(E), which can be downloaded from

```
http://standards.iso.org/ittf/PubliclyAvailableStandards/
c067367_ISO_IEC_TR_19075-6_2017.zip
```

The data consists of two columns, K and J of a table T. K is the primary key of the table, and J is the data, consisting of key-value pairs and arrays of key-value pairs. JSON_EXISTS tests for the existence of a given character string literal in the JSON path specification. For example:

```
SELECT T.K
FROM T
WHERE JSON_EXISTS (T.J, 'lax $.where') ;
```

The primary keys of the rows that contain the word 'where' are returned as the result set of the SELECT query. The keyword 'lax' refers to error handling that is more forgiving than "strict" error handling. It has no effect on the result of this query. $ is the accessor that accesses the word 'where' in the current JSON object.

JSON_VALUE

The `JSON_VALUE` function extracts an SQL scalar value from a JSON value. The syntax is

```
<JSON value function> ::=
  JSON VALUE <left paren>
    <JSON API common syntax>
    [ <JSON returning clause> ]
    [ <JSON value empty behavior> ON EMPTY ]
    [ <JSON value error behavior ON ERROR ]
  <right paren>
<JSON returning clause> ::= RETURNING <data type>
<JSON value empty behavior> ::=
    ERROR
  | NULL
  | DEFAULT <value expression>
<JSON value error behavior> ::=
    ERROR
  | NULL
  | DEFAULT <value expression>
```

As you can probably surmise, `<JSON value empty behavior>` tells what to return if the result of the SQL/JSON path expression is empty.

» `NULL ON EMPTY` means the result of JSON_VALUE is empty.

» `ERROR ON EMPTY` means an exception is raised.

» `DEFAULT <value expression> ON EMPTY` means that the value expression is evaluated and cast to the target type.

» `<JSON value error behavior>` is similar. It specifies what to do if there is an unhandled error.

In the previous `JSON_EXISTS` example, all the rows where the keyword `'where'` was present in the J value column were returned. With `JSON_VALUE`, the value associated with a target keyword is returned. Using the same data set as the `JSON_EXISTS` example, where the keyword `'who'` is paired with a person's name, the following SQL code will return the names of people from all the rows where the keyword `'who'` is present.

```
SELECT T.K,
   JSON_VALUE (T.J, 'lax $.who') AS Who
FROM T ;
```

The result set will contain a column named K, containing the primary keys of the rows being returned, and a column named Who, containing the names that were paired with the 'who' keyword in the source data.

By default, JSON_VALUE returns an implementation-defined character string data type. The user can specify other types with a RETURNING clause.

JSON_QUERY

JSON_VALUE does a fine job of extracting a scalar from an SQL/JSON value, but is unable to extract an SQL/JSON array or an SQL/JSON object from an SQL/JSON value. JSON_QUERY is designed to perform those functions. The syntax for JSON_QUERY is

```
<JSON query> ::=
   JSON_QUERY <left paren>
      <JSON API common syntax>
      [ <JSON output clause> ]
      [ <JSON query wrapper behavior> ]
      [ <JSON query quotes behavior> QUOTES
        [ ON SCALAR STRING ] ]
      [ <JSON query empty behavior> ON EMPTY ]
      [ <JSON query error behavior> ON ERROR ]
   <right paren>
```

The ON EMPTY and ON ERROR clauses are similar to the ones in JSON_VALUE and are handled the same way, the difference here being that the user can specify behavior when either the empty case or the error case arises.

» If <JSON output clause> is not specified, RETURNING JSON FORMAT is the default.

» If <JSON query empty behavior> is not specified, then NULL ON EMPTY is the default.

» If <JSON query error behavior> is not specified, then NULL ON ERROR is the default.

» If <JSON query wrapper behavior> is not specified, then WITHOUT ARRAY is the default.

» If <JSON query wrapper behavior> specifies WITH and if neither CONDITIONAL nor UNCONDITIONAL is specified, then UNCONDITIONAL is the default.

» If the value of the <JSON context item> simply contained in the <JSON API common syntax> is the null value, then the result of <JSON query> is the null value.

Using the same sample data that was used for the JSON_EXISTS sample query and the JSON_VALUE sample query, you can add array data to the result set, along with the results obtained with the JSON_VALUE clauses.

```
SELECT T.K,
   JSON_VALUE (T.J, 'lax $.who') AS Who,
   JSON_VALUE (T.J, 'lax $.where' NULL ON EMPTY)
     AS Nali,
   JSON_QUERY (T.J, 'lax $.friends') AS Friends
FROM T
WHERE JSON_EXISTS (T.J, 'lax $.friends')
```

The WHERE JSON_EXISTS clause eliminates any rows that do not have a key-value pair for friends. If WITH ARRAY WRAPPER is specified, then array elements returned are enclosed in a pair of square brackets.

JSON_TABLE

The JSON_TABLE function is significantly more complex than the other query functions. It takes JSON data and generates a relational output table from the valid input data. The syntax definition for the simplest variant of the JSON_TABLE function takes up more than a full page of text. Adding nested paths and plan clauses adds enormous complexity to what is already pretty complex. I do not have enough room here to cover JSON_TABLE in the depth that it deserves, so instead, I refer you to page 35 and following of the SQL Technical Report ISO/IEC TR 19075-6:2017(E), which can be downloaded from

```
http://standards.iso.org/ittf/PubliclyAvailableStandards/
c067367_ISO_IEC_TR_19075-6_2017.zip
```

Constructor functions

The SQL/JSON constructor functions serve to construct JSON objects, arrays, and aggregates, based on information stored in relational tables. They are performing operations that take data in the opposite direction from the direction that SQL/JSON query functions take.

JSON_OBJECT

The JSON_OBJECT function constructs JSON objects from explicit name/value pairs. The syntax is

```
<JSON object constructor> ::=
   JSON_OBJECT <left paren>
```

```
      [ <JSON name and value> [ { <comma>
            <JSON name and value> } ... ]
        [ <JSON constructor null clause> ]
        [ <JSON key uniqueness constraint> ] ]
      [ <JSON output clause> ]
   <right paren>
<JSON name and value> ::=
      [KEY] <JSON name> VALUE <JSON value expression>
    | <JSON name> <colon> <JSON value expression>
<JSON name> ::= <character value expression>
<JSON constructor null clause> ::=
      NULL ON NULL
    | ABSENT ON NULL
<JSON key uniqueness constraint> ::=
      WITH UNIQUE [ KEYS ]
    | WITHOUT UNIQUE [ KEYS ]
```

There are a few rules that must be followed along with the preceding syntax:

» `<JSON name>` may not be NULL.

» `<JSON value expression>`s may be NULL.

» The `<JSON constructor null clause>`, if NULL ON NULL, produces a SQL/JSON null. If ABSENT ON NULL, it omits the key-value pair from the resulting SQL/JSON object.

» If no JSON constructor null clause is present, the default is NULL ON NULL.

JSON_OBJECTAGG

An application developer may want to construct a JSON object as an aggregation of the data in a relational table. If such a table contains two columns, one with JSON names and the other with JSON values, the JSON_OBJECTAGG function can act on that data to create a JSON object. The syntax to perform this operation is

```
<JSON object aggregate constructor> ::=
   JSON_OBJECTAGG <left paren>
      <JSON name and value>
        [ <JSON constructor null clause> ]
        [ <JSON key uniqueness constraint> ]
      [ <JSON output clause> ]
   <right paren>
```

If `<JSON constructor clause>` is not present, NULL ON NULL is the default.

JSON_ARRAY

To create a JSON array, based on a list of data items in a relational database table, the JSON_ARRAY function can be used. The syntax is

```
<JSON array constructor> ::=
    <JSON array constructor by enumeration>
  | <JSON array constructor by query>
<JSON array constructor by enumeration ::=
  JSON_ARRAY <left paren>
    [ <JSON value expression> [ { <comma>
        <JSON value expression> }... ]
      <JSON constructor null clause> ] ]
    <JSON output clause>
  <right paren>
<JSON array constructor by query> ::=
  JSON_ARRAY <left paren>
    <query expression>
    [ <JSON input clause> ]
    [ <JSON constructor null clause> ]
    [ <JSON output clause> ]
```

JSON_ARRAY has two variants, one that produces its result from an input list of SQL values, and the other that produces its results from a query expression invoked from within the function. If the optional <JSON constructor null clause> is absent, the default is ABSENT ON NULL, which is the opposite of the default behavior for JSON_OBJECT.

JSON_ARRAYAGG

Just as you may want to construct a JSON object based on an aggregation of relational data, you may also want to construct a JSON array based on an aggregation of relational data. To do that, the JSON_ARRAYAGG function is now part of the SQL standard. The syntax is

```
<JSON array aggregate constructor> ::=
  JSON_ARRAYAGG <left paren>
    <JSON value expression>
    [ <JSON array aggregate order by clause> ]
    [ <JSON constructor null clause> ]
    [ <JSON output clause> ]
  <right paren>
<JSON array aggregate order by clause> ::=
  ORDER BY <sort specification list>
```

If there is no `<JSON constructor null clause>`, the default is ABSENT ON NULL. The `<JSON array order by clause>` enables the developer to order output array elements according to one or more sort specifications, similar to the way ORDER BY works on ordinary SQL data.

IS JSON predicate

The IS JSON predicate tests whether a string purported to be JSON data is indeed valid JSON data. The syntax for use of the IS JSON predicate is

```
<JSON predicate> ::=
    <string value expression> [ <JSON input clause> ]
        IS [NOT] JSON
    [ <JSON predicate type constraint> ]
    [ <JSON key uniqueness constraint> ]
<JSON predicate type constraint> ::=
    VALUE
  | ARRAY
  | OBJECT
  | SCALAR
```

If the optional `<JSON input clause>` is not specified, then FORMAT JSON is the default. If `<JSON key uniqueness constraint>` is not specified, then WITHOUT UNIQUE KEYS is the default.

JSON nulls and SQL nulls

JSON nulls are not exactly the same as SQL nulls. In SQL, a zero-length string ("") is distinct from an SQL null value, which represents the absence of a definite value. In JSON, null is an actual value, and is represented by a JSON literal ("null"). JSON nulls must be distinguishable from SQL nulls. SQL/JSON syntax enables the application author to select whether SQL null values are included in a JSON object or array being constructed, or whether they should be omitted from the JSON object or array being constructed.

SQL/JSON Path Language

SQL/JSON Path language is a query language used by the SQL/JSON query functions. It accepts a context item, a path specification, and a PASSING clause as inputs, potentially along with ON ERROR and other clauses, to execute the JSON_EXISTS,

JSON_VALUE, JSON_QUERY, and JSON_TABLE functions. These functions are executed by a path "engine" that returns results to the function, and ultimately back to the user.

In path language, the dollar sign ($) represents the current context element, and the period (.) represents an object member. Square brackets enclose array elements. Thus:

>> $.name denotes the value of the name attribute of the current JSON object.

>> $.phones[last] denotes the last element of the array stored in the phones attribute of the current JSON object.

There's More

JSON is a complex subject and there is much more to it than I have had space to cover here. For additional information on how Microsoft uses JSON with their SQL Server database products, you can find information specific to that implementation here:

```
https://docs.microsoft.com/en-us/sql/relational-databases/json/
json-data-sql-server?view=sql-server-2017
```

6
Advanced Topics

Chapter **20**

Stepping through a Dataset with Cursors

major incompatibility between SQL and the most popular application development languages is that SQL operates on the data of an entire set of table rows at a time, whereas the procedural languages operate on only a single row at a time. A *cursor* enables SQL to retrieve (or update, or delete) a single row at a time so that you can use SQL in combination with an application written in any of the popular languages.

A cursor is like a pointer that locates a specific table row. When a cursor is active, you can SELECT, UPDATE, or DELETE the row at which the cursor is pointing.

Cursors are valuable if you want to retrieve selected rows from a table, check their contents, and perform different operations based on those contents. SQL can't perform this sequence of operations by itself. SQL can retrieve the rows, but procedural languages are better at making decisions based on field contents. Cursors enable SQL to retrieve rows from a table one at a time and then feed the result to procedural code for processing. By placing the SQL code in a loop, you can process the entire table row by row.

In a pseudocode representation of embedded SQL, the most common flow of execution looks like this:

```
EXEC SQL DECLARE CURSOR statement
EXEC SQL OPEN statement
Test for end of table
Procedural code
Start loop
    Procedural code
    EXEC SQL FETCH
    Procedural code
    Test for end of table
End loop
EXEC SQL CLOSE statement
Procedural code
```

The SQL statements in this listing are DECLARE, OPEN, FETCH, and CLOSE. Each of these statements is discussed in detail in this chapter.

TIP

If you can perform the operation that you want with normal SQL (set-at-a-time) statements, then do so. Declare a cursor, retrieve table rows one at a time, and use your system's host language only when you can't do what you want to do with SQL alone.

Declaring a Cursor

To use a cursor, you first must declare its existence to the DBMS. You do this with a DECLARE CURSOR statement. The DECLARE CURSOR statement doesn't actually cause anything to happen; it just announces the cursor's name to the DBMS and specifies what query the cursor will operate on. A DECLARE CURSOR statement has the following syntax:

```
DECLARE cursor-name [<cursor sensitivity>]
    [<cursor scrollability>]
CURSOR [<cursor holdability>] [<cursor returnability>]
FOR query expression
    [ORDER BY order-by expression]
    [FOR updatability expression] ;
```

Note: The cursor name uniquely identifies a cursor, so it must be unlike that of any other cursor name in the current module or compilation unit.

TIP

To make your application more readable, give the cursor a meaningful name. Relate it to the data that the query expression requests or to the operation that your procedural code performs on the data.

Here are some characteristics that you must establish when you declare a cursor:

» **Cursor sensitivity:** Choose SENSITIVE, INSENSITIVE, or ASENSITIVE (default).

» **Cursor scrollability:** Choose either SCROLL or NO SCROLL (default).

» **Cursor holdability:** Choose either WITH HOLD or WITHOUT HOLD (default).

» **Cursor returnability:** Choose either WITH RETURN or WITHOUT RETURN (default).

Query expression

REMEMBER

You can use any legal SELECT statement as a *query expression*. The rows that the SELECT statement retrieves are the ones that the cursor steps through one at a time. These rows are the scope of the cursor.

The query is not actually performed when the DECLARE CURSOR statement is read. You can't retrieve data until you execute the OPEN statement. The row-by-row examination of the data starts after you enter the loop that encloses the FETCH statement.

ORDER BY clause

You may want to process your retrieved data in a particular order, depending on what your procedural code will do with the data. You can sort the retrieved rows before processing them by using the optional ORDER BY clause. The clause has the following syntax:

```
ORDER BY sort-specification [ , sort-specification]...
```

You can have multiple sort specifications. Each has the following syntax:

```
(column-name) [COLLATE BY collation-name] [ASC|DESC]
```

You sort by column name, and to do so, the column must be in the select list of the query expression. Columns that are in the table but not in the query select list do not work as sort specifications. For example, suppose you want to perform an operation that is not supported by SQL on selected rows of the CUSTOMER table. You can use a DECLARE CURSOR statement like this:

```
DECLARE cust1 CURSOR FOR
    SELECT CustID, FirstName, LastName, City, State, Phone
        FROM CUSTOMER
    ORDER BY State, LastName, FirstName ;
```

In this example, the SELECT statement retrieves rows sorted first by state, then by last name, and then by first name. The statement retrieves all customers in Alaska (AK) before it retrieves the first customer from Alabama (AL). The statement then sorts customer records from Alaska by the customer's last name (*Aaron* before *Abbott*). When the last name is the same, sorting then goes by first name (*George Aaron* before *Henry Aaron*).

Have you ever made 40 copies of a 20-page document on a photocopier without a collator? What a drag! You must make 20 stacks on tables and desks, and then walk by the stacks 40 times, placing a sheet on each stack. This process of putting things in the desired order is called *collation*. A similar process plays a role in SQL.

A collation is a set of rules that determines how strings in a character set compare. A character set has a default collation sequence that defines the order in which elements are sorted. But, you can apply a collation sequence other than the default to a column. To do so, use the optional COLLATE BY clause. Your implementation probably supports several common collations. Pick one and then make the collation *ascending* or *descending* by appending an ASC or DESC keyword to the clause.

In a DECLARE CURSOR statement, you can specify a calculated column that doesn't exist in the underlying table. In this case, the calculated column doesn't have a name that you can use in the ORDER BY clause. You can give it a name in the DECLARE CURSOR query expression, which enables you to identify the column later. Consider the following example:

```
DECLARE revenue CURSOR FOR
    SELECT Model, Units, Price,
            Units * Price AS ExtPrice
        FROM TRANSDETAIL
    ORDER BY Model, ExtPrice DESC ;
```

In this example, no COLLATE BY clause is in the ORDER BY clause, so the default collation sequence is used. Notice that the fourth column in the select list is the result of a calculation of the data in the second and third columns. The fourth column is an extended price named ExtPrice. In my example, the ORDER BY clause is sorted first by model name and then by ExtPrice. The sort on ExtPrice is descending, as specified by the DESC keyword; transactions with the highest dollar value are processed first.

The default sort order in an ORDER BY clause is ascending. If a sort specification list includes a DESC sort and the next sort should also be in descending order, you must explicitly specify DESC for the next sort. For example:

```
ORDER BY A, B DESC, C, D, E, F
```

is equivalent to

```
ORDER BY A ASC, B DESC, C ASC, D ASC, E ASC, F ASC
```

Updatability clause

Sometimes, you may want to update or delete table rows that you access with a cursor. Other times, you may want to guarantee that such updates or deletions can't be made. SQL gives you control over this issue with the updatability clause of the DECLARE CURSOR statement. If you want to prevent updates and deletions within the scope of the cursor, use the clause:

```
FOR READ ONLY
```

For updates of specified columns only — leaving all others protected — use the following:

```
FOR UPDATE OF column-name [, column-name]...
```

REMEMBER

Any columns listed must appear in the DECLARE CURSOR's query expression. If you don't include an updatability clause, the default assumption is that all columns listed in the query expression are updatable. In that case, an UPDATE statement can update all the columns in the row to which the cursor is pointing, and a DELETE statement can delete that row.

Sensitivity

The query expression in the DECLARE CURSOR statement determines the rows that fall within a cursor's scope. Consider this possible problem: What if a statement in your program, located between the OPEN and the CLOSE statements, changes the contents of some of those rows so that they no longer satisfy the query? Does the cursor continue to process all the rows that originally qualified, or does it recognize the new situation and ignore rows that no longer qualify?

A normal SQL statement, such as UPDATE, INSERT, or DELETE, operates on a set of rows in a database table (or perhaps the entire table). While such a statement is active, SQL's transaction mechanism protects it from interference by other statements acting concurrently on the same data. If you use a cursor, however, your window of vulnerability to harmful interaction is wide open. When you open a cursor, data is at risk of being the victim of simultaneous, conflicting operations until you close the cursor again. If you open one cursor, start processing through a table, and then open a second cursor while the first is still active, the actions you take with the second cursor can affect what the statement controlled by the first cursor sees.

REMEMBER

Changing the data in columns that are part of a DECLARE CURSOR query expression after some — but not all — of the query's rows have been processed results in a big mess. Your results are likely to be inconsistent and misleading. To avoid this problem, make sure that the cursor doesn't change as a result of any of the statements within its scope. Add the INSENSITIVE keyword to your DECLARE CURSOR statement. As long as your cursor is open, it is insensitive to (unaffected by) table changes that affect qualified rows in the cursor's scope. A cursor can't be both insensitive and updatable. An insensitive cursor must be read-only.

For example, suppose that you write these queries:

```
DECLARE C1 CURSOR FOR SELECT * FROM EMPLOYEE
    ORDER BY Salary ;
DECLARE C2 CURSOR FOR SELECT * FROM EMPLOYEE
    FOR UPDATE OF Salary ;
```

Now, suppose you open both cursors and fetch a few rows with C1 and then update a salary with C2 to increase its value. This change can cause a row that you have fetched with C1 to appear again on a later fetch of C1.

REMEMBER

The peculiar interactions that are possible with multiple open cursors, or open cursors and set operations, are the sort of concurrency problems that transaction isolation avoids. If you operate this way, you're asking for trouble. So remember: Don't operate with multiple open cursors. For more information about transaction isolation, check out Chapter 15.

The default condition of cursor sensitivity is ASENSITIVE. Although you might think you know what this means, nothing is ever as simple as you'd like it to be. Each implementation has its own definition. For one implementation ASENSITIVE could be equivalent to SENSITIVE, and for another it could be equivalent to INSENSITIVE. Check your system documentation for its meaning in your own case.

Scrollability

Scrollability gives you the capability to move the cursor around within a result set. With the SCROLL keyword in the DECLARE CURSOR statement, you can access rows in any order you want. The syntax of the FETCH statement controls the cursor's movement. I describe the FETCH statement later in this chapter.

Opening a Cursor

Although the DECLARE CURSOR statement specifies which rows to include in the cursor, it doesn't actually cause anything to happen because DECLARE is just a declaration and not an executable statement. The OPEN statement brings the cursor into existence. It has the following form:

```
OPEN cursor-name ;
```

To open the cursor that I use in the discussion of the ORDER BY clause (earlier in this chapter), use the following:

```
DECLARE revenue CURSOR FOR
    SELECT Model, Units, Price,
            Units * Price AS ExtPrice
        FROM TRANSDETAIL
    ORDER BY Model, ExtPrice DESC ;
OPEN revenue ;
```

REMEMBER

You can't fetch rows from a cursor until you open the cursor. When you open a cursor, the values of variables referenced in the DECLARE CURSOR statement become fixed, as do all current date-time functions. Consider the following example of SQL embedded in a host language program:

```
EXEC SQL DECLARE C1 CURSOR FOR SELECT * FROM ORDERS
    WHERE ORDERS.Customer = :NAME
        AND DueDate < CURRENT_DATE ;
NAME :='Acme Co';      //A host language statement
EXEC SQL OPEN C1;
NAME :='Omega Inc.';   //Another host statement
...
EXEC SQL UPDATE ORDERS SET DueDate = CURRENT_DATE;
```

The OPEN statement fixes the value of all variables referenced in the declare cursor and also fixes a value for all current date-time functions. As a result, the second assignment to the name variable (NAME := 'Omega Inc.') *has no effect* on the rows that the cursor fetches. (That value of NAME is used the *next* time you open C1.) And even if the OPEN statement is executed a minute before midnight and the UPDATE statement is executed a minute after midnight, the value of CURRENT_DATE in the UPDATE statement is the value of that function at the time the OPEN statement executed — even if DECLARE CURSOR doesn't reference the date-time function.

Fetching Data from a Single Row

Processing cursors involves three steps:

1. The DECLARE CURSOR statement specifies the cursor's name and scope.

2. The OPEN statement collects the table rows selected by the DECLARE CURSOR query expression.

3. The FETCH statement actually retrieves the data.

The cursor may point to one of the rows in the cursor's scope, or to the location immediately before the first row in the scope, or to the location immediately after the last row in the scope, or to the empty space between two rows. You can specify where the cursor points with the orientation clause in the FETCH statement.

Syntax

The syntax for the FETCH statement is

```
FETCH [[orientation] FROM] cursor-name
   INTO target-specification [, target-specification]... ;
```

Seven orientation options are available:

>> NEXT

>> PRIOR

>> FIRST

>> LAST

>> ABSOLUTE

>> RELATIVE

>> <simple value specification>

The default option is NEXT, which, incidentally, was the *only* orientation available in versions of SQL prior to SQL-92. The NEXT orientation moves the cursor from wherever it is to the next row in the set specified by the query expression. That means that if the cursor is located before the first record, it moves to the first record. If it points to record *n*, it moves to record *n*+1. If the cursor points to the last record in the set, it moves beyond that record, and notification of a no data condition is returned in the SQLSTATE system variable. (Chapter 22 details SQL-STATE and the rest of SQL's error-handling facilities.)

The target specifications are either host variables or parameters, depending on whether embedded SQL or a module language, respectively, is using the cursor. The number and types of the target specifications must match the number and types of the columns specified by the query expression in the DECLARE CURSOR. So in the case of embedded SQL, when you fetch a list of five values from a row of a table, five host variables must be there to receive those values, and they must be the right types.

Orientation of a scrollable cursor

Because the SQL cursor is scrollable, you have other choices besides NEXT. If you specify PRIOR, the pointer moves to the row immediately preceding its current location. If you specify FIRST, it points to the first record in the set, and if you specify LAST, it points to the last record.

When you use the ABSOLUTE and RELATIVE orientation, you must specify an integer value, as well. For example, FETCH ABSOLUTE 7 moves the cursor to the seventh row from the beginning of the set. FETCH RELATIVE 7 moves the cursor seven rows beyond its current position. FETCH RELATIVE 0 doesn't move the cursor.

FETCH RELATIVE 1 has the same effect as FETCH NEXT. FETCH RELATIVE −1 has the same effect as FETCH PRIOR. FETCH ABSOLUTE 1 gives you the first record in the set, FETCH ABSOLUTE 2 gives you the second record in the set, and so on. Similarly, FETCH ABSOLUTE −1 gives you the last record in the set, FETCH ABSOLUTE −2 gives you the next-to-last record, and so on. Specifying FETCH ABSOLUTE 0 returns the no-data exception condition code, as will FETCH ABSOLUTE 17 if only 16 rows are in the set. FETCH <simple value specification> gives you the record specified by the simple value specification.

Positioned DELETE and UPDATE statements

You can perform delete and update operations on the row to which a cursor is currently pointing. The syntax of the DELETE statement looks like this:

```
DELETE FROM table-name WHERE CURRENT OF cursor-name ;
```

If the cursor doesn't point to a row, the statement returns an error condition, and no deletion occurs.

The syntax of the UPDATE statement is as follows:

```
UPDATE table-name
    SET column-name = value [,column-name = value]...
    WHERE CURRENT OF cursor-name ;
```

The value you place into each specified column must be a value expression or the keyword DEFAULT. If an attempted positioned update operation returns an error, the update isn't performed.

Closing a Cursor

WARNING

After you finish with a cursor, make a habit of closing it immediately. Leaving a cursor open as your application goes on to other issues may cause harm. Also, open cursors use system resources.

If you close a cursor that was insensitive to changes made while it was open, when you reopen it, the reopened cursor reflects any such changes.

You can close the cursor that I opened earlier in the TRANSDETAIL table with a simple statement such as the following:

```
CLOSE revenue ;
```

Chapter **21**

Adding Procedural Capabilities with Persistent Stored Modules

S ome of the leading practitioners of database technology have been working on the standards process for years. Even after a standard has been issued and accepted by the worldwide database community, progress toward the next standard doesn't slow down. A seven-year gap separated the issuance of SQL-92 and the release of the first component of SQL:1999. During the intervening years, ANSI and ISO issued an addendum to SQL-92, called SQL-92/PSM (Persistent Stored Modules). This addendum formed the basis for a part of SQL:1999 with the same name. SQL/PSM defines a number of statements that give SQL flow of control structures comparable to the flow of control structures available in full-featured programming languages. It enables you to use SQL to perform tasks that programmers previously were forced to use other tools for. Can you imagine what your life would have been like in the caveman times of 1992, when you'd have to repeatedly swap between SQL and its procedural host language just to do your work?

Compound Statements

Throughout this book, SQL is represented as a nonprocedural language that deals with data a set at a time rather than a record at a time. With the addition of the facilities covered in this chapter, however, this statement is not as true as it used to be. Although SQL still deals with data a set at a time, it is becoming more procedural.

Archaic SQL (defined by SQL-92) doesn't follow the procedural model — where one instruction follows another in a sequence to produce a desired result — so early SQL statements were standalone entities, perhaps embedded in a C++ or Visual Basic program. With these early versions of SQL, posing a query or performing other operations by executing a series of SQL statements was discouraged because these complicated activities resulted in a performance penalty in the form of network traffic. SQL:1999 and all following versions allow compound statements, made up of individual SQL statements that execute as a unit, easing network congestion.

All the statements included in a compound statement are enclosed between a BEGIN keyword at the beginning of the statement and an END keyword at the end of the statement. For example, to insert data into multiple related tables, you use syntax similar to the following:

```
void main {
   EXEC SQL
      BEGIN
         INSERT INTO students (StudentID, Fname, Lname)
            VALUES (:sid, :sfname, :slname) ;
         INSERT INTO roster (ClassID, Class, StudentID)
            VALUES (:cid, :cname, :sid) ;
         INSERT INTO receivable (StudentID, Class, Fee)
            VALUES (:sid, :cname, :cfee)
      END ;
/* Check SQLSTATE for errors */
   }
```

This little fragment from a C program includes an embedded compound SQL statement. The comment about SQLSTATE deals with error handling. If the compound statement doesn't execute successfully, an error code is placed in the status parameter SQLSTATE. Of course, placing a comment after the END keyword doesn't correct the error. The comment is placed there simply to remind you that in a real program, error-handling code belongs in that spot. (I discuss error handling in detail in Chapter 22.)

Atomicity

Compound statements introduce a possibility for error that you don't face when you construct simple SQL statements. A simple SQL statement either completes successfully or doesn't, and if it doesn't complete successfully, the database is unchanged. This is not necessarily the case when a compound statement creates an error.

Consider the example in the preceding section. What if the INSERT to the STUDENTS table and the INSERT to the ROSTER table both took place, but because of interference from another user, the INSERT to the RECEIVABLE table failed? A student would be registered for a class but would not be billed. This kind of error can be hard on a university's finances.

The concept that is missing in this scenario is *atomicity*. An atomic statement is indivisible — it either executes completely or not at all. Simple SQL statements are atomic by nature, but compound SQL statements are not. However, you can make a compound SQL statement atomic by specifying it as such. In the following example, the compound SQL statement is safe by introducing atomicity:

```
void main {
    EXEC SQL
        BEGIN ATOMIC
            INSERT INTO students (StudentID, Fname, Lname)
                VALUES (:sid, :sfname, :slname) ;
            INSERT INTO roster (ClassID, Class, StudentID)
                VALUES (:cid, :cname, :sid) ;
            INSERT INTO receivable (StudentID, Class, Fee)
                VALUES (:sid, :cname, :cfee)
        END ;
/* Check SQLSTATE for errors */
}
```

By adding the keyword ATOMIC after the keyword BEGIN, you ensure that either the entire statement executes, or — if an error occurs — the entire statement rolls back, leaving the database in the state it was in before the statement began executing. Atomicity is discussed in detail in Chapter 15 in the course of the discussion of transactions.

You can find out whether a statement executed successfully. Read the section "Conditions," later in this chapter, for more information.

Variables

Full computer languages such as C and Java have always offered *variables,* but SQL didn't offer them until the introduction of SQL/PSM. A variable is a symbol that takes on a value of any given data type. Within a compound statement, you can declare a variable, assign it a value, and use it in a compound statement.

After you exit a compound statement, all the variables declared within it are destroyed. Thus, variables in SQL are local to the compound statement within which they are declared.

Here's an example:

```
BEGIN
   DECLARE prezpay NUMERIC ;
   SELECT salary
   INTO prezpay
   FROM EMPLOYEE
   WHERE jobtitle = 'president' ;
END;
```

Cursors

You can declare a *cursor* within a compound statement. You use cursors to process a table's data one row at a time. (See Chapter 20 for details.) Within a compound statement, you can declare a cursor, use it, and then forget it because the cursor is destroyed when you exit the compound statement. Here's an example of this usage:

```
BEGIN
   DECLARE ipocandidate CHARACTER(30) ;
   DECLARE cursor1 CURSOR FOR
           SELECT company
           FROM biotech ;
   OPEN CURSOR1 ;
   FETCH cursor1 INTO ipocandidate ;
   CLOSE cursor1 ;
END;
```

Conditions

When people say that a person has a condition, they usually mean that something is wrong with that person — he or she is sick or injured. People usually don't bother to mention that a person is in *good* condition; rather, they talk about people who are in serious condition or, even worse, in critical condition. This idea is similar to the way programmers talk about the condition of an SQL statement. The execution of an SQL statement leads to a successful result, a questionable result, or an outright erroneous result. Each of these possible results corresponds to a *condition.*

Every time an SQL statement executes, the database server places a value into the status parameter SQLSTATE. SQLSTATE is a five-character field. The value that is placed into SQLSTATE indicates whether the preceding SQL statement executed successfully. If it did not execute successfully, the value of SQLSTATE provides some information about the error.

The first two of the five characters of SQLSTATE (the class value) give you the major news as to whether the preceding SQL statement executed successfully, returned a result that may or may not have been successful, or produced an error. Table 21-1 shows the four possible results.

TABLE 21-1 **SQLSTATE Class Values**

Class	Description	Details
00	Successful completion	The statement executed successfully.
01	Warning	Something unusual happened during the execution of the statement, but the DBMS can't tell whether there was an error. Check the preceding SQL statement carefully to ensure that it is operating correctly.
02	Not found	No data was returned as a result of the execution of the statement. This may or may not be good news, depending on what you were trying to do with the statement. You may be hoping for an empty result table.
Other	Exception	The two characters of the class code, plus the three characters of the subclass code, comprise the five characters of SQLSTATE. They also give you an inkling about the nature of the error.

Handling conditions

You can have your program look at SQLSTATE after the execution of every SQL statement. What do you do with the knowledge that you gain?

>> **If you find a class code of 00, you probably don't want to do anything.** You want execution to proceed as you originally planned.

>> **If you find a class code of 01 or 02, you may want to take special action.** If you expected the "Warning" or "Not Found" indication, then you probably want to let execution proceed. If you didn't expect either of these class codes, then you probably want to have execution branch to a procedure that is specifically designed to handle the unexpected, but not totally unanticipated, warning or not found result.

>> **If you receive any other class code, something is wrong.** You should branch to an exception-handling procedure. Which procedure you choose to branch to depends on the contents of the three subclass characters, as well as the two class characters of SQLSTATE. If multiple different exceptions are possible, there should be an exception-handling procedure for each one because different exceptions often require different responses. You may be able to correct some errors or find workarounds. Other errors may be fatal; no one will die, but you may end up having to terminate the application.

Handler declarations

You can put a *condition handler* within a compound statement. To create a condition handler, you must first declare the condition that it will handle. The condition declared can be some sort of exception, or it can just be something that's true. Table 21-2 lists the possible conditions and includes a brief description of what causes each type of condition.

TABLE 21-2

Conditions That May Be Specified in a Condition Handler

Condition	Description
SQLSTATE VALUE 'xxyyy'	Specific SQLSTATE value
SQLEXCEPTION	SQLSTATE class other than 00, 01, or 02
SQLWARNING	SQLSTATE class 01
NOT FOUND	SQLSTATE class 02

The following is an example of a condition declaration:

```
BEGIN
   DECLARE constraint_violation CONDITION
         FOR SQLSTATE VALUE '23000' ;
END ;
```

This example is not realistic, because typically the SQL statement that may cause the condition to occur — as well as the handler that would be invoked if the condition did occur — would also be enclosed within the BEGIN...END structure.

Handler actions and handler effects

If a condition occurs that invokes a handler, the action specified by the handler executes. This action is an SQL statement, which can be a compound statement. If the handler action completes successfully, then the handler effect executes. The following is a list of the three possible handler effects:

>> CONTINUE: Continue execution immediately after the statement that caused the handler to be invoked.

>> EXIT: Continue execution after the compound statement that contains the handler.

>> UNDO: Undo the work of the previous statements in the compound statement and then continue execution after the statement that contains the handler.

If the handler can correct whatever problem invoked the handler, then the CONTINUE effect may be appropriate. The EXIT effect may be appropriate if the handler didn't fix the problem, but the changes made to the compound statement do not need to be undone. The UNDO effect is appropriate if you want to return the database to the state it was in before the compound statement started execution. Consider the following example:

```
BEGIN ATOMIC
    DECLARE constraint_violation CONDITION
        FOR SQLSTATE VALUE '23000' ;
    DECLARE UNDO HANDLER
        FOR constraint_violation
        RESIGNAL ;
    INSERT INTO students (StudentID, Fname, Lname)
        VALUES (:sid, :sfname, :slname) ;
    INSERT INTO roster (ClassID, Class, StudentID)
        VALUES (:cid, :cname, :sid) ;
END ;
```

If either of the INSERT statements causes a constraint violation, such as trying to add a record with a primary key that duplicates a primary key already in the table, SQLSTATE assumes a value of '23000', thus setting the constraint_violation condition to a true value. This action causes the handler to UNDO any changes that have been made to any tables by either INSERT command. The RESIGNAL statement transfers control back to the procedure that called the currently executing procedure.

If both INSERT statements execute successfully, execution continues with the statement following the END keyword.

The ATOMIC keyword is mandatory whenever a handler's effect is UNDO. This is not the case for handlers whose effect is either CONTINUE or EXIT.

Conditions that aren't handled

In the example in the preceding section, consider this possibility: What if an exception occurred that returned an SQLSTATE value other than '23000'? Something is definitely wrong, but the exception handler that you coded can't handle it. What happens now?

Because the current procedure doesn't know what to do, a RESIGNAL occurs. This bumps the problem up to the next higher level of control. If the problem isn't handled there, it continues to be elevated to higher levels until either it is handled or it causes an error condition in the main application.

WARNING

The idea that I want to emphasize here is that if you write an SQL statement that may cause exceptions, then you must write exception handlers for all such possible exceptions. If you don't, you will have more difficulty isolating the source of a problem when it inevitably occurs.

Assignment

With SQL/PSM, SQL gained a function that even the lowliest procedural languages have had since their inception: the ability to assign a value to a variable. Essentially, an assignment statement takes the following form:

```
SET target = source ;
```

In this usage, target is a variable name, and source is an expression. Several examples include the following:

```
SET vfname = 'Joss' ;
```

```
SET varea = 3.1416 * :radius * :radius ;
```

```
SET vWIMPmass = NULL ;
```

Flow of Control Statements

Since its original formulation in the SQL–86 standard, one of the main drawbacks that has prevented people from using SQL in a procedural manner has been its lack of flow of control statements. Until SQL/PSM was included in the SQL standard, you couldn't branch out of a strict sequential order of execution without reverting to a host language like C or Java. SQL/PSM introduces the traditional flow of control structures that other languages provide, thus allowing SQL programs to perform needed functions without switching back and forth between languages.

IF. . .THEN. . .ELSE. . .END IF

The most basic flow of control statement is the IF...THEN...ELSE...END IF statement. This statement, roughly translated from computerese, means IF a condition is true, then execute the statements following the THEN keyword. Otherwise, execute the statements following the ELSE keyword. For example:

```
IF
    vfname = 'Joss'
THEN
    UPDATE students
        SET Fname = 'Joss'
        WHERE StudentID = 314159 ;
ELSE
    DELETE FROM students
        WHERE StudentID = 314159 ;
END IF
```

In this example, if the variable vfname contains the value 'Joss', then the record for student 314159 is updated with 'Joss' in the Fname field. If the variable vfname contains any value other than 'Joss', then the record for student 314159 is deleted from the STUDENTS table.

The IF...THEN...ELSE...END IF statement is great if you want to choose one of two actions based on the value of a condition. Often, however, you want to make a selection from more than two choices. At such times, you should probably use a CASE statement.

CASE. . .END CASE

CASE statements come in two forms: the simple CASE statement and the searched CASE statement. Both kinds allow you to take different execution paths based on the values of conditions.

Simple CASE statement

A simple CASE statement evaluates a single condition. Based on the value of that condition, execution may take one of several branches. For example:

```
CASE vmajor
    WHEN 'Computer Science'
    THEN INSERT INTO geeks (StudentID, Fname, Lname)
            VALUES (:sid, :sfname, :slname) ;
    WHEN 'Sports Medicine'
    THEN INSERT INTO jocks (StudentID, Fname, Lname)
            VALUES (:sid, :sfname, :slname) ;
    WHEN 'Philosophy'
    THEN INSERT INTO skeptics (StudentID, Fname, Lname)
            VALUES (:sid, :sfname, :slname) ;
    ELSE INSERT INTO undeclared (StudentID, Fname, Lname)
            VALUES (:sid, :sfname, :slname) ;
END CASE
```

The ELSE clause handles everything that doesn't fall into the explicitly named categories in the THEN clauses.

You don't need to use the ELSE clause — it's optional. However, if you don't include it, and the CASE statement's condition is not handled by any of the THEN clauses, SQL returns an exception.

Searched CASE statement

A searched CASE statement is similar to a simple CASE statement, but it evaluates multiple conditions rather than just one. For example:

```
CASE
    WHEN vmajor
        IN ('Computer Science', 'Electrical Engineering')
        THEN INSERT INTO geeks (StudentID, Fname, Lname)
            VALUES (:sid, :sfname, :slname) ;
    WHEN vclub
        IN ('Amateur Radio', 'Rocket', 'Computer')
        THEN INSERT INTO geeks (StudentID, Fname, Lname)
            VALUES (:sid, :sfname, :slname) ;
    WHEN vmajor
        IN ('Sports Medicine', 'Physical Education')
        THEN INSERT into jocks (StudentID, Fname, Lname)
            VALUES (:sid, :sfname, :slname) ;
```

```
    ELSE
        INSERT INTO skeptics (StudentID, Fname, Lname)
            VALUES (:sid, :sfname, :slname) ;
END CASE
```

You avoid an exception by putting all students who are not geeks or jocks into the SKEPTICS table. Because not all nongeeks and nonjocks are skeptics, this may not be strictly accurate in all cases. If it isn't, you can always add a few more WHEN clauses.

LOOP...ENDLOOP

The LOOP statement allows you to execute a sequence of SQL statements multiple times. After the last SQL statement enclosed within the LOOP...ENDLOOP statement executes, control loops back to the first such statement and makes another pass through the enclosed statements. The syntax is as follows:

```
SET vcount = 0 ;
LOOP
    SET vcount = vcount + 1 ;
    INSERT INTO asteroid (AsteroidID)
        VALUES (vcount) ;
END LOOP
```

This code fragment preloads your ASTEROID table with unique identifiers. You can fill in other details about the asteroids as you find them, based on what you see through your telescope when you discover them.

Notice the one little problem with the code fragment in the preceding example: It is an infinite loop. No provision is made for leaving the loop, so it will continue inserting rows into the ASTEROID table until the DBMS fills all available storage with ASTEROID table records. If you're lucky, the DBMS will raise an exception at that time. If you're unlucky, the system will merely crash.

For the LOOP statement to be useful, you need a way to exit loops before you raise an exception. That way is the LEAVE statement.

LEAVE

The LEAVE statement works just like you might expect it to work. When execution encounters a LEAVE statement embedded within a labeled statement, it proceeds to the next statement beyond the labeled statement. For example:

```
AsteroidPreload:
SET vcount = 0 ;
```

```
LOOP
    SET vcount = vcount + 1 ;
    IF vcount > 10000
        THEN
            LEAVE AsteroidPreload ;
    END IF ;
    INSERT INTO asteroid (AsteroidID)
        VALUES (vcount) ;
END LOOP AsteroidPreload
```

The preceding code inserts 10,000 sequentially numbered records into the ASTEROID table and then passes out of the loop.

WHILE. . .DO. . .END WHILE

The WHILE statement provides another method of executing a series of SQL statements multiple times. While a designated condition is true, the WHILE loop continues to execute. When the condition becomes false, looping stops. For example:

```
AsteroidPreload2:
SET vcount = 0 ;
WHILE
    vcount< 10000 DO
        SET vcount = vcount + 1 ;
        INSERT INTO asteroid (AsteroidID)
            VALUES (vcount) ;
END WHILE AsteroidPreload2
```

This code does exactly the same thing that AsteroidPreload did in the preceding section. This is just another example of the often-cited fact that with SQL, you usually have multiple ways to accomplish any given task. Use whichever method you feel most comfortable with, assuming your implementation allows both.

REPEAT. . .UNTIL. . .END REPEAT

The REPEAT loop is very much like the WHILE loop, except that the condition is checked after the embedded statements execute rather than before. For example:

```
AsteroidPreload3:
SET vcount = 0 ;
REPEAT
    SET vcount = vcount + 1 ;
```

```
    INSERT INTO asteroid (AsteroidID)
        VALUES (vcount) ;
    UNTIL vcount = 10000
END REPEAT AsteroidPreload3
```

Although you can perform the same operation three different ways (with LOOP, WHILE, and REPEAT), you will encounter some instances when one of these structures is clearly better than the other two. Have all three methods in your bag of tricks so that when a situation like this arises, you can decide which one is the best tool available for the situation.

FOR. . .DO. . .END FOR

The SQL FOR loop declares and opens a cursor, fetches the rows of the cursor, executes the body of the FOR statement once for each row, and then closes the cursor. This loop makes processing possible entirely within SQL, instead of switching out to a host language. If your implementation supports SQL FOR loops, you can use them as a simple alternative to the cursor processing described in Chapter 20. Here's an example:

```
FOR vcount AS Curs1 CURSOR FOR
    SELECT AsteroidID FROM asteroid
DO
    UPDATE asteroid SET Description = 'stony iron'
        WHERE CURRENT OF Curs1 ;
END FOR
```

In this example, you update every row in the ASTEROID table by putting 'stony iron' into the Description field. This is a fast way to identify the compositions of asteroids, but the table may suffer some in the accuracy department. Perhaps you'd be better off checking the spectral signatures of the asteroids and then entering their types individually.

ITERATE

The ITERATE statement provides a way to change the flow of execution within an iterated SQL statement. The iterated SQL statements are LOOP, WHILE, REPEAT, and FOR. If the iteration condition of the iterated SQL statement is true or not specified, then the next iteration of the loop commences immediately after the ITERATE statement executes. If the iteration condition of the iterated SQL statement is false or unknown, then iteration ceases after the ITERATE statement executes. For example:

```
AsteroidPreload4:
SET vcount = 0 ;
WHILE
    vcount< 10000 DO
        SET vcount = vcount + 1 ;
        INSERT INTO asteroid (AsteroidID)
            VALUES (vcount) ;
        ITERATE AsteroidPreload4 ;
        SET vpreload = 'DONE' ;
END WHILE AsteroidPreload4
```

Execution loops back to the top of the WHILE statement immediately after the ITERATE statement each time through the loop until vcount equals 9999. On that iteration, vcount increments to 10000, the INSERT performs, the ITERATE statement ceases iteration, vpreload is set to 'DONE', and execution proceeds to the next statement after the loop.

Stored Procedures

Stored procedures reside in the database on the server rather than execute on the client — where all procedures were located before SQL/PSM. After you define a stored procedure, you can invoke it with a CALL statement. Keeping the procedure located on the server rather than on the client reduces network traffic, thus speeding performance. The only traffic that needs to pass from the client to the server is the CALL statement. You can create this procedure in the following manner:

```
EXEC SQL
    CREATE PROCEDURE ChessMatchScore
        ( IN score  CHAR (3),
          OUT result CHAR (10) )
    BEGIN ATOMIC
        CASE score
            WHEN '1-0' THEN
                SET result = 'whitewins' ;
            WHEN '0-1' THEN
                SET result = 'blackwins' ;
            ELSE
                SET result = 'draw' ;
        END CASE
    END ;
```

After you have created a stored procedure like the one in this example, you can invoke it with a CALL statement similar to the following statement:

```
CALL ChessMatchScore ('1-0', :Outcome) ;
```

The first argument is an input parameter that is fed to the ChessMatchScore procedure. The second argument is an embedded variable that accepts the value assigned to the output parameter that the ChessMatchScore procedure uses to return its result to the calling routine. In this case, it returns 'white wins'.

SQL:2011 added a couple of enhancements to stored procedures. The first of these is the introduction of named arguments. Here's the equivalent of the preceding call, with named arguments:

```
CALL ChessMatchScore (result => :Outcome,score =>'1-0');
```

Because the arguments are named, they can be written in any order without a danger of them being confused.

The second enhancement added in SQL:2011 is the addition of default input arguments. You can specify a default argument for the input parameter. After you do that, you don't need to specify an input value in the CALL statement; the default value is assumed. (Of course, you would want to do this only if the default value were in fact the value you wanted to send to the procedure.)

Here's an example of that usage:

```
EXEC SQL
    CREATE PROCEDURE ChessMatchScore
        ( IN score  CHAR (3)   DEFAULT '1-0',
          OUT result CHAR (10) )
    BEGIN ATOMIC
        CASE score
            WHEN '1-0' THEN
                SET result = 'whitewins' ;
            WHEN '0-1' THEN
                SET result = 'blackwins' ;
            ELSE
                SET result = 'draw' ;
        END CASE
    END ;
```

You can now call this procedure thusly with the default value:

```
CALL ChessMatchScore (:Outcome) ;
```

Stored Functions

A stored function is similar in many ways to a stored procedure. Collectively, the two are referred to as *stored routines*. They are different in several ways, including the way in which they are invoked. A stored procedure is invoked with a CALL statement, and a stored function is invoked with a *function call*, which can replace an argument of an SQL statement. The following is an example of a function definition, followed by an example of a call to that function:

```
CREATE FUNCTION PurchaseHistory (CustID)
   RETURNS CHAR VARYING (200)

   BEGIN
      DECLARE purch CHAR VARYING (200),
         DEFAULT '' ;
      FOR x AS SELECT *
               FROM transactions t
               WHERE t.customerID = CustID
      DO
         IF a <>''
            THEN SET purch = purch || ', ' ;
         END IF ;
         SET purch = purch || t.description ;
      END FOR
      RETURN purch ;
   END ;
```

This function definition creates a comma-delimited list of purchases made by a customer that has a specified customer number, taken from the TRANSACTIONS table. The following UPDATE statement contains a function call to PurchaseHistory that inserts the latest purchase history for customer number 314259 into her record in the CUSTOMER table:

```
SET customerID = 314259 ;
UPDATE customer
   SET history = PurchaseHistory (customerID)
   WHERE customerID = 314259 ;
```

Privileges

I discuss the various privileges that you can grant to users in Chapter 14. The database owner can grant the following privileges to other users:

- » The right to DELETE rows from a table

- » The right to INSERT rows into a table

- » The right to UPDATE rows in a table

- » The right to create a table that REFERENCES another table

- » The right of USAGE on a domain

SQL/PSM adds one more privilege that can be granted to a user — the EXECUTE privilege. Here are two examples:

```
GRANT EXECUTE on ChessMatchScore to TournamentDirector ;
```

```
GRANT EXECUTE on PurchaseHistory to SalesManager ;
```

These statements allow the tournament director of the chess tournament to execute the ChessMatchScore procedure, and the sales manager of the company to execute the PurchaseHistory function. People lacking the EXECUTE privilege for a routine aren't able to use it.

Stored Modules

A stored module can contain multiple routines (procedures and/or functions) that can be invoked by SQL. Anyone who has the EXECUTE privilege for a module has access to all the routines in the module. Privileges on routines within a module can't be granted individually. The following is an example of a stored module:

```
CREATE MODULE mod1
    PROCEDURE MatchScore
        ( INscore    CHAR (3),
          OUT result CHAR (10) )
    BEGIN ATOMIC
        CASE result
            WHEN '1-0' THEN
                SET result = 'whitewins' ;
            WHEN '0-1' THEN
                SET result = 'blackwins' ;
            ELSE
                SET result = 'draw' ;
        END CASE
    END ;
```

```
        FUNCTION PurchaseHistory (CustID)
        RETURNS CHAR VARYING (200)
        BEGIN
            DECLARE purch CHAR VARYING (200)
                DEFAULT '' ;
            FOR x AS SELECT *
                    FROM transactions t
                    WHERE t.customerID = CustID
            DO
                IF a <>''
                    THEN SET purch = purch || ', ' ;
                END IF ;
                SET purch = purch || t.description ;
            END FOR
            RETURN purch ;
        END ;
    END MODULE ;
```

The two routines in this module (a procedure and a function) don't have much in common, but they don't need to. You can gather related routines into a single module, or you can stick all the routines you're likely to use into a single module, regardless of whether they have anything in common.

Chapter **22**

Handling Errors

Wouldn't it be great if every application you wrote worked perfectly every time? Yeah, and it would also be really cool to win $314.9 million playing Powerball. Unfortunately, both possibilities are equally unlikely to happen. Error conditions of one sort or another are inevitable, so it's helpful to know what causes them. SQL's mechanism for returning error information to you is the *status parameter* (or *host variable*) SQLSTATE. Based on the contents of SQLSTATE, you can take different actions to remedy the error condition.

For example, the WHENEVER directive enables you to take a predetermined action whenever a specified condition (if SQLSTATE has a non-zero value, for example) is met. You can also find detailed status information about the SQL statement that you just executed in the diagnostics area. In this chapter, I explain these helpful error-handling facilities and how to use them.

SQLSTATE

SQLSTATE specifies a large number of anomalous conditions. SQLSTATE is a five-character string in which only the uppercase letters *A* through *Z* and the numerals 0 through 9 are valid characters. The five-character string is divided into two groups: a two-character class code and a three-character subclass code. The class code holds a status after the completion of an SQL statement. That status could indicate successful completion of the statement, or one of a number of major types of error conditions. The subclass code provides additional detail about this particular execution of the statement. Figure 22-1 illustrates the SQLSTATE layout.

The SQL standard defines any class code that starts with the letters *A* through *H* or the numerals 0 through 4; therefore, these class codes mean the same thing in any implementation. Class codes that start with the letters *I* through *Z* or the numerals 5 through 9 are left open for implementors (the people who build database management systems) to define because the SQL specification can't anticipate every condition that may come up in every implementation. However, implementors should use these nonstandard class codes as little as possible to avoid migration problems from one DBMS to another. Ideally, implementors should use the standard codes most of the time and the nonstandard codes only under the most unusual circumstances.

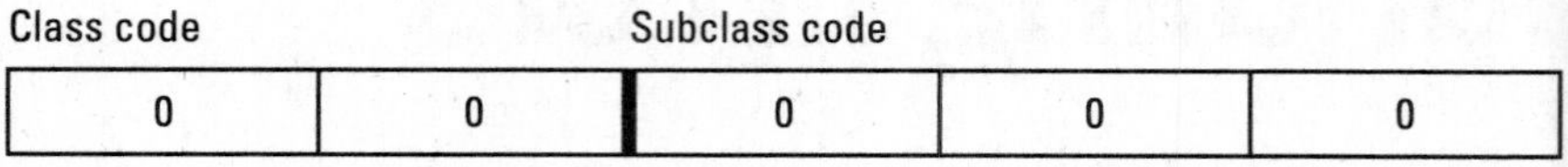

FIGURE 22-1:
SQLSTATE of
00000 indicates
successful
completion of an
SQL statement.

Class code		Subclass code		
0	0	0	0	0

I introduce SQLSTATE in Chapter 21, but here's a recap. A class code of 00 indicates successful completion. Class code 01 means that the statement executed successfully but produced a warning. Class code 02 indicates a no data condition. Any SQLSTATE class code other than 00, 01, or 02 indicates that the statement did not execute successfully.

Because SQLSTATE updates after every SQL operation, you can check it after every statement executes. If SQLSTATE contains 00000 (successful completion), you can proceed with the next operation. If it contains anything else, you may want to branch out of the main line of your code to handle the situation. The specific class code and subclass code that an SQLSTATE contains determine which of several possible actions you should take.

To use SQLSTATE in a module language program (which I describe in Chapter 16), include a reference to it in your procedure definitions, as the following example shows:

```
PROCEDURE NUTRIENT
   (SQLSTATE, :foodname CHAR (20), :calories SMALLINT,
      :protein DECIMAL (5,1), :fat DECIMAL (5,1),
      :carbo DECIMAL (5,1))
```

```
INSERT INTO FOODS
    (FoodName, Calories, Protein, Fat, Carbohydrate)
    VALUES
    (:foodname, :calories, :protein, :fat, :carbo) ;
```

At the appropriate spot in your procedural language program, you can make values available for the parameters (perhaps by soliciting them from the user) and then call up the procedure. The syntax of this operation varies from one language to another, but it looks something like this:

```
foodname = "Okra, boiled" ;
calories = 29 ;
protein = 2.0 ;
fat = 0.3 ;
carbo = 6.0 ;
NUTRIENT(state, foodname, calories, protein, fat, carbo) ;
```

The state of SQLSTATE is returned in the variable state. Your program can examine this variable and then take the appropriate action based on the variable's contents.

WHENEVER Clause

What's the point of knowing that an SQL operation didn't execute successfully if you can't do anything about it? If an error occurs, you don't want your application to continue executing as if everything is fine. You need to be able to acknowledge the error and do something to correct it. If you can't correct the error, at the very least you want to inform the user of the problem and bring the application to a graceful termination. The WHENEVER directive is the SQL mechanism for dealing with execution exceptions.

The WHENEVER directive is actually a declaration and is therefore located in your application's SQL declaration section, before the executable SQL code. The syntax is as follows:

```
WHENEVER condition action ;
```

REMEMBER

The condition may be either SQLERROR or NOT FOUND. The action may be either CONTINUE or GOTO address. SQLERROR is True if SQLSTATE has a class code other than 00, 01, or 02. NOT FOUND is True if SQLSTATE is 02000.

If the action is CONTINUE, nothing special happens, and the execution continues normally. If the action is GOTO *address* (or GO TO *address*), execution branches to the designated address in the program. At the branch address, you can put a conditional statement that examines SQLSTATE and takes different actions based on what it finds. Here are some examples of this scenario:

```
WHENEVER SQLERROR GO TO error_trap ;
```

or

```
WHENEVER NOT FOUND CONTINUE ;
```

The GO TO option is simply a macro: The *implementation* (that is, the embedded language precompiler) inserts the following test after every EXEC SQL statement:

```
IF SQLSTATE <>'00000'
   AND SQLSTATE <>'00001'
   AND SQLSTATE <>'00002'
THEN GOTO error_trap ;
```

The CONTINUE option is essentially a NO-OP that says "ignore this."

Diagnostics Areas

Although SQLSTATE can give you some information about why a particular statement failed, the information is pretty brief. So SQL provides for the capture and retention of additional status information in diagnostics areas.

Multiple diagnostics areas are maintained in the form of a *last-in-first-out* (LIFO) stack. That is, information on the most recent error can be found at the top of the stack, with info on older errors farther down in the list. The additional status information in a diagnostics area can be particularly helpful in cases in which the execution of a single SQL statement generates multiple warnings followed by an error. SQLSTATE reports the occurrence of only one error, but the diagnostics area has the capacity to report on multiple (hopefully all) errors.

The diagnostics area is a DBMS-managed data structure that has two components:

>> **Header:** The header contains general information about the most recent SQL statement that was executed.

>> **Detail area:** The detail area contains information about each code (error, warning, or success) that the statement generated.

Diagnostics header area

In the SET TRANSACTION statement (described in Chapter 15), you can specify DIAGNOSTICS SIZE. The SIZE that you specify is the number of detail areas allocated for status information. If you don't include a DIAGNOSTICS SIZE clause in your SET TRANSACTION statement, your DBMS assigns its default number of detail areas, whatever that happens to be.

The header area contains several items, as listed in Table 22-1.

TABLE 22-1

Diagnostics Header Area

Fields	Data Type
NUMBER	Exact numeric with no fractional part
ROW_COUNT	Exact numeric with no fractional part
COMMAND_FUNCTION	VARCHAR (implementation defined max length)
COMMAND_FUNCTION_CODE	Exact numeric with no fractional part
DYNAMIC_FUNCTION	VARCHAR (implementation defined max length)
DYNAMIC_FUNCTION_CODE	Exact numeric with no fractional part
MORE	Exact numeric with no fractional part
TRANSACTIONS_COMMITTED	Exact numeric with no fractional part
TRANSACTIONS_ROLLED_BACK	Exact numeric with no fractional part
TRANSACTION_ACTIVE	Exact numeric with no fractional part

The following list describes these items in more detail:

>> The NUMBER field is the number of detail areas that have been filled with diagnostic information about the current exception.

>> The ROW_COUNT field holds the number of rows affected if the previous SQL statement was an INSERT, UPDATE, or DELETE.

>> The COMMAND_FUNCTION field describes the SQL statement that was just executed.

>> The COMMAND_FUNCTION_CODE field gives the code number for the SQL statement that was just executed. Every command function has an associated numeric code.

- The DYNAMIC_FUNCTION field contains the dynamic SQL statement.

- The DYNAMIC_FUNCTION_CODE field contains a numeric code corresponding to the dynamic SQL statement.

- The MORE field may be either a 'Y' or an 'N'. 'Y' indicates that there are more status records than the detail area can hold. 'N' indicates that all the status records generated are present in the detail area. Depending on your implementation, you may be able to expand the number of records you can handle by using the SET TRANSACTION statement.

- The TRANSACTIONS_COMMITTED field holds the number of transactions that have been committed.

- The TRANSACTIONS_ROLLED_BACK field holds the number of transactions that have been rolled back.

- The TRANSACTION_ACTIVE field holds a '1' if a transaction is currently active and a '0' otherwise. A transaction is deemed to be active if a cursor is open or if the DBMS is waiting for a deferred parameter.

Diagnostics detail area

The detail areas contain data on each individual error, warning, or success condition. Each detail area contains 28 items, as Table 22-2 shows.

TABLE 22-2 ### Diagnostics Detail Area

Fields	Data Type
CONDITION_NUMBER	Exact numeric with no fractional part
RETURNED_SQLSTATE	CHAR (6)
MESSAGE_TEXT	VARCHAR (implementation defined max length)
MESSAGE_LENGTH	Exact numeric with no fractional part
MESSAGE_OCTET_LENGTH	Exact numeric with no fractional part
CLASS_ORIGIN	VARCHAR (implementation defined max length)
SUBCLASS_ORIGIN	VARCHAR (implementation defined max length)
CONNECTION_NAME	VARCHAR (implementation defined max length)
SERVER_NAME	VARCHAR (implementation defined max length)
CONSTRAINT_CATALOG	VARCHAR (implementation defined max length)

Fields	Data Type
CONSTRAINT_SCHEMA	VARCHAR (implementation defined max length)
CONSTRAINT_NAME	VARCHAR (implementation defined max length)
CATALOG_NAME	VARCHAR (implementation defined max length)
SCHEMA_NAME	VARCHAR (implementation defined max length)
TABLE_NAME	VARCHAR (implementation defined max length)
COLUMN_NAME	VARCHAR (implementation defined max length)
CURSOR_NAME	VARCHAR (implementation defined max length)
CONDITION_IDENTIFIER	VARCHAR (implementation defined max length)
PARAMETER_NAME	VARCHAR (implementation defined max length)
PARAMETER_ORDINAL_POSITION	Exact numeric with no fractional part
PARAMETER_MODE	Exact numeric with no fractional part
ROUTINE_CATALOG	VARCHAR (implementation defined max length)
ROUTINE_SCHEMA	VARCHAR (implementation defined max length)
ROUTINE_NAME	VARCHAR (implementation defined max length)
SPECIFIC_NAME	VARCHAR (implementation defined max length)
TRIGGER_CATALOG	VARCHAR (implementation defined max length)
TRIGGER_SCHEMA	VARCHAR (implementation defined max length)
TRIGGER_NAME	VARCHAR (implementation defined max length)

CONDITION_NUMBER holds the sequence number of the detail area. If a statement generates five status items that fill up five detail areas, the CONDITION_NUMBER for the fifth detail area is 5. To retrieve a specific detail area for examination, use a GET DIAGNOSTICS statement (described later in this chapter in the "Interpreting the information returned by SQLSTATE" section) with the desired CONDITION_NUMBER. RETURNED_SQLSTATE holds the SQLSTATE value that caused this detail area to be filled.

CLASS_ORIGIN tells you the source of the class code value returned in SQLSTATE. If the SQL standard defines the value, the CLASS_ORIGIN is 'ISO 9075'. If your DBMS implementation defines the value, CLASS_ORIGIN holds a string identifying the source of your DBMS. SUBCLASS_ORIGIN tells you the source of the subclass code value returned in SQLSTATE.

CLASS_ORIGIN is important. If you get an SQLSTATE of '22012', for example, the values indicate that it is in the range of standard SQLSTATEs, so you know that it means the same thing in all SQL implementations. However, if the SQLSTATE is '22500', the first two characters are in the standard range and indicate a data exception, but the last three characters are in the implementation-defined range. And if SQLSTATE is '90001', it's completely in the implementation-defined range. SQLSTATE values in the implementation-defined range can mean different things in different implementations, even though the code itself may be the same.

So how do you find out the detailed meaning of '22500' or the meaning of '90001'? You must look in the implementor's documentation. Which implementor? If you're using CONNECT, you may be connecting to various products. To determine which one produced the error condition, look at CLASS_ORIGIN and SUBCLASS_ORIGIN: They have values that identify each implementation. You can test the CLASS_ORIGIN and SUBCLASS_ORIGIN to see whether they identify implementors for which you have the SQLSTATE listings. The actual values placed in CLASS_ORIGIN and SUBCLASS_ORIGIN are implementor-defined, but they also are expected to be self-explanatory company names.

If the error reported is a constraint violation, the CONSTRAINT_CATALOG, CONSTRAINT_SCHEMA, and CONSTRAINT_NAME identify the constraint being violated.

Constraint violation example

The constraint violation information is probably the most important information that GET DIAGNOSTICS provides. Consider the following EMPLOYEE table:

```
CREATE TABLE EMPLOYEE
    (ID CHAR(5) CONSTRAINT EmpPK PRIMARY KEY,
     Salary DEC(8,2) CONSTRAINT EmpSal CHECK Salary > 0,
     Dept CHAR(5) CONSTRAINT EmpDept,
        REFERENCES DEPARTMENT) ;
```

and this DEPARTMENT table:

```
CREATE TABLE DEPARTMENT
    (DeptNo CHAR(5),
     Budget DEC(12,2) CONSTRAINT DeptBudget
        CHECK(Budget >= SELECT SUM(Salary)
                        FROM EMPLOYEE
                        WHERE
            EMPLOYEE.Dept=DEPARTMENT.DeptNo),
     ...) ;
```

Now consider an INSERT as follows:

```
INSERT INTO EMPLOYEE VALUES(:ID_VAR, :SAL_VAR, :DEPT_VAR) ;
```

Suppose that you get an SQLSTATE of '23000'. You look it up in your SQL documentation and discover that this means that the statement is committing an "integrity constraint violation." Now what? That SQLSTATE value means that one of the following situations is true:

>> **The value in ID_VAR is a duplicate of an existing ID value:** You have violated the PRIMARY KEY constraint.

>> **The value in SAL_VAR is negative:** You have violated the CHECK constraint on Salary.

>> **The value in DEPT_VAR isn't a valid key value for any existing row of DEPARTMENT:** You have violated the REFERENCES constraint on Dept.

>> **The value in SAL_VAR is large enough that the sum of the employees' salaries in this department exceeds the BUDGET:** You have violated the CHECK constraint in the BUDGET column of DEPARTMENT. (Recall that if you change the database, all constraints that may be affected are checked, not just those defined in the immediate table.)

Under normal circumstances, you would need to do a great deal of testing to figure out what is wrong with that INSERT. But you can find out what you need to know by using GET DIAGNOSTICS as follows:

```
DECLARE ConstNameVar CHAR(18) ;
GET DIAGNOSTICS EXCEPTION 1
    ConstNameVar = CONSTRAINT_NAME ;
```

Assuming that SQLSTATE is '23000', this GET DIAGNOSTICS sets ConstNameVar to 'EmpPK', 'EmpSal', 'EmpDept', or 'DeptBudget'. Notice that, in practice, you also want to obtain the CONSTRAINT_SCHEMA and CONSTRAINT_CATALOG to uniquely identify the constraint given by CONSTRAINT_NAME.

Adding constraints to an existing table

This use of GET DIAGNOSTICS — determining which of several constraints has been violated — is particularly important in the case where ALTER TABLE is used to add constraints that didn't exist when you wrote the program:

```
ALTER TABLE EMPLOYEE
    ADD CONSTRAINT SalLimit CHECK(Salary < 200000) ;
```

Now if you insert data into EMPLOYEE or update the Salary column of EMPLOYEE, you get an SQLSTATE of '23000' if Salary exceeds $200,000. You can program your INSERT statement so that, if you get an SQLSTATE of '23000' and you don't recognize the particular constraint name that GET DIAGNOSTICS returns, you can display a helpful message, such as Invalid INSERT: Violated constraint SalLimit.

Interpreting the information returned by SQLSTATE

CONNECTION_NAME and ENVIRONMENT_NAME identify the connection and environment to which you are connected at the time the SQL statement is executed.

If the report deals with a table operation, CATALOG_NAME, SCHEMA_NAME, and TABLE_NAME identify the table. COLUMN_NAME identifies the column within the table that caused the report to be made. If the situation involves a cursor, CURSOR_NAME gives its name.

Sometimes a DBMS produces a string of natural language text to explain a condition. The MESSAGE_TEXT item is for this kind of information. The contents of this item depend on the implementation; the SQL standard doesn't explicitly define them. If you do have something in MESSAGE_TEXT, its length in characters is recorded in MESSAGE_LENGTH, and its length in octets is recorded in MESSAGE_OCTET_LENGTH. If the message is in normal ASCII characters, MESSAGE_LENGTH equals MESSAGE_OCTET_LENGTH. If, on the other hand, the message is in kanji or some other language whose characters require more than an octet to express, MESSAGE_LENGTH differs from MESSAGE_OCTET_LENGTH.

To retrieve diagnostic information from a diagnostics area header, use the following:

```
GET DIAGNOSTICS status1 = item1 [, status2 = item2]... ;
```

statusn is a host variable or parameter; itemn can be any of the keywords NUMBER, MORE, COMMAND_FUNCTION, DYNAMIC_FUNCTION, or ROW_COUNT.

To retrieve diagnostic information from a diagnostics detail area, use the following syntax:

```
GET DIAGNOSTICS EXCEPTION condition-number
    status1 = item1 [, status2 = item2]... ;
```

Again `statusn` is a host variable or parameter, and `itemn` is any of the 28 keywords for the detail items listed in Table 22-2. The condition number is (surprise!) the detail area's `CONDITION_NUMBER` item.

Handling Exceptions

When `SQLSTATE` indicates an exception condition by holding a value other than `00000`, `00001`, or `00002`, you may want to handle the situation in one of the following ways:

>> Return control to the parent procedure that called the subprocedure that raised the exception.

>> Use a `WHENEVER` clause (as described earlier in this chapter) to branch to an exception-handling routine or perform some other action.

>> Handle the exception on the spot with a *compound* SQL statement (as described in Chapter 21). A compound SQL statement consists of one or more simple SQL statements, sandwiched between `BEGIN` and `END` keywords.

The following is an example of a compound-statement exception handler:

```
BEGIN
DECLARE  ValueOutOfRange EXCEPTION FOR SQLSTATE '73003' ;
    INSERT INTO FOODS
        (Calories)
        VALUES
        (:cal) ;
    SIGNAL ValueOutOfRange ;
    MESSAGE 'Process a new calorie value.'
    EXCEPTION
        WHEN ValueOutOfRange THEN
            MESSAGE 'Handling the calorie range error' ;
        WHEN OTHERS THEN
            RESIGNAL ;
END
```

With one or more `DECLARE` statements, you can give names to specific `SQLSTATE` values that you suspect may arise. The `INSERT` statement is the one that might cause an exception to occur. If the value of `:cal` exceeds the maximum value for a

SMALLINT data item, SQLSTATE is set to "73003". The SIGNAL statement signals an exception condition. It clears the top diagnostics area. It sets the RETURNED_SQLSTATE field of the diagnostics area to the SQLSTATE for the named exception. If no exception has occurred, the series of statements represented by the MESSAGE 'Process a new calorie value' statement is executed. However, if an exception has occurred, that series of statements is skipped, and the EXCEPTION statement is executed.

If the exception was a ValueOutOfRange exception, then a series of statements represented by the MESSAGE 'Handling the calorie range error' statement is executed. The RESIGNAL statement is executed if the exception isn't a ValueOutOfRange exception.

TIP

RESIGNAL merely passes control of execution to the calling parent procedure. That procedure may have additional error-handling code to deal with exceptions other than the expected value-out-of-range error.

Chapter **23**

Triggers

I n the course of executing a database application, occasions may arise where if some specific action occurs, you want that action to cause another action, or perhaps a succession of actions, to occur. In a sense, that first action *triggers* the execution of the following actions. SQL provides the TRIGGER mechanism to provide this capability.

Triggers, of course, are best known as those parts of a firearm that cause it to fire. More generally, a trigger is an action or event that causes another event to occur. In SQL, the word *trigger* is used in this more general sense. A triggering SQL statement causes another SQL statement (the *triggered* statement) to be executed.

Examining Some Applications of Triggers

The firing of a trigger is useful in a number of situations. One example is to perform a logging function. Certain actions that are critical to the integrity of a database — such as inserting, editing, or deleting a table row — could trigger the making of an entry in a log that documents that action. Log entries can record not only what action was taken, but also when it was taken and by whom.

Triggers can also be used to keep a database consistent. In an order entry application, an order for a specific product can trigger a statement that changes the status of that product in the inventory table from available to reserved. Similarly, the deletion of a row in the orders table can trigger a statement that changes the status of the subject product from reserved to available.

Triggers offer even greater flexibility than is illustrated in the preceding examples. The triggered item doesn't have to be an SQL statement. It can be a host language procedure that performs some operation in the outside world, such as shutting down a production line or causing a robot to fetch a cold beer from the fridge.

Creating a Trigger

You create a trigger, logically enough, with a CREATE TRIGGER statement. After the trigger is created, it lies in wait — waiting for the triggering event to occur. When the triggering event occurs, bang! The trigger fires.

The syntax for the CREATE TRIGGER statement is fairly involved, but you can break it down into understandable pieces. First take a look at the overall picture:

```
CREATE TRIGGER trigger_name
    trigger_action_time trigger_event
    ON table_name
    [REFERENCING old_or_new_value_alias_list]
    triggered_action
```

The trigger name is the unique identifier for this trigger. The trigger action time is the time you want the triggered action to occur: either BEFORE or AFTER the triggering event. The fact that a triggered action can occur *before* the event that is supposedly causing it to happen may seem a little bizarre, but in some cases, this ability can be very useful (and can be accomplished without invoking time travel). Because the database engine knows that it is about to execute a triggering event before it actually executes it, it has the ability to sandwich in the triggered event ahead of the execution of the triggering event, if a trigger action time of BEFORE has been specified.

Three possible trigger events can cause a trigger to fire: the execution of an INSERT statement, a DELETE statement, or an UPDATE statement. These three statements have the power to change the contents of a database table. Thus, any insertion of one or more rows into the subject table, any deletion of one or more rows from the subject table, or any update of one or more columns in one or more rows in the subject table can cause a trigger to fire. ON table_name, of course, refers to the table for which an INSERT, DELETE, or UPDATE has been specified.

Statement and row triggers

The `triggered_action` in the preceding example has the following syntax:

```
[ FOR EACH { ROW | STATEMENT }]
   WHEN <left paren><search condition><right paren>
   <triggered SQL statement>
```

You can specify how the trigger will act:

» **Row trigger:** The trigger will fire once upon encountering the INSERT, DELETE, or UPDATE statement that constitutes the triggering event.

» **Statement trigger:** The trigger will fire multiple times, once for every row in the subject table that is affected by the triggering event.

As indicated by the square brackets, the FOR EACH clause is optional. Despite this, the trigger must act one way or the other. If no FOR EACH clause is specified, the default behavior is FOR EACH STATEMENT.

When a trigger fires

The search condition in the WHEN clause enables you to specify the circumstances under which a trigger will fire. Specify a predicate, and if the predicate is true, the trigger will fire; if it's false, it won't. This capability greatly increases the usefulness of triggers. You can specify that a trigger fires only after a certain threshold value has been exceeded, or when any other condition can be determined to be either True or False.

The triggered SQL statement

The triggered SQL statement can be a single SQL statement or a sequence of SQL statements executed one after another. In the case of a single SQL statement, the triggered SQL statement is merely an ordinary SQL statement. For a sequence of SQL statements, however, you must guarantee atomicity to ensure that the operation is not aborted midstream, leaving the database in an unwanted state. You can do this with a BEGIN–END block that includes the ATOMIC keyword:

```
BEGIN ATOMIC
     { SQL statement 1 }
     { SQL statement 2 }
     ...
     { SQL statement n }
END
```

An example trigger definition

Suppose the corporate human resources manager wants to be informed whenever one of the regional managers hires a new employee. The following trigger can handle this situation nicely:

```
CREATE TRIGGER newhire
   BEFORE INSERT ON employee
   FOR EACH STATEMENT
     BEGIN ATOMIC
       CALL sendmail ('HRDirector')
       INSERT INTO logtable
        VALUES ('NEWHIRE', CURRENT_USER, CURRENT_TIMESTAMP);
     END;
```

Whenever a new row is inserted into the NEWHIRE table, an email is fired off to the HR manager with the details, and the logon name of the person making the insertion and the time of the insertion are recorded in a log table, providing an audit trail.

Firing a Succession of Triggers

You can probably see a complication in the way triggers operate. Suppose you create a trigger that causes an SQL statement to be executed on a table upon the execution of some preceding SQL statement. What if that triggered statement itself causes a second trigger to fire? That second trigger causes a third SQL statement to be executed on a second table, which may itself cause yet another trigger to fire, affecting yet another table. How is it possible to keep everything straight? SQL handles this machine-gun-style trigger firing with something called *trigger execution contexts.*

A succession of INSERT, DELETE, and UPDATE operations can be performed by nesting the contexts in which they occur. When a trigger fires, an execution context is created. Only one execution context can be active at a time. Within that context, an SQL statement may be executed that fires a second trigger. At that point, the existing execution context is suspended in an operation analogous to pushing a value onto a stack. A new execution context, corresponding to the second trigger, is created, and its operation is performed. There is no arbitrary limit to the depth of nesting possible. When an operation is complete, its execution context is destroyed, and the next higher execution context is "popped off the stack" and reactivated. This process continues until all actions are complete and all execution contexts have been destroyed.

Referencing Old Values and New Values

The one part of the CREATE TRIGGER syntax that I have not talked about yet is the optional REFERENCING old_or_new_value_alias_list phrase. It enables you to create an alias or correlation name that references values in the trigger's subject table. After you create a correlation name for new values or an alias for new table contents, you can then reference the values that will exist after an INSERT or UPDATE operation. In a similar way, after you create a correlation name for old values or an alias for old table contents, you can then reference the values that existed in the subject table before an UPDATE or DELETE operation.

The old_or_new_values_alias_list in the CREATE TRIGGER syntax can be one or more of the following phrases:

```
OLD [ ROW ] [ AS ] <old values correlation name>
```

or

```
NEW [ ROW ] [ AS ] <new values correlation name>
```

or

```
OLD TABLE [ AS ] <old values table alias>
```

or

```
NEW TABLE [ AS ] <new values table alias>
```

The table aliases are identifiers for transition tables, which are not persistent, but which exist only to facilitate the referencing operation. As you would expect, NEW ROW and NEW TABLE cannot be specified for a DELETE trigger, and OLD ROW as well as OLD TABLE cannot be specified for an INSERT trigger. After you delete a row or table, there is no new value. Similarly, OLD ROW and OLD TABLE cannot be specified for an INSERT trigger. There are no old values to reference.

In a row-level trigger, you can use an old value correlation name to reference the values in the row being modified or deleted by the triggering SQL statement as that row existed before the statement modified or deleted it. Similarly, an old value table alias is what you use to access the values in the entire table as they existed before the triggering SQL statement's action took effect.

You may not specify either OLD TABLE or NEW TABLE with a BEFORE trigger. The transition tables created by the OLD TABLE or NEW TABLE keyword are too likely to be affected by the actions caused by the triggered SQL statement. To eliminate this potential problem, using OLD TABLE and NEW TABLE with a BEFORE trigger is prohibited.

Firing Multiple Triggers on a Single Table

One final topic that I want to cover in this chapter is the case in which multiple triggers are created, all causing an SQL statement to be executed that operates on the same table. All those triggers are primed and ready to fire. When the triggering event occurs, which one goes first? This conundrum is solved by an executive decision. Whichever trigger was created first is the first to fire. The trigger created second fires next, and so on down the line. Thus the potential ambiguity is avoided, and execution proceeds in an orderly fashion.

7

The Parts of Tens

Chapter **24**

Ten Common Mistakes

I f you're reading this book, you must be interested in building relational database systems. Face it — nobody studies SQL for the fun of it. You use SQL to build database applications, but before you can build one, you need a database. Unfortunately, many projects go awry before the first line of the application is coded. If you don't get the database definition right, your application is doomed — no matter how well you write it. Here are ten common database-creation mistakes that you should be on the lookout for.

Assuming That Your Clients Know What They Need

Generally, clients call you in to design a database system when they have a problem getting the information they need because their current methods aren't working. Clients often believe that they have identified the problem and its solution. They figure that all they need to do is tell *you* what to do.

Giving clients exactly what they ask for is usually a sure-fire prescription for disaster. Most users (and their managers) don't possess the knowledge or skills necessary to accurately identify the problem, so they have little chance of determining the best solution.

Your job is to tactfully convince your client that you are an expert in systems analysis and design and that you must do a proper analysis to uncover the real cause of the problem. Usually the real cause of the problem is hidden behind the more obvious symptoms.

Ignoring Project Scope

Your client tells you what he or she expects from the new application at the beginning of the development project. Unfortunately, the client almost always forgets to tell you something — usually several things. Throughout the job, these new requirements crop up and are tacked onto the project. If you're being paid on a project basis rather than an hourly basis, this growth in scope can change what was once a profitable project into a loser. Make sure that everything you're obligated to deliver is specified in writing before you start the project.

Considering Only Technical Factors

Application developers often consider potential projects in terms of their technical feasibility, and they base their time and effort estimates on that determination. However, issues of cost maximums, resource availability, schedule requirements, and organization politics can have a major effect on the project. These issues may turn a project that is technically feasible into a nightmare. Make sure that you understand all relevant nontechnical factors before you start any development project. You may decide that it makes no sense to proceed; you're better off reaching that conclusion at the beginning of the project than after you have expended considerable effort.

Not Asking for Client Feedback

Your first inclination might be to listen to the managers who hire you. After all, the users themselves don't have any clout and they sure as heck don't pay your fee. On the other hand, there may be good reason to ignore the managers, too. They usually don't have a clue about what the users really need. Wait a minute! Don't ignore everyone or assume that you know more than a manager or user about what a database should do and how it should work. Data-entry clerks don't typically have much organizational clout, and many managers have only a dim understanding of some aspects of the work that data-entry clerks do. But isolating yourself from either group is almost certain to result in a system that solves a problem that nobody has. You can learn a lot from managers and from users by asking the right questions.

Always Using Your Favorite Development Environment

You've probably spent months or even years becoming proficient in the use of a particular DBMS or application development environment. But your favorite environment — no matter what it is — has strengths and weaknesses. Occasionally, you come across a development task that makes heavy demands in an area where your preferred development environment is weak. So rather than kludge together something that isn't really the best solution, bite the bullet. You have two options: Either climb the learning curve of a more appropriate tool and then use it, or candidly tell your clients that their job would best be done with a tool that you're not an expert at using. Then suggest that the client hire someone who can be productive with that tool right away. Professional conduct of this sort garners your clients' respect. (Unfortunately, if you work for a company rather than for yourself, that conduct may also get you laid off or fired. It's best to go with option one — dive on into a new development environment.)

Using Your Favorite System Architecture Exclusively

Nobody can be an expert at everything. Database management systems that work in a teleprocessing environment are different than systems that work in client/server, resource sharing, web-based, or distributed database environments. The one or two systems that you are expert in may not be the best for the job at hand. Choose the best architecture anyway, even if it means passing on the job. Not getting the job is better than getting it and producing a system that doesn't serve the client's needs.

Designing Database Tables in Isolation

If you incorrectly identify data objects and their relationships to each other, your database tables are likely to introduce errors into the data and destroy the validity of any results. To design a sound database, you must consider the overall organization of the data objects and carefully determine how they relate to each other. Usually, no single *right* design exists. You must determine what is appropriate, considering your client's present and projected needs.

Neglecting Design Reviews

Nobody's perfect. Even the best designer and developer can miss important points that are evident to someone looking at the situation from a different perspective. Presenting your work before a formal design review can actually make you more disciplined in your work — probably helping you avoid numerous problems that you may otherwise have experienced. Have a competent professional review your proposed design before you start development. You should have a database designer check it over, but you may want to show it to the client, as well.

Skipping Beta Testing

Any database application complex enough to be truly useful is also complex enough to contain bugs. Even if you test it in every way you can think of, the application is sure to contain failure modes that you don't uncover. Beta testing means giving the application to people who don't know how it was designed. They're likely to have problems that you never encountered because you know too much about the application. If they're familiar with the data, but not the database, they're also more likely to use the application as they would on a daily basis, so they can pinpoint queries that take a long time to generate results. You can then fix the bugs or performance shortfalls that others find before the product goes officially into use.

Not Documenting Your Process

If you think your application is so perfect that it never needs to be looked at, even once more, think again. The only thing you can be absolutely sure of in this world is change. Count on it. Six months from now, you won't remember why you designed things the way you did, unless you carefully document what you did and why you did it that way. If you transfer to a different department or win the lottery and retire, your replacement has almost no chance of modifying your work to meet new requirements if you didn't document your design. Without documentation, your replacement may need to scrap the whole thing and start from scratch.

Don't just document your work adequately — over-document your work. Put in more detail than you think is reasonable. If you come back to this project after six or eight months away from it, you'll be glad you documented it in detail.

- » **Using test databases**

- » **Scrutinizing any queries containing joins**

- » **Examining queries containing subselects**

- » **Using GROUP BY with the SET functions**

- » **Being aware of restrictions on the GROUP BY clause**

- » **Using parentheses in expressions**

- » **Protecting your database by controlling privileges**

- » **Backing up your database regularly**

- » **Anticipating and handling errors**

Chapter **25**

Ten Retrieval Tips

A database can be a virtual treasure trove of information, but like the treasure of the Caribbean pirates of long ago, the stuff that you really want is probably buried and hidden from view. The SQL SELECT statement is your tool for digging up this hidden information. Even if you have a clear idea of what you want to retrieve, translating that idea into SQL can be a challenge. If your formulation is just a little off, you may end up with the wrong results — but results that are so close to what you expected that they mislead you. To reduce your chances of being misled, use the following ten principles.

Verify the Database Structure

If you retrieve data from a database and your results don't seem reasonable, check the database design. Many poorly designed databases are in use, and if you're working with one, fix the design before you try any other remedy. Remember — good design is a prerequisite of data integrity.

Try Queries on a Test Database

Create a test database that has the same structure as your production database, but with only a few representative rows in the tables. Choose the data so that you know in advance what the results of your queries should be. Run each test query on the test data and see whether the results match your expectations. If they don't, you may need to reformulate your queries. If a query is properly formulated but you end up with bad results all the same, you may need to restructure your database.

Build several sets of test data and be sure to include odd cases, such as empty tables and extreme values at the very limit of allowable ranges. Try to think of unlikely scenarios and check for proper behavior when they occur. In the course of checking for unlikely cases, you may gain insight into problems that are more likely to happen.

Double-Check Queries That Include Joins

Joins are notoriously counterintuitive. If your query contains one, make sure that it's doing what you expect before you add WHERE clauses or other complicating factors.

Triple-Check Queries with Subselects

Queries with subselects take data from one table and, based on what is retrieved, take some data from another table. Therefore, by definition, such queries can really be hard to get right. Make sure the data that the inner SELECT retrieves is the data that the outer SELECT needs to produce the desired result. If you have two or more levels of subselects, you need to be even more careful.

Summarize Data with GROUP BY

Say that you have a table (NATIONAL) that contains the name (Player), team (Team), and number of home runs hit (Homers) by every baseball player in the National League. You can retrieve the team homer total for all teams with a query like this:

```
SELECT Team, SUM (Homers)
    FROM NATIONAL
    GROUP BY Team ;
```

This query lists each team, followed by the total number of home runs hit by all that team's players.

Watch GROUP BY Clause Restrictions

Suppose that you want a list of National League power hitters. Consider the following query:

```
SELECT Player, Team, Homers
    FROM NATIONAL
    WHERE Homers >= 20
    GROUP BY Team ;
```

In most implementations, this query returns an error. Generally, only columns used for grouping or columns used in a set function may appear in the select list. However, if you want to view this data, the following formulation works:

```
SELECT Player, Team, Homers
    FROM NATIONAL
    WHERE Homers >= 20
    GROUP BY Team, Player, Homers ;
```

Because all the columns you want to display appear in the GROUP BY clause, the query succeeds and delivers the desired results. This formulation sorts the resulting list first by Team, then by Player, and finally by Homers.

Use Parentheses with AND, OR, and NOT

Sometimes when you mix AND and OR, SQL doesn't process the expression in the order that you expect. Use parentheses in complex expressions to make sure that you get the desired results. Typing a few extra keystrokes is a small price to pay for better results.

TIP

Parentheses also help to ensure that the NOT keyword is applied to the term or expression that you want it to apply to.

Control Retrieval Privileges

Many people don't use the security features available in their DBMS. They don't want to bother with them because they think misuse and misappropriation of data are things that only happen to other people. Don't wait to get burned. Establish and maintain security for all databases that have any value.

Back Up Your Databases Regularly

Understatement alert: Data is hard to retrieve after a power surge, a fire, an earthquake, or some other disaster destroys your hard drive. (Remember, sometimes computers just die for no good reason.) Make frequent backups and put the backup media in a safe place.

REMEMBER

What constitutes a safe place depends on how critical your data is. It might be a fireproof safe in the same room as your computer. It might be in another building. It might be in the cloud. It might be in a concrete bunker under a mountain that has been hardened to withstand a nuclear attack. Decide what level of safety is appropriate for your data.

Handle Error Conditions Gracefully

Whether you're making ad hoc queries from a workstation or embedding queries in an application, occasionally SQL returns an error message rather than the desired results. At a workstation, you can decide what to do next, based on the message returned. In an application, the situation is different. The application user probably doesn't know what action is appropriate. Put extensive error handling into your applications to cover every conceivable error that may occur. Creating error-handling code takes a great deal of effort, but it's better than having the user stare quizzically at a frozen screen.

ISO/IEC SQL: 2016 Reserved Words

ABS	BEGIN	CHAR	CORR
ALL	BEGIN_FRAME	CHAR_LENGTH	CORRESPONDING
ALLOCATE	BEGIN_PARTITION	CHARACTER	COUNT
ALTER	BETWEEN	CHARACTER_LENGTH	COVAR_POP
AND	BIGINT	CHECK	COVAR_SAMP
ANY	BINARY	CLASSIFIER	CREATE
ARE	BLOB	CLOB	CROSS
ARRAY	BOOLEAN	CLOSE	CUBE
ARRAY_AGG	BOTH	COALESCE	CUME_DIST
ARRAY_MAX_CARDINALITY	BY	COLLATE	CURRENT
AS	CALL	COLLECT	CURRENT_CATALOG
ASENSITIVE	CALLED	COLUMN	CURRENT_DATE
ASYMMETRIC	CARDINALITY	COMMIT	CURRENT_DEFAULT_TRANSFORM_GROUP
AT	CASCADED	CONDITION	CURRENT_PATH
ATOMIC	CASE	CONNECT	CURRENT_ROLE
AUTHORIZATION	CAST	CONSTRAINT	CURRENT_ROW
AVG	CEIL	CONTAINS	CURRENT_SCHEMA
	CEILING	CONVERT	

CURRENT_TIME	DISTINCT	EXTRACT	HOLD
CURRENT_TIMESTAMP	DO	FALSE	HOUR
	DOUBLE	FETCH	IDENTITY
CURRENT_TRANSFORM_GROUP_FOR_TYPE	DROP	FILTER	IF
	DYNAMIC	FIRST_VALUE	IN
CURRENT_USER	EACH	FLOAT	INDICATOR
CURSOR	ELEMENT	FLOOR	INITIAL
CYCLE	ELSE	FOR	INNER
DATE	ELSEIF	FOREIGN	INOUT
DAY	EMPTY	FRAME_ROW	INSENSITIVE
DEALLOCATE	END	FREE	INSERT
DEC	END-EXEC	FROM	INT
DECFLOAT	END_FRAME	FULL	INTEGER
DECIMAL	END_PARTITION	FUNCTION	INTERSECT
DECLARE	EQUALS	FUSION	INTERSECTION
DEFAULT	ESCAPE	GET	INTERVAL
DEFINE	EVERY	GLOBAL	INTO
DELETE	EXCEPT	GRANT	IS
DENSE_RANK	EXEC	GROUP	ITERATE
DEREF	EXECUTE	GROUPING	JOIN
DESCRIBE	EXISTS	GROUPS	JSON_ARRAY
DETERMINISTIC	EXP	HANDLER	JSON_ARRAYAGG
DISCONNECT	EXTERNAL	HAVING	JSON_EXISTS

JSON_OBJECT	MATCH	NOT	OVERLAY
JSON_OBJECTAGG	MATCHES	NTH_VALUE	PARAMETER
JSON_QUERY	MATCH_NUMBER	NTILE	PARTITION
JSON_TABLE	MATCH_RECOGNIZE	NULL	PATTERN
JSON_TABLE_ PRIMITIVE	MAX	NULLIF	PER
	MEMBER	NUMERIC	PERCENT
JSON_VALUE	MERGE	OCCURRENCES_ REGEX	PERCENT_RANK
LAG	METHOD		PERCENTILE_CONT
LANGUAGE	MIN	OCTET_LENGTH	PERCENTILE_DISC
LARGE	MINUTE	OF	PERIOD
LAST_VALUE	MOD	OFFSET	PORTION
LATERAL	MODIFIES	OLD	POSITION
LEAD	MODULE	OMIT	POSITION_REGEX
LEADING	MONTH	ON	POWER
LEAVE	MULTISET	ONE	PRECEDES
LEFT	NATIONAL	ONLY	PRECISION
LIKE	NATURAL	OPEN	PREPARE
LIKE_REGEX	NCHAR	OR	PRIMARY
LN	NCLOB	ORDER	PROCEDURE
LOCAL	NEW	OUT	RANGE
LOCALTIME	NO	OUTER	RANK
LOCALTIMESTAMP	NONE	OVER	READS
LOWER	NORMALIZE	OVERLAPS	REAL

RECURSIVE	ROLLBACK	SOME	SYSTEM_USER
REF	ROLLUP	SPECIFIC	TABLE
REFERENCES	ROW	SPECIFICTYPE	TABLESAMPLE
REFERENCING	ROW_NUMBER	SQL	THEN
REGR_AVGX	ROWS	SQLEXCEPTION	TIME
REGR_AVGY	RUNNING	SQLSTATE	TIMESTAMP
REGR_COUNT	SAVEPOINT	SQLWARNING	TIMEZONE_HOUR
REGR_INTERCEPT	SCOPE	SQRT	TIMEZONE_MINUTE
REGR_R2	SCROLL	START	TO
REGR_SLOPE	SEARCH	STATIC	TRAILING
REGR_SXX	SECOND	STDDEV_POP	TRANSLATE
REGR_SXY	SEEK	STDDEV_SAMP	TRANSLATE_REGEX
REGR_SYY	SELECT	SUBMULTISET	TRANSLATION
RELEASE	SENSITIVE	SUBSET	TREAT
REPEAT	SESSION_USER	SUBSTRING	TRIGGER
RESIGNAL	SET	SUBSTRING_REGEX	TRIM
RESULT	SHOW	SUCCEEDS	TRIM_ARRAY
RETURN	SIGNAL	SUM	TRUE
RETURNS	SIMILAR	SYMMETRIC	TRUNCATE
REVOKE	SKIP	SYSTEM	UESCAPE
RIGHT	SMALLINT	SYSTEM_TIME	UNION

UNIQUE	USING	VARCHAR	WIDTH_BUCKET
UNKNOWN	VALUE	VARYING	WINDOW
UNNEST	VALUES	VERSIONING	WITH
UNTIL	VALUE_OF	WHEN	WITHIN
UPDATE	VAR_POP	WHENEVER	WITHOUT
UPPER	VAR_SAMP	WHERE	YEAR
USER	VARBINARY	WHILE	

Index

Symbols and Numerics

transaction-starting statement, 341
transferring data, 158–161
transitive dependency, 138
TRANSLATE function, 198
TRANSLATE_REGEX function, 196–197
translation tables, 67
translations, 116
triggers
  applications of, 457–458
  defined, 324
  example trigger definition, 459–460
  firing multiple on single table, 462
  firing succession of, 460
  general discussion, 457
  referencing old and new values, 461–462
  row triggers, 459
  specifying when triggers fire, 459
  statement triggers, 459
  trigger action time, 325
  trigger events, 325
  triggered actions, 325
  triggered SQL statement, 459
TRIM function, 198
TRIM_ARRAY function, 203
tuples, 14–15
two-dimensional arrays, 14–15

U

UDTs (user-defined types)
  from collection types, 48
  distinct types, 45–46
  overview, 44–45
  structured types, 46–47
underscore (_) character, 231
UNION ALL operation, 261
union joins, 276–282
UNION operator
  CORRESPONDING operation, 262
  overview, 259–261
  UNION ALL operation, 261
unique keys, 240–241
UNIQUE predicate, 237–238

update anomalies, 124–127
UPDATE statements
  nested queries and, 299–301
  positioned, 424
updating data, 155–158
UPPER function, 198
user access levels
  database administrator, 317
  database object owners, 317–318
  overview, 316
  public, 318
user names, 320
user privileges. *See* privileges
user-defined types. *See* UDTs
user-defined value expressions, 71

V

VALID predicate, 391
valid time, 164
value expressions
  advanced
    CASE conditional expressions, 210–217
    CAST expression, 217–220
    overview, 209
    row value expressions, 221–222
  conditional value expression, 189
  datetime value expressions, 187–188
  DML, 68–71
  interval value expressions, 188
  numeric value expressions, 187
  string value expressions, 186–187
value functions
  datetime, 207–208
  interval, 208
  numeric, 199–206
  string, 193–199
values
  column references, 185
  literal values, 180–182
  overview, 179–180
  row values, 180
  special variables, 184

About the Author

Allen G. Taylor is a 30-year veteran of the computer industry and the author of over 40 books, including *Develop Microsoft HoloLens Apps Now, Crystal Reports 2008 For Dummies, Database Development For Dummies, Access Power Programming with VBA,* and *SQL All-in-One For Dummies.* He lectures internationally on databases, innovation, astronomy, and entrepreneurship. He also teaches database development through a leading online educational program. For the latest news on Allen's activities, check out http://www.allengtaylor.com. You can contact Allen at allen.taylor@ieee.org.

Dedication

This book is dedicated to Joyce Taylor, my partner in life.

Author's Acknowledgment

First and foremost, I would like to acknowledge the help of Jim Melton, editor of the ISO/ANSI specification for SQL. Without his untiring efforts, this book, and indeed SQL itself as an international standard, would be of much less value. Andrew Eisenberg has also contributed to my knowledge of SQL through his writing. I would like to thank Michael Durthaler for helpful suggestions regarding the coverage of cursors, as well as SQL wizard Markus Winand for insights into the latest additions to the ISO/IEC standard. I would also like to thank my project manager Maureen Tullis, my project editor Scott Tullis, my technical editor Russ Mullen, and my executive editor Steve Hayes for their key contributions to the production of this book. Thanks also to my agent, Carole McClendon of Waterside Productions, for her support of my career.

Publisher's Acknowledgments

Associate Publisher: Katie Mohr

Development/Copy Editor: Scott Tullis

Technical Editor: Russ Mullen

Production Editor: Vasanth Koilraj

Project Manager: Maureen Tullis

Cover Image: © luismmolina/iStock.com